LIBRARY OF LIVING CATHOLIC THOUGHT

(Under the direction of the West Baden College faculty)

A Guide to the Thought of
Saint Augustine

A GUIDE TO THE THOUGHT OF
SAINT AUGUSTINE

by
EUGÈNE PORTALIÉ, S.J.

With an Introduction by
VERNON J. BOURKE

Translated by
RALPH J. BASTIAN, S.J.

Library of Living Catholic Thought
HENRY REGNERY COMPANY
Chicago   *1960*

Imprimi potest
William J. Schmidt, S.J.
Praepositus Provincialis Provinciae Chicagiensis, S.J.

Nihil obstat
Austin G. Schmidt, S.J.
Censor deputatus

Imprimatur
Albert Cardinal Meyer, S.T.D., S.S.L.
Archiepiscopus Chicagiensis
March 9, 1960

This translation is from the article, "Saint Augustin," which appeared in the *Dictionnaire de Théologie Catholique*, published by Editions Letouzey et Ané, Paris.

MADE AND PRINTED IN GREAT BRITAIN BY
WILLIAM CLOWES AND SONS, LIMITED, LONDON AND BECCLES

Acknowledgments

The translator's task was made lighter by many helping hands. While it is impossible to mention by name everyone who helped with this book, acknowledgment must be made for the outstanding work performed by the following: Rev. Raymond V. Schoder, S.J., encouraged the beginning of the translation and expedited the work in all stages until its completion. Rev. Robert F. Harvanek, S.J., Robert W. Schmidt, S.J., and Roland Turenne, S.J., gave valuable advice on grammatical difficulties. Rev. Walter P. Krolikowski, S.J., Thomas G. Savage, S.J., and D. Clayton Schario, S.J., read the typed copy and suggested many improvements. Rev. Eugene P. Simon, S.J., and Peter J. Moloney checked the footnotes, correcting many misprints in the original article. Rev. Thomas L. Kenealy, S.J., and Francis T. Gignac, S.J., worked up the preliminary material for the bibliography. Daniel L. Flaherty, S.J., and Norman G. McKendrick, S.J., read the proofs. To these and to all who helped in any way the translator extends his sincere appreciation and gratitude.

RALPH J. BASTIAN, S.J.

West Baden College

Acknowledgement

The handsome book was made richer by the helpful supplied...

While it is impossible to mention by name everyone who contributed to this book, acknowledgement must be made for the outstanding work performed by the software water for Kauppsad...

... encouraged the beginning of the translation and supervised the work in all stages and its completion. Bhas, Robert W. Prasad, S.J., Robert W. Schmidt, S.J., and Roland Teuno, S.J., gave valuable advice on grammatical points; Father P. Krohmchicki, S.J., Thomas G. Barry, S.J., and D. Clayton Sharp, S.J., read the final text and suggested many improvements; Rev. Eugene B. Simon, S.J., and Rev. J. Maloney checked the footnotes, correcting many inaccuracies in the original; Rev. Thomas L. Ren...de, S.J., and Francis C. Cramer, S.J., worked up the preliminary material for the bibliography; Daniel L. Flaherty, S.J., and Thomas C. McConamara, S.J., read the proofs. To these and to all with helped in any way, the author sincerely expresses his sincere appreciation and gratitude.

John J. Kilgallen, S.J.

West Baden College

Contents

vii

xvi

CONTENTS

Introduction

IT is a remarkable thing to find a scholarly work written more than fifty years ago which is still among the best in its field. There is little doubt that this is true of Eugène Portalié's study of St. Augustine of Hippo.[1] Etienne Gilson, himself the author of an excellent general work on Augustine, has called Portalié's the indispensable introduction.[2] Similar encomia are found in other Augustinian studies of our day.[3] Such universal esteem is all the more unusual when the study in question is a relatively inaccessible article in an encyclopedic dictionary. Clearly, the publication in book form of an English translation of this work is well advised.

Eugène Portalié lived and worked quietly; he was not too well known, even by his fellow Jesuits. Born on January 3, 1852, at Mende, France, he entered the Jesuit Novitiate for the Toulouse Province, in December, 1867. His scholarship was completely the product of his training in the Society of Jesus, and of his own efforts. Distinguishing himself in the regular course in theology, he spent at least two years in advanced studies. Portalié held a "Grand Act" (a rare type of disputation reserved for a few brilliant Jesuit scholars) at Uclès. The Papal Nuncio of Madrid presided, attended by his secretary, the future Pope Benedict XV.

In his theological teaching at several Jesuit centers of study, Father Portalié was a successful and highly personal professor.

[1] "Augustin, Saint," *Dictionnaire de Théologie Catholique* (Paris, Letouzey, 1902; reprinted 1923), tome I, col. 2268–2472.
[2] *Introduction à l'étude de s. Augustin* (Paris, 1947), p. 329; see also, *History of Christian Philosophy in the Middle Ages* (New York, 1955), p. 591.
[3] See for example the works of Sciacca, Most, Pope, Boyer, and Wolfson, cited later in this *Introduction*.

His knowledge of the history of his subject made his lectures informative and interesting. Central in his scholarly interests were the problems of faith and grace. Most of his writing was done for the Jesuit periodical, *Etudes*. Though some of these articles have been separately published, notably a collection concerned with the Diana Vaughan affair,[4] the magistral article on St. Augustine remains as his only publication of major size.[5] In 1899 he was called to the chair of positive theology at the Institut Catholique, Toulouse, where he was an associate of Msgr. Pierre Battifol, another enthusiastic student of St. Augustine. From 1899 to 1902, Portalié wrote six articles for the newly projected *Dictionnaire de Théologie Catholique*; of these the one on Augustine has been the most influential.

In his later years, Father Portalié became much concerned with the Modernist movement in French Catholicism. He engaged in energetic polemic against Loisy and his colleagues. This activity is thought to have sapped his energies and contributed to his death, April 20, 1909.[6]

Interest in St. Augustine has not dwindled since Father Portalié's time. Hundreds of valuable works have been written in the ensuing fifty years. Augustine's original writings have been partly re-edited and translated into modern languages. Archaeological discoveries have brought precious information about Augustine's world. His religious and philosophical teachings have been studied by an ever-increasing number of interpreters. New journals and publication series are devoted in whole or in part to the study of his writings. While it is not possible to cover all this material adequately, a brief survey of some of the main trends and publications of the last fifty years may serve to supplement this already excellent work.

[4] *La fin d'une mystification* (Paris, 1897).
[5] For a list of his writings see *Bulletin de littérature ecclésiastique* (Paris, 1909).
[6] F. Cavallera, "Portalié, Eugène," *DTC*, 12, 2 (1934), col. 2590–2593; see also: *Etudes*, 119 (May 5, 1909) 297–302, for a memorial note.

I. BIOGRAPHY

Dozens of biographies of St. Augustine have been published in this century. Some very popular lives have been written by prominent literary figures (Louis Bertrand, Rebecca West, Giovanni Papini) but these have added little that is new. One of the best scholarly biographies is that by Canon Bardy.[7] This book describes very fully the later life of Augustine—a period often passed over briefly because it is not covered in the autobiographical section of the *Confessions*. Much material can be gathered on Augustine's mature work as a bishop from his letters and sermons, and from the contemporary *Life* by Possidius.[8]

Several remarkable archaeological discoveries, related to Augustine studies, have been made in North Africa; extensive investigations have been made of the ruins of the old cities. Père Delattre and others have verified Augustine's description of the waterfront and topography of ancient Carthage.[9] At Hippo, the ruins of two cathedrals (apparently Augustine's and the Donatist church) have been uncovered.[10] The mosaic floor, partially preserved in Augustine's cathedral, shows that the building was large (162 × 65 feet). A baptismal font, episcopal throne, and several tombs have been found in this church. Meanwhile, in Italy, striking evidence of the historicity of the account of St. Monica's death and burial at Ostia (*Conf.*, 9, 11, 28) came to light about ten years ago. A stone bearing a partial text of what seems to be an epitaph for Augustine's

---

[7] Gustave Bardy, *Saint Augustin, l'homme et l'œuvre*, 6me éd. (Paris, 1946); my book, *Augustine's Quest of Wisdom* (Milwaukee, 1945), is listed by Father Boyer (*Gregorianum*, 36, 1955, 486) as an "un ouvrage semblable de langue anglaise."

[8] Now unfortunately out-of-print in the best English version: *S. Augustini vita scripta a Possidio episcopo* (Latin and English), ed. H. T. Weiskotten (Princeton, 1919). There is also an English version in: E. A. Foran, *The Augustinians* (London, 1938).

[9] For details, see the report in Pope, *op. cit.*, p. 10; also G. G. Lapeyre, "Saint Augustin et Carthage," *Miscellanea Agostiniana* (Roma, 1931), II, 92–100.

[10] Reported by M. Leglay and Erwan Marec in "L'Afrique Chrétienne," *Augustinus Magister* (Paris, 1954), I, 1–17.

mother was found in the yard of the church of St. Aurea at Ostia.[11]

Concerning the personal life of Augustine, one of the most significant controversies had started before Father Portalié wrote and has continued to the present day. This is the dispute about the details of his conversion. Briefly, certain writers[12] claim that, at the time of his baptism, Augustine was a devotee of Greek philosophy rather than a convinced Christian. Implied in this interpretation is the non-historicity of certain parts of the *Confessions*. Opposition to the early versions of this thesis is found in Portalié, of course, and elsewhere.[13] The outstanding later rebuttal to Alfaric, and this whole position, was written by Father Charles Boyer.[14] He strongly supports the historicity of the *Confessions*, and maintains the sincerity of Augustine's religious conversion. More recent works have stressed the complexity of the problem.[15] The present tendency among Catholic scholars is to grant the intellectual impact of Plotinus, Porphyry, even of Stoicism, on Augustine's mental development—but also to maintain his acceptance of the essentials of Christianity at the time of his baptism.[16]

It is impossible to review here the many new studies of detailed

[11] R. Arbesmann, "A Lucky Archaeological Find," *Classical Bulletin*, 28 (1946) 9 ff.; V. Grumel, "Découverte à Ostie d'un inscription relative à sainte Monique," *Revue des études latines*, 24 (1946) 70–71.

[12] Older advocates of this thesis are Adolf Harnack, S. Loofs, L. Gourdon, and W. Thimme. The most discussed later work, in the same category, is: P. Alfaric, *L'Evolution intellectuelle de saint Augustin*, I (Paris, 1918; the second volume was never published).

[13] F. Wörter, *Die Geistesentwicklung des hl. Aurelius Augustinus* (Paderborn, 1892). A still useful study.

[14] *Christianisme et néoplatonisme dans la formation de saint Augustin* (Paris, 1920). Much the same argument in English is found in: Garvey, Sister M. Patricia, *St. Augustine: Christian or Neo-Platonist?* (Milwaukee, 1939).

[15] In *Recherches sur les Confessions de s. Augustin* (Paris, 1950), P. Courcelle argues that Milan was an important center of Neo-Platonism, during Augustine's residence, and that even St. Ambrose was well read in this philosophy. J. J. O'Meara, *The Young Augustine: The Growth of St. Augustine's Mind up to his Conversion* (London, 1954), criticizes some of Courcelle's findings but admits the strong influence of Porphyry.

[16] Cf. J.-M. Le Blond, *Les conversions de saint Augustin* (Paris, 1950); M. Sciacca, *S. Agostino* (Brescia, 1954).

points in the biography of Augustine—of his illnesses (Legewie), the location of Cassiciacum (Morin, Meda, Rota), his ethnic background (Poittier), his association with Carthage (Lapeyre), his priestly development (Pincherle), and his preaching (De Bruyne, Pope).[17] A great deal of such patient research remains to be done.

II. WRITINGS

No complete, critical edition of the Latin works of St. Augustine has been published. Many scholars still use the Migne reprint of the famous Renaissance edition by the Benedictines of St-Maur.[18] Critical texts of about one third of Augustine's writings are to be found in the *Corpus Scriptorum Ecclesiasticorum Latinorum* (Vienna, 1864–   ). Augustine volumes in CSEL are not grouped in one numerical sequence; hence it is necessary to use a table (such as Portalié gives) to locate his works therein.[19] Inexpensive and useful for the small library is the Latin-French printing of the works of Augustine, now in progress.[20] Publication of a new critical edition of the Fathers has started in Holland; Augustine's writings are to be in volumes XXVII to LIX.[21] There is also an edition of the Latin works under way in Spain.[22]

[17] Many such studies appear in the centenary publications listed at the head of the Bibliography. The *Bibliographia Augustiniana* (Rome, 1928) by C. M. F. Nebreda is not well done; of greater help are: Gonzalez, R., "Bibliografía Augustiniana del Centenario," *Religion y Cultura*, XV (1931) 461–509; F. Van Steenberghen, "La philosophie de s. Augustin d'après les travaux du Centenaire," *Revue Néoscolastique de Philosophie*, 34 (1932) 366–387; 35 (1933) 106–126, 230–281. For more recent material, see the bibliographical sections of the *Revue Philosophique de Louvain*; the *Revue des Etudes Augustiniennes* (Paris); and the new Spanish journal, *Augustinus* (Madrid), which began publication in 1956.

[18] *Patrologia Latina*, volumes 32–47.

[19] This table forms the appendix of this book. Later listings include some writings added in the twentieth century: Ueberweg-Geyer, *Grundriss der Geschichte der Philosophie*, Bd. II (Berlin, 1928), p. 96; Pope, *op. cit.*, pp. 368–383; Bourke, *op. cit.*, pp. 303–307.

[20] *Œuvres de saint Augustin* (Paris, Desclée, 1948–   ). Sixteen volumes now printed; to contain about 85 vols.

[21] *Corpus Christianorum*, under the direction of the Abbey of St. Pierre de Steenbrugge (The Hague, Nijhoff, 1953–   ).

[22] In the *Biblioteca de Autores Cristianos* (Madrid-Escorial, 1931–   ).

We also lack a complete English version of St. Augustine. For the older collected translations in English, and for some versions of individual treatises up to 1937, Father Pope's table may be consulted.[23] Two translation series are in progress in the U.S.A. *Ancient Christian Writers* now contains many of the shorter works, well annotated.[24] The *Fathers of the Church* series[25] includes some of the short works and also certain major treatises have been printed.[26] A practical two-volume collection of shorter works plus most of the *Confessions* and *City of God* has been assembled from available versions by Protestant scholars.[27]

For up-to-date information on the authenticity and chronology of these writings, with bibliographical references in this field, Bardy's annotated edition and translation of the *Retractationes* is recommended.[28] There is an earlier general study of the chronology of all the works.[29] Several important articles on major writings (De Bruyne, Kunzelmann, Wilmart) are printed in the second volume of *Miscellanea Agostiniana* (Roma, 1931). Many points connected with the literary and philological study of St. Augustine were discussed by outstanding scholars (Marrou, Courcelle, Mohrmann, Henry, etc.) at the International Augustinian Congress of Paris, 1954. The first and third volumes of these proceedings contain much information in this area.[30] Hundreds of special studies of various works of Augustine have been printed since Father Portalié worked. Many volumes of the *Patristic Studies*

[23] *Op. cit.*, pp. 368–389.

[24] ACW is edited by J. Quasten and J. C. Plumpe; published by the Newman Press, Westminster, Md.; first Augustine volume, 1946; 17 volumes of Augustine have now appeared.

[25] FOC was founded by L. Schopp, is now directed by R. J. Deferrari; first Augustine vol. in 1947; 18 vols. of his works now in print (Fathers of the Church, Inc., 475 Fifth Ave., New York).

[26] *City of God*, translated by G. G. Walsh et al., 3 vols. (1950–1954); this version is now available, with some deletions, in a paper-back volume (Doubleday Image Books, New York, 1958); *Confessions*, translated by V. J. Bourke (1953).

[27] *Basic Writings of St. Augustine*, ed. W. J. Oates (New York, 1948).

[28] *Les Révisions*, par G. Bardy, in *Œuvres de s. Augustin*, XII (Paris, 1950).

[29] S. M. Zarb, *Chronologia Operum S. Augustini* (Roma, 1934).

[30] See *Augustinus Magister* (Paris, Etudes Augustiniennes, 1954), tome I, in toto; III, 27–50.

(Catholic U. of America) fall in this category. New work has been done on the editing of the *Sermons*.[31] Several critical editions of the *Confessions* have appeared; it is generally agreed that Skutella's text is the best.[32] In the first volume of the *City of God* (FOC translation, 1950), Etienne Gilson has provided a brilliant *Foreword* of almost one hundred pages. On the historicity of the early dialogues, and their relation to the *Confessions*, there is now an abundant literature.[33] Goldbacher's edition of the *Epistulae* (CSEL, vols. 34, 44, 57, and 58) is well annotated and conveniently indexed.

Because of Augustine's care in reviewing most of his literary production, in the *Retractationes*, there has never been great difficulty about matters of authenticity and chronology. Portalié's information on such questions is still sound. It might be noted that *De octo quaestionibus ex veteri Testamento*, formerly suspect, is now considered quite authentic.[34] But the *Speculum 'Quis ignorat'* seems to be spurious.[35]

III. THOUGHT

Introductions. Of the many introductions to the thought of St. Augustine, some stress the interests of the philosopher.[36] However,

---

[31] Dom G. Morin has devoted the whole first volume of *Miscellanea Agostiniana* (Roma, 1930) to the texts of previously unprinted *Sermones*, and notes thereon; cf. A. Kunzelmann, "Die Chronologie der Sermones des hl. Augustinus," *ibid.*, II, 417–520.

[32] *Confessionum Libri Tredecim*, post P. Knoell, iteratis curis edidit Martinus Skutella (Leipzig, Teubner, 1934).

[33] Consult J. J. O'Meara's translation, *Against the Academics*, ACW, 12 (Westminster, Md., 1950), and also his *The Young Augustine*, for further documentation.

[34] See De Bruyne in *Miscellanea Agostiniana*, II, 327–340.

[35] G. De Plinval, "Une œuvre apocryphe de saint Augustin: Le speculum 'Quis ignorat'," *Augustinus Magister*, I, 187–196.

[36] E. Gilson, *Introduction à l'étude de saint Augustin*, 3me éd. (Paris, 1949); the bibliography (pp. 325–351) covers work up to 1943. F. Cayré, *Initiation à la philosophie de saint Augustin* (Paris, 1947).

it is admittedly difficult to maintain a distinction between philosophic and religious thought in Augustine. He is a theocentric thinker; some introductory works emphasize this.[37] Augustine scholarship is by no means exclusively Catholic; it would seem that Protestant interest is now increasing in America.[38] There is also an impressive three-volume study of patristic thought, by a noted Jewish scholar, which stresses the contributions of Augustine.[39] Despite the title, the problems explored in this large work are primarily theological.

Sources. There is an abundant literature on the backgrounds of Augustine's thought. One of the most useful bibliographies of this material is found in Courcelle's *Recherches sur les Confessions* (pp. 259–278). This work emphasizes the importance of Plotinus and Neo-Platonism as influences on Augustine.[40] Some reaction to this emphasis, with the claim that Porphyry is at least as important a source as Plotinus, is found in the works of J. J. O'Meara, already mentioned.[41] The influence of Plato and Cicero has also been studied.[42] It has even been argued that there was considerable Aristotelian influence on St. Augustine.[43] If there was, it was indirect; apart from the *Categories*, he read none of Aristotle's

[37] S. J. Grabowski, *The All-Present God. A Study in St. Augustine* (St. Louis, 1954); thoroughly documented. H. Weinand, *Die Gottesidee, der Grundzug der Weltanschauung des hl. Augustinus* (Paderborn, 1910). For an introductory anthology: E. Przywara, *An Augustine Synthesis*, introd. by C. C. Martindale, S.J., (New York, 1936).

[38] For this trend, see: R. W. Battenhouse, *A Companion to the Study of St. Augustine* (New York, 1955).

[39] H. A. Wolfson, *The Philosophy of the Church Fathers* (Cambridge, Mass., 1956). Only the first volume has appeared, as yet.

[40] On the same theme, there are several French studies by Paul Henry; his "Augustine and Plotinus," *Journal of Theological Studies,* 38 (1937) 1–23, gives a brief summary in English.

[41] In the same vein: W. Theiler, *Porphyrios und Augustin* (Halle, 1933).

[42] Hans Dyroff, "Ueber Form und Begriffsgehalt der augustinischen Schrift De Ordine," in *Aurelius Augustinus* (Köln, 1930), pp. 16–62; see also his introduction to L. Schopp's translation: *Augustinus Selbstgespräche* (München, 1938)

[43] N. Kaufman, "Les éléments aristotéliciens dans la cosmologie et la psychologie de s. Augustin," *Rev. Néoscol. de Philos.,* II (1904) 140–156.

works. Some Stoic themes, however, are apparent in his thought, especially in the *City of God*.[44]

Holy Scripture, of course, was a most important source of information for Augustine. It appears that a general index of his biblical citations is now under way in Europe.[45] Another religious influence, largely negative, was Manichaeism. In the past few decades, new texts have been discovered which indicate that Augustine's reports on this religion were precise, but also that this sect had much more variety in its teaching than was realized either by Augustine or the historians of the nineteenth century.[46] A recent tendency is to stress the special and restricted character of this religion in North Africa.[47]

Psychology and Theory of Knowledge. There are several works in English on the psychology of St. Augustine which are consciously omitted here, for they are not reliable.[48] The outstanding study of the "trinitarian" analysis of the human soul has not been translated.[49] A key part of his psychology is the "active" theory of sensation, in which the mind makes within itself its images of certain events in the bodily world. This is a quite different explanation from that of later scholasticism.[50] It is very important to our understanding of the body-soul relations in St. Augustine.

[44] Bushman, Sister Rita Marie, "St. Augustine's Metaphysics and Stoic Doctrine," *New Scholasticism*, 26 (1951) 283–302.

[45] Briefly mentioned as the "fichier de de Lagarde" in *Augustinus Magister*, II, 243.

[46] P. Alfaric, *Les Ecritures manichéennes* (Paris, 1918); A. V. W. Jackson, *Researches in Manichaeism* (London, 1931); Schmidt-Polotsky, *Ein Mani-Fund in Aegypten* (Berlin, 1933); H. C. Puech, *Le Manichéisme* (Paris, 1949); still useful is: F. C. Burkitt, *The Religion of the Manichees* (Cambridge, 1925); for further data, see *Catholic Biblical Quarterly*, VII (1945) 206–222, 306–325.

[47] L. Tondelli, *Mani: Rapporti con Bardesane, S. Agostino, Dante* (Milano, 1932); L. H. Grondijs, "Manichéisme Numidien au IVme siècle," *Augustinus Magister*, III, 391–410.

[48] Though not a formal treatment of the psychology, Pegis' "Mind of St. Augustine," *Mediaeval Studies*, 6 (1944) 1–61, gives the essential information; see also, Gilson, *Introduction*, pp. 31–147.

[49] M. Schmaus, *Die psychologische Trinitätslehre des hl. Augustinus* (Münster W., 1927).

[50] Cf. Gannon, Sister M. Ann Ida, "The Active Theory of Sensation in St. Augustine," *New Scholasticism*, 30 (1956) 154–180.

Twentieth-century explanations of Augustine's theory of knowledge, and especially of the divine illumination texts, have continued to follow much the same diverse paths described by Portalié. There are still some exponents of the notion of a rather direct vision of the divine truths.[51] Opposed to this intuitionist interpretation is the abstractionist view; this takes Augustine's theory of intellection as an early form of Thomistic abstraction. The "light" of the mind is thus identified with the agent intellect.[5] A third (and, to this writer, better) position lies somewhere between the foregoing interpretations. It would appear that St Augustine's divine illumination doctrine is not so much a theory of the origin of concepts as of the manner in which the human mind is enabled to make some *judgments* with certitude. These judgments correspond with those which would be called first principles of logic, mathematics, morals, and possibly metaphysics in later Scholasticism. Father Portalié makes a start on such an interpretation: his view has had other distinguished followers.[5] It should be noted, however, that "illumination" is still a bone of contention among Augustine scholars; some now doubt that the text of Augustine offers an intelligible account of the light metaphor.[54]

On God and His Works. Since Augustine lived long before the teaching of Catholic theology became scientifically organized

[51] J. Hessen, *Die unmittelbare Erkenntnis nach dem hl. Augustinus* (Paderborn 1919); *Augustins Metaphysik der Erkenntnis* (Berlin, 1931). For a survey of recent German interpretations of "Illumination" see: F. Körner, *Das Prinzip der Innerlichkeit in Augustins Erkenntnislehre* (Würzburg, 1952).

[52] C. Boyer, *L'Idée de vérité dans la philosophie de s. Augustin* (Paris, 1921); "La philosophie augustinienne ignore-t-elle l'abstraction?" *Nouvelle Revue Théo-logique* (1930) 1–14; I. Sestili, "Thomae Aquinatis cum Augustino de illumina-tione concordia," *Divus Thomas* (Piacenza), 31 (1928) 50–82.

[53] B. Kälin, *Die Erkenntnislehre des hl. Augustinus* (Sarnen, 1920); E. Gilson *Introduction*, pp. 88–170; for an English statement of Gilson's views on the rela-tion of Augustine to Aquinas, see: *A Gilson Reader* (ed. A. C. Pegis [New York 1957], pp. 68–81). Consult also: L. Keeler (ed.), *S. Augustini Doctrina de Cogni-tione* (Romae, 1934).

[54] Notably R. Allers ("Illumination et vérités éternelles," *Augustinus Magister* I, 477–498) and Canon F. Van Steenberghen (*Augustinus Magister*, III, 190).

(twelfth and thirteenth centuries), he can hardly be regarded as a systematic theologian like Thomas Aquinas. However, Augustine is the greatest and most influential religious writer among the Fathers; there are many introductions to his religious doctrine.[55] Especially valuable is the study of trinitarian thinking by Michael Schmaus, already mentioned.[56] Later literature on the theology of St. Augustine is fully cited in the most recent printing of his *De Trinitate*.[57]

St. Augustine's thinking on creation[58] has continued to be the subject of much argument, particularly regarding his possible anticipation of transformistic evolution. His theory of the *rationes seminales* has been taken by some interpreters as a type of evolutionism.[59] Others have vigorously denied that Augustine gives any support to Darwinism.[60] Indeed, Augustine does grant the actual appearance on earth of living members of "new" species; but, in the view of the present writer, he thinks that the *rationes* of such species have always existed in the creative mind of God. Hence, he combines a fixity of species theory (after the first six days of creation, no new *rationes seminales* are made) with a recognition

[55] Recommended for English readers: S. J. Grabowski, *The Church: An Introduction to the Theology of St. Augustine* (St. Louis, 1957); and his previously cited book: *The All-Present God*. The section by F. Cayré in *Les directions doctrinales de s. Augustin* (Paris, 1948), is an excellent survey. See also: A. Pincherle, *La formazione teologica di S. Agostino* (Roma, 1948); M. Grabmann, *Die Grundgedanken des hl. Augustinus über Seele und Gott* (Köln, 1929); F. Cayré, "The Great Augustinism," *Theology Digest*, II (1954) 169–173.

[56] *Supra*, note 49.

[57] *Œuvres de saint Augustin*, tome 15: *La Trinité* (Livres I–VII), texte, traduction et notes par M. Mellet et Th. Camelot, introduction par E. Hendriks (Paris, 1955); tome 16: *La Trinité* (Livres VIII–XV), par P. Agaësse et J. Moingt (Paris, 1955).

[58] C. J. O'Toole, *The Philosophy of Creation in the Writings of St. Augustine* (Washington, 1944).

[59] H. de Dorlodot, *Le Darwinisme au point de vue de l'orthodoxie catholique* (Bruxelles-Paris, 1921). In a less extreme sense: L. Pera, *La creazione similtanea e virtuale secondo S. Agostino* (Firenze, 1928).

[60] H. Woods, *Augustine and Evolution* (New York, 1924); M. J. McKeough, *The Meaning of the Rationes Seminales in St. Augustine* (Washington, 1926); C. Boyer, "La théorie des raisons séminales," in *Essais sur la doctrine de s. Augustin* (Paris, 1932), pp. 97–137. For a more qualified view: E. C. Messenger, *Evolution and Theology* (New York, 1931).

of the fact that the "seeds" of certain species may lie dormant in the texture of matter, for long periods of time, before conditions are right for the actual growth of living members of these species.

Reality, as Augustine sees it, falls on three levels. God and the *rationes aeternae* constitute the top layer, characterized by absolute immutability of being. Human souls (and in a sense angelic spirits) dwell on the middle level: immutable in regard to place but mutable in time. On the lowest level are all bodily things: mutable both in space and time.[61] So situated, the soul of man is able to look upward to God and the eternal truths (this is the *conversio ad Deum*), or downward to mutable creatures (the *perversio animae*). In the upward gaze of the soul, we find the working of the *ratio superior*; in the downward glance, the *ratio inferior*. These are not two faculties of the soul but two dispositions of one and the same mind; there are no "faculties" in the psychology of Augustine. It is on the same basis that two "loves" are distinguished, and so two societies of intellectual creatures, as described in the *City of God*.[62] Similarly, the distinction of time and eternity, a topic dear to the heart of Augustine, depends on the foregoing.[63] The same theme runs through Augustine's esthetics.[64]

Grace and Predestination. Though Augustine's writings on divine grace are of major import in the history of theology, they are difficult to interpret today. One source of difficulty is the very complexity of later thinking (even among Catholics), resulting from the Renaissance controversies on grace. St. Augustine, moreover, did not stress the distinction between the natural and the super-

[61] Cf. B. J. Cooke, "The Mutability-Immutability Principle in St. Augustine's Metaphysics," *The Modern Schoolman*, XXIII (1946) 174–193; XXIV (1946) 37–49. The same theme is developed in my article, "Wisdom in the Gnoseology of St. Augustine," in *Augustinus* (Madrid, 1958).

[62] See my introduction to the Image Book edition (New York, 1958) for this socio-political application of the mutability-immutability principle.

[63] J. Guitton, *Le temps et l'éternité chez Plotin et saint Augustin* (Paris, 1933); J. F. Callahan, *Four Views of Time in Ancient Philosophy* (Cambridge, Mass., 1948).

[64] E. Chapman, *St. Augustine's Philosophy of Beauty* (New York, 1939); K. Svoboda, *L'Esthétique de s. Augustin et ses sources* (Paris, 1933).

natural, as later writers do.[65] He spoke of the original state of Adam as the "natural"[66] (as did St. Anselm of Canterbury and many Anglican theologians), and so fallen man is, for Augustine, in a less than "natural" state. On the same basis, the *libertas* which characterizes man's highest freedom is found at its best in this original state, before the Fall. Man is helped by grace to regain something of what was lost by Adam's sin. In opposition to Pelagius, Augustine came in later life to insist more and more on the necessity of grace for good and meritorious human action.[67] A thorough study, in English, of Augustine's whole teaching on grace is much to be desired.

The rôle of divine predestination in Augustinism is well explained by Father Portalié. Augustine's views on divine foreknowledge and the influence of God's will on man's destiny were distorted by some of the reformation thinkers. Indeed, few authors have exalted the liberty of man as did Augustine; yet few have so strongly affirmed the certainty and extent of God's knowledge of the ways in which man will use and abuse his freedom. That the relation of these two themes involves mystery and obscurity for the imperfect human mind, Augustine readily admits.[68]

Ecclesiology. While Augustine wrote no separate treatise on the Church, his whole later life was devoted to his diocese, to the

[65] On this point the research of H. de Lubac, *Surnaturel* (Paris, 1946), is fundamental.

[66] *Retractationes*, I, 10, 3: "hoc dictum ad naturam talem referatur, qualis sine vitio primitus condita est: ipsa enim vere ac proprie natura hominis dicitur." Cf. J.-B. Kors, *La Justice primitive et le péché originel d'après s. Thomas* (Le Saulchoir, 1922), p. 11.

[67] C. Boyer, "Le système de s. Augustin sur la grâce," in *Essais* (Paris, 1932), pp. 206–236; V. Capanaga, *La teologia agustiniana de la gracia* (Madrid-Escorial, 1933); K. Janssen, *Die Entstehung der Gnadenlehre des hl. Augustinus* (Rostock, 1936); L. Bovy, *Grâce et liberté chez s. Augustin* (Montreal, 1939); P. Platz, *Der Römerbrief in der Gnadenlehre Augustins* (Würzburg, 1937); E. J. Carney, *The Doctrine of St. Augustine on Sanctity* (Washington, 1945).

[68] Gilson, *Introduction*, p. 204. On the whole question of predestination in Augustine: J. Saint-Martin, *Le pensée de s. Augustin sur la prédestination* (Paris, 1930); A. M. Jacquin, "La prédestination d'après s. Augustin," *Miscellanea Agostiniana* (Roma, 1931), II, 855–868; A. Polman, *De Predestinatie van Augustinus, Thomas van Aquino, en Calvijn* (Franeker, 1936); T. Deman, "La théologie de la grâce," in *Augustinus Magister*, III, 247–257, cites more recent studies.

ecclesiastical problems in North Africa, and indeed to Catholicism in the civilized world of his day. Of course, the Church figures prominently throughout the *City of God*.[69] Important in his ecclesiological thinking were his successive polemics against Manichaeism, Donatism, and Pelagianism.[70]

Much contemporary writing has been done on Augustine's contribution to sacramental theology. While it is clear that the term, *sacramentum*, had not yet achieved its technical usage in Augustine's time, the doctrine of the sacraments was well presented in his writings.[71] Numerous special studies of his teaching on the individual sacraments are now available.[72]

Moral Teaching. The outstanding study of Augustine's moral theory is still that of Joseph Mausbach.[73] Since he did not know the *Nicomachean Ethics* of Aristotle, St. Augustine has a different approach to moral theory from that of the later Scholastics. He

[69] S. J. Grabowski, "St. Augustine and the Primacy of the Roman Bishops," *Traditio*, 4 (1946) 89–113; his later book, *The Church*, has been mentioned *supra*, note 55. Father Portalié's colleague, P. Battifol produced a fundamental study: *Le Catholicisme de s. Augustin* (Paris, 1920). See also: F. Hofmann, *Der Kirchenbegriff des hl. Augustinus* (München, 1933); G. Spaneddo, *Il misterio della Chiesa nel pensiero di Sant' Agostino* (Sassari, 1944).

[70] G. Bardy, "Manichéisme," *DTC*, IX (1927), col. 1841–1895; P. Monceaux, *Histoire Littéraire de l'Afrique Chrétienne*, tome VI: Donatisme (Paris, 1923); A. Guzzo, *Agostino contro Pelagio* (Torino, 1934); for criticism of the moral position of these sects, see: J. Mausbach, *Die Ethik des hl. Augustinus* (Freiburg i. B., 1909), volume II. Consult also: W. B. O'Dowd, "Development of Augustine's Opinions on Religious Toleration," *Irish Theol. Quarterly* (1919), pp. 337–348.

[71] J. P. Christopher (ed.), St. Augustine, *The First Catechetical Instruction* (Westminster, Md., 1946), pp. 108–109. See also: J. Hymnen, *Die Sakramentlehre Augustins* (Bonn, 1905); G. Pierse, "The Origin of the Doctrine of the Sacramental Character," *Irish Theol. Quarterly* (1911), pp. 196–211; C. Spallanzani, "La nozione di sacramento in S. Agostino," *Scuola Cattolica*, IX (1927) 175–188, 258–266.

[72] A. Gendreau, *S. Augustini Doctrina de Baptismo* (Baltimore, 1939); B. Busch, *De initiatione christiana secundum doctrinam S. Augustini* (Romae, 1939); K. Adam, *Die geheime Kirchenbusse nach dem hl. Augustin* (Kempten, 1931); A. Reuter, *S. Augustini doctrina de bonis matrimonii* (Romae, 1942); B. A. Pereira, *La doctrine du mariage selon s. Augustin* (Paris, 1930).

[73] Cited above, note 70. See also: B. Roland-Gosselin, *La morale des s. Augustin* (Paris, 1925); C. Boyer, *Saint Augustin* (*Les Moralistes Chrétiens*: Paris, 1932);

makes no distinction between moral theology and ethics, stresses the love of God above all else, regards the eternal law as the immediate rule of man's life on earth.[74] Of course, in the work of a man who has written and preached so much, it is possible to find texts in which Augustine faces nearly all the problems treated in a complete course in moral theology.[75] However, his way of handling these questions (man's end and beatitude, voluntariness, principles and laws, virtues, moral conscience, and so on) is frequently rhetorical and non-technical. There are few significant differences between Augustine's answers to special moral problems and the later tradition of Catholic morality. The Decalogue supplies the foundation for the whole tradition.

Much work has been done on the political and social views of the Bishop of Hippo, particularly by English writers.[76] Gilson's *Foreword* to the *City of God* has been mentioned; it refers to many foreign language studies in this area.[77] Augustine's vision of a Christian state of mind imbued with the love of God was operative in, and distorted by, many of the political efforts of mediaeval rulers.[78]

The problem of the mysticism of St. Augustine has occasioned much controversy. Some historians consider him the most impor-

S. J. Grou, *Morality Extracted From the Confessions*, introd. by R. Hudleston (London, 1934); J. F. Harvey, *Moral Theology of the Confessions of St. Augustine* (Washington, 1951).

[74] G. Combès, *La Charité d'après s. Augustin* (Paris, 1934); A. Schubert, *Augustins Lex-aeterna-Lehre nach Inhalt und Quellen* (Münster, 1924).

[75] Such a systematic collection of Augustine's moral texts has recently been made: G. Armas, *La moral de San Agustin* (Latin and Spanish) (Madrid, 1955), pp. 1, 181.

[76] J. N. Figgis, *The Political Aspects of St. Augustine's City of God* (London, 1921); E. G. Sihler, *From Augustus to Augustine* (London, 1924); E. Humphries, *Politics and Religion in the Days of Augustine* (New York, 1927).

[77] Deserving of special mention: O. Schilling, *Die Staats- und Soziallehre des hl. Augustinus* (Freiburg i. B., 1910); G. Combès, *La doctrine politique de s. Augustin* (Paris, 1927); A. Brucculeri, *Il pensiero sociale di S. Agostino* (Roma, 1932).

[78] H. X. Arquillière, *L'Augustinisme politique. Essai sur la formation des théories politiques du moyen âge* (Paris, 1934); V. Bourke, "The Political Philosophy of St. Augustine," *Proc. Amer. Cath. Philos. Assoc.*, VII (1931), 45–55.

tant writer on mysticism in the early Church.[79] Others deny that Augustine was a mystic at all.[80] The latter group uses a much restricted definition of mysticism. Thus the problem reduces not so much to the interpretation of Augustine as to the finding of an accepted definition. Father Boyer sums up the difficulty in these penetrating words: "M. Meyer sets up an opposition between intellectualism and mysticism. I say: if we admit this, then even the intuitive vision in Heaven will not be mystical. In that case, I wonder what mysticism is."[81] It should be understood that some hesitancy regarding the validity of Augustine's mystical experience stems from an almost disconcerting resemblance of certain ecstatic passages in the *Confessions* to texts in Plotinus' *Enneads*.[82]

Eschatology. Regarding the future life of man, Augustine's teaching is basically the same as that of present-day Catholic theology.[83] Heaven and hell are very real sanctions.[84] One editor of the *City of God* (F. W. Bussell, 1903) has tried to get rid of hell by omitting the passages which mention it.

IV. Influence

Contemporary scholarship continues to rank Augustine among the great minds in western civilization. His authority as a Christian writer is second only to the canonical writings and the official pronouncements of his Church. He is still regarded as the outstanding Father of the Church.[85] It is probably impossible to exaggerate the influence of his life and thought.

[79] C. Butler, *Western Mysticism* (London, 1927); F. Cayré, *La contemplation augustinienne* (Paris, 1927).

[80] E. Hendriks, *Augustins Verhältnis zur Mystik* (Würzburg, 1936); H. Meyer, "War Augustinus Intellektualist oder Mystiker?" *Augustinus Magister*, III, 429–437; see the same volume (pp. 103–168) for a survey of the whole problem, and for bibliography.

[81] *Augustinus Magister*, III, 168.

[82] Cf. P. Henry, *La vision d'Ostie* (Paris, 1938).

[83] D. J. Leahy, *St. Augustine on Eternal Life* (New York, 1939); H. Eger, *Die Eschatologie Augustins* (Paderborn, 1933).

[84] A. Lehaut, *L'Eternité des peines de l'enfer dans saint Augustin* (Paris, 1912).

[85] P. von Sokolowski, *Der hl. Augustin und die christliche Zivilisation* (Halle, 1927); C. Dawson, "St. Augustine and his Age," in *Monument to St. Augustine* (London, 1930), pp. 34–76.

Augustine's contribution to the development of monasticism was fundamental. His *Rule* for the religious life has been followed not only by the Order which bears his name, the Augustinians, but has formed the basis for the regulation of many other religious communities.[86] Prominent among such groups is the Order of Preachers, founded by St. Dominic. The fifth Master General, Humbert de Romans, perfected the Dominican rule by means of a famous commentary on the *Rule* of St. Augustine.[87] As mediaeval philosophy is becoming better known, our appreciation of Augustine's rôle in its development is increasing. From Boethius to Nicholas Cusa, the story of intellectualism in the middle ages is replete with references to his works.[88] In the growth of Christian theology, Augustine is always a key author.[89]

Among modern and contemporary philosophers Augustine is read by people of widely diversified interests. We have seen how many of his works have been printed, both in Latin and in the vernaculars, throughout this century. Existentialists, phenomenologists, philosophers of history, actionists, idealists, introspective psychologists, representatives of a dozen other movements, find or think they find a patron in St. Augustine.[90]

VERNON J. BOURKE

St. Louis University

---

[86] E. A. Foran, *The Augustinians* (London, 1938).

[87] P. Mandonnet, *Saint Dominique. L'Idée, l'homme et l'œuvre* (Paris, 1937), vol. I, 188.

[88] E. Gilson, *History of Christian Philosophy in the Middle Ages* (New York, 1955); "Pourquoi saint Thomas a critiqué saint Augustin," *Archives d'Histoire Doctrinale et Littéraire*, I (1926-7) 5-127; M. Grabmann, *Mittelalterliches Geistesleben* (München, 1926), I, 1-62.

[89] M. Grabmann, *Geschichte der katholischen Theologie* (Freiburg i. B., 1933); see also the *Patrologies* of Cayré, Quasten, and Altaner.

[90] J. Geyser, *Augustin und die phaenomenologische Religionsphilosophie der Gegenwart* (Münster, 1923); E. Przywara, "St. Augustine and the Modern World," *Monument to St. Augustine*, pp. 249-286; M. Blondel, "The Latent Resources of St. Augustine's Thought," *Ibid.*, pp. 317-353; V. Capanaga, "San Agustin en Nuestro Tiempo," *Augustinus*, II, 6 (1957) 155-175; for further references, see: P. Vignaux, "Influence Augustinienne," *Augustinus Magister*, III, 265-273.

A Guide to the Thought of
Saint Augustine

Part One

LIFE

CHAPTER I

Aberrations and Conversion
(354–386)

URELIUS AUGUSTINE, Bishop of Hippo, one of the greatest
saints and the most renowned doctor of the Church, was
born November 13, 354, and died August 28, 430. Without
a doubt his writings have had a very powerful influence in directing the course of Western thought. It is precisely his life as a
scholar, as a matter of fact, which will be presented in this book,
which is an account of the history of his thought rather than of
his virtues or his episcopal ministry. The documents concerning
him are of unsurpassed richness, for the *Confessions*, the *Retractations*, and the *Life of Augustine* by his friend Possidius provide
far more autobiographical and historical references than we have
for any other ancient author.

The first part of this book will be limited to a mere indication
of the principal characteristics of each period of his life.

1. Christian Education

Augustine was born November 13, 354, at Tagaste, the modern
Souk Arrhas, about sixty miles from Bône, the ancient city of
Hippo Regius. Tagaste was a free village of the Roman province
of Numidia Proconsularis, recently converted to the Donatist
schism. Aurelius, his second name, never appears in his correspondence, but was given him by his contemporaries.[1] His family,
which occupied a respectable place in society, was not rich. His
father Patricius, one of the Roman administrators of the town,
was still a pagan; but the exemplary virtues which have exalted

Monica (or Monnica, according to the spelling of the manuscripts) as the model of Christian motherhood finally resulted in the baptism and holy death of her husband about the year 371.

Augustine received a Christian education. His mother took care that he was marked with the sign of the cross and enrolled among the catechumens.[2] He shared the faith of Monica and, having fallen sick, asked for baptism. However, since the danger quickly disappeared, it was put off, in keeping with the deplorable custom of that time.

He came into contact with some men of prayer, *homines rogantes*.[3] From then on three important ideas, formed in his conversations with them, made a deep impression on him. The first of these was the existence of a provident God, whom he conceived as "some Great Being, who, though not evident to our senses, might hear us and help us";[4] and he prayed fervently "that I might not be beaten in school" for his giddiness. For, although he was a talented youth, he was also trifling, inattentive, lazy, and an enemy of Greek. The second idea was the thought of Christ the Savior. "This name of my Savior, Thy Son, my youthful heart had drunk in piously with my mother's milk and until that time had retained it in its depths; whatever was without this name could not completely win me, however well expressed, polished, and truthful."[5] Finally, he was impressed by the idea of the future life and its sanctions: "While still a boy, I had indeed heard of the eternal life promised us."[6] Elsewhere he tells about the thought of the judgment, fear of which, "despite the vagaries of my opinions, never departed from my breast."[7]

Augustine soon learned all that he could at the school of Tagaste. He studied literature in the town of Madaura with such success that his father's hopes for him grew very strong. Although it called for greater sacrifices than he could afford, Patricius decided to send him to Carthage to prepare for a legal career. Unfortunately it took him some months to gather the necessary funds, and Augustine had to pass his sixteenth year at Tagaste in an idleness which proved fatal to his virtue.

2. THE MORAL CRISIS (369)

The second book of the *Confessions* deprecates this first victory of his passions. Left to himself, Augustine gave himself over to seeking out pleasures with all the impetuosity of a passionate nature. At the beginning of this critical period he prayed, but without a sincere desire of being heard: "Give me chastity, but not just yet."[8] When he arrived at Carthage towards the end of the year 370, every attraction swept him along with it: the enticements of that great half-pagan city, the free and easy morals of the other students, the attendance at the theater, the exhilaration of his literary successes ("I was puffed up with vanity."),[9] and the arrogant desire to be the leader, even in evil ("I was ashamed not to be shameless.").[10] It was not long before he had to confess to Monica a sinful union from which a son had been born to him (372), "the son of his sin." He did not separate from this woman until he was at Milan, after fifteen years of enslavement.

In the evaluation of this critical period two excesses must be avoided. Some, deceived by the protestations of sorrow in the *Confessions*, have, with Mommsen, played it up too much. Loofs rightly reproaches him for this opinion, but, for his own part, frees Augustine from blame too readily when he maintains that the Church permitted one to keep a concubine at that period.[11] The *Confessions*, even apart from other evidence, prove that Loofs had no understanding of the seventeenth canon of the Council of Toledo. Indeed, it could be said that even in his fall Augustine kept a certain dignity, a sense of compunction which does him credit, and also, from his nineteenth year on, a true desire to burst the bonds of his captivity. In the year 373, as a matter of fact, a whole new outlook on life was brought home to him by the reading of the *Hortensius*. From it he drank in a love of the wisdom which Cicero had so magnificently eulogized. Thereafter a new ideal arose in his soul; he already dreamed—and it was then only a dream—to give up everything for truth. "Suddenly, every vain hope became worthless to me and I yearned with unbelievable ardor of heart for the immortality of wisdom."[12] From this moment rhetoric no longer held any interest for Augustine except as a means of livelihood, for his heart had turned to philosophy. The solitude of Cassiciacum will see the fulfillment of his dream, put off till then by the double allure of his passions and of Manicheism.

3. THE MANICHEAN CRISIS (373-382)

It was also in his nineteenth year that Augustine with his friend Honoratus fell into the snares of the Manicheans. He was their disciple for nine years, "nine entire years," he says,[13] that is, until the time of his departure from Africa for Rome.

a. MOTIVES

How could a mind so noble be led astray by Oriental musings which the Persian Mani (in Greek Μάνης, lived 215-276) had synthesized into a coarse and materialistic dualism and introduced into Africa hardly fifty years previously? Augustine himself enumerated the motives which carried him along. (1) His pride allowed him to be taken in by the promises of a liberal philosophy unhampered by the bridle of faith. The Manicheans kept repeating "that faith was demanded of us before reason, while they, on the other hand, were forcing no one to believe without first hunting for and disentangling the truth. Who would not be enticed by these promises? And would there not be special enticement for a youthful mind desirous of truth, . . . yet haughty and talkative?"[14] "And they repeated: 'Truth, truth'; and they said it often."[15] (2) The contradictions which they thought they proved in Holy Scripture, for example, the one between the two genealogies of Matthew and Luke.[16] (3) The hope of finding in their sect a *scientific* explanation of nature and of its most mysterious phenomena. The inquisitive mind of Augustine took a deep interest in the natural sciences and the Manicheans assured him that nature held no secrets for Faustus, their teacher. (4) The origin of evil distressed his mind, and, for want of a solution, he admitted the conflict of two principles. (5) The materialism which is latent in a system which explained everything by the opposition of light and darkness attracted Augustine, for his mind could not picture a spiritual substance.[17]

In addition, other motives of a moral character succeeded in winning his allegiance. On the one hand, he let himself be taken in by the apparent austerity and the affected virtues of the initiated Manicheans, who, calling themselves "the elect" or "the perfect," made a great show of extremely rigorous abstinence and chastity. Later on, this hypocrisy, unmasked for what it was, brought about his conversion. On the one hand, what a powerful attraction, what moral irresponsibility resulted from a doctrine which denied liberty and attributed its crimes to an extrinsic principle! "For, up to that time, it seemed to me that it is not we who sin, but some other unknown nature within us which sins. It was a joy to my pride to be freed from culpability."[18]

Once he had been won over to the sect, Augustine devoted himself to it with his characteristic impetuosity. He read all their books; he adopted and defended all their opinions. He attacked the Catholic faith "with wretched and violent bombast"[19] and his impassioned proselytism soon drew into the error his friend Alypius; his patron of Tagaste Romanianus, a friend of his father whose fortune had been used to defray the expenses of his studies;[20] and finally the friend whose conversion, baptism, and death he recounts in the *Confessions*.[21]

b. PROFESSOR AT CARTHAGE

This Manichean period coincides with the full development of Augustine's literary powers. He was still a student at Carthage when he embraced the false doctrine. At the termination of his course of studies he should normally have entered the law courts, but he preferred a literary career and returned to Tagaste to teach "grammar."[22] The youthful professor knew how to capture the attention of his pupils; and one of them, Alypius, hardly younger than Augustine himself, was unwilling ever to leave him again.

After having followed him into the error of Manicheism, he was to be baptized with him in Milan and still later was to become bishop of Tagaste, his native city. Meanwhile Monica mourned her son's heresy "far more than do mothers who weep at bodily deaths."[23] A holy bishop, no doubt the Bishop of Tagaste, consoled her with these words: "It is impossible for the son of those tears of yours to perish."[24] She had at first banned Augustine from her home, but soon she consented to receive him into her house and at her table.

The death of a very close friend made Augustine's further residence at Tagaste unendurable. To divert his mind from his grief through public acclaim, he went to Carthage to continue his lectures in rhetoric. On this broader stage of action, to which his pupils, Alypius and the two sons of Romanianus, followed him, his native talents shone with all their true brilliance. Here he put the finishing touches to the complete formation of his mind by his tireless study of all the liberal arts. "I read by myself and understood all the books I could on the arts which are proper to a free man."[25] Having taken part in a famed poetic contest, he carried off the trophy. The proconsul Vindicianus crowned him with the laurel of victory before all the people in the theater. At this time he composed his first work, no longer extant. It was on esthetics, entitled *On the Beautiful and Fitting.*[26]

C. DISILLUSIONMENT WITH MANICHEISM

Basically, even during the period of his first enthusiasm, the teaching of Manes left his mind somewhat uneasy and disturbed; he was never fully satisfied. Far from having been a priest in the sect, as he was accused later on,[27] he was never initiated into the elect, but remained only in the grade of hearer, the lowest rank of the hierarchy, somewhat like a catechumen. His restive mind kept looking for an answer to the mysteries of nature. Although he had always abominated the art of magic,[28] he went from the study of astronomy to the musings of the astrologers, well content with blaming his faults on the stars.[29] In vain did the magistrate Vindicianus and the young Nebridius try to drag him away from these studies; it took the story of two infants born the same day to shake him in his belief.[30] The fact of the matter was that the problem of evil always bothered him and the more acquainted he became with Manicheism, the less he was able to put his anxiety to rest.

He himself revealed the causes of his disappointment. (1) The frightful emptiness of the Manichean philosophy. "They tore everything down and were unable to construct anything in its place. . . . And so they did to us what bird catchers are accustomed to do. . . . They cover over and conceal in any way they can the surrounding waters . . . so that the birds fall into their snares, not through choice, but of necessity."[31] (2) Their immorality in contrast to their affectation of virtue. He observed that beneath an austere exterior the lives of the elect were really scandalous and this hypocrisy revolted him.[32] (3) Their inferiority in polemics with Catholics. Against texts from Holy Scripture they had only one reply: "They have falsified the Scriptures."[33] He himself did not know what answer to make to Nebridius, who had remained a Catholic, when asked why God could not prevent the evil principle from taking portions of His divinity from Him.[34] (4) Especially did he not find any science at all among them. And it was science, in the modern sense of the knowledge of nature and its laws, that had been promised him. Now, when he asked about the movements of the stars and their causes, none of the Manicheans knew how to answer him. "Wait for Faustus," they told him, "he will explain everything." Faustus of Milevis, the noted Manichean bishop, finally did come to Carthage. Augustine saw him and questioned him. His answers showed that he was a popular orator, but an absolute stranger to all scientific learning.[35] The spell was broken. Although he did not immediately make an open break from the sect, his mind was completely detached from its teachings. The delusion had lasted for nine years.

d. CONVERSION BY PHILOSOPHY

A little while after this intellectual revolution, Augustine, at the age of twenty-nine (383), wished to seek at Rome, in more respectable surroundings, some disciples who would be more worthy of him than the *eversores* of Carthage.[36] Since his mother had guessed that he was departing and did not wish to be separated from him, he resorted to a subterfuge and sailed during the night. Scarcely had he arrived at Rome when he became seriously ill, but he had no thought of asking for baptism. Once he was well, he started a school of oratory. Disgusted, however, by the stratagems of the students to default on their tuition, he put in an application for a vacant professorship at Milan and was approved by Symmachus, the Roman prefect. In a visit he had with the bishop Ambrose, the charm of the saint captivated him and he decided to attend his sermons.

Two years of struggle yet separated him from the victory of the faith. The mind of Augustine, from 383 to 386, passed through three different phases. First, there was a period of Academic philosophy and discouraged scepticism. At heart he was not in favor of Manicheism, but he still mingled with its adherents and had lodgings in the home of one of them at Rome. But the philosophy which he preferred to it offered him nothing but doubts. "Thus, in the traditional manner of the Academics, I was in doubt about all things and took no definite position on anything, but I decided that the Manicheans were to be abandoned."[37] He remained, therefore, a catechumen in the Catholic Church, as he had been since his infancy, "until some light of certainty might appear, by which I could direct my course."[38]

The second period was one of enthusiastic Neoplatonism. No sooner had he finished reading, at Milan, certain works of Plato and especially of Plotinus, than his hope of finding truth blazed up again. Formerly he had found it impossible to think of a spiritual being.[39] Now when he meditated the profound theories about the "unchangeable light" of truth,[40] about evil, which is essentially a privation,[41] about God, an immaterial and infinite Being who is the source of other beings,[42] and about the Word itself, which he thought that he found in these works,[43] he was carried out of himself and seized by a new passion, a passion for philosophy. Then he dreamt of a life entirely consecrated to the quest after truth, a life in common with his friends who were smitten with the same desire.[44] It was to be a pure life, free from all the ordinary concerns about honors, fortune, or pleasures, with celibacy as a guiding principle. But it was only a dream, for he still remained a prisoner to his passions.[45] Monica, who had joined her son at Milan, persuaded him to make arrangements for marriage, but his fiancee was not yet of age. Augustine had sent away the mother of Adeodatus, but now, alas, another followed in her place.

Then he went through a final period of anguish and struggle. Light began to illumine his mind from the reading of the Scriptures,[46] for they revealed to him two fundamental truths which the Platonists did not know: Christ the Savior and all-conquering grace. Soon he was certain that Jesus Christ was the only way to truth and salvation.[47] Resistance came no longer except from his heart. A talk with Simplicianus, the future successor of Ambrose, and the story of the conversion of the famous Neoplatonic orator Victorinus[48] prepared the way for the decisive stroke of grace which vanquished him in a garden of Milan. It was September, 386; Augustine was thirty-three.[49]

A few days afterwards, taking advantage of the autumn holidays, Augustine, who was sick, gave up his chair and went with Monica, Adeodatus, and his friends to the country home of Verecundus. There he devoted himself to true philosophy, which he no longer differentiated from Christianity.

CHAPTER II

From His Conversion to the Episcopate (386–396)

THE ten years from 386–396 comprise a period when Augustine became acquainted with Christian dogma. During this time he developed in his mind a blend of Platonic philosophy and revealed doctrine. The principle which governed the evolution of his thought has been misunderstood recently and deserves a clear explanation.

1. THE SOLITARY OF CASSICIACUM (SEPTEMBER, 386–MARCH, 387)

a. THE PHILOSOPHER

The long-cherished dream had finally come true. In the third book of *Against the Academics* Augustine has described this life of perfect repose, enlivened only by his passion for truth. In charge of the administration of the villa, he complains of the time lost in giving orders to the servants, although his health demanded this diversion. At the same time he brought to completion the education of his young friends, partially by classes in literature for all of them, partially by philosophical discussions to which he occasionally invited Monica. Accounts of these talks, taken down by a scribe, have furnished the substance of the dialogues *Against the Academics*, *On the Happy Life*, and *On Order*.

Later Licentius will recall these delightful morning and evening sessions spent on philosophy.[1] Augustine, when speaking of everyday occurrences, raises problems of the deepest profundity. An example of this is seen in the exquisite passage of *On Order*.[2] One of his principles is that "the most sublime topics, when discussed by lowly people, tend to share their own greatness with them."[3]

He knew well how to impart his passion for philosophy to his disciples so that they had only a distaste for the world and a sovereign contempt for the life of the senses.[4] The subjects which he especially loved to discuss in these meetings can be gleaned from the writings of this period: truth and certitude in *Against the Academics*; true happiness in philosophy in *On the Happy Life*; the divinely providential order in the world and the problem of evil in *On Order*; and to bring all these together, God and the soul in the *Soliloquies* and *On the Immortality of the Soul*.

b. CHRISTIAN OR NEOPLATONIST?

Until modern times no one had doubted that Augustine at Cassiciacum was a Christian. All the historians, relying on the account of the *Confessions*, had been of the opinion that the conversion of Augustine dated from the scene in the garden and that the retirement to Cassiciacum, necessary to restore his health, also served the purpose of preparing him for baptism. Today, however, some critics uncover a radical opposition between the philosophical dialogues which were written during this seclusion and the state of soul described in the *Confessions*. According to Harnack,[5] the author of the *Confessions* must have superimposed the feelings of the bishop in 400 on the solitary of 386. Others, Loofs for instance,[6] and especially Gourdon in a thesis presented to the faculty of Protestant Theology of Paris,[7] go even further. The solitary of the villa at Milan, they maintain, was not a Christian at heart but a Platonist; the scene in the garden was not a conversion to Christianity but to philosophy. According to Gourdon the truly Christian stage of Augustine's life did not begin until 390.[8]

Wörter has anticipated and treated these assertions as they deserve.[9] The discussion is quickly resolved by means of these solidly established facts: (1) Augustine was baptized, as all admit, at Easter, 387. Who will believe that this was a meaningless and empty ceremony? (2) The material facts of the *Confessions* (and not only the state of his soul) would have to have been falsified with unashamed brazenness: the scene in the garden, the example of the solitaries, the reading of St. Paul, the conversion of Victorinus, the ecstasy of Augustine when reading the Psalms with Monica—all that fabricated after the deed was done! (3) Finally, Augustine composed such apologetic works as *On the Morals of the Catholic Church* in 388, when he would not even have been a Christian! The reader is free, moreover, to consult the dialogues themselves.

C. CHRISTIAN DEVELOPMENT ACCORDING TO THE WRITINGS OF CASSICIACUM

Undoubtedly there is all the difference between the *Confessions* and the philosophical dialogues that such diverse literary types and purposes demand. The dialogues are a purely philosophical work, composed in his youth, although, as Augustine candidly admits, not without pretension: "in writings which now served You indeed, but still, at unguarded moments, smacked of my proud desires."[10] How could works of this nature tell of the victories of grace? Only incidentally do they reveal the state of soul of the solitary, but they tell enough of it to prove that their author is the converted Augustine of the *Confessions*.

The first thing to consider is the ruling purpose which directs these philosophical inquiries. It was revealed already in 386 in the first work written at Cassiciacum. The third book of *Against the Academics* contains the following conclusions: From the outset the purpose of his investigations is to unite reason to authority and then his faith to the authority of Christ: "I am certain that I can never entirely withdraw from the authority of Christ, for I can find none more cogent."[11] Finally the law governing his philosophy is given. In his study of the Platonists he is seeking only those explanations which are in harmony with the faith: "I am confident that I will find in the Platonists meanwhile nothing that will be at variance with our sacred literature."[12] This excessive confidence would have its dangers, as will be seen later when the Neoplatonic doctrine of Augustine is explained. But it is clear that it is not a Platonist who is speaking in these dialogues, but a Christian; or, to be more exact, a man who is both. There are not two truths for Augustine; there is only the one which he has

found in the Gospel. He is now seeking reasons for it in philosophy. The illusion of Gourdon and Loofs has been to graft our
modern distinctions onto the mind of Augustine. But to do
that, they, Gourdon especially, must have refused to read the
texts.

The faith of Augustine shows itself in the dialogues under
various guises. (1) An account of his conversion. In the second
book of *Against the Academics* he tells of the irrepressible passion
which drew him towards philosophy once the religion of his child-
hood had again laid hold of him. "I only looked upon that
religion, I confess, as from afar . . . but all the time it was drawing
me to itself without my knowledge."[13] Disturbed and hesitant, he
had taken up the Apostle Paul: "I read all of him with the greatest
attention and care."[14] He reveals the argument which convinced
him, namely, the panorama of the life and conquests of the
Apostles. "For not even they would have been able to do so
much. . . ."[15] (2) A beautiful act of faith in the Trinity and the
Incarnation.[16] (3) A typical conversation about the divinity of
Christ. Nothing can give a better proof of the intimate relationship which united philosophical wisdom and the Christian faith
in that group of Augustine and his friends than this delightful
scene.[17] In connection with a definition of the providential order
in the world, a discussion took place. The subject of this dispute
was not the faith in Christ which all those young Christians themselves defended: " 'That's a fine statement you are making,' said
Licentius. 'Are we to deny that the Son of God is God?' "[18] The
discussion was rather concerned with the way of understanding
His divine filiation, and it was Augustine who exclaimed, "Just
a minute, for the Son is not called God in any improper sense."[19]
He is God in the strictest meaning of the word. Immediately
young Trygetius, in confusion, begged that the unfortunate phrase
be stricken from the account.

Monica also was admitted to these philosophical discussions, for
she was no stranger in these "hallowed halls of philosophy."[20]
The philosophy which Augustine was in quest of was not that
condemned in Holy Scripture, but that which Monica loved,

which she loved even more than her son himself, "and I know how much you love me."[21]

The wondrous transformations which faith is working in his soul also appear in the dialogues. There is the prayer which he offers to God each day: "I arose and paid my daily homage to God."[22] And what prayer! An echo of it sounds in the *Soliloquies* (written at Cassiciacum at the beginning of 387), which open with that wonderful outpouring of a heart that is thoroughly steeped in the words of the Gospel: "O God, who take care that the door is open to those who knock (Matt. 7:8); O God, who give us the bread of life (John 6:35); O God, through whom we thirst for that draught which will quench our thirst forever (John 4:13). . . ."[23] And for what does he pray? "Increase my faith, increase my hope, increase my charity."[24] Is this the prayer of a non-Christian Platonist?

The repentance of Augustine shines forth much less frequently here than in the *Confessions*, but its beams are none the less piercing: "My wounds are enough for me, to heal which I pray to God with almost daily tears."[25] In the prayer of the *Soliloquies* he deplores his intellectual aberrations: "Receive, I beg, Your fugitive, O Lord. . . . Long enough . . . have I served . . . Your enemies, long enough have I been the plaything of errors. Receive me, Your servant, fleeing from all these things."[26] Boissier stated that "the penitent had definitely taken the ascendancy in Augustine, although he still remained a philosopher."[27] Nevertheless, Gourdon dares to deny that the penitent had yet appeared![28]

The moral victory was the climax of everything, a victory over the intellectual pride created previously by his readings in Platonism.[29] Now, the big obstacle to wisdom, "very much to be feared, and cautiously avoided," is pride, "the proud seeking after vain glory."[30] His ignorance appalls him.[31] His moral wretchedness strikes terror into him: "I who am healed so quickly am unworthy."[32] There is a victory also over his passions which are subsiding little by little. Finally, he made the decisive step to forgo marriage; wisdom is the only partner which appeals to him and for it he gives up all earthly joy: "For the freedom of my soul I laid a command on myself . . . not to take a wife."[33]

Thus the heart of Augustine, as well as his mind, was ready for baptism.

2. The Neophyte and Religious (Lent, 387–391)

a. MILAN AND ROME

Towards the beginning of Lent, 387, Augustine returned to Rome and placed himself, along with Adeodatus and Alypius, among the formal candidates for baptism. The *Confessions* testify to the mortifications and fervor of these young men.[34] On Easter day, or at least during the Paschal season, Augustine was baptized by Ambrose. The legend that the *Te Deum* was sung that day in turn by the bishop and the neophyte has no foundation, but seems to stem from a bishop of the fifth century, Nicetas of Remesiana.[35] This story but serves to illustrate how much the Church rejoiced at receiving a son who was to be her most illustrious doctor. This date also marks the resolution taken together with Alypius and Evodius of retiring to Africa to live in solitude. He undoubtedly remained at Milan until the autumn of the year, continuing his works on the immortality of the soul and on music. In the autumn of 387 he was on the verge of embarking at Ostia when Monica departed from this earth. Nowhere in literature are pages of more tender feeling to be found than the account of her blessed death and the sorrow of Augustine.[36] Augustine remained at Rome several months, occupied principally with the refutation of Manicheism. He embarked for Africa after the death of the tyrant Maximus in August, 388, and, after a short visit to Carthage,[37] he returned to his native town.

b. ESTABLISHMENT OF THE MONASTERY OF TAGASTE

Scarcely had Augustine arrived when he wished to bring into being his plan for a perfect life. He sold all his goods and gave the proceeds to the poor.[38] Then he retired with his friends onto his property, which was already sold, to live a life of poverty, prayer, and study of sacred literature.[39] The book on *Eighty-three Different Questions* is the fruit of his conversation in this solitude. There he also composed *On Genesis Against the Manicheans*, *On the Teacher*, and *On the True Religion*.

3. The Priest of Hippo (391–396)

Augustine did not think of the priesthood. He even fled from towns where an episcopal election was being held for fear of being chosen bishop. One day, when he had been called to Hippo by a friend for his spiritual welfare, he was praying in the church. The people raised a sudden clamor, begging the bishop Valerius to raise him to the priesthood. Despite the tears of Augustine, he had to yield and was ordained at the beginning of 391 (not 390).[40]

The new priest saw in his priesthood additional reasons for taking up again the religious life of Tagaste. Valerius assisted him and granted him property from the dependencies of the Church. This marked the second monastery which he founded.

A list of the principal achievements of the five-year period of his priestly ministry includes the following: (1) The office of preaching was entrusted to him, despite the custom which, in Africa, reserved this function to the bishop.[41] Valerius, far from being jealous of the talents of his priest, made an exception in his favor and soon, notwithstanding the complaints of some bishops, his example was followed by others. The *Incomplete Literal Commentary on Genesis* and *On Our Lord's Sermon on the Mount* are a summary of these sermons. (2) He fought against heresies, especially Manicheism, with overwhelming success. For example, one of the Manicheans' noted teachers, Fortunatus, challenged by Augustine to a public debate, was so ashamed of his defeat that he fled from Hippo.[42] From this period come *On the Advantage of Believing* (391), *On Two Souls* (391–392), *Against Adimantus* (394), and the completion of *On Freedom of Choice*. (3) He participated in the Plenary Council of Africa in October, 393,[43] which took place at Hippo under the presidency of Aurelius, one of the greatest bishops of Carthage. At the request of the bishops, Augustine had to give a discourse which in its completed form is *On Faith and Creed*.[44] (4) He stamped out the abuse of holding banquets in the chapels of the martyrs. Emboldened by the confidence which Aurelius had displayed in him, Augustine urged him to abolish this practice in his diocese.[45] Hefele sees his influence in the thirty-third canon of the Council of Hippo in 393 on this subject.[46] Finally, this scandalous custom was wiped out at Hippo itself in 395, but not without the gargantuan battles described in his twenty-ninth letter.[47]

CHAPTER III

The Episcopate (396–430)

VALERIUS, worn out by old age and wishing to make sure that Hippo would have a man of the caliber of Augustine as its shepherd, obtained from Aurelius, the primate of Africa, permission to associate Augustine with himself as co-adjutor. But Augustine would not consent to be consecrated until he had been given proof that the eighth canon of Nicaea permitted exceptions.[1] He was consecrated by Megalius, bishop of Calama and primate of Numidia, although there is some doubt whether the year of his consecration was 395 or 396. With Rauscher and Rottmanner[2] we prefer 396. Augustine, then forty-two years old, was destined to remain the ruler of the flock of Hippo for thirty-four years. The joy of the Church is expressed in the beautiful letter from Paulinus of Nola to Romanianus.[3]

1. THE DEVOUT BISHOP AND PASTOR

Augustine left his monastic foundation behind and moved to the episcopal residence, but his palace became a monastery in which he established the practice of common life with his clerics, who entered upon the observance of poverty and religious discipline. A frequent question is whether the Bishop of Hippo had founded an order of monks or of regular clerics, or two distinct orders. He undoubtedly gave little thought to these distinctions. But he certainly required a formal promise of poverty from his clerics. His sharing of these intimate details with his people in his sermons is most unusual.[4] He praises his clerics' life of self-denial. Augustine relates that once, following an infraction of the rule by one of the monks, all of them were given time to reconsider this life and choose it anew. They all chose to live in poverty, but it was agreed that thereafter a fall would exclude one from ordination.

The episcopal residence of Hippo became a nursery of founders who quickly covered Africa with monasteries and bishops for the sees of the neighboring dioceses. Possidius enumerates ten friends and disciples of the saint who were promoted to the episcopate.[5] Thus Augustine merited the title of the patriarch of the religious life and the reformer of clerical life in Africa. He also won others over by his example. The catalog of his virtues in Possidius[6] ought to be noted: extreme poverty and simplicity in all things, excessive austerity of life, charity which inspired the sale of the sacred vessels to ransom captives. He had a hospital and five churches erected, in one of which the relics of the first deacon, St. Stephen, were preserved.

Above all Augustine was the pastor of souls and the defender of truth. His activity in defense of orthodoxy—the influence of which was to endure as long as the Church herself—ranged over every field. He frequently preached the Word, often for five days in succession, with such evident charity that he won souls. His correspondence carried replies to questions concerning temporary problems on a world-wide scale. He offered guidance to the different African Councils in which he took part: Carthage (398, 401, 407, 419) and Milevis (416, 418). Finally, Augustine unceasingly fought against every sort of error. To do full justice in recounting these struggles would be an endless task. It is possible to mention only those chronological facts which afford a fuller understanding either of his writing or of changes in his life.

2. Struggle Against the Manicheans

The zeal which Augustine had shown since his baptism in trying to bring back his former coreligionists took a very paternal form, without losing any of its earnestness: "Let them rage against you, O Manicheans, who do not know with what great pains truth is found. . . . I will have such patience in my dealings with you as I experienced from my brethren when I wandered from the truth and followed your teachings, blinded and maddened."[7] Without going into detail, we must single out the great victory won in 404 over Felix, who was an "elect" of the Manicheans and a teacher of some of the most celebrated members of the sect. When Felix was propagating his errors in Hippo, Augustine invited him to a public discussion. Its outcome created a deep impression. Felix acknowledged that he was defeated, embraced the faith, and signed the proceedings of the discussion with Augustine.[8] In his writings Augustine successively refuted Manes (397), the noted Faustus (400), and Secundinus (405). About 415 he wrote against the fatalistic Priscillianists and astrologers who were denounced to him by Paul Orosius. Finally, about 420 he answered a Marcionite work.

3. STRUGGLE AGAINST DONATISM

This schism had been in existence almost a century. It was in 312 that the bishops of Numidia had illegally deposed Caecilianus, bishop of Carthage, on the grounds that he had been consecrated by a *traditor*.[9] They nominated as bishop an intruder, Majorinus, whom Donatus the Great succeeded. Although condemned by the pope and the emperors, the schism spread to the point that in the year 330 a synod of the movement included 270 bishops. It had brought back to life and blended two ancient errors, that of the rebaptizers and that of the Novatians. Like the rebaptizers, the Donatists held that sacramental validity was dependent upon the faith and even the moral integrity of the minister. In the spirit of the Novatians, they barred sinners from the Church. Further, it is difficult not to see in Donatism a current of antisocial claims against which the emperors had to fight with rigorous legislation.

The strange sect called the "Soldiers of Christ," known to the Catholics as the "Circumcellions" (vagrants, ruffians),[10] resembled the revolutionary sects of the Middle Ages in their destructive fanaticism. Perhaps there was evidence here, as Thummel, Döllinger, and Harnack contended, of a national movement against Roman domination. From 373 to 379, the emperors Valentinian I and Gratian re-enacted the ancient decrees forbidding this schismatic creed and taking away their churches. The Donatists in Numidia were powerful enough to render these laws useless. But there was an internal ferment of disintegration and a multitude of different sects had split up the party.

At the time when Augustine arrived at Hippo, a savage war had just broken out between two factions. On June 24, 393, a synod of one hundred bishops at Cabarsussi condemned Primianus, the successor of Parmenianus, and set Maximianus up in his place. Primianus, however, at the synod of Bagaia, assembled 310 partisan bishops who excommunicated Maximianus. Then, with the help of the public authority, he took their churches away from his adversaries. But all the sects presented a united front against the Catholics. In Hippo, their stronghold, this hatred even led them to forbid the baking of bread for the Catholics.[11]

The history of Augustine's struggles against the Donatists is contemporaneous with a change in his mental attitude regarding the use of harshness in dealing with heretics. Because Augustine was the soul of its councils, this change was mirrored in the Church of Africa.

a. PERIOD OF MILDNESS AND CALM DISCUSSION

The Bishop of Hippo preferred to re-establish unity through discussions and friendly controversy. As early as 393, at the synod of Hippo, where he assisted as a simple priest, the Fathers mitigated the law which specified that Donatist clerics were to be taken back only as members of the laity. An exception was made for those who had not rebaptized or who brought back their flock to the bosom of the Church.[12] It was then that Augustine published his *Psalm Against the Donatists*. In 397 the Council of Carthage renewed the provisions of 393. The Donatists answered the advances of the Catholics and the writings of Augustine with silence. They were afraid. They did not even dare affix their signatures to their letters and booklets. They shunned the attention of others and refused to enter into conversation.[13] Augustine was able to obtain a copy of the letter of Petilianus only after a year of inquiry. There were, however, two controversies: in 397 or 398 a discussion with Fortunius, the Donatist bishop of Tubursicum;[14] and then in 398 a controversy carried on by letter at the request of the Donatist Honoratus.[15] Augustine proposed a third discussion to Crispinus, bishop of Calama, in 399, but without success.[16] From 398 to 400, in the lost work *Against the Donatists*, he pleaded for tolerance and mildness. About 400 he wrote his great treatises against Parmenianus, *On Baptism Against the Donatists*, and in 400 to 402, *Against the Letters of Petilianus*.

The councils of Africa, following the lead of Augustine, continued to display a fine spirit of conciliation. On June 16, 401, the Fifth Council of Carthage asked Pope Anastasius to admit Donatist children to orders. On September 13, 410, the Sixth Council decided to allow clerics converted from Donatism to retain their orders; of special note was its decree to send ambassadors to the Donatists to invite them to return to the Church.[17] On August 25, 403, the Eighth Synod of Carthage decided to invite the Donatists, through the mediation of the civil magistrates, to send their representatives to a conference.[18]

The Donatists answered at first with abusive refusals. At Hippo, Proculeianus refused even to speak in the name of the sect;[19] at Calama, Crispinus insulted the Catholics.[20] Then the violence redoubled. Possidius, the bishop of Calama and friend of the saint, escaped only by flight;[21] the bishop of Bagaia was abandoned covered with terrible wounds;[22] several attempts were made on the life of the Bishop of Hippo.[23] These outrages led to a change in the dispositions of the African Fathers.

b. PERIOD OF RIGOROUS REPRESSION

Saint Augustine has pointed out the two reasons for which he approved the severity of the laws which formerly was displeasing to him: "I had not yet experienced either how much evil their [the Donatists] brash boldness was capable of or how much the constant pressure of discipline would aid in their reformation."[24] The sight of the numerous conversions encouraged him, of course, but the chief factor in his decision was the fury of the Circumcellions.

In June, 404, the Ninth Council of Carthage sent two bishops, one of whom was Augustine's friend Evodius, as ambassadors to the emperors Arcadius and Honorius to describe the Donatists' refusal to meet in a conference and the outrages committed by them and to ask for the enforcement of the laws of Theodosius.[25] Augustine explains the meaning of this petition: They asked the emperor to exact the fine of ten gold pounds only in those places where the Catholics would suffer violence at the hands of the heretics.[26] In February, 405, Honorius, who had been informed by his officials of the atrocities committed even before the arrival of the ambassadors, published a series of decrees which were designed to take their churches away from the Donatists. They resisted and the battles started all over again. On August 23, 405, the Tenth Council of Carthage thanked the emperors but again urged the Donatists to send an equal number of representatives with plenary powers to a conference, a "free legation." In 406, Augustine had to write a letter of protest to the Donatist bishop Januarius complaining, in the name of the entire clergy of Hippo, of the cruelties of the Circumcellions.[27]

From 407 to 410 there were fluctuations between severity and leniency on the part of the civil authority. It is certain that a considerable number of conversions took place and these annoyed the stubborn. On June 13, 407, the Eleventh Council of Carthage made some provisions for the converted churches: The bishops who brought back their flocks before the imperial decrees could retain their care over them; the other churches were to be joined to the Catholic dioceses. Various letters of Augustine justify these strict laws.[28] An important stipulation of St. Augustine must be mentioned. By no means did he wish that death should be the penalty for heresy: "We ask that you do not kill them."[29] Ceaselessly he extended the invitation to a conference, so much did he count on its success.

C. THE CONFERENCE OF 411

An edict of Honorius of October 14, 410, setting up a conference between the Catholic and Donatist bishops put an end to the refusal of the latter. In a joint letter, drawn up by Augustine,[30] the Catholic bishops promised to give up their sees if they were proven guilty of error and to keep the Donatists in their bishoprics if they recognized their mistake.

The meeting took place at Carthage on June 1, 3, and 8, 411, a hundred years after the origin of the schism. The sessions were held in conclave at the baths under the presidency of the imperial tribune Marcellinus. Present were 286 Catholic and 279 Donatist bishops. Petilianus of Constantine, Primiamus of Carthage, and Emeritus of Caesarea spoke for the Donatists; Aurelius and especially St. Augustine presented the Catholic view. The first two days were spent in worthless wrangling over questions raised by the Donatists. On the third day Augustine succeeded in entering into the heart of the debate. The historical question of the innocence of Caecilianus and of his consecrator Felix was established by authentic documents. Dealing with questions of dogma, Augustine proved, by means of texts from Holy Scripture, the Catholic contention that the Church, inasmuch as she is on earth, can tolerate sinners in her bosom for the purpose of leading them back to the truth, without losing her sanctity.

The tribune Marcellinus, in the name of the emperor, conceded victory to the Catholics on all counts. Augustine published a synopsis of the proceedings of the congress for the use of the faithful[31] with an appeal to the Donatists. There were many conversions. Thus, for instance, the visit of Augustine to Constantine, or Cirta, led to the conversion of the town.[32]

The stern measures against the Donatists were resumed. A law of 411 even went as far as to punish with death participants in their secret assemblies. Augustine recommended greater mildness in many instances.[33] In a letter to Count Boniface in 417 he expressed his complete theory on the repression of the heretics.[34]

Donatism waned little by little, but did not disappear entirely until after the invasion of the Vandals. As late as 419 Augustine, chancing to be at Iol Caesarea, the modern Cherchel, held a public debate with Emeritus, one of the spokesmen of the Donatists at Carthage.[35] In 420, at the request of Dulcitus, the imperial tribune, he refuted a short work of the Donatist bishop Gaudentius.[36] But now Pelagianism was beginning to demand his active attention.

4. STRUGGLE AGAINST PELAGIANISM

a. BEGINNINGS TO THE CONDEMNATION BY INNOCENT I (417)

About 400 there lived at Rome Pelagius (in Gaelic, Morgan), a monk, but not a priest. Though surnamed the Breton, he was really of Irish or Scottish extraction. Influenced by Rufinus the Syrian, a disciple of Theodore of Mopsuestia, Pelagius attacked the dogma on grace and became exasperated one day when he heard a bishop quote Augustine's saying: *"Da quod jubes et jube quod vis."*[37]

Coelestius, a former lawyer who had become a monk, became the propagator of this doctrine. After 410 the two heresiarchs, fleeing Rome after Alaric's seizure of the city, arrived in Africa. Pelagius stayed there a short while and then went to see John of Jerusalem. Augustine mentions that he had heard Pelagius spoken of with honor.[38] He was not at Hippo when Pelagius passed through there and he could hardly have seen him at Carthage, for the meeting of 411 with the Donatists was demanding all his attention for the moment. Since Pelagius wrote a respectful letter to him, Augustine answered him in a friendly manner. Later at Diospolis the heresiarch took advantage of Augustine's kindness[39] by failing to mention the warning contained in this letter.[40]

After 411, however, Coelestius was exposed at Carthage, where in the same year (according to Quesnel it was 412) the assembled council condemned six propositions denounced by the deacon Paulinus of Milan.[41] Coelestius, having refused to make a retractation, was excommunicated. He appealed the decision to Rome, but instead of going there he withdrew to Ephesus where he was clever enough to obtain sacerdotal ordination.

Augustine had not taken part in the Council of Carthage, for Hippo belonged to the province of Numidia. But at the request of the faithful and especially of Marcellinus, he refuted the errors of Coelestius in *On the Punishment and Remission of Sins* and *On the Spirit and the Letter* in 412, and in *On the Perfection of Justice* in 415. The name Pelagius did not appear in these works. Augustine mentions that he wished to treat him kindly.[42] But, in 415, without yet mentioning his name, he vigorously refuted one of Pelagius' books on nature in *On Nature and Grace*. At the same time he sent his friend Paul Orosius to Jerome to help him check the progress of the error in Jerusalem. But Pelagius found Bishop John a skillful protector. In June, 415, the topic was discussed in a diocesan synod. John so directed the discussion that Pelagius appeared the victor. Six months afterwards, in December, 415, a council of fourteen bishops met at Diospolis, or Lydda, to pass judgment on Pelagius, who had been officially denounced by the two Gallic bishops Heros of Arles and Lazarus of Aix. But because of the influence of John of Jerusalem and in the absence of the accusers, the synod, too easily satisfied with the hypocritical denials or the ambiguous explanations of Pelagius, admitted him into communion with the Catholic Church. Although there was no doctrinal compromise, the effect was deplorable. St. Jerome called the council a "wretched synod."[43]

In 416 also, the Synod of Carthage, as soon as it had been informed of the happenings at Diospolis by Heros and Lazarus, renewed the sentence of 411 and sent to Pope Innocent a detailed synodal letter.[44] The same year Augustine took part with sixty bishops in the Synod of Numidia at Milevis which adopted the same resolutions and also sent a letter to Innocent.[45] In addition, another personal letter from Augustine, Aurelius, and three other bishops informed the pope of the rumor, which was spreading in Africa, that Rome approved the Pelagian teaching, and demanded a condemnation.[46]

On January 27, 417, Innocent I examined the question in a synod at Rome. Three responses to the letters from Africa praised the bishops and confirmed the excommunication of Pelagius and

Coelestius until the withdrawal of their errors.[47] Nevertheless, to offset the evil effects of the Synod of Diospolis, Augustine wrote to the priest Hilary[48] and to John of Jerusalem to request from him the proceedings of the council, about which he wrote *On the Deeds of Pelagius in the Synod of Diospolis* at the beginning of the year 417.

b. INTRIGUES UNDER ZOZIMUS AND THE SECOND CONDEMNATION

Pelagius had sent to Innocent I a *libellus fidei* which was received by Zozimus, his successor, in March, 417.[49] Driven from Ephesus, Coelestius meanwhile had returned to Constantinople where he was condemned by the bishop Atticus. Seeking refuge at Rome, he too presented Zozimus an ambiguous *libellus fidei*.[50] All these things worked together to deceive Zozimus: the false protests of Coelestius, the suspected character of the accusers Heros and Lazarus, and finally a defense of Pelagius by Praile, the successor of John of Jerusalem.

The pope therefore accepted the appeal and, in a Roman Synod, questioned Coelestius, who did not scruple to condemn everything which Innocent I had condemned. Two letters from Zozimus to the African bishops, the second dated September, 417, charged the African Fathers with too much haste, approved the statements of Coelestius and Pelagius, and asked that the accusers be sent to Rome.[51]

Immediately the bishops of Africa, assembled in council at Carthage at the end of 417 or the beginning of 418, wrote to the pope, warning him of the Pelagian trickery and begging him to uphold the decision of Innocent.[52] In a third letter, March 21, 418, Zozimus answered the bishops of Africa that since he wished to handle the affair together with them, he had left everything untouched.[53] When they had received this letter on May 1, 418, the General Synod of Carthage, made up of more than 224 bishops,[54] drew up eight or nine canons against the Pelagian teaching. They were placed in the *Code of Canons of the African Church*.[55] These canons have been falsely attributed to the Second Council of Milevis in 416.[56]

Meanwhile, at Rome, Zozimus had seen through the trickery of Coelestius. The latter, indicted to appear again before the Roman Synod for a definitive judgment, fled from Rome. The pope pronounced the condemnation of the two heresiarchs in 418.[57] Soon afterward, in the summer of 418, the pope expounded the Catholic position in an encyclical letter (the famous *Epistola Tractoria*) which was signed by the bishops of the entire world.[58] This document has been lost, but from the fragments preserved in St. Augustine's writings[59] we know that the pontiff ratified the decrees of the councils of Africa, condemned Coelestius and Pelagius, and defined in particular the teaching on original sin and the necessity of grace for every good work, "for all goods must be referred to their author, whence they come." [60]

During this period of papal indecision, the position of Augustine proved to be quite delicate. He it was who drew up the letter of the African bishops to Zozimus and suggested the eight canons of the Council of Carthage. On the other hand, since the Pelagians first boasted of being upheld at Rome by the pope and the priests of his curia (especially Sixtus, who was to be Pope St. Sixtus III), and then after the condemnation accused Rome of lying, the Bishop of Hippo instructed Sixtus by letters which were gentle but insistent.[61] Then he took up the defense of Zozimus.

Distinguishing between the dogmatic question and the personal problem, he showed that the pope had never approved the Pelagian teaching, but had only conditionally accepted the declarations of Coelestius when he promised that "he would condemn everything which the Apostolic See condemned." [62] The prominent place of Augustine in the condemnation of the Pelagians is set in relief by a letter of St. Jerome[63] and by the commission which the emperors Honorius and Theodosius entrusted to him of obtaining the signatures of the bishops to the condemnation.[64]

C. AFTER THE CONDEMNATION OF ZOZIMUS

The encyclical of Zozimus, signed by the bishops and ratified by imperial laws,[65] marked the decline of Pelagianism. But long afterwards it still made attempts at resistance. Three facts are most noticeable in this new phase of the struggles of St. Augustine: the entry of Julian into the lists, the retractation of Leporius, and the birth of Semipelagianism.

(1) *Julian.* Julian was the son of the bishop Memorius and the well-known Christian Juliana, an early friend of Augustine. He had been admired until then for his knowledge and his bountiful almsgiving and promoted by Pope Innocent I to the bishopric of Eclanum in Apulia. This figure suddenly became the leader of the Pelagian forces. A quick and penetrating thinker as well as a truly formidable though stubborn dialectician, he took the place of Pelagius and Coelestius, who for all practical purposes passed out of the picture. After 418 he persuaded seventeen bishops of Italy to join him in refusing to sign the encyclical; they sent their protest to the pope, with appeal for a plenary council.[66] They were all canonically deposed and banished by the emperor. Julian, exiled from Italy in 421, continued to write pamphlet after pamphlet against Augustine, insultingly labeling him a Manichean and the leader of the traducianists.[67] His teaching is preserved in the lengthy citations of St. Augustine quoted in Marius Mercator.[68]

About 419 Augustine published a work in reply to Julian, *On Marriage and Concupiscence*, a summary defense of the first book which Julian had attacked in a work of four volumes. About 420 he wrote *Against Two Pelagian Letters*, an answer to the two manifestoes of Julian and the eighteen bishops protesting the sentence of Zozimus. About 421 he completed *Against Julian the Defender of the Pelagian Heresy*, a more detailed reply to the chief work of Julian. When the latter had answered *On Marriage and Concupiscence* with a work of eight volumes addressed to Florus, another Pelagian bishop, the Bishop of Hippo, in 429, set himself the task of refuting it line by line. However, he was able to complete only the first six books before he was taken by death. Julian remained stubborn in his heresy. He tried vainly to renew his intrigues with Coelestius under Pope Celestine I and died in poverty in Sicily in 454.

(2) *The retraction of Leporius* (426). This Gallic monk was both a Pelagian and a Nestorian. Evicted from Gaul by the imperial

laws, he had taken refuge in Africa where he was converted by St. Augustine. The Council of Carthage in 426 received the *libellus emendationis*, or retractation, of Leporius and sent him back to the bishops of Gaul with a letter of recommendation.[69]

(3) *Struggle against incipient Semipelagianism.* It is not at all doubtful that the teaching of the Bishop of Hippo, especially his occasional overly heated statements, had perplexed a good number of Catholics. In particular, his teaching that grace furnishes the ability to will and to act seemed to destroy liberty. The first attack came from a monastery of Hadrumetum in 426 or 427. The monks were shocked at the letter sent to Sixtus.[70] Augustine was not just when he blamed us for our faults, they said, because it is grace that we are lacking. Augustine wrote the treatises *On Grace and Freedom of Choice* and *On Punishment and Grace* for them along with several letters to the abbot Valentinus, which, it seems, managed to restore peace.[71]

At the same time a certain Vitalis of Carthage, probably a monk also, was keeping certain elements of the Pelagian virus alive. He thought that the acceptance of faith is a work of freedom alone and merits subsequent graces. Augustine wrote him a letter which was more like a treatise.[72] In it he depended especially on the writings of St. Cyprian, whose authority Vitalis had invoked.

In the southern part of Gaul, however, especially at Marseilles, the work *On Punishment and Grace* aroused livelier opposition which continued throughout a whole century. Several priests and monks of Marseilles,[73] being unable to admit the absolute gratuity of predestination, were looking for a *via media* between Augustine and Pelagius. Grace, they said, must be given to those who merit it, and refused to others. Otherwise, would God be just? Good will, therefore, takes the lead; it desires, it asks, and God rewards it. Two disciples of the holy bishop, Prosper of Aquitaine and Hilary, zealous and learned members of the laity, informed him in 428 or 429 of the progress of this teaching.[74] The holy doctor again showed in two works, *On Predestination* and *On the Gift of Perseverance*, how the very first aspirations toward salvation were themselves due to the grace of God, who is thus the absolute master of our predestination.

5. Last Years: Struggles against Arianism

Since he wished to spare his city the trials of an election after his death, the saintly bishop, seventy-two years of age in 426, prevailed upon the clergy and people to accept the choice of the deacon Heraclius as his auxiliary with right of succession and he handed over to him the external administration of the diocese.[75] He would have finally enjoyed a little quiet had not the unwarranted disgrace and the revolt of Count Boniface in 427 thrown Africa into disorder. The Goths sent by the empress Placidia to fight against Boniface, as well as the Vandals summoned by him, were Arians. Maximinus, an Arian bishop, entered Hippo with the imperial armies. The holy doctor defended the faith in a public conference in 428 and in various works.[76]

Ten years previously the Bishop of Hippo, at the request of the faithful, had refuted an Arian sermon, copies of which had been distributed among the people.[77]

Nevertheless, the holy bishop, distressed by the devastation of Africa, worked to reconcile Count Boniface and the empress.[78] Peace was made indeed, but not with Genseric, the king of the Vandals. The vanquished Boniface fled to Hippo where a number of bishops had already withdrawn. This place, then well fortified, was to suffer the horrors of a siege of eighteen months. The saintly old man, disregarding his pains, continued his refutation of Julian of Eclanum when, at the beginning of the siege, he felt that death was at hand. After three months of wonderful patience and fervent prayers, he left this world on August 28, 430, seventy-six years of age.

The body of the saintly bishop was laid to rest with honor in the Basilica of Saint Stephen. But Hippo, freed for a time, succumbed eventually to new assaults and fell a victim to the flames. The library of Augustine was providentially rescued from the disaster.

In 486, St. Fulgentius and some other African bishops, in exile because of the Vandal persecution, took the venerated body of their noble teacher with them to Sardinia. Two centuries later, when the Saracens seized the island, Luitprand, the Lombard king, ransomed the precious relics, which were buried in the church of San Pietro at Pavia. There it is that they were supposed to have been found in a marble sarcophagus in 1695; but, following Muratori, Father Rottmanner[79] does not trust the authenticity of the findings. Today a magnificent basilica built by Cardinal Lavigerie to the honor of its immortal doctor rises over the ruins of Hippo.

Part Two

WORKS

CHAPTER IV

Writings of St. Augustine

A DETAILED analysis of all his works is impossible here; Tillemont and Ceillier both give one in their books.[1] The limits of this study permit only the most important characteristics to be singled out, especially those which refer to chronology or authenticity. The apocryphal writings will be examined separately at the end of the chapter. In the rear of the book will be found a table giving the chronological listing of all his works.[2]

The present chapter follows a systematic order, although this is occasionally somewhat arbitrary. The writings are divided into nine classes: (1) Autobiography and correspondence; (2) philosophy and liberal arts; (3) general apologetics and polemics against the infidels; (4) polemics against the heretics; (5) scriptural exegesis; (6) dogmatic and moral exposition; (7) pastoral theology and preaching; (8) apocryphal works; (9) lost writings.

1. AUTOBIOGRAPHY AND CORRESPONDENCE

The *Confessions* portray for us the history of his heart; the *Retractations*, of his mind; and the *Letters*, of his activity in the Church.

(1) *Confessions.*[3] The *Confessions* were written about 400.

(*a*) *Purpose.* Their aim is clearly indicated by a correct understanding of the meaning of the title: "confession" here does not mean an admission of guilt or a narration; it is used in the biblical sense of the word *confiteri*, the praise of a soul which recognizes and admires the divine activity in contrast with its own wretchedness.[4] "The thirteen books of my *Confessions*," says the author, "praise the just and good God for my evils and my goods; they elevate the mind and heart of man to God."[5] Therefore the author speaks to God Himself with unequalled transports of faith, humility, and love; nowhere will the emptiness and uneasiness of a soul without God be found more graphically portrayed. "You have made us for Yourself and our heart is restless until it finds rest in You."[6]

(b) *Division*. The first nine books of the *Confessions* are the canticle of praise offered by the soul of Augustine at the remembrance of his sinful life and the graces of God. The second part, a sublime contemplation of creation narrating the glory of God, is not just a digression, as some have thought; it is the natural complement of the story. Augustine had to give us an intimate portrayal of his soul in the state consequent to its transfiguration by faith and grace.

(c) *Judgment*. None of the works of the holy doctor has been more universally praised and admired; none has caused more people to shed salutary tears. Whether for its penetrating analysis of the most complex experiences of the soul, or its communicative emotion, or its loftiness of feeling, or its depth of philosophical concepts, this book has no equal in all literature.

(2) *Retractations*.[7] This work was written in his last years, 426 to 427, or even into 428, according to Tillemont.[8] The title should be understood not so much in the sense of a revocation or retraction as in the primitive meaning of a revision or critical examination by the author of his works. "I was revising my writings, and, if any passage offended me or could possibly offend others, I either corrected it or justified it by clarifying the meaning which could and ought to be given it."[9] He enumerated his writings in their chronological order, explaining the purpose, occasion, and dominant theme of each. Book I covers the period from his conversion to his episcopate, 386 to 395; Book II, from his episcopate to the year 426. Altogether he mentions ninety-four works divided into 232 books. This work, a monument to the humility of the saint, is an invaluable guide for grasping the progress of the holy doctor's thought.

(3) *Letters*.[10] The Benedictine edition (1865) includes 270 letters.

Two more and a fragment discovered since then must be added to that figure.[11] Subtracting, then, fifty-three letters which are directed to Augustine, there remain 220 authentic letters, divided into four classes by the Benedictines: (1) before the episcopate, nn. 1–30; (2) from the episcopate to the conference of 411, nn. 31–123; (3) from 411 to his death, nn. 124–231; (4) letters belonging to the third period without a definite date, nn. 232–270.

This correspondence is of the greatest value for knowledge of the life, influence, and even the teaching of the Bishop of Hippo. Mere personal letters are rare and do not display Augustine's distinctive style. "Nowhere," says Ebert, "is there more conclusive evidence of the eminent authority which St. Augustine enjoyed in his time."[12] Consulted from all parts of the world as the oracle of the West, he answers questions on every topic imaginable. A good number of his letters are really treatises which are so listed in the table of his works. The Benedictines have distinguished eight classes of letters in a very useful analytic index:[13] (1) theological; (2) polemical; (3) exegetical; (4) ecclesiastical or liturgical; (5) moral; (6) philosophical; (7) historical; (8) personal. Fessler has drawn up a similarly precise and detailed division.[14]

2. Philosophy and the Liberal Arts

These writings, which have as their background the discussions of the solitaries of Cassiciacum, were all written or at least begun at that villa, from his conversion to his baptism (September, 386–March, 387). Two elements stand out in them: they continue the autobiography of the saint by acquainting us with the investigations and doubts of his mind and also with its achievements. But there is less abandon than in the *Confessions*; these works are literary essays, written, it is true, with simplicity, but with a simplicity which is the apogee of art and elegance. Nowhere else is the style of Augustine so polished, nowhere his language so pure. The holy doctor seems to have had some remorse about these works. "I wrote these works while already a catechumen, but I was still proud, as one writing secular literature."[15] The dialogue form in which these works are cast shows that he was imitating Plato and Cicero. Besides Augustine, the speakers are his friend Alypius; the young Licentius, son of Romanianus, whose worldly life troubled Augustine until he had converted him;[16] and Trygetius, brother of Licentius. Wörter makes a thorough examination of all these philosophical writings.[17]

(4) *Against the Academics.*[18] This was the first work of Augustine after his conversion (autumn, 386) and he dedicated it to his fellow-countryman and friend Romanianus who had entrusted his two sons to him. In it he opposes the scepticism of the new Academy from which he had suffered so much: happiness lies not in the search after truth, but in knowledge of it (Book I); the mind can attain certitude and ought not be content with probability (II–III).

(5) *On the Happy Life.*[19] This summary of a conversation begun on November 13, 386, his thirty-second birthday, is dedicated to Theodore Manlius, probably the consul of the year 399 mentioned in the *City of God.*[20] After a magnificent vista of humanity sailing over the ocean of life towards the harbor of philosophy which is, however, closed to it by the steep promontory of pride, Augustine proves that true happiness lies only in the knowledge of God, which will be realized in the life to come, as he adds in the *Retractations.*[21]

(6) *On Order.*[22] Dedicated to Zenobius, a rich friend of Milan, this work of 386 examines the role of evil in the plan of providence. Of note are a delightful scene in the first book (nn. 29–33) and, in the second book, the union of reason and authority and the function of the liberal arts in education (26–45).

(7) *Soliloquies.*[23] Under the form of a conversation of Augustine with his reason, the *Soliloquies* foreshadow the *Confessions* in the magnificent prayer with which they begin (Book I, nn. 1–6), in the ardent expression of his passion for the knowledge of God (7–10), and in the lofty virtues which he demands of the wise man (14–26). Book II, showing that truth is immortal, concludes from

this fact that the soul, the abode of truth, cannot die. The work was written in 387.

Apocryphal works. Three pious booklets have often been published together, a *Book of Soliloquies of the Soul with God*, some *Meditations*, and a *Manual*, all of which are certainly not authentic. They are collections of passages (in themselves quite attractive) taken from various authors by an unknown compiler not earlier than the twelfth century. In the *Book of Soliloquies*[24] there are borrowings from the true *Soliloquies*, from the *Confessions*, from Hugh of St. Victor's *De arrha animae*, and from the Lateran Council of 1198. Some of the *Meditations*[25] are already found in the miscellany of Anselm,[26] while some others seem to be from John, abbot of Fécamp (†1178). The *Manual*,[27] which was also published in part under the names of Anselm and Hugh of St. Victor, assembles fragments of Saints Augustine, Cyprian, Gregory, and Isidore of Seville. The Benedictine edition carefully notes the source of each chapter.

(8) *On the Immortality of the Soul*.[28] This book was written at Milan in 398 as a companion piece to the *Soliloquies*. It takes up again the proof for the immortality of the soul from the eternity of truth. Later, in the *Retractations*,[29] the arguments appeared inadequate to the author himself and their expression too obscure.

(9) *On the Quantity of the Soul*.[30] This dialogue with Evodius, written at Rome toward the beginning of 388, studies the grandeur and the dignity of the soul, which are consequent upon its immateriality.

(10) *On the Teacher*.[31] Written in 389, this is a dialogue between Augustine and his son Adeodatus, then sixteen years old, who was to die two years later. Augustine has told us that "I stood in awe of his native ability."[32] After an interesting study of the role of language (chaps. 1–8), Augustine develops his celebrated theory of the Word as the only interior teacher; this will be explained later under his theory of knowledge.[33]

(11) An encyclopedia of the liberal arts. St. Augustine had undertaken a collection of treatises on all the branches of education: grammar, rhetoric, dialectic, the categories, and so forth.

Several of them were completed, but all have been lost except for the treatise *On Music*. The treatises long attributed to St. Augustine, the *Book on Grammar*,[34] the *Principles of Dialectic*,[35] the *Ten Categories taken from Aristotle*,[36] and the *Principles of Rhetoric*[37] are all apocryphal according to the Benedictines. Nevertheless, Father Rottmanner says that *On Grammar* has been preserved in excerpts, although the original text has been reworked.[38]

(12) *On Music*.[39] This work, begun at Milan in 387 and finished at Tagaste in 391, first explains the technique of rhythm, meter, and verse (Books I–IV). The purpose of the dialogue, however, is to raise the mind from the changeable rhythm of bodies and souls to the changeless rhythm of the eternal truth (VI, chaps. 11–17). The last book is well worth reading; the mystics of the Middle Ages loved to draw inspiration from it. Augustine himself judged the other five books very difficult to understand.[40]

3. GENERAL APOLOGETICS AND POLEMICS AGAINST THE INFIDELS

(13) *On the City of God*.[41] This work was written from 413 to 426 with frequent interruptions. Book X was written after 415, and Books XX–XXII date from 426.

(a) *Purpose*. The pagans attributed the fall of Rome in 410, like all public calamities, to the abolition of pagan worship. Despite the defense sketched in letters to Volusianus and to the tribune Marcellinus,[42] the latter asked for a more complete vindication of the faith. Augustine set himself to the task. Finding himself faced with the problem of explaining divine providence over the Roman empire, he widens the scope of his work yet further and, in a flash of genius which transformed his apology into a philosophy of history, he encompasses in one glance the destinies of the nations of the world. These destinies, he saw, were centered around the Christian religion, the unique religion, which, completely understood, goes back to the beginning and leads humanity to its final goal. The "city of God," an association of all the servants of God in all times and countries of the world,[43] the "city of this earth" or of the devil, an association of all the enemies of God, these two moral cities constructed by contrary loves—there is the true objective of providence and the triumph of the city of God is the true focal point of the divine plan.

(b) *Analysis*. The great doctor retraces in detail the compass of his work, with its divisions into two great parts.[44] The first part, Books I–X, is apologetic. Pagan polytheism is equally unable to give the prosperity in this life which the people hope for or to prepare for the happiness of the future life as the philosophers assert. Books I–V give a history of the calamities which occurred even under the protection of the gods and the true explanation of the grandeur of Rome. Books VI–X are a concise, profound, and caustic criticism of pagan theology in all its forms, especially of Neoplatonic demonology.

The second part, Books XI–XXII, is expository. Christianity gives the key to providence by showing that the city of God, although entangled here below in the city of this earth, is nevertheless on the march toward its eternal destiny. Augustine describes the three great phases of this history, devoting four books to each stage. Books XI–XIV recount the rise of the two cities, treating creation, the fall of the angels, the fall of Adam, and original sin. Books XV–XVIII explain the progress or evolution of the two cities in history, covering the great periods of the Bible marked by the flood, Abraham, David, and the captivity, in the first three books and concluding in Book XVIII with a description of the terrestrial city, or the history of empires. Books XIX–XXII study the purpose of these two cities or their final end: happiness, judgment, hell, and heaven. Within this majestic outline dogmatic, moral, or historical digressions are common. But his contemporaries, who snatched up each book as it came from his pen, were less worried about the whole than about the burning questions of the day which were considered from such a lofty point of view.

(c) *Judgment*. The *City of God* is considered as the most important work of the great bishop. The tremendous scope of the subject encompasses the whole gamut of problems which torment the mind of man; the author, in solving them, is lavish with profound and original insights. This book, with the *Confessions*, merits a place by itself; while his other works chiefly interest theologians, these two belong to the general legacy of literature and powerfully attract every soul. The *Confessions* are theology as experienced in one soul and the history of God's action in individuals; the *City of God* is theology as living in the historical framework of humanity and explains the action of God in the world. Augustine's erudition would be behind the times today, but his general views, whatever has been said about them, govern events and people of which he had not even heard.

(14) *On the True Religion.*[45] This work, a product of the solitude of Tagaste (389–391) and addressed to Romanianus, is a gem of apologetics not only against the Manicheans, against whom he particularly directed it, but also against all the infidels. The true religion is found only in the Catholic Church (chaps. 1–7), founded on the history of religion and the prophecies (10–20, a sketch of the *City of God*). Later, in 415, Augustine, when consulted about the proofs for the existence of God, referred Evodius to this book.[46]

(15) *On the Advantage of Believing.*[47] Addressed to his friend Honoratus who was still a Manichean (391), this work proves that faith, which he is mocking, is not conferred blindly, but is based on the divine proofs of the infallible authority of the Catholic Church.

(16) *On Faith in Things Unseen.*[48] This book treats the same subject. It was written in 400 and is not mentioned in the *Retractations*, but only in a letter.[49] Possibly it was only a sermon.

(17) *On the Divination of Demons.*[50] This was written between 406 and 411 on the occasion of a discussion between the Bishop of Hippo and several educated laymen about the predictions attributed to false gods.

(18) *Six Questions against the Pagans.*[51] This letter of 408 or 409 to Deogratius, a priest of Carthage, answers the mocking insults of Porphyry and the pagans about the resurrection, the newness of Christianity, its cult, and its sacrifices.

(19) *Letter 118.*[52] This letter of 410 to the pagan Dioscorus is indirectly an apologetic essay in reply to the questions from profane rhetoric to which Augustine avoids a direct answer. The picture which Augustine draws of the errors of all the schools of philosophy makes the authority of the Christian faith stand out. He invites Dioscorus to embrace the faith.

(20) *Treatise against the Jews.*[53] This is a sermon, perhaps of 428, on the mission of Christ and the rejection of the Jewish people and of their worship. For the Messianic character of Christ, see *Sermon 91.*

4. POLEMICS AGAINST THE HERETICS

a. HISTORY OF HERESIES

(21) *On Heresies.*[54] Composed at the request of the deacon of Carthage, Quodvultdeus, in 428 to 429, this is a list, very valuable for the history of the doctrines, of each of the eighty-eight heresies which Augustine enumerates from Simon Magus to Pelagius. Death unfortunately prevented the author from writing his proposed refutation of them.

b. AGAINST THE MANICHEANS

(22) *On the Morals of the Catholic Church and the Morals of the Manicheans.*[55] Augustine wrote these two books at Rome immediately after his baptism in 388. The comparison drawn is an answer to the insolent charges of the Manicheans and unveils the hypocritical austerity of the moral life of their "elect." Book I, after establishing the theory that charity is the source of all holiness (nn. 1–61), extols the virtues of the Church in its religious, its clerics, and its lay people (62–74). Book II condemns the Manichean principles concerning the origin of evil (nn. 1–18) and discloses the hidden vices of its adherents (67–75).

(23) *On Two Souls.*[56] This work was written at the beginning of the priestly ministry of Augustine (before August, 392) to refute the doctrine of the two souls, one of which was an emanation from God and the other the work of the evil principle. Augustine

shows that every soul comes from God (nn. 1–9) and that the origin of sin is in freedom of the will (11–15).

(24) *Disputation against Fortunatus.*[57] These proceedings are the written report of the two-day public debate (August 28–29, 392) between Augustine and Fortunatus, whom he calls a Manichean priest. The debate centered on the nature of evil, which Fortunatus claimed to be coeternal with God; Augustine held that it had its origin in freedom of the will. On the second day Fortunatus had to confess that he was at a loss for an answer and he soon left Hippo.

(25) *Against Adimantus.*[58] Among the secret documents of the Manicheans were the writings of Adimantus, perhaps the most renowned disciple of Manes, on the supposed contradictions between the Old and New Testaments. Having been able to obtain these books, Augustine published their text and refuted them (393–396) by reconciling the passages which were cited. According to the *Retractations* many of these questions were treated from the pulpit at Hippo; others were left unanswered due to lack of time.[59]

(26) *Against a Letter of the Manicheans.*[60] This letter of Manes was like a catechism of Manicheism. Augustine published its text and refuted the first part with great moderation (393–396); he was satisfied with a few remarks at the end. The questions under discussion were the two principles, creation, and the origin of evil.

(27) *On Freedom of Choice.*[61] The three books of his work were begun at Rome in 388 in the form of a dialogue like the other works of this period. Book I is really the result of the conversation of Augustine with his friend Evodius on the origin of evil, which is found in freedom of the will. Later, at Hippo, he completed the other two books sometime before the end of 395. Book II inquires why God gave us a free will which is able to sin, especially, Book III adds, since His foreknowledge showed him our future falls. Subsequently the Pelagians and Semipelagians appealed to several passages from this work, but, according to St. Augustine,[62] incorrectly.

(28) *Against Faustus.*[63] This Faustus, "an African of the city of Milevis, persuasively eloquent and shrewdly talented,"[64] is the

same one whose ignorance had disillusioned Augustine of Manicheism.[65] In a work published about 400 "he blasphemed against
the Law and the prophets, against their God, and against the
Incarnation of Christ." Augustine refuted him and, following his
favorite method, answered his work line by line through thirty-
three books or treatises, thus giving an admirable defense of
Judaism and Christianity. Unfortunately, the disorder of Faustus'
book had repercussions, for its repetitions and a certain amount
of confusion appear in Augustine's work. Fessler has drawn up an
analytic table of the questions handled.[66]

(29) *Proceedings with Felix the Manichean.*[67] This is the official
written report of a two-day discussion in 404 between Augustine
and the Manichean Felix, who acknowledged his defeat and
signed the anathema against Manes. The discussion centered
around the mission of Manes (nn. 1–15), the immutability of God,
freedom of the will as the source of evil, and redemption by
Christ.

(30) *On the Nature of Good.*[68] Written in 405, this booklet
developed the contention that every being, material or immaterial,
is good in its essence, since God is its creator, that evil is always
a deficiency, and that it is impossible to conceive an absolutely
evil principle of things.

(31) *Against Secundinus.*[69] Written about 405 or 406, this is
Augustine's reply to Secundinus, a Manichean hearer, who had
read Augustine's books against the sect and had written to try to
win him back to Manicheism.[70] St. Augustine states that he prefers
this work to all his other writings against the Manicheans.[71]

In connection with the Manichean controversy, we may take
up here the works against the Priscillianists and Marcionites.

(32) *Against the Priscillianists and the Followers of Origen.*[72]
The Spaniard Paul Orosius, having had recourse to Augustine in
414, gave him an "inquiry or reminder concerning the errors of
the Priscillianists"[73] which was a list of the Manichean doctrines,
intermingled with astrology, which Priscillian, deluded by the
noted Mark of Memphis, had bequeathed to Spain. Augustine
refuted these summarily in 415 in this book addressed to Orosius,

since his anti-Manichean writings had already exhausted the subject. In a letter to Ceretius[74] he reproaches the Priscillianists chiefly for their shameless falsifications and their famous motto: "Give your word, break it, but don't betray the secret." In regard to Origenism, Augustine preferred to direct Orosius to St. Jerome.[75]

(33) *Against an adversary of the Law and the Prophets.*[76] In 420 the faithful of Hippo turned over to their bishop an anonymous document which was being read and sold publicly to the harm of the faith. The author, a Marcionite or one of a similar sect—Augustine could not guess which (chap. 1, n. 1)—pretended that creation and the entire Old Testament were the work of the devil. The reply of Augustine is therefore a new defense of the Old Testament, which the New has never proven false.[77]

C. AGAINST THE DONATISTS

These works, most of which were written from 400 to the conference of 411, develop the fundamental theories of the visibility of the Church, which harbors even sinners in her bosom, the efficacy of the sacraments independently of the disposition of the minister, and the impossibility of validly repeating baptism, even if originally conferred outside the Church.

(34) *Psalm against the Donatists.*[78] This is a purely rhythmical chant of 240 verses, the oldest of its type, composed by Augustine between 393 and 396 for the use of the people. Each of the twenty stanzas of twelve verses was indicated by the letter of the alphabet with which the first word began, whence it received its title, abecedarian. After the letter "v" Augustine added a personification of the Church calling to her lost children. The fundamental theme of the work is the account of the schism and a brief refutation of it.[79]

(35) *Against the Letter of Parmenianus.*[80] These three books were written in 400 following the laws of Honorius in 399 against idolatry (Book I, chap. 9). The occasion of the work was the letter in which Parmenianus, the Donatist bishop of Carthage (already dead by 400), had reproached Tichonius his coreligionist and the author of some famous rules of asceticism. Tichonius, so Parmeniamus felt, was too conciliatory in granting that the Church should

be universal and could not be confined to the Northern coast of Africa. The holy doctor then established the catholicity of the Church and examined the origin of the Donatist schism. *De facto*, the charge that the consecrators of Caecilianus were *traditores* could not be proved (I, 3–5); *de jure*, the Church does not perish because she admits unworthy members in her bosom (II–III). There are also digressions on the laws against the Donatists.[81]

(36) *On Baptism against the Donatists*.[82] These seven books are of the same period, about 400. The thesis of the validity of baptism conferred outside the Church is examined in them with special emphasis on the historical side of the question in order to deprive the Donatists of the authority of St. Cyprian. Augustine clearly proves that Cyprian had condemned the schism, despite his error on the repetition of baptism (Book II). He then successively criticizes the letters to Jubaianus (III–V), to Quintus (V, 18–19), the synodal letter to the bishops of Numidia (V, 20–22), the letter of Pompey (V, 23–28), and finally the opinions of the eighty-seven bishops at the Council of Carthage in 256 (VI–VII).[83]

(37) *Against the Letters of Petilianus*.[84] These three books open the controversy with the Donatist bishop of Cirta (Constantine). They were written from 400 to 402 as the Donatist documents reached the Bishop of Hippo.

Petilianus, although born a Catholic, had been violently snatched away from the Church, rebaptized, and ordained against his will by the Donatists. Afterwards, having become bishop of Cirta and one of the bulwarks of the sect—he was appointed one of their speakers at the conference of 411—he had sent a letter against the Catholic Church to his priests. Augustine, having obtained portions of it, immediately addressed a pastoral letter to his faithful to forewarn them. This is the content of Book I. Afterwards, when the full text of the Donatist letter had been sent to him, he refuted it sentence by sentence in the eighteen chapters of Book II. Finally, after Petilianus had answered Book I with a second letter which was full of invective, Augustine, in Book III, showed the weakness of his adversary. Of note are the discussion of the Donatist principle that the justification of the baptized depends on the moral standing of the minister (Book I, chaps. 2–9), the contradiction of the Donatists who condemn the Maximianists and yet do not rebaptize them (I, 10–18), and the debate on the imperial laws of suppression.[85]

(38) *Letter to the Catholics against the Donatists.*[86] This pastoral letter, bearing Augustine's name and supposedly written in 402 between Book II and III of the preceding work before Augustine learned of the second letter of Petilianus (n. 1), is of very doubtful authenticity. It has in its favor the list of Possidius which mentions an *Epistola contra donatistas ad catholicos fratres*[87] (but is this it?) and a citation by the Second Council of Constantinople in 553 which attributes it to Augustine.[88] But against its authenticity are the silence of the *Retractations*, which, however, mention the preceding pastoral letter *Against the Letters of Petilianus*,[89] and a style which is not only inferior, but of an entirely different character. It is labored, bombastic, frequently obscure in thought, with occasional barbarisms, and contains opinions opposed to Augustine's. The Benedictines have grave doubts about it;[90] we think that a minute comparison with the other treatises will show that this work should be rejected, for, among other things, it treats the same questions as the preceding work and is likewise directly against Petilianus, although Possidius does not think this last point is certain.

(39) *Against Cresconius, the Donatist Grammarian.*[91] These four books carry on the same polemic. They were written shortly after Honorius' laws of suppression in 405;[92] therefore sometime in 406. The orator Cresconius had taken up the defense of the first letter of Petilianus, his bishop, and attacked Book I of *Against the Letters of Petilianus*. Noteworthy are the uselessness of the baptism of the heretics, although it is valid (I, 21–34), and the notions of heresy and schism, where Augustine shows that the Donatists are heretics (II, 3–9). The entire fourth book deals with the famous secession of the Maximianists.

(40) *On Single Baptism.*[93] This is the last section of this polemic, written about 410. Petilianus had renewed his charge in a book entitled *On Single Baptism*; the Bishop of Hippo gave the same

title to his reply which covers the same ideas and touches on the historical question of Caecilianus (chaps. 16–17).

(41) *Letter 108 to Macrobius.*[94] Written to the Donatist bishop of Hippo, this letter belongs to the same period (410) and ought to be considered in this controversy. Augustine reproaches the successor of Proculeianus for rebaptizing Catholics though he does not rebaptize Maximianists and for cutting himself off from the unity of the Church.

(42) *Résumé of a Conference with the Donatists.*[95] Just a summary of the official written report of the controversial three-day discussion between the Catholic and Donatist bishops in June, 411, this work was intended for the faithful.

(43) *To the Donatists after the Conference.*[96] This is an appeal addressed to the Donatist laity after the conference to invite them to union and to caution them about the errors spread by their bishops. *Letter 141* is a similar invitation, although shorter, in the name of the bishops of the Synod of Zerta.[97]

(44) The discussion with Emeritus, the Donatist bishop of Caesarea, is a sequel to the one at Carthage. Augustine had come to Caesarea in 418 in a mission from Pope Zozimus whose purpose has remained a secret. Emeritus, who had been one of the Donatist spokesmen in 411, came to greet the Bishop of Hippo, who invited him that same day to go with him to the Catholic church for a discussion before the people. Emeritus agreed, and the conference took place before several bishops who were friends of Augustine. The Bishop of Hippo delivered his *Sermon to the People of the Church of Caesarea in the Presence of Emeritus,*[98] which treated of peace and of the conference of 411. Emeritus, doubtless feeling that he was vanquished, refused to accept the challenge that day, September 16, 418.

Two days later there was a new conference in the church, which is recounted in the *Proceedings with Emeritus.*[99] Emeritus remained obstinate and persisted in his silence without being converted.

(45) *Against Gaudentius.*[100] These two books, written in 420, are the last of the anti-Donatist writings. Vexed by the emperor's

severe laws, Gaudentius, the Donatist bishop of Thamugadi and one of the spokesmen of 411, encouraged the madness of suicide among his faithful. He wrote two letters to that effect to Dulcitius, the imperial commissioner, which he in turn gave to the Bishop of Hippo for refutation. That is the subject of the first book. When Gaudentius made his reply to Augustine, the latter answered in the second book. The principal question discussed is that of the severe laws and of suicide.[101]

d. AGAINST THE PELAGIANS

Since the Augustinian concept of grace will be studied in the next part of this book, we will limit ourselves here to the necessary chronological data.[102] There are three classes of writings: (1) against Pelagius and Coelestius; (2) against Julian; (3) against the Semipelagians.

(1) *Against Pelagius and Coelestius (412–419)*

(46) *On the Punishment and Remission of Sins.*[103] This work was written at the request of the tribune Marcellinus in 412. Book I asserts that the fall of Adam was the cause of death and of the sin which baptism forgives in infants; Book II is directed against the Pelagian theory of impeccability; Book III is a letter added subsequently to refute the explanation of Romans 5:12 given by Pelagius.

(47) *On the Spirit and the Letter.*[104] This book answers the worries of Marcellinus who was troubled after he had read in the preceding work that man could be free from sin with the help of grace, but, as a matter of fact, is not. It was written towards the end of 412, certainly before the murder of Marcellinus in September, 413. The terms "spirit" and "letter" of the title are borrowed from Second Corinthians 3:6 and stand for "grace" and "law."[105] The law alone is the letter which kills; the grace of the Holy Spirit gives life by inspiring the "delights" of charity.

(48) *On Nature and Grace.*[106] This is a refutation, written in 415, of Pelagius' book *On Nature*, which was passed on to Augustine by two young monks whom Pelagius had won over to the religious

life. Of note are the consideration shown to Pelagius (chap. 6), the exposition of his theory (7–10, 19), and the discussion of the testimony of Saints Hilary, Ambrose, Jerome, and others.[107]

(49) *On the Perfection of Justice.*[108] This book of 415 was addressed to the bishops Eutropius and Paul who had sent Augustine a document brought from Sicily, the *Definitions*, or arguments attributed to Coelestius and certainly in agreement with a work of his (chap. 1). St. Augustine refutes the sixteen arguments of Coelestius (1–7) and then explains the texts from Scripture adduced by him in favor of the possibility of impeccability.

(50) *On the Deeds of Pelagius.*[109] Dedicated in 417 to Bishop Aurelius of Carthage, this book is the most valuable source for the history of the Council of Diospolis because its proceedings are quoted and explained. It contains a series of articles imputed to Pelagius which he had to disavow or condemn to receive absolution. St. Augustine concludes with a summary of the work (nn. 60–66).

(51) *Letter 186 to Paulinus of Nola.*[110] This was also written in 417. It gives a summary of the Synod of Diospolis (n. 32) and shows the influence of Pelagius on St. Paulinus (n. 1). *Letter 188 to Juliana,*[111] mother of the virgin Demetrias, belongs to the same period, the end of 417 or the beginning of 418, and shows the dangerous influence of Pelagius on this noble family to which Julian of Eclanum was related by his marriage with Ia. Paulinus himself, since he was related to the Anicii, had composed a nuptial poem for the occasion.[112] Father Garnier, S.J., even fears that Demetrias may have been favorable to the heresy.[113]

(52) *On the Grace of Christ and Original Sin.*[114] These two books were written against Pelagius and Coelestius in 418, after the condemnation of the heresy at Rome and in Africa. Augustine had stayed at Carthage after the council of May 1 and had not yet carried out his mission to Caesarea. The noble and saintly Romans Pinianus,[115] Melania, and Albina, influenced by Pelagius who kept affirming his orthodoxy, addressed themselves to the Bishop of Hippo. Augustine unmasks in Book I, *On the Grace of Christ*, the wiles of Pelagius who calls freedom of the will or law or

remission of sins grace. Book II, *On Original Sin*, establishes the existence and the dogmatic character of original sin even in infants.

(53) *Letter 194 to Sixtus*.[116] This letter, also written in 418, has to be mentioned because of the Semipelagian misunderstandings which it occasioned. In it Augustine insists on the mystery of predestination, which, because of grace, is entirely gratuitous (nn. 4–5, 20, 30, 34). Here (n. 19) occurs the famous expression: "When God rewards our merits, he rewards nothing else than his own gifts." Augustine also witnesses that the Pelagians had prior recourse to the purely possible future merits of infants so as to deny the gratuity of grace (35–43).

(54) *On the Soul and Its Origin*.[117] These four books can be noted here, although they were written in 420. Vincentius Victor, a young man recently converted to Donatism, astonished at the hesitant handling of the problem of the origin of the soul by the Bishop of Hippo, wrote a libelous statement of two books against him. In this work he mingled the most outlandish errors, borrowing, for instance, the doctrine of emanation from the Manicheans, the preexistence of souls from the Origenists, and salvation without baptism from the Pelagians.

Augustine answered him in this work of four books. The first is addressed to the monk Renatus who had sent him the work of Victor; the second to Peter the Spaniard to whom Victor had dedicated his book; the third and fourth to Victor himself, whom he treats with gracious kindness. He refutes emanationism (Book I, nn. 4, 23–24; II, 4, 7), justifies his doubts between traducianism and creationism, and finally affirms that neither the joys of paradise nor the prayers of the Church can be expected by those who die without baptism.

(2) *Against Julian of Eclanum* (419–430)

(55) *On Marriage and Concupiscence*.[118] The first book of this work of the beginning of 419 was addressed to Count Valerius,

whom the Bishop of Hippo wished to caution against the Pelagian writings (clearly those of Julian) which he had received (chap. 2, n. 2). There he proves that the teaching of original sin is not a condemnation of marriage. Julian of Eclanum immediately published a statement against Augustine's work in four books, fragments of which were transmitted to the Bishop of Hippo by Count Valerius. Augustine then wrote the second book, which is a defense of the first against the calumnies of Julian. The debate with Julian centered on concupiscence—an innocent propensity, according to Julian—material sin, and the cause of sin according to the holy doctor.

(56) *Against Two Pelagian Letters*.[119] These four books were addressed, about 420, to Pope St. Boniface I (418–422), who had sent to Augustine two letters: one, it was said, of Julian, sent to Rome; the other of the eighteen Pelagian bishops, sent to Rufus, the bishop of Thessalonica. There is some doubt about the first letter.[120] Book I refutes the first letter which accuses Augustine of being a Manichean, of denying the freedom of the will, and of condemning marriage. Books II–IV refute the similar charges of the second letter and give the heart of the Pelagian teaching.

(57) *Against Julian the Defender of the Pelagian Heresy*.[121] These six books were written in 421 after the death of St. Jerome, when Julian's entire work of four books had reached Augustine. Books I–II constitute a general refutation of Julian based on the testimony of the Greek and Latin Fathers, whom Julian is accusing of Manicheism. Passages from Irenaeus, Cyprian, Reticius, Olympius, Ambrose, Basil, John Chrysostom, and others are examined. The last four books refute line by line, according to the method of the illustrious doctor, each sentence in Julian's four books, treating original sin and marriage (III), concupiscence (IV–V), and the baptism of infants (VI).

(58) *Incomplete Work against Julian*.[122] These six books are the last work of the great doctor and were interrupted by his death. Julian, who had fled to Sicily, learned of Augustine's first answer.[123] He immediately wrote a virulent diatribe of eight books against him which did not reach the Bishop of Hippo until 428

while he was preparing the third book of the *Retractations*. At the request of Alypius, he refuted, book by book and point by point, Julian's text which is quoted in its entirety. The replies are consequently too scattered to preserve their real cogency unless the reader synthesizes them. The debate centers chiefly on original sin (Books II–III), concupiscence (IV–V), and freedom of the will after the fall (VI).

(3) *Against the Semipelagians (426–430)*

(59) *On Grace and Freedom of Choice.*[124] This was written in 426 or 427 for the monks of Hadrumetum, the modern city of Sousse in Tunisia. *Letter 194 to Sixtus*, sent to the monastery by the monk Florus, had stirred up vehement disputes, many believing that freedom of the will had been annihilated by Augustine. The abbot Valentinus sent two of his monks, Cresconius and Felix, to consult the Bishop of Hippo. Augustine instructed them and sent back two letters, one to the abbot Valentinus, the other to his community.[125] At the same time he wrote this treatise to assert the gratuity of grace without prejudice to freedom of the will. Peace was restored, but not entirely. Valentinus sent Florus to the holy doctor with his letter of thanks.[126]

(60) *On Punishment and Grace.*[127] This book answers the question proposed in 427 by Florus on behalf of the disturbed monks: "If grace alone is responsible for perseverance in good, why are we blamed for our faults?" Augustine replies that, inasmuch as freedom of the will remains, the punishment is legitimate. "O man," he said to the faithful, "you would have persevered in that which you had heard and believed, if your will had remained the same."[128] Then he develops the dogma of the gratuity of total predestination, the gift of perseverance. In connection with this he distinguishes between the grace of Adam and that of his redeemed children, a distinction which has caused torrents of ink to flow and which Jansenius wished to make the key to the Augustinian teaching on grace.[129]

(61) *Letter 217 to Vitalis of Carthage.*[130] This was written in 427, according to the Benedictines, although Garnier believes it is earlier, somewhere around 420 to 424. It is quite important for the history of Semipelagianism, which had its advocates at Carthage as well as at Marseilles. Of note are the "twelve sentences" or rules of faith on the gratuity of grace (n. 16) which mark a tremendous development of the question since the canons of Carthage in 418.

(62) *On the Predestination of the Saints.*[131] (63) *On the Gift of Perseverance.*[132] Both these works were written after the *Retractations*, in 428–429, against the Semipelagians in France. Two educated and zealous laymen, Prosper and Hilary, witnessing the agitation in the regular and secular clergy of southern France caused by the writings of Augustine, especially by the work *On Punishment and Grace*, informed the Bishop of Hippo of the new doctrines.[133] People were claiming first that the beginning of salvation ought to come from the will, which prays for and desires salvation; they also maintained that perseverance is not a gift, but depends on us. Against the first error Augustine wrote *On the Predestination of the Saints*, which established the necessity of the gift of God both for the beginning of salvation and for every prayer or aspiration. The gratuity of the first grace is the basis of the dogma of predestination, which is the eternal preparation of the graces to be given in time (n. 19). The second error he refutes in *On the Gift of Perseverance*, also known as the *Second Book on Predestination*.

c. AGAINST ARIANISM

(64) *Against an Arian Sermon.*[134] This is a refutation, written in 418, of an anonymous Arian sermon which had been distributed among the faithful. The complete text of the sermon is quoted. The unknown author affirmed the inferiority of Christ in comparison with the Father.

(65) *Conference with Maximinus.*[135] *Against Maximinus.*[136] These works relate to the celebrated conference of 428 at Hippo between the great doctor and the Arian bishop Maximinus who

had arrived in Africa with the Goths of Segisvult. The *Conference* is the official written report of the meeting. After some attacks on both sides, Maximinus filibustered with a long speech[137] which lasted through the rest of the day. Instead of continuing the debate again the next day, he announced his departure for Carthage. Augustine explicitly pointed out his unfair procedure in the written report and refuted the speech in his two books *Against Maximinus*. Maximinus granted Augustine the distinction of three persons in God, but he denied the unity of operation and of substance. It is this consubstantiality and equality of the three persons which the Bishop of Hippo demonstrated.[138]

5. SCRIPTURAL EXEGESIS

After a few words on Augustine's theory of exegesis, we will enumerate the exegetical writings in the order of the Bible.

a. THEORY OF EXEGESIS

(66) *On Christian Doctrine*.[139] This is a genuine treatise of exegesis, the earliest of its kind, since St. Jerome wrote rather as a controversialist. It was written in large part after 397,[140] finally being completed in 426. It is divided into two parts. Viewing the Bible as a great source of Christian doctrine, although not the only or the primary one, Augustine outlines the method of discovering its meaning in the first part, really a treatise on hermeneutics (Books I–III). Then he shows how to explain its meaning to the people. Thus the second part gives the principles of homiletics or preaching rather than of scientific exposition. It is impossible to go into detail here; the book is a very useful historical monument for becoming acquainted with the nature of the exegesis of that time.

b. COMMENTARIES ON THE OLD TESTAMENT

Three commentaries on Genesis, not counting a fourth inserted in chapters eleven to thirteen of the *Confessions*, show how the mind of Augustine searched with increasing anxiety for the scientific explanation of the beginning of things.

(67) *On Genesis against the Manicheans.*[141] This commentary was written by the neophyte on his return from Italy (388–390) to refute the objections of the Manicheans against the account of creation. In his explanation of the first three chapters of Genesis he also found fault with the abuse of the allegorical sense.

(68) *Incomplete Literal Commentary of Genesis.*[142] Augustine ventured this attempt at literal exegesis after he had been ordained a priest, about 393 or 394. "But," he states, "his inexperience weakened under the burden,"[143] and he decided not to complete it. In the revision of 426 he added numbers 61 and 62.

(69) *Literal Commentary on Genesis.*[144] These twelve books are the definitive work of literal exegesis on the account of creation. They were written from 401 to 415, after the more allegorical interpretation given in the *Confessions*. His purpose was to settle in proper manner any disagreement between the biblical account and true science. But he said himself, "In this work more questions were raised than answered, and among those which were answered, still fewer were settled. The rest are proposed so as to provoke further inquiry."[145] Digressions are frequent: on astrology (Book II, chap. 8), on the knowledge of the angels (III, 19), a complete treatise on psychology (III, X) with the addition of one on anthropology (VI), a study on the rapture of St. Paul in Second Corinthians 12:24 and supernatural visions (XII).

(70) *Expressions in the Heptateuch.*[146] These are critical linguistic notes on the Hebraisms or Hellenisms which obscure the meaning of the Latin translation. They were written about 419.

(71) *Questions on the Heptateuch.*[147] These are more developed notes calling attention to problems which the text raises. They also were written about 419.

(72) *Notes on Job.*[148] These are marginal notes written by Augustine from 397 to 400 and published by others in a somewhat clumsy fashion "as they were able or wished."[149] Hence there is disorder, obscurity, and a certain hesitation on Augustine's part to claim authorship of them.

(73) *Discourses on the Psalms.*[150] This book is a lifetime work of Augustine. He was just ordained priest when he set himself to

explain, although not in any definite order, the various Psalms. Only much later did he put his sermons in order. Many were never delivered; thus, in 415, he wrote many commentaries which are really not sermons, for example, the ones on Psalms 67, 71, and 77. The thirty-three sermons on Psalm 68 were the last to be written, well after 415. There is no use looking for a literal explanation of the Psalms here, but according to the admission of Ellies Dupin, hostile as he is to allegory, they are masterpieces of popular eloquence, with a warmth and originality which are inimitable.

C. WRITINGS ON THE GOSPELS

(74) *On the Agreement of the Evangelists.*[151] This work, written about 400, is a defense of the Gospels against the infidels and an attempt to reconcile the apparent contradictions of the four accounts. Book I, on the authority, nature, and purpose of the Evangelists, refutes the charge of their having changed the teaching of Christ. Books II–III reconcile Matthew with Mark, Luke, and John. Book IV studies specific points in the last three Evangelists. Doubtless some of the observations are more subtle than solid, but in the opinion of the Protestant Clausen, Augustine has nowhere displayed greater finesse and ingenuity.[152]

(75) *Questions on the Gospels.*[153] These two books are a collection of replies sent at different times to a reader who was in love with the Scriptures. They were collected afterwards, about 400, without being put in order. The moral and mystical element is predominant. The first book is on St. Matthew; the second, on St. Luke.

(76) *On Our Lord's Sermon on the Mount.*[154] These two books are the fruit of Augustine's sacerdotal ministry (393–396). Taking as a basis chapters five to seven of Matthew, he groups the other sayings of Christ around the framework of the Sermon on the Mount, especially of the beatitudes. In this synthesis, remarkable for its eloquence and profundity, he summarizes the whole of what we call today the moral theology of Christ.

(77) *Commentary on the Gospel of St. John.*[155] These homilies were delivered about 416. This connected commentary on St. John, which has both dogmatic and moral aspects, is rightly listed

among the magisterial works of Augustine. Arians, Pelagians, and Donatists are successively combated and he always leaves a deep impression on the soul of his hearer.

(78) *Commentary on the First Epistle of St. John.*[156] These sermons also date from the year 416 and end with chapter 5, verse 3. The orator is particularly concerned with charity (VIII–X) and the unity of the Church (II; III; X, 8–10).

d. ON THE EPISTLES OF ST. PAUL

Augustine has left us three essays dating from his sacerdotal ministry.

(79) *Explanation of some Questions from Romans.*[157] This is the fruit of his conversations with his brethren at the monastery of Hippo (393–396). As they read the Epistle to the Romans, they questioned Augustine about the difficult passages. His answers, written down by his brethren with his approbation, make up this collection. The Semipelagians made use of his explanation of the ninth chapter (chap. 55); Augustine confessed that he had not yet grasped the idea of grace as the beginning of salvation.[158]

(80) *Partial Explanation of the Epistle to the Romans.*[159] This work develops only the salutations (I, 1–7) and the question of the sin against the Holy Spirit (14–23).[160] The difficulty of the task made him abandon the undertaking.

(81) *Explanation of the Epistle to the Galatians.*[161] This is a true commentary explaining the literal sense of each verse.[162]

e. SCRIPTURAL ANALECTA

(82) *The Mirror of Scripture.*[163] This is a simple collection of moral injunctions gathered in the same order as they appear in the sacred books, without any attempt at systematization. Augustine wrote this as a mirror of the divine law for the purpose of edification at the end of his life.[164]

6. DOGMATIC AND MORAL EXPOSITION

a. GENERAL EXPOSITION OF THE FAITH

(83) *On Faith and the Creed.*[165] This discourse on the Creed was delivered at the Council of Hippo in 393 while Augustine was

only a priest. He could not refuse his consent to have it published in its completed form.

(84) *On the Christian Struggle.*[166] This is a manual of the Christian life, "explaining, in extremely simple language for our brethren who have little facility in the Latin tongue, the rule of faith and morals."[167] It is a handbook for the common folk and, like the longer *Enchiridion*, develops dogmatic problems more extensively than moral questions.

(85) *Enchiridion.*[168] Laurentius, a holy and educated Roman, brother of the tribune Dulcitius, asked Augustine for an enchiridion of the Christian faith. In the Greek sense of the word, an enchiridion is a handbook of essential truths. The reply was this most valuable booklet of 421, an admirable synthesis of Augustinian theology arranged according to the three theological virtues. To the virtue of faith he attaches the explanation of the whole Apostles' Creed; this forms the largest part of the book (chaps. 8–113). The commentary on the Lord's Prayer is treated under the virtue of hope (114–116) and the commandments are explained under the virtue of charity (117–122). Theologians have always prized this as a manual of genuine Augustinianism.

b. VARIOUS QUESTIONS OR COLLECTIONS

(86) *On Eighty-three Different Questions.*[169] This work is the product of theological discussions with the solitaries of Tagaste and Hippo (393–396). When Augustine became bishop, he collected the notes on which his answers had been recorded and published them without further organization. All kinds of topics are considered: philosophical (8, 9, 12, 15, etc.), exegetical (49; on St. Paul, 66–74), and especially dogmatic.[170]

(87) *On Various Questions for Simplicianus.*[171] This is the first work of Augustine after he became bishop; it was addressed to Simplicianus,[172] the successor of Ambrose in the see of Milan. The first book, by far the most important, answers two questions: on grace from Romans 7:7–25, and, at greater length, on predestination from Romans 9:10–29. The better critics, whether Catholic

like Fessler or Protestant like Loofs and Reuter, consider this work the expression of the true Augustinian teaching on grace.[173]

(88) *On Eight Questions of Dulcitius*.[174] Addressed to the tribune Dulcitius in 422 this book "is made up of passages taken from other works which I had previously written."[175] He retained it, however, because of its new line of development and because of one new question.

C. PARTICULAR DOGMATIC QUESTIONS

(89) *On the Trinity*.[176] This is the best developed and the most profound dogmatic work of Augustine. He labored over it for more than fifteen years from 400 to 416 and he tells us that, when the first twelve books were distributed to the public without his knowledge before their final revision, it was necessary for his brethren to plead with him to complete the work.[177] He sets himself the task of justifying the mystery of the Trinity. The first part (Books I–VII) establishes the dogma and resolves objections from Scripture and reason. The second part (VIII–XV) tries to throw some light on the mystery by means of the analogies which Augustine discovered in the soul which knows and loves itself (IX), in its three faculties of memory, understanding, and will (X), even in bodily sight (XI), and finally in knowledge, faith, and wisdom (XII–XIV). This last section is both the subtlest and the most disputed. The holy doctor himself proclaims that these were only farfetched analogies and elsewhere admits the great obscurity of these concluding books.[178]

(90) *Letter 120 to Consentius*.[179] This short treatise on the Trinity, written about 410 in answer to *Letter 119*, insists on the subordination of reason to faith (nn. 2–10) and on the infinite simplicity which does not permit singling out some one thing as the "divinity of the Trinity" which would be other than the Trinity itself (13–20).

(91) *On Faith and Works*.[180] About 413 some educated members of the faithful sent certain writings to Augustine in which salvation was guaranteed to all baptized persons; faith, without amendment of life, was the only requirement for baptism. Against this

form of error about the mercy of God, the Bishop of Hippo showed that only believers who had resolved to live good lives could be baptized and that, despite his faith, the impenitent sinner will be damned forever.[181]

d. MORAL OR ASCETICAL QUESTIONS

Under this heading are gathered all the works with a more practical purpose. Thus there are two on lying, five on continence or marriage, and so forth.

(92) *On Lying*.[182] Written in 395, this work had first been condemned to oblivion because of its obscurity. But Augustine, in the revision of 426, corrected and preserved it because of certain features which are lacking in the following work. Only the following work is addressed to Consentius.

(93) *Against Lying*.[183] The motive for this work, written about 420, was the question proposed by Consentius: "Could not a member of the Church pass himself off for a Priscillianist to discover the mysteries of that sect, which, to guard its secrets, imposes the obligation of lying on its adherents?" Augustine's reply to his friend is negative, for every lie is wrong, but even more so where religion is concerned.

(94) *On Continence*.[184] This is really a sermon of 395 on the struggles necessary to preserve the continence required by one's state, despite the false excuses alleged by sinners, especially the Manicheans.

(95) *On Conjugal Good*.[185] About 400 the partisans of Jovinianus were repeating the charge that no one had been able to oppose him without playing down the importance of marriage. Augustine replies by showing its dignity and purpose. This is the most complete patristic treatise on the duties of the married state.

(96) *On Holy Virginity*.[186] This book immediately followed the above and completed it. It is a defense of virginity as explained in First Corinthians 7:26 and a fervent exhortation to the vow of perpetual continence, provided that it is made with humility (nn. 29–57).

(97) *On the Good of Widowhood*.[187] This letter was written in

414 at the request of the noble widow Juliana, the mother of Demetrias. Although it is perfectly all right to remarry (nn. 1–15), Augustine extols the merit and the virtues of a saintly widowhood (16–19), provided that it relies on grace.

(98) *On Adulterous Marriages.*[188] Augustine answers the questions of Pollentius in 419 by stating that Christian marriage is absolutely indissoluble even in the case of adultery. Pollentius had denied this. He also studies the famous Pauline privilege (Book I, chap. 20).

(99) *On Patience.*[189] This is really a sermon delivered before 418.[190] The leading idea is that the patience of the just and of true martyrs is a gift of grace (nn. 12–26).

(100) *On the Care to be shown the Dead.*[191] About 421 Augustine was asked by Paulinus of Nola about the advantage of being buried near the tombs of the martyrs. Explaining the efficacy of prayers for the departed, especially the Holy Sacrifice, Augustine adds that these prayers are ordinarily more fervent when said near the remains of the martyrs.[192]

(101) *On the Labor of the Monks.*[193] This was written about 400 at the request of Aurelius, bishop of Carthage, to settle a question which was dividing the monks and, through them, the faithful. In recently founded monasteries, some made use of Matthew 6:25–34 to exclude and scorn the corporal labor which others practiced for their livelihood. Augustine embraces the second viewpoint and recommends labor, which was practiced by St. Paul (nn. 1–26) and is in keeping with the Gospels (nn. 27–35), as a preservative against vices.[194]

7. Pastoral Theology and Preaching

The Bishop of Hippo set forth his theory of preaching in the fourth book of *On Christian Doctrine.*[195] In Augustine's mind the preacher is above all the "trustee and the teacher of the divine Scriptures."[196] He therefore had the obligation of learning Holy

Writ by memory and of fathoming its meaning.[197] But Christian wisdom ought also to make use of the resources of eloquence.[198]

(102) *On Catechizing the Uneducated.*[199] This work was written about 400 at the request of the deacon Deogratias, who was in charge of instructing the catechumens. Augustine tells him to forewarn their minds against the scandal of the vices of unworthy Christians and to teach without boring or fatiguing his listeners. His zealous interest in their conversion will suggest means of attaining this objective. He even gives two sample instructions (nn. 24–55).

(103) *Sermons.*[200] The oratorical output of Augustine was tremendous; it includes the *Discourses on the Psalms,*[201] the *Commentary on St. John,*[202] and so forth. Under the category of *Sermons* the Benedictines have listed 363 of the more isolated discourses which are certainly authentic. They have divided these into four classes: (1) On the Scriptures (1–183), also called On the Words of our Lord, On the Words of the Apostle, and so forth. It was the custom to read a passage of the Old Testament or Epistles before the singing of the Gradual, which was followed by the Gospel. Augustine, as the spirit moved him would enlarge upon one of the two passages, or even join the two.[203] (2) On the season of the year, referring to the various feasts (184–272). (3) On the saints, panegyrics on the martyrs (273–340). (4) On various subjects, including dogmatic, moral, or occasional sermons.

In general the sermons are quite short. The listeners were standing and could take notes if they wished. Augustine reexamined the shorthand notes or occasionally dictated the text himself, most of the time after the sermon. This process explains various versions of the same sermon. The Manichean Secundinus even then called Augustine "the greatest orator and the guiding spirit of the whole field of eloquence."[204] And in this he only mirrored the general impression of his contemporaries which has been ratified by posterity. If the teacher in him dominates the orator, if there is less figure of speech, abundance of detail, and Oriental charm than in John Chrysostom, there is in its place a stronger logic, bolder comparisons, greater elevation, and sublimer thought content. Sometimes, in his bursts of emotion and his daring lapses into dialogue style, he matches the irresistible power of the Greek orator. The critics of our time have highlighted the oratorical excellence of St. Augustine which his role as teacher had kept from proper attention.[205]

8. Apocryphal Works

These will be listed in the same order as the authentic works.

a. letters

(1) *Letter to Demetrias*.[206] This was written by Pelagius either in 413 after Demetrias, moved by a sermon of Augustine, took the veil and received the congratulations of Jerome, Augustine, and Innocent I on the occasion, or perhaps in 414, when she returned to Rome. It is strange that this could have been attributed to Augustine, who denounced its Pelagian tendencies[207] and named the author in *On the Grace of Christ*,[208] also citing the admission of Pelagius.[209] Paul Orosius attributes it to Pelagius in his *Apologeticus*, edited in 415, and he mentions that a secretary named Anianus had written it in the name of Pelagius. Bede refuted this opinion and attributed it to Julian of Eclanum.[210]

(2) *Rule for Monks*.[211] This adaptation to monks of *Letter 211* for religious women postdates St. Augustine.

(3) *Letter to Probus*.[212] Although Migne regarded this letter of consolation as authentic, the Benedictines rightly reject it.

(4) *Correspondence with Count Boniface*.[213] These sixteen short notes were absolutely unknown to the ancients, although admitted as authentic by Baronius. They are an exercise in rhetoric by an unknown author.

(5) *Correspondence between Augustine and Cyril of Jerusalem*.[214] These letters on the virtues and miracles of St. Jerome are the work of a clumsy Monothelite impostor. Cyril died long before Jerome.[215]

b. philosophy

(1) *On the Spirit and the Soul*.[216] This work, falsely attributed to St. Augustine, was also published in the works of Hugh of St.

Victor, where it constitutes Book II of *On the Soul*. This theoretical and ascetical work on psychology is a curious compilation quoting or summarizing the theories of the Latin Fathers from Augustine, Gennadius, and Boethius all the way to St. Bernard and Hugh, including Isidore, Alcuin, and Anselm. St. Thomas in his *De Anima*, a. 12 *ad* 1, attributes it to a Cistercian and is little disturbed that he does not agree with the Cistercian's distinction of the soul and its faculties. The Benedictines and Stöckl[217] think that it is the work of Alcher of Clairvaux.

C. APOLOGETICS AGAINST THE INFIDELS

(1) *Treatise against Five Heresies*.[218] This is later than Augustine, dating from the time of the Vandal persecution. The subtitle is the only exact one, since the pagans and Jews are refuted together with the Manicheans, Sabellians, and Arians. The *Lovanienses*, Bellarmine, and others thought that it was authentic.

(2) *Sermon on the Creed against the Jews, Pagans, and Arians*.[219] This belongs to the same era. The Benedictines have noted the passages borrowed from St. Augustine.

(3) *Dispute between the Church and the Synagogue*.[220] This seems to be the work of a lawyer, according to the Benedictines,[221] but it seems more likely that it is the declamation of a rhetorician.

d. APOLOGETICS AGAINST THE HERETICS

(1) *Against the Manicheans*

(1) *On the Faith against the Manicheans*.[222] This is an imitation of Augustine, especially of *On the Nature of Good against the Manicheans*. Sirmond attributes it to Evodius on the strength of one manuscript.

(2) *Warning how one should deal with Converted Manicheans*.[223] This work, falsely attributed to St. Augustine, gives in ten anathemas the formula of abjuration for Manichean converts, together with the rules to be followed.[224]

(2) *Against the Donatists*

(1) *Sermon on Rusticianus the Subdeacon*.[225] This is not Augustine's work,[226] but, according to Harnack, a forgery of the famous Jerome Vignier.[227]

(2) *Against Fulgentius.*[228] Likewise apocryphal, this work seemingly belongs to Vigilius of Thapsus.

(3) *Testimonies of Faith against the Donatists.*[229] Written by a more recent author, this document is neither Augustinian nor against the Donatists, but against the Arians and Macedonians. Perhaps it is the *Parvus libellus adversus arianos et macedonianos* of Faustus of Riez.[230]

(3) Against the Pelagians

(1) *Hypomnesticon against the Pelagians and Coelestians.*[231] This book of warnings is also entitled the *Hypognosticon*, that is, a book of notes, both titles being used by Marius Mercator. It is a refutation of the five central Pelagian theses divided into six books of real value. Although Julian is not mentioned by name, the author seems to be writing against him, for the whole of Book IV is against his theory of concupiscence. In the ninth century, Remi, archbishop of Lyons, had already proved against Hincmar that it is not from the pen of Augustine.[232] Prudentius of Troyes did the same against Scotus Erigena.[233] The author is unknown; the Benedictines lean towards Marius Mercator, despite the difference in style. According to Garnier, the author is the priest Sixtus—later Sixtus III—who would have wished to make reparation in this way for the favor which he first showed Coelestius.[234]

(2) *On Predestination and Grace.*[235] This short and insignificant treatise certainly belongs neither to Augustine nor to Fulgentius of Ruspe. Bellarmine and others have seen traces of Semipelagian inspiration in the ninth chapter.

(3) *Booklet on Predestination.*[236] This is a short protest against predestination to evil, which is well characterized in the third chapter as an irresistible impulse.

(4) Against the Arians

(1) *Discussion of Augustine with Pascentius.*[237] This is presented as the official report of a conference which supposedly took place

at Hippo. The Benedictines have shown that it is not historical[238] and that it is the work of Vigilius of Thapsus, who used Augustine's name on certain works which the Vandal persecution prevented him from publishing under his own.

(2) *Against Felicianus.*[239] The same explanation holds for this work, a dialogue between Augustine and Felicianus, which was forged by the true author, Vigilius of Thapsus.

(3) *On the Trinity and Unity of God.*[240] This is made up of sections borrowed both from an apocryphal dialogue between Crosius and Augustine and from the work *Against an Arian Sermon.*

c. EXEGESIS

(1) *On the Marvels of Holy Scripture.*[241] These three books are not the work of Augustine, as St. Thomas had already pointed out,[242] but of someone with the same name who wrote in 661, most likely in Ireland.[243] The work is an examination of all the miracles of the Bible according to the knowledge of the time; it is not too interesting.

(2) *On the Blessings of the Patriarch Jacob.*[244] This commentary is an extract from the *Questions on Genesis* of Alcuin who, in his turn, had imitated St. Jerome and St. Gregory the Great.

(3) *Questions on the Old and New Testaments.*[245] This lengthy collection of widely varying questions, some from the Old, some from the New Testament, and some from both together, cannot be Augustine's, as everybody admits.[246] Besides, the collection has been rearranged and amplified at least once, for a more recent family of manuscripts interweaves new questions.[247] The first collection, according to Garnier,[248] was composed about 370 by Ambrosiaster (the author of the *Commentary on the Epistles of St. Paul*), although the Benedictines hold that it is the work of several authors at different periods.[249] Jansenius accused it of Pelagianism.[250]

(4) *Seventeen Questions on Matthew.*[251] This is also very probably apocryphal.[252]

(5) *Psalter for His Mother*.[253] This is attributed to John XXII (?).

(6) *Explanation of the Magnificat*.[254] This is a horribly mutilated extract from Hugh of St. Victor.

f. DOGMATIC OR MORAL EXPOSITION

(1) *On Faith to Peter*.[255] The explanation of the faith with its forty rules is of Augustinian inspiration, but the author is Fulgentius of Ruspe.

(2) *On the Dogmas of the Church*.[256] This was long ago restored to its rightful author, Gennadius of Marseilles.

(3) *On the Incarnation of the Word*.[257] These two books are made up of excerpts from the Περὶ ἀρχῶν of Origen, translated by Rufinus.

(4) *On the Essence of the Divinity*.[258] Attributed also to Jerome, Ambrose, and others, this is mostly an extract from the *De formulis spiritualis intelligentiae* of Eucherius of Lyons.

(5) *On the Unity of the Holy Trinity*.[259] This is of an unknown author, but quite early.

(6) *Questions on the Trinity and on Genesis*.[260] These are excerpts from Alcuin.

(7) *Dialogue of Sixty-five Questions*.[261] This is a collection of extracts taken at random from the works of Augustine and from the commentaries *On Genesis* attributed to Eucherius.

(8) *Book of Twenty-one Sentences*.[262] This is a shorter, poorly edited collection of various excerpts.

(9) *On Antichrist*.[263] Although this was also attributed to Alcuin, it is the work of the English monk, Adson of Derby.

(10) *On the Assumption*.[264] This is a reply to a question about the reality of the assumption. The author, perhaps Fulbert of Chartres in the eleventh century, shows why the doctrine is fitting.

(11) *On the Christian Life*.[265] This work displays a Pelagian rigorism, which Tillemont had already recognized.[266] Until recently critics attributed it to the Breton bishop Fastidius, an ardent Pelagian who was the author of a book *On the Christian Life*. Caspari has published several of his works.[267] Dom Morin

has identified *On the Christian Life* of Fastidius as the first letter published by Caspari. On the other hand, the *On the Christian Life* under consideration included in its text the proud prayer for which Pelagius was reproached so violently. Dom Morin concluded that this work was very probably the famous book of Pelagius, *To a Widow*, which was believed to have been lost. If so, the writing of the heresiarch himself had been attributed to Augustine!

(12) *On True and False Penance.*[268] Although this was cited almost in its entirety by Gratian and Peter Lombard under Augustine's name, it is certainly not his work. It quotes the apocryphal *Acts of St. Andrew* (n. 22) and describes an economy of penance belonging to a later period than Augustine.[269] The author of this interesting document is unknown.

(13) *Book of Exhortation.*[270] A collection of counsels of an exalted asceticism, this is certainly the work of Paulinus of Aquileia (†802–803).

(14) *On the Knowledge of the True Life.*[271] This is the work of Honorius of Autun (†1152) under the form of a dialogue between a teacher and his disciples. The Greeks translated and attributed it to Augustine.

(15) *On Friendship.*[272] This is a summary, rather poorly done by an unknown hand, of the beautiful treatise in three books of the English monk, Ethelred Rievaulx.

(16) *On the Eremetical Life.*[273] This work quotes the Rule of St. Benedict (chap. 14) and transcribes the *Anselmian Meditations* (chaps. 15–18). The author seems to be the same Ethelred.

(17) *Mirror.*[274] This is the first part of the *Confessio fidei* attributed to Alcuin, which is itself made up of excerpts from Augustine and other Fathers. This work has in its turn been the source of parts of the *Meditations of St. Augustine*.

(18) *Mirror of the Sinner.*[275] This was written after the tenth century.

(19) *Book on Loving God.*[276] This pious collection is carefully composed of sections taken from Hugh of St. Victor, St. Bernard, and the *Proslogium* of Anselm.

(20) *Soliloquies, Meditations, Manual.*[277] These works all appear to be the work of the same author as the preceding book. They were described above.[278]

(21) *On the Triple Dwelling.*[279] This anonymous work, which is not without its merits, is a study of hell, earth or the place of trial, and heaven.

(22) *On Contrition of Heart.*[280] These are pious extracts from the *Anselmian Meditations.*

(23) *Ladder of Paradise.*[281] This is not the work of St. Augustine or of St. Bernard, but of the Carthusian monk, Gui.

(24) *On the Seven Vices and Gifts.*[282] This is found in the *Allegories* of Hugh of St. Victor.

(25) *On the Conflict of the Vices and Virtues.*[283] Although attributed to four of the Fathers, this is the work of the Benedictine monk Ambrose of Autbert, the abbot of St. Vincent-en-Vulturne.

(26) *On the Twelve Degrees of Abuses.*[284] This study of twelve faults is falsely attributed to St. Ambrose; its true author is unknown.

(27) *On Sobriety and Chastity.*[285] The author is unknown.

(28) *On Visiting the Sick.*[286] The author of this book on the art of preparing for death is unknown.

g. PREACHING

To the 317 apocryphal sermons listed by the Benedictines the following should be added.

(1) *Sermons to the Brethren in the Desert.*[288] There are seventy-six of these sermons, put into circulation by the celebrated Augustinian friar Jordan of Saxony. (Jordan of Quedlinberg, †1380.) The first forty-eight are the work of one author who palmed himself off as the Bishop of Hippo. But the sermons are unworthy of him, filled as they are with ridiculous tales.[289] The *Lovanienses* editors see them as exercises of a Gallic-Flemish orator; Christianus Lupus says they are the work of an ignorant impostor of the tenth or eleventh century.

(2) Various sermons or parts of sermons collected by the Benedictines.[290] Among these are two sermons *On Consoling the*

Dead,[291] attributed by one manuscript to St. Chrysostom. Others, under the title of *On the Correctness of Catholic Conversation*,[292] are excerpts from St. Caesarius, not St. Eligius.

(3) In the series of eleven sermons edited among the opuscules,[293] the first four were formerly called *On the Creed*.[294] Really they are sermons for catechumens to explain the Creed.[295] Only the first is authentic. From the other three apocryphal sermons Hahn has extracted a formulation of the Creed slightly different from Augustine's.[296] He has also pointed out, according to Usher, the relationship of these sermons with the *Sermon of the Creed against the Jews, Pagans, and Arians* which was mentioned above.[297]

The other seven sermons, *On Christian Discipline*, *On the New Chant* (at baptism), *On Wednesday*, *On the Cataclysm*, and *On the Barbaric Age* are likewise apocryphal and probably written by the same author as the preceding sermons, during the Vandal domination.[298]

(4) *Sermon 351*, recognized as authentic by the Benedictines, is held suspect by Erasmus and, it seems, rightly. When examined carefully, it bears no relationship in style or language to the other writings of Augustine.[299]

9. LOST WRITINGS[300]

a. PHILOSOPHICAL AND LITERARY WORKS

(1) *On the Fitting and Beautiful*, written under Manichean influence as a young professor of rhetoric at Carthage.[301] (2) Almost all the parts of his great study on the *Liberal Arts*,[302] for example, *Principles of Geometry*, and so forth, which were begun at Milan in 387.

b. ANTI-DONATIST WRITINGS

The *Retractations* mention a number of these works which we no longer have: (1) *Against the Donatists*,[303] written between 397 and 400. (2) *Against the Assertions of Centurius*,[304] after 400. (3) *Proofs and Witnesses against the Donatists*,[305] after 406.

(4) *Against a Donatist*,[306] written at the same time. (5) *Warning of the Donatists*.[307] (6) *On the Maximinianists*,[308] about 407. (7) *To Emeritus*,[309] about 407. Besides, Possidius mentions other anti-Donatist writings not listed in the *Retractations*.[310] (8) *Against Primianus*.[311] (9) *On Surrendering the Scriptures in Persecution*.[312] (10) *On Baptism*.[313]

C. VARIOUS SUBJECTS

In the *Retractations* the following are mentioned: *Book against Hilary* and the *Answer to the Objections of Hilary*;[314] *Explanation of the Epistle of St. James*.[315] Following Possidius, Cave, and Schönemann add these titles: *Against the Pagans*; *Exhortation to the Pagans*; *On Spiritual Sacrifices*; *On the Lord's Day*; various treatises against the Arians; *On Charity*.[316]

Part Three

TEACHING

CHAPTER V

Augustine's Unexcelled Teaching Role

WHEN the critics endeavor to determine "Augustine's place in the history of the Church and of civilization,"[1] there can be no question of exterior or political influence such as was exercised by Saints Leo, Gregory, or Bernard. Reuter has rightly remarked that Augustine was bishop of a third-rate city and wielded scarcely any direct political control.[2] Harnack adds that he probably was not even qualified to be a statesman.[3] All his influence has been interior, on the minds of men.

If his life marked a turning point in the destiny of the Church, as everyone agrees, it is in the history of dogma that this activity had its repercussions. If he occupies a place apart in the history of humanity—a fact agreed upon by reflective thinkers such as Rudolph Eucken—it is in his capacity as a thinker, for even outside the realm of theology he has played an important role in the orientation of Western thought. To study his teaching is at the same time to study his influence on the world. In this vast field it is impossible to be complete. However, omitting detailed points which can be found in any comprehensive bibliography, we have attempted to fix precisely Augustine's position in reference to the fundamental problems which are primarily Augustinian problems.

As an introduction to the study of his specific theories we do not wish to emphasize the uncontested truth that Augustine's doctrinal influence has been tremendous. Emphasis is rather concentrated on the even more astounding conclusion, acknowledged by the most important critics, that this influence is altogether exceptional and unrivaled even by St. Thomas Aquinas. In brief, Augustine's teaching marks a distinct epoch in the history of

Christian thought and opens a new phase in the development of the Church. This fact could have been held in abeyance as a conclusion to the study of his teaching. It is, however, mentioned now only to determine better the precise points on which we shall fix our attention: (1) the degree of influence which must be attributed to Augustine; (2) the nature, or the elements, of his doctrinal influence; (3) the general characteristics of his teaching.

1. THE GREATEST OF THE FATHERS

a. JUDGMENT OF CATHOLICS

That Augustine was the foremost of the Fathers was certainly the opinion of his contemporaries, if one can judge from their expressions of enthusiasm collected in the *Acta Sanctorum*.[4] Jerome, to mention only one, did not hesitate to write to him: "Catholics venerate you as the second founder of their ancient faith."[5] But the judgment of his contemporaries would have been suspect if posterity had not ratified it. The popes have attributed such exceptional authority to the Doctor of Hippo that it deserves separate study.[6] Peter the Venerable accurately recapitulated the thought of the Middle Ages when he ranked Augustine immediately after the Apostles.[7] The sixteenth century expressed the same admiration through the writings of two men of widely divergent character. Erasmus exclaimed ecstatically on this subject: "What more golden or hallowed possession has the Christian world than this writer?"[8] Sixtus of Sienna names Augustine the greatest genius of humanity: "Teacher above all mortals who have already lived before or after him."[9] In modern times Bossuet, whose genius was most like that of Augustine, assigns him the place of honor among the Doctors. He does not simply call him "the incomparable Augustine" or "the teacher so intelligent and, to coin a phrase, so teacherly,"[10] but he names him "the Eagle of Doctors"[11] and "the Doctor of Doctors."[12] If the Jansenistic misuse of his works and the exaggerations of certain Catholics as well as the attacks of critics imitating Richard Simon have dismayed some minds, the general judgment has not wavered. In the nineteenth century Stöckl expressed the thought of all when he said: "Augustine has been justly called the greatest Doctor of the Catholic world"[13]

b. JUDGMENT OF PROTESTANTS

A marvelous fact is that it would seem that the Protestant critics have been particularly captivated in recent times by the great figure of Augustine, in view of the fact that so many of them have devoted learned works to him (to mention only German authors: Bindemann, Schaff, Dorner, Reuter, Harnack, Eucken, Scheel, and others). Their admiration, for all its dispassionate reasoning, is not any less enthusiastic. All of them more or less accept Harnack's comment: "But where, then, in the history of the West is there a man to be compared to him?"[14]

The reformers Luther and Calvin were satisfied to treat Augustine with a little less irreverence than the other Fathers.[15] Their descendants, however, do him full justice, although honestly recognizing him as the Father of Roman Catholicism.[16] According to Bindemann, "Augustine is a star of extraordinary brilliance in the firmament of the Church. No other has outshone him since the time of the Apostles; the position of honor among the Fathers of the Church is his rightful due. . . . He marks the highest point of development of the Western Church before the Middle Ages. From him both mediaeval Mysticism and Scholasticism have drawn their life. He is the staunchest support of Roman Catholicism." He adds, it is true, that from him the leaders of the Reformation have also drawn "the principles which have given birth to a new era."[17] Dr. Kurtz entitled Augustine "the greatest, the most powerful of all the Fathers, the one whose influence is the most profound, from whom proceeds all the doctrinal and ecclesiastical development of the West and to whom each crisis and each new orientation of thought periodically brings us back."[18] Schaff is of the same opinion: "Although the other great men in the history of the Church are claimed by either Catholics or Protestants, he alone enjoys a respect at once profound and lasting with men of both creeds."[19] Rudolph Eucken has ventured this even bolder statement: "Only one great philosopher has appeared in the sphere of Christianity proper, and that is Augustine."[20]

Adolph Harnack is the one most insistent upon Augustine's unique role. He has studied "Augustine's place in the history of the world as a reformer of Christian piety and his influence as Doctor of the Church."[21] In his study on the *Confessions* he comes back to this point: "No man since the time of Paul can be compared to him"[22]—with the exception of Luther, he adds. "We still live on Augustine today, on his thought, on his spirit. We are, it is said, sons of the Renaissance and the Reformation, but both of these depend upon him." That is the principal theme of his book, *What Is Christianity?*,[23] in which he explains at length the role of Augustine in the formation of Catholicism.

2. NATURE OF AUGUSTINE'S INFLUENCE

a. LINK BETWEEN ANCIENT AND MODERN CIVILIZATION

Augustine collects and condenses in his writings the intellectual treasures of the old world and transmits them to the new. It is truly remarkable that precisely at the time when the migrations of nations were about to bury civilization under the ruins of the Roman world and new nations needed the traditions of the ancient world to nurture their growth, a man of the stature of Augustine came forward to collect in one vast synthesis the heritage of the sublimest contributions of ancient thought and especially the developments of Christian thought which had taken place in the two previous centuries and to implant it in the new world like a salutary ferment which was to bring about in those fertile but yet uncultivated natures the rise of the religious philosophy of the future.[24]

The providential mission of Augustine is sharply defined. Harnack went so far as to say: "It would seem that the sorry existence of the Roman empire in the West had been prolonged until then only to permit Augustine's influence to be exercised on universal history."[25] To carry out this tremendous job Providence put him in contact with the three worlds whose thought he was to transmit. He had lived in the environment of the Roman and Latin world; his study of Manicheism had partially opened up to him the Oriental world; the Platonists had shown him the Greek world. In philosophy he had been initiated into all the subtleties of the teachings of the various schools with which he had come into contact, but he retained his independence, not committing himself to any one of them. In theology he was the one who introduced the Latin Church to the great dogmatic work accomplished in the East during the fourth century and the early part of the fifth. He popularized its results by putting them into the briefer and more exact form in which the spirit of the Latin language expresses itself.

Moreover, unlike an eclectic Scholastic, Augustine did not summarize this knowledge of the past in a cold and impersonal synthesis. Nor did he analyze, classify, and combine all these ideas without so leaving his own stamp upon them in the new edifice that the origin of each could still have been recognized. Eucken put it well: "Augustine made his own all the influences of the past as well as all the movements of his own age. He gathered them together in himself only to achieve something that was both greater and newer. Although his cultural roots were in the Latin tradition, he underwent strong Greek and Oriental influences. From primitive Christianity and Neoplatonism he worked out a new synthesis in which the Christian element, with his own originality, is predominant. The result of this synthesis could be debated, but it was to dominate the entire history of Christianity." [26]

b. LEADER IN DEVELOPMENT OF DOGMAS

Augustine has been the most powerful instrument of Providence for the development and progress of dogma. Here the danger has not lain in denying, but in exaggerating, this progress. It has often been said that the dogmatic mission of Augustine calls to mind (although in a more limited way and exclusive of inspiration) that of Paul in the preaching of the Gospel. It has also been subject to the same vagaries of criticism. As Paulinism has been pictured as the true source of present-day Christianity which has smothered the primitive germ of the Gospel of Jesus, so people have imagined, under the name of Augustinism, that Augustine has implanted in the Church some sort of syncretism of the ideas of Paul and Neoplatonism which was a deviation from early Christianity, deplorable according to some, but very fortunate in the eyes of others. Such fanciful conjectures fail to stand up against a reading of the texts. Even Harnack shows that Augustine was the heir of the tradition which preceded him.

On the other hand, is it necessary, as is sometimes done, to identify all his concepts with the views of the writers, in particular the Greek Fathers, whom he succeeded? Is his doctrinal work to be limited merely to a question of synthesis, methodology, better ordering, or new expression? Certainly not, and the share of inventiveness and originality which Providence reserved for this incomparable genius must not be disregarded, although here and there, on particular questions, human weaknesses appear. More than any other Father he has brought into reality that progress in dogma so well expressed by Vincent of Lerins, his contemporary, in a book which some have thought to be directed against him. The living germ develops into the full blossoming of life— what a change occurs from the almost imperceptible seed to the great tree! But it is still the same being. Thus the words of the Gospel increase, rendered fruitful by providential geniuses of whom Augustine, even to this day, seems to be the very greatest of all.

In general, the whole of Christian dogma is in debt to him for new theories which better justify and explain revelation, for new outlooks, for greater clearness and precision. The many struggles in which he was involved, coupled with the speculative bent of his mind, left almost no question untouched by his investigations. Always on the watch, he had to fight the enemies of all the truths of Christianity from the infidels and Manicheans to the Semi-pelagians, those otherwise fervent Catholics. His subtle and penetrating mind, versed in all the fine points of dialectics, knew how to lay bare sophisms and dispel equivocations. Moreover, in each question which he took up his profound and clever mind opened up clear proofs and new approaches. Even his way of stating the problems so left his impress on them that there is scarcely a single question where the theologian is not obliged to study his thought.

In particular, he developed certain dogmas with such fullness, so clearly disengaging the fruitful germ of these truths from their envelope of tradition, that many of them have been (incorrectly, in our opinion) designated as "Augustinism." Augustine was not their inventor; he was merely the first one to throw full light on them. The dogmas in question are particularly those of the Fall, the Atonement, Grace, and Predestination. "Augustine's appearance in the history of dogma was an epoch-making event," says Schaff, "especially in regard to anthropological and soteriological doctrines, whose limits he advanced considerably and which he raised to a degree of clearness and accuracy they had never before had in the consciousness of the Church."[27]

But he is not only the Doctor of Grace; he is also the Doctor of the Church. His twenty-year struggle with Donatism resulted in a complete dogmatic system on the Church, the great work and mystical body of Christ and the true kingdom of God, on its part in salvation, and on the intimate efficacy of its sacraments.[28] The Manichean controversy forced him to explain clearly the great problems of the divine Being and the nature of evil, for which reason he could also be called the Doctor of the Good, of the good principle of all things. Finally, we will show that the very character of his genius and the practical, supernatural, and divine direction which it impressed on all his intellectual speculations have made him the Doctor of Charity.

The last advance due to the works of Augustine is that accomplished in theological language. His principal contribution lay not so much in creating the terminology as in giving it a definite form. Theology is indebted to him for a host of concise formulas, as full of meaning as they are terse, which the Scholastics later adopted from his works. In addition, the Latin language, briefer and more precise than Greek and less fluid in its inflection, was a marvelous vehicle for this task; Augustine made it the language of dogma par excellence. Both Anselm and Thomas Aquinas modeled their language on his.

Attempts have been made from time to time to attribute the pseudo-Athanasian Creed to him. Undoubtedly it is later, but the critics are not mistaken when they seek its inspiration in the formulas of *On the Trinity*.[29] Whoever its author may have been,[30] he knew Augustine and drew from his works. It is undoubtedly this gift of precise expression, as well as his charity, which has caused this celebrated dictum to be attributed to him: "In essentials unity, in non-essentials liberty, in all things charity." Actually he did not say this, but it is redolent of his mentality.[31]

C. INSPIRER OF RELIGIOUS THOUGHT

Augustine also stands forth as the great inspirer of religious thought in the following centuries. An entire volume would not be sufficient to relate his influence on posterity. Here we will simply mention the facts and indicate their importance.

In the first place, with Augustine the center of dogmatic and theological development shifted, moving from the East to the West. This is an added reason for calling Augustine's part in the history of dogma epoch-making. "Until his time," rightly remarks Bonifas, "the predominant influence had belonged to the Greek Church; the East had been the classical land of theology, the great workshop for the elaboration of dogma. From Augustine's time, however, the preponderant influence begins to pass over to the West. . . . The practical, realistic spirit of the Latin race supplants the speculative and idealistic spirit of the East and Greece."[32]

Similarly, Augustine was the inspiration of two seemingly antagonistic currents of thought in the bosom of the Church, Scholasticism and Mysticism. From Gregory the Great to the Fathers of Trent, his theological authority, unquestionably the highest, dominates all thinkers. The representatives of Scholasticism—Anselm, Peter Lombard, Thomas Aquinas—and the representatives of Mysticism—Bernard, Hugh of St. Victor, and Tauler —both appealed to his authority, nourished themselves upon his writings, and were penetrated with his spirit.

Finally, there is not a single one of even modern trends of thought the truth and profound religious sentiment of which does not depend on him. Some of the more learned critics have called Augustine "the first modern man."[33] As a matter of fact he so shaped the Latin world that it is basically his influence that has educated modern minds. Even without going that far, one can cite the statement of Eucken: "It is perhaps not paradoxical to say that if our age wishes to take up and treat the problem of religion independently it should not go back to Schleiermacher or Kant, nor even to Luther or St. Thomas, but to Augustine. . . . And leaving aside the question of religion, the modern world, the moment it overlooks his somewhat strange formulas in order to uncover his basic teaching, will find more than one bond by which it is attached to Augustine. . . . On many questions Augustine is more modern than Hegel and Schopenhauer."[34]

3. General Characteristics of his Teaching

a. PROGRESSIVE DEVELOPMENT OF HIS THOUGHT

The Doctor of Hippo did not reach the full development of his thought overnight. Often aided by circumstances and the necessities of controversy, Augustine advanced by stages until he attained the precise expression of each truth and a clear insight into its place in the whole of revelation. Therefore students of Augustine must learn how to "advance with him." For study of St. Augustine's works in their historical order is a necessity if one does not wish to be deceived; that is especially true, as we will see, in his teaching on grace.

But even here there is an excess to be avoided: the tendency is to prolong beyond bounds his periods of doubt or error. Neither the Jansenists of yesterday nor Protestant critics of today knew how to avoid this pitfall. Harnack, speaking of Augustine's Christology, interpreted too freely a statement of the *Confessions*.[35] In that passage Augustine acknowledged that at the beginning he did not distinguish too well the Catholic teaching on the Incarnation from the adoptionist error of Photinus; he saw in Jesus Christ only an inspired person and a teacher. Harnack avails himself of this opportunity to affirm that what Augustine had not understood then he never did comprehend fully, and that his Christology has a profound affinity with that of Paul of Samosata and Photinus.[36] As a matter of fact, the words "for a little while afterwards" in the text of the *Confessions* limit this moment of doubt to a very short period of time which began even before the scene of his conversion in the garden. It is, therefore, rather a stage in his return to the faith than a phase of his thought once he had become a Christian. After 388 he expressed the most Catholic of ideas on the Son of God begotten equal to His Father.[37] As for the persistent affinities to Photinus mentioned by Harnack, they are disproved by the most explicit texts, and even by those which the German critic adduces to confirm his position.[38]

b. THEOLOGICAL CHARACTER OF HIS TEACHING, WITH GOD ITS CENTER

Without doubt Augustine is a great philosopher, and Fénelon could say of him: "If an enlightened man were to gather from St. Augustine's books all the sublime truths which this great figure has scattered quite casually throughout them, such a selected collection would be far superior to Descartes' *Meditations*."[39] This collection has actually been made.[40] Clearly, then, there is a philosophy of St. Augustine, but so intimately is it linked with his theology that the two cannot be separated. Therefore no separate study will be made of Augustine the theologian and Augustine the philosopher. Augustine is not the kind of man you can cut in two. There was never more than one truth to his way of thinking and this truth he seized and embraced with all his soul; it is for him like an emanation from God and becomes the law of his being. An example of this: Augustine is one of the deepest and most profound of psychologists, a psychologist by preference, by desire. *"Noverim me,"* he exclaimed after having said to God, *"Noverim te."* God and the soul: those are the objects he desired to know. And truly in the study of the complicated and impenetrable workings of our soul he has gone far deeper than any psychologist of note. For him, however, this study of the soul is a religious study, inspired by the desire to know the mysterious ways of God in our soul and of our soul towards God. Protestant historians also have noticed this characteristic of the writings of Augustine. "The world," says Eucken, "holds less interest for him than the action of God in the world and particularly in ourselves. God and the soul are the only subjects whose knowledge should fire us with enthusiasm. All knowledge becomes a moral-religious knowledge, or rather a moral-religious conviction, an act of faith on the part of man, who gives himself up entirely."[41] With even more vigor Böhringer has stated: "The axis on which the heart, life, and theology of Augustine turn is God."[42]

Even in his theology it is remarkable that Augustine always places the knowledge of God in the most prominent position, whereas the Oriental discussions on the Word had forced Athanasius and the Greek Fathers to put faith in the Word and the God-man who redeems us at the summit of their theology. Revelation was also being developed all through the fourth century as the teaching of Christ. Augustine, too, places the Incarnation at the center of the divine plan, but he views it as the great historical manifestation of God to humanity—the idea of God dominates everything: God considered in His essence (*On the Trinity*), in His government (*On the City of God*), or as the goal of all Christian life (*Enchiridion* and *On the Christian Struggle*).

C. CATHOLIC CHARACTER OF HIS TEACHING

Augustine's teaching, essentially Catholic, is the very antithesis of Protestantism. It is important to establish this fact here. One reason is that thus we will not have to return to it as regards each particular dogma. The principal reason, however, is the change of attitude of Protestant criticism towards St. Augustine. Nothing is more deserving of attention than the development of this criticism, so creditable to the impartiality of these modern writers.

(1) *Former contention of Protestants.* Attempts to monopolize Augustine and make him an ante-Reformation reformer were not lacking. Luther naturally had to admit that he did not find in his

works the doctrine of justification by faith alone, that generating principle of all Protestantism; he consoled himself, according to Schaff,[43] when he wrote: "Augustine has often erred and is not to be trusted. Good and holy though he was, he was often in error about the true faith just like the other Fathers." But in general the Reformation did not make its mind up about him so easily, and it was long the custom to oppose the great name of Augustine to Catholicism. The *Confession of Augsburg* dared to attribute to him justification without works,[44] and Melanchthon called on his authority in his *Apologia confessionis*.[45]

(2) *Recent admissions.* In the last thirty or forty years all this has been changed, and the best Protestant critics vie with one another in proclaiming the eminently Catholic nature of Augustinian teaching. In fact, some go to the other extreme of seeing him as the founder of Catholicism. Here is the comment of Reuter at the conclusion of his important studies on the Doctor of Hippo: "Augustine is, in my opinion, the founder of Roman Catholicism in the West. . . . This is not a new discovery, as Kattenbusch seemed to think, but a truth long known by Neander, Julius Köstlin, Dorner, Schmidt, and others."[46] Then, asking whether Evangelicalism is found in Augustine, he says: "On this point, modern reasoning is quite different from that of the past. . . . Phrases much used from 1830 to 1870, such as 'Augustine is the Father of evangelical Protestantism and Pelagius is the Father of Catholicism' are found but rarely to-day. They have since been found to be untenable, although they do contain a particle of truth."[47] Schaff arrives at the same conclusions,[48] and Dorner says: "It is an error to ascribe to Augustine the ideas which inspired the Reformation."[49] No one, however, has insisted on this idea more strongly than Harnack. Quite recently, in his lectures on "What Is Christianity?" he characterized the Roman Church by three elements, the third of which is Augustinism: the spirit and piety of St. Augustine. "So far as the inner life of this Church is religious life and religious thought, it follows the standard which St. Augustine authoritatively fixed."[50] In the fifth century," he continues, "at the very time when the Church was setting itself to acquire

the inheritance of the Roman empire, it came into possession of a religious genius of extraordinary depth and power, accepted his ideas and feelings, and up to the present day has been unable to get rid of them."[51]

The same critic dwells at length upon the ideas of what he calls "popular Catholicism," of which Augustine forms a part.[52] The characteristics of it are: (1) the Church as a hierarchical institution with doctrinal authority; (2) the meriting of eternal life and the disregard for the Protestant thesis of salvation by faith, "that is, salvation by that constant trust in God which the certainty of the forgiveness of sins brings about";[53] (3) forgiveness of sins in the Church and by the Church; (4) the distinction between the commands and the counsels; between venial and mortal sins; the scale of good and bad men; the degree of heavenly beatitude according to the measure of one's merits. (5) Augustine is accused "of improving on the superstitious ideas" of this popular Catholicism: the infinite value of the satisfaction of Christ; salvation considered as the enjoyment of God in heaven; the mysterious efficacy of the sacraments (*ex opere operato*); the idea of the virginity of Mary, even in childbirth; "the idea of her purity and her conception, unique in their class." Harnack does not dare to state openly that Augustine taught the Immaculate Conception, but Schaff has no doubts: "Augustine," he states, "is responsible for many serious errors of the Roman Church; . . . he has anticipated the dogma of the Immaculate Conception, and his prophetic statement, 'Rome has spoken, the subject is closed,' can almost be cited in favor of the Vatican decree on papal infallibility."[54]

(3) *Theory of contradictions*. It would be a mistake, however, to think that modern Protestants have given up Augustine entirely. They like to say that it was this doctor, although basically a Catholic, who had inspired Luther and Calvin. The new thesis is, then, that each of the two Churches can make use of his name. Burke's expression is characteristic: "In Augustine ancient and modern ideas are mingled and the papal Church has as much right to call on his authority as the Churches of the Reformation."[55] No one sets this contradiction forth more clearly than

Loofs.[56] After stating that Augustine has emphasized the characteristic elements of Western (Catholic) Christianity, that because of this he has become its Father in following ages, and that "the Ecclesiasticism of Roman Catholicism, Scholasticism, Mysticism, and even the claims of the papacy to temporal government are founded on a tendency imparted by him," Loofs affirms that Augustine is the teacher of all the reformers and their bond of union, and concludes with this strange paradox: "The history of Roman Catholicism is the history of the progressive elimination of Augustinism." This facility among the critics in presuming violent contradictions in a genius like Augustine is less startling when one remembers that, with Reuter, they justify this theory by the reflection: "In whom are more contradictions to be found than in Luther!"[57] Others, with Harnack, pretend that in a genius like Augustine there are many distinct personalities which express in turn the dominant thought of the moment.[58] We will show when speaking of his teaching on grace—and there especially they wish to find contradictions—that the theories of the critics rest on a false interpretation of the thought of St. Augustine, which is frequently misconstrued by those who are not sufficiently acquainted with his language and terminology.

CHAPTER VI

Neoplatonic Influences

1. THE FACTS

a. A REAL INFLUENCE

THE reality of this influence cannot be seriously questioned by anyone who has read Augustine's works, in particular those written in the first years following his conversion.[1] Evidence enough to convince one of this influence is the arrangement of texts of Plotinus and Augustine in parallel columns by Grandgeorge.[2] The *Confessions* describe the enthusiasm enkindled in him by Platonic writings; this enthusiasm, a source of magnificent and repeated eulogies, was to die a slow death in the heart of Augustine.[3]

b. AN EXCLUSIVE INFLUENCE

No other philosophy has played an important role in the shaping of Augustine's thought. The only other possibility would be Pythagoras, or rather the Pythagoreans, whose doctrine Augustine called "venerable and almost divine,"[4] praise noted in the *Retractations* as excessive.[5] The only thing he owes them is some overly subtle inquiries into the allegory of numbers. Aristotle is cited only three times by Augustine[6] and despite his recognized merits[7] Augustine considers him far inferior to Plato. The Stoics and the Epicureans, although cited quite often (twenty-three and twenty-two times respectively), always receive severe treatment at his hands.

c. PLATONIC SOURCES

Augustine certainly knew the *Timaeus* directly, for he cites it in the *City of God*.[8] In *On the Happy Life* he says that he has "read very few of the books of Plato,"[9] and that is about all that can be conceded; five manuscripts, in fact, substitute the word

"Plotinus" for "Plato." Augustine read Greek poorly and the works of Plato were not translated into Latin as those of Plotinus had been by Victorinus.[10] The influence, therefore, came from the Neoplatonists rather than from Plato, but a closer examination will show that the imprint left on Augustine's soul derives from the fundamental Platonic doctrine rather than from Neoplatonic variations.

In Grandgeorge the precise passages of the works of Plotinus and Porphyry cited by Augustine, or at least known by him, are indicated.[11] Iambilichus remained a stranger to him, for he never quoted him and mentioned his name hardly once.[12]

d. METHOD USED BY AUGUSTINE

The rule imposed by Augustine's faith is the factor which determined the extent of the influence felt by him. The charge has often been made that for a long time Augustine was a Neoplatonist who had adopted Christian formulas. Nothing could be farther from the truth. Both at Cassiciacum and still later he was a Neoplatonist who had become a very sincere Christian, but he was still trying to couch the dogmas of his faith in Neoplatonic expressions.

The formal statement of this method is established from the start in one of the autobiographical notations which depict the history of his thought. In *Against the Academics* he informs us that there are two ways of arriving at the truth, authority and reason.[13] "Now," he adds, "in the matter of authority I have chosen Christ for my leader, from whose direction I will never deviate." As for philosophy, he gives the following rule: "As regards the matters which are to be investigated by close reasoning, I am of such a mind that I impatiently desire to grasp the truth not only through faith but also by understanding. I am confident that I will find in the Platonists nothing that will be at variance with our sacred literature."[14] Therefore he believes in Christ, but he still continues his investigations with the certainty that in Platonism he will find a philosophy which will fit in with the explanation of his faith.

The dispositions of his mind, then, are unconditionally those of a believer. He is not ready to condemn the Gospel in the name of Plato, but rather to explain it by his philosophy. Grandgeorge puts the case well: "Therefore, insofar as his philosophy is in agreement with his religious doctrines, St. Augustine is unreservedly Neoplatonic, but whenever a contradiction presents itself, he does not hesitate for a moment to subordinate his philosophy to his religion, reason to faith. . . . He was above all a Christian. Philosophical questions in his mind are found relegated to the background, the more so as he grew older."[15] This remark is sufficient to show how much Dorner has exaggerated the Neoplatonic influence.[16]

His method was nevertheless dangerous. Seeking as he did of set purpose for the common ground between the two doctrines, he could come to believe, without basis for it, that he found Christianity in Plato or Platonism in the Gospels. In turn he exaggerated the elements that could be borrowed from the Platonists and then those which the Platonists owed to revelation. He made the Platonists dependent upon Scripture and in the *Retractations*[17] he had to correct his statement in *On Christian Doctrine*[18] that Plato had drawn inspiration from Jeremias. Augustine saw this so well that after the year 400 he thanked God in the *Confessions*[19] that he had known the Scriptures only after the Platonic writings, because thus he was able to be certain that he had drawn great truths and noble sentiments from the sacred books which no Platonist had ever been able to inspire in him. If he had experienced these sentiments before reading the Platonists, he could have imagined that they also aroused them in him, whereas, having read them first, he had proved their impotency. This prior experience opened his eyes ever afterward. In the *City of God* he found fault with this tendency of Christian writers to discover their dogmas in Plato: "Because they esteem Plato, they say that he had an opinion similar to ours even on matters like the Resurrection."[20] The *Retractations* contain the admission that he himself had not always avoided this pitfall.[21]

97

2. The Results

Not being in a position to make a detailed study, we will single out four areas of contact in Augustine between Platonism and Christianity.

a. CHRISTIAN THEORIES WRONGLY THOUGHT TO BE PLATONIC

The most celebrated of these is the teaching on the Word. When one reads in the *Confessions*[22] that he has found the whole prologue of St. John in Platonic works—"the very same thing"—including the divine generation—"but He was born of God"—one should not forget, in explaining these exaggerations, his state of soul at this period. For him an immaterial God was still inconceivable. The intelligible world of Plato fascinated him and straightway he thought he sensed all mysteries in it. Even in 416, in *On St. John's Gospels*, he thought that he could find proof in the philosophers "that God had an only-begotten Son, through whom all things exist."[23]

On the subject of the Trinity Augustine was less of an enthusiast for Platonism. In 419 he declared formally that those philosophers had not known the Holy Spirit: "They philosophized without the Holy Spirit, although they were acquainted with the Father and the Son."[24] In the *City of God* he makes a milder statement and says of Porphyry: "You proclaim the Father and his Son, whom you call the paternal intellect or mind, and an intermediary between them, whom we think you call the Holy Spirit. But according to your custom, you call them three gods."[25] However, he warns that the likeness is only apparent,[26] that Plotinus and Porphyry do not agree on the place of this soul in their Trinity, and that lastly the thought of Porphyry remains obscure.

One other imaginary likeness is mentioned in the *Retractations*.[27] In the words "My kingdom is not of *this* world" Augustine understood a reference to the Platonic theory of the intelligible world of ideas, opposed to the real world!

b. PLATONIC THEORIES ALWAYS APPROVED FOR USE IN DOGMA

These theories constitute the real influence exercised by the Platonists on Augustine and, through him, on Christian philosophy in the West. Most of them moreover belonged to that sage and true philosophy which Leibniz names *philosophia perennis*; only the expression of the theories and the way of considering the problems were borrowed from the Neoplatonists.

(1) *Concept of philosophy.* Augustine's entire concept of philosophy was borrowed from the Platonists. He took from them (1) the very notion of philosophy as a "love of wisdom,"[28] a definition which immediately protects Augustinian teaching from all dry and cold intellectualism;[29] (2) the object of philosophy, and this object is the greatest thing that there is in the world: God and the soul, our origin and nature;[30] (3) the purpose of wisdom, which leads to true happiness so that Augustine identifies philosophy and the happy life even to excess as we will point out;[31] (4) the esteem and the enthusiastic love of this wisdom which is the true treasure of the soul. It is so noble that all things should be sacrificed for it, even honors and pleasures;[32] (5) the essential distinction between intellection, a knowledge of the eternal truths which alone merits the name of wisdom, and discursive knowledge of temporal things which constitutes science;[33] (6) the necessity of curbing the imagination to arrive at true understanding and perception of incorporeal objects, a thing which had been long impossible for Augustine. This was one of the great insights which he received from Platonism, the ability to conceive a being without a body;[34] (7) the degrees by which one rises to the contemplation of the eternal truth;[35] (8) the divine characteristics of the eternal and unchangeable truth.[36]

(2) *Theodicy.* Augustine was grateful to the Platonists for having inspired in him two leading ideas. The first of these was the notion of God considered by Himself in His infinite attributes. In the *City of God* he congratulates them for having understood that "God is not a body . . . ,"[37] that is to say, for rising above all sensible objects to the incomprehensible, ineffable simplicity of one in whom being, knowledge, love, and life are all identified. He

was stirred to a keen appreciation of this extreme simplicity of the supreme One and made it the foundation stone of his theodicy.[38]

The second idea gleaned from the Platonists was the synthesis of the triple role of God, the principle of things. In God, the supreme and first cause, everything has its source. Although certainly Platonic, that is also a commonplace idea. But concerning this same subject of the causality of God there is a profound Neoplatonic theory which has been little noted and which throws extraordinary light on Augustine's teaching: God, he says, is the principle of things through a threefold influence. He is the source of the being of things, as their creator; the source of the truth of things, as intellectual light; and the source of the (moral) goodness of things through His grace. Thus he reduces to unity the three great theories of his theology: the theory of creation, the theory of the Word as the source of all truth, and the theory of the supreme Good, at once the object of our happiness and, through grace, the principle of the sanctity which leads us there. Augustine explains that the Word is the source of truth in itself since it is nothing else than the divine, eternal idea; it is the source of truth in beings since the existing world is only a representation of the divine ideas;[39] it is the source of truth as known by us since the Word is the sun of our minds, the only teacher,[40] the light which puts us in contact with truth.[41] It is impossible to understand either the Augustinian theory of knowledge or his explanation of grace if they are considered in isolation from this synthesis of the threefold role of God to which the holy doctor continually returns.

Of capital importance is the passage explaining his reasons for admiring the Platonists, in which he develops the threefold role of God.[42] The following is especially to the point: "Our nature by which we are made to His image comes from the one true and great God, as also the doctrine by which we know Him and ourselves and grace through which, adhering to Him, we become blessed."[43] The Platonists, he continues, knew that in God was "the cause of the entire created universe, the light of all truth that can be known, and the source of all happiness which can be enjoyed."[44] St. Augustine based his division of philosophy into physics, logic, and moral—the science of being, the science of the true, and the science of the good—on this threefold influence of God.

(3) *Nature of the created world.* To Platonism he owed his knowledge of the good and the evil in beings. For him, the goodness of all beings was axiomatic; they are good in themselves because of their matter and their origin (imitations of the eternal ideas); they are good in their destiny, since every being praises God.[45] The nature of evil was also explained to his satisfaction by the Platonists; that was the great service which they rendered his troubled mind. Thus, following their lead, he taught that evil is not a being, but a privation, a limitation;[46] that evil is useful for the general order of the world, since it is one of the components of advance;[47] and that moral evil has its source in human freedom.[48]

(4) *Cosmology.* He borrowed from the Neoplatonists their complicated theory of *rationes seminales*, but with such profound modifications that he seems to have made it his very own.[49]

(5) *Rational psychology.* The immaterial psychology of the Platonists accustomed him to thinking about incorporeal beings and kept him from the error into which some other Fathers fell of attributing some sort of subtle, corporal envelope even to the soul.[50]

(6) *Foundation and formulation of moral philosophy.* The fundamental and noble moral concepts of the Platonists passed over into the works of Augustine. We find, for example, their theory of happiness in the contemplation of God,[51] their fundamental laws of perfection: (1) The truly wise man is he who imitates God, knows and loves Him;[52] (2) To become like God, one must detach himself from all temporal and transient things.[53]

C. NEOPLATONIC THEORIES ALWAYS REJECTED

(1) *Ignorance of fundamental dogmas.* Augustine always reproached the Platonists for their ignorance or rejection of the three fundamental Christian dogmas. The Incarnation is missing

from their philosophy;[54] it is even declared impossible: "The statement is not true," Augustine tells them, "which that same Platonist (Apuleius) says that Plato once made: 'No God will mingle with a man.' "[55] Equally unknown to them is everything concerning the person of Christ, the mystery of the cross, the ineffable humiliations of the Son of God and the great lesson of humility which flows from them.[56] Finally they have no knowledge of grace as the source of all virtue.[57] They lay down some sublime moral precepts, but without any helps to put them into execution.

(2) *History of creation*. Augustine refuted six major errors in their cosmogony: (1) Their lower gods were types of demiurges which they ranked between God and creatures, whose function was to produce the souls of the animals.[58] (2) The creative principle for them was only one of the three hypostases of which they composed their triad. Augustine taught that creation is the work of the three persons.[59] (3) God produced the world by generation or emanation, according to the Platonists. Augustine always defended a true creation *ex nihilo*.[60] (4) In their view creation is necessary; for Augustine it is always an act of the free will of God.[61] (5) Creation is eternal for the Platonists, and in particular they wished the soul to be coeternal with God. Augustine quotes their argument and refutes it.[62] He does not even hesitate to reject the possibility of an eternal creation, for time begins with creation and, since it is limited, is essentially finite.[63] A vigorous affirmation of his position is the following: "Nevertheless, I have no doubts that absolutely no creature is coeternal with the Creator."[64] And this refers to the possibility as well as the fact, and he has given proof of it in two principles.[65] The first is that the angels have a successive duration, because one act of theirs follows another. The second is that all successive duration is finite: "Time, because it passes by in changeableness, cannot be coeternal with the eternal unchangeableness." (6) The final point is that Neoplatonic creation seems to entail a dynamic pantheism as Zeller proved. Now the system of Augustine, as shown in the texts already quoted, cries

out against the accusations of Loesche[66] and Ritschl, for he rejects all types of pantheism forcefully.[67]

(3) *Psychology.* Augustine rejected two Platonic doctrines in psychology. The first was metempsychosis, which filled him with abhorrence, although the preexistence of souls did not surprise him at all.[68] The Platonists also attributed all the vices of the soul to the influence of the body. Augustine thought that the soul had its own proper imperfections.[69] Curiously enough, in the Middle Ages this Platonic thesis was taken up again by St. Thomas and his followers.

(4) *Personal lives.* Augustine stigmatized the idolatry and polytheism practiced by the Platonists, which they paraded before the people in spite of their teaching to the contrary. "They had disagreeing factions and common temples."[70]

d. NEOPLATONIC THEORIES FIRST ADOPTED, THEN REJECTED

This list is found in the first book of the *Retractations*, where the works written before his episcopate, the period of his really fervent Neoplatonism, were corrected.

(1) *Excessive admiration.* In general, he found fault with his excessive admiration of philosophy and the philosophers. Thus he took back the exaggerated eulogies of the Platonists in *Against the Academics.*[71] In the *Retractations* he says: "I praised them much more than was becoming impious men."[72] In the *City of God* he had already written: "We do not compare Plato to a prophet or Apostle . . . or to any Christian."[73] A second retrenchment concerned the too prominent role assigned to their philosophy, as if it could give complete happiness.[74] Finally, he retracted the statement of the *Soliloquies*[75] that knowledge is always reserved for the virtuous man.[76]

(2) *Theory of happiness.* In particular, the Neoplatonic theory of happiness had led him astray. He had truly thought when he was dreaming of a life devoted to philosophy that the knowledge of God gave true happiness, even in this life—an illusion which reversed the order of our destinies. He corrected this concept in the *Retractations*, where he showed that happiness is the know-

ledge and love of God, but only in the future life, and the sole way leading there is Christ.[77]

(3) *Platonic demonology.* The theory of the demiurges had been the cause of some doubts, uncertainties, and even errors on the role of the angels. For example, in one place he corrects the Neoplatonic terminology which confuses angels and souls.[78] He also tells of his hesitations on the nature of the tempting spirits: Are they good? Are they lower than man?[79]

(4) *Platonic cosmology.* The Platonic explanation of the world led him to adopt at first the famous thesis that there existed a universal soul which made the world an immense living being.[80] But in the *Retractations*, without absolutely condemning the idea, he admits that it is lacking proof, "an opinion rashly stated."[81]

(5) *Platonic psychology.* He had been too tolerant of two major errors in the field of psychology. He had adopted at first the Platonic theory on the origin of ideas which holds that all knowledge is a reminiscence. Augustine of course never admitted a previous life, whose sins were being punished in the present one.[82] But he did have recourse to memory for an explanation of the origin of ideas[83] and he subsequently rejected that error.[84] He also admitted doubts on a question of no less importance: Is there only one soul for all men, or a separate one for each?[85]

(6) *Platonic eschatology.* He had drawn two errors from their teaching on the last things. The first was a false theory about the resurrection, for the Platonists exaggerated the hatred that we ought to have for the body to the point where the resurrection became impossible. Augustine had adopted this principle in the *Soliloquies*.[86] He had also believed that the resurrected bodies would have neither limbs nor flesh nor bones.[87] Secondly, the Platonic thesis about the evolution of things which leads to a reestablishment of the primeval order had led Augustine astray. He had formulated this theory in a vague way[88] and showed the danger of Origenism in it.[89]

CHAPTER VII

Religious Knowledge

1. CERTITUDE AND ITS LIMITS

THE modern character of Augustine's teaching shows up here especially, both in the problems which occupy his attention and in the wise and moderate character of his statements.

a. TRUE CERTITUDE VERSUS THE SCEPTICISM OF THE ACADEMY

Augustine opposes the scepticism of the New Academy and lays claim to true certitude for the understanding. His first concern is to establish the certitude of the first and most fundamental truths: the principle of contradiction: "I hold it for certain that the world is either a unit or is not a unit. . . . Tell me that those two disjunctions are false";[1] mathematical truths: "It is necessarily true that three times three is nine even if the whole human race were fast asleep";[2] he shows moreover that these truths are eternal.[3] Finally, we have certitude about logic, the foundation of philosophy.[4]

Then, anticipating Descartes and the moderns, he takes psychology, in particular the consciousness of the ego which senses, thinks, and lives, as a point of departure for arriving at the objectivity of our knowledge.[5] Even doubt, when expertly analyzed, becomes a solid base for certitude, for this doubt, when known by the mind, becomes a first truth: "Everyone who understands that he is doubting understands the truth and is certain about this thing which he understands."[6] Secondly, the doubt serves as a proof for one's existence: "If you did not exist, you would certainly not be able to be deceived."[7] "Even the state of ignorance is a sign of a living being."[8] Finally, no one doubts except in virtue of prior certitude which convinces him of the danger of a premature decision: "Even if he doubts, he is alive; if he doubts, he remembers the source of his doubt; if he doubts, he wishes to be certain; if he doubts, he is thinking; if he doubts, he knows that he does not have certitude; if he doubts, he judges that he should not rashly consent to the proposition."[9]

b. LIMITS OF INTELLECTUAL CERTITUDE AND THE ROLE OF THE WILL

Augustine assigns limits to intellectual certitude and underlines the great influence the will has upon the judgments of the intellect. There arises the problem of determining the great doctor's position on the question, still as much discussed today as it was formerly by the Scotists and Thomists, whether the proofs of religious truths are so clear and evident that they necessarily demand assent, or whether the will can play an active part in ordering this assent. Properly understood, the teaching of Augustine seems to us calculated to reconcile the opposing parties by showing what truth is present in each of the two extremes. His teaching is equally removed from that exaggerated intellectualism which would not recognize any other certitude than that which is necessarily dictated to the mind by the absolutely irresistible cogency of logical evidence, as it is from that sentimental mysticism which would impose a complete and irrevocable assent without any convincing proofs and is based on probabilities alone.

For Augustine realized that we ascend to God by means of creatures and that His existence is evinced as clearly to our mind as the sun appears to our eyes: "For your reason which converses with you promises that it will make the existence of God as clear to your mind as the sun is to your eyes."[10] It is not, therefore, quite exact to compare Augustine's theory with the famous wager of Pascal as Jules Martin had done when commenting on the text of *On the Advantage of Believing*.[11] Augustine never presumed that these proofs were only probable, and that sooner or later one must leap into the unknown, relying on a belief which lacked convincing motives.

On the other hand, no doctor has indicated with like insistence the limitations of our proofs and the mystery which arises in conjunction with, or better, at the very heart of, our best proofs, even in the purely philosophical order prescinding from revealed dogma. As soon as we draw near to God, mystery surrounds us, alarms the understanding, and prevents it from being irresistibly drawn by the arguments unless the will adds its command. In this sense Augustine can be said to be the doctor of the will, and to have granted it a certain primacy over the understanding.

As a fundamental principle of his theory he holds that the mind cannot attain the truth without the moral qualities of the heart. It is a law of Providence that God grants truth only to those who seek for it "piously, chastely, and diligently."[12] Again: "Pay attention therefore diligently and piously, as best you can, for to such does God give His help."[13] This principle is reiterated often in *On the Morals of the Catholic Church*, but especially in this passage: "Not all who desire to learn are worthy; both diligence and piety must be employed."[14] "You will think the more fruitfully as you think more piously."[15] According to *On Order*: "The vision of truth is the prerogative of him who lives well, prays well, and studies well."[16] In particular, pride of spirit is the great obstacle to the acquiring of truth; when philosophers do not yield to the proofs of the faith, it is because they persist in this pride, "remaining in pride and envy."[17]

One reason for this law is that religious truths are not presented to man as a cold theory for contemplation, but as a good which he must embrace with all his soul and adopt as a rule of life. The great doctor, it is true, does not state (as some moderns do) that religion is a way of life and not a body of doctrine, although he does insist on the fact that religion is not only a doctrine but also the life of the soul. Already in *Against the Academics* he demands that the whole soul hand itself over to the truth: "You will not see the truth itself unless you have entered wholly into philosophy."[18] Later he made this vigorous pronouncement about revealed truth: "Love it is that asks, love that seeks, love that knocks, love that reveals, love, finally, that assures the permanence of what is revealed."[19] Take away love, that is, the influence of the ever-free will, and the proofs will no longer hold good.[20]

Nor is Augustine afraid to affirm that knowledge of truth is the result of virtue, not its cause: "In the correct education of man, the hard work of doing what is right precedes the delight of understanding what is true."[21] The same thought occurs in the beautiful prayers at the beginning of the *Soliloquies*: "O God, . . . whom no one finds unless first he is entirely purified."[22] Very significant also is the passage in *On the Advantage of Believing* where he formulates this law, so striking at first sight: It is an illusion and perversion of right order to seek after truth to purify the soul; one must rather purify the soul to see truth: "It is certainly out of order and incorrect to wish to see truth that you may purify your soul, which should rather be purified that you may see."[23]

The characteristic note of every religious demonstration which best explains how there can be place for free choice is, in Augustine's opinion, the mystery which pervades every concept about God, the infinite, and the eternal. He is not an adherent of that school which seeks only absolute proofs in a religious philosophy and thinks that it can resolve all difficulties. He describes the state of soul of these overly dogmatic spirits at the beginning of *On the Trinity*. As an example he chooses the reconciliation of the divine immutability with creation, for him an unfathomable mystery: "But when you speak in this way to certain individuals, they become indignant. . . ."[24] He recognizes that he erred in this way before his conversion when he demanded absolutely cogent and almost mathematical proofs: "For I wished to be as sure about those things which I could not see as I am that seven and three are ten."[25] He concludes that our knowledge of God is always mysterious, for "the soul has no knowledge of God beyond the fact that it knows how much it does not know about Him."[26]

More than that, Augustine discovers even in natural philosophy this note of mystery which, without destroying the validity of our proofs, does allow a certain degree of latitude to the mind and liberty of assent to the will. Thus the union of soul and body seems to him, not without reason, an impenetrable mystery.[27] Speaking of the origin of the soul, he addresses this precious bit of advice to Vincentius Victor, who represents all who exaggerate the intellectual: "Understand what you do not understand lest you understand nothing at all."[28]

2. AUGUSTINIAN THEORY OF INTELLECTUAL KNOWLEDGE

This problem assumes a singular importance not only because of its difficulty (Augustine recognized that this type of knowledge is a mystery)[29] and because of the various interpretations often attempted in the nineteenth century and recently revived, but especially because of the role which this theory plays in the Augustinian system. It is not just an isolated problem; it is part and parcel of the great general question of our dependance on God. For Augustine, the understanding has need of the light of God, its sun, to attain truth just as the will needs the grace of God, the supreme good, to attain virtue. Many of his interpreters have gone astray because they have not noticed this resemblance between the role of illumination and that of grace.

a. THE THEORY AND ITS FORMULATIONS IN HIS WORKS

(1) *Preliminary suppositions.* The problem under consideration is the explanation of the origin of intellectual ideas which, according to Augustine, are totally different from the inferior knowledge given by the senses. Sense cognition constitutes only science, whereas he is searching for the origin of wisdom. In the beginning Augustine had admitted the Neoplatonic theory of reminiscence, but later he rejected it.[30] No one doubts that St. Augustine admitted the intelligible world of Plato, with the important exception that he did not make those ideas which are truth itself a real world apart from God, but the very ideas of the divine wisdom. The question then comes up, how can we gain access to them?

(2) *Principal formulations and their sources.* The following expressions of Augustine's theory on intellectual cognition are taken from his works in chronological order.

(1) God is the sun of the soul. In 387 he says that intellectual truths "cannot be understood unless they are illuminated by another as by their sun."[31] (2) God is the only teacher and the inner teacher of the soul. In 389, in the exceptional document *On the Teacher* and in the letter to Nebridius (before 391), he adds that the soul understands "by consulting God."[32] (3) God is the light of our soul in which we see all things, a statement Augustine makes in explaining the difficult passage of the vision of St. Paul.[33] He reiterates this in *On the Punishment and Remission of Sins* where he says: "The soul is the eye; God is the light."[34] In the *City of God*, written after 415, he develops the idea that the Word is this light of every soul (he is speaking of natural knowledge).[35] (4) The soul has in its nature an intimate relation with the intelligible world which it sees "in some sort of incorporeal light of a special kind."[36] In these two passages, found in *On the Trinity* (415) and the *Retractations* (426–427), Augustine tries to avoid the use of metaphors in an effort to present his theory more clearly.

We could go on to examine the citations collected by André Martin[37] and Jules Martin,[38] but we would only arrive at the following conclusion: "We see the unchangeable truth" and this metaphor: "We see it in the divine light." The whole problem revolves around the meaning of this metaphor.

b. VARIOUS INTERPRETATIONS

(1) *Pantheist interpretation.* God, the universal reason and the unique intelligence, sees the truth in us and we see it in and through Him. This interpretation, held by many, makes Augustine an Averroist; but this is hardly plausible, such was his care to exclude all pantheism from his teaching.[39]

(2) *Ontologist interpretation.* Our soul contemplates the Divine Being itself and sees in it the divine ideas, the eternal and immutable truths. This perhaps was the understanding of some of the earlier scholastics, and certainly of Malebranche. Fénelon and Bossuet held this theory in most part; more recently the Ontologists, and certainly Abbé Jules Martin, embraced it.

A criticism of this interpretation is found in the definitive explanations of Augustine teaching the contrary. First, every kind of vision of God was rejected by Augustine in the most decisive manner. He had first seemed to allow this sight of God to Moses and St. Paul,[40] but he later refused it to them also, even by way of a privilege.[41] In addition to this, St. Augustine held that God, the sun of the soul, never appears as an object which we see, but as an agent which produces in our soul that by which we are able to know. Here is the heart of the question which the Ontologists do not sufficiently investigate. The comparisons of Augustine have already put us on the trail: the teacher, the sun, the light—these do not have a direct influence as objects which have been perceived and in which other objects are known. But in addition to this there is one text in which his meaning is unmistakable. In *On the Trinity* he describes the influence of this incorporeal light as a transcription which transports eternal truth from the divine book into our soul where it is imprinted, just as a seal leaves its mark in wax: "Whence [from the book of light] every just law [the moral truths he is discussing] is copied, brought over, and imprinted in the heart of man, just as the image from a ring passes into the wax and yet does not leave the ring."[42] Here is the influence of the divine teacher, the sun, the intellectual light: It transcribes, it imprints the image of truth in the soul, although the teacher or the sun is in no way the object which we see.

The explanation just given is not isolated in Augustine's work, but is a commonplace with him. Explaining the famous text of the fourth Psalm, *"Signatum est in nobis lumen vultus tui,"* he says: "He said that it was imprinted in us as a coin is marked with the image of the king."[43] In *On Order* he tells us that the "law of God is as it were transcribed in the souls of the wise."[44] An impression of an image, a transcription—this is the divine influence, and this influence comes into play at the precise moment of intellectual cognition. It is not, for example, the gift of innate ideas, made once for all to the soul, which are then called into consciousness by the stimulus of sense cognition.

(3) *Scholastic interpretation.* According to St. Thomas and his followers God is the light of the soul first as the creative cause of

the understanding, for it is He who through creation has enkindled the torch of reason, and secondly as the source of all truth, for the divine ideas are the type and model to which all knowledge, to be true, must be conformed.[45] This is also the current interpretation of the Scholastics.[46]

A criticism of this explanation is that it is deficient. We have seen that St. Augustine's texts themselves go further than this interpretation. Just one reflection decides the whole issue: If this explanation were satisfactory, then one would have to say that St. Augustine had never touched upon the real problem of knowledge, which, however, seems to have been a major care of his whole life. All his answers would be reduced to this: We know because all knowledge is an image of the divine ideas and because God has given us our intellect in order to know. But when this is said, the whole problem still remains. Just what is this intellect given by God and how does it, finite and created as it is, arrive at a perception of the eternal truth? Plato's answer was reminiscence; Aristotle's and the Schoolmen's, the result of abstraction; others, innate ideas, a mysterious deposit of truths. Augustine alone would have no answer to give. His whole book *On the Teacher* would be reduced to this statement: God has created our reason.

Such a stand is unthinkable; St. Thomas sensed this, for here and there he tried to align St. Augustine with the Aristotelian system.[47] But his efforts were in vain, for Augustine's texts cannot fit into that framework and St. Thomas often admits that Augustine was too much a Platonist.

C. SOLUTION

(1) *Explanation of the system.* In our opinion, Augustine's doctrine is the theory of the divine illumination of our understanding, so much in favor in the Middle Ages which borrowed it from him. It can be formulated this way: Our soul cannot attain to intellectual truth without a mysterious influence of God which does not consist in the objective manifestation of God to us, but in the effective production of a kind of image in our soul of those

truths which determine our knowledge. In Scholastic language, the role of producing the impressed species which the Aristotelians attribute to the agent intellect is assigned to God in this system. He it is, the teacher, who speaks to the soul in the sense that He imprints that representation of the eternal truths which is the cause of our knowledge. The ideas are not innate as in the angels, but successively produced in the soul which knows them in itself.

This explanation must not be confused with Averroism which attributes the knowledge itself to a separated intellect. According to the Arabs, God or the universal mind supplies not only the function of the agent intellect but also of the possible intellect, the whole process of knowledge going on in the self without its aid. This is nothing but an intellectual pantheism which was opposed, as being destructive of the faith, by St. Thomas and all the Scholastics. The system of illumination, on the contrary, has always been regarded as a tenable theory, as Suarez, for example, affirmed: "In a subject so mysterious," he says, "the problem is so obscure that complete liberty remains." [48] Augustine has had illustrious proponents, especially in Bonaventure's camp. [49] Moreover, this is, more or less, the interpretation of Augustine adopted by Leibniz and Gerdil. [50] St. Thomas even hints at it in his work *De spiritualibus creaturis*. [51]

(2) *Proofs for this interpretation*. This explanation is formally demanded by the texts quoted above. Everything is explained and solved. We understand clearly the transcription; the imprinting of an image; the comparisons of the seal, the sun, the teacher who speaks interiorly, and the angel illuminating men; [52] and the affirmation of necessary assistance: "unless God aids us interiorly." [53] See the *Soliloquies* for the comparison with the sun. [54] In *On the Trinity* he tells us that we contemplate the truth "in some sort of incorporeal light of a special kind just as the bodily eye sees the objects which surround it in its corporeal light." [55] This light of a special kind is not God, then, but it is produced by Him.

This explanation is especially demanded by the general theory of St. Augustine. The illumination of the understanding is ordinarily compared to the influence of grace on the will: that is one of the favorite theses of the Doctor of Hippo.[56] Now no one doubts that grace exerts its influence effectively; the same holds true for intellectual illumination. *On the Trinity* provides a very interesting text where the light which illumines the soul is compared to justifying grace, both being created forms in the soul.[57]

This explanation is demanded finally by its historical origins. It would be quite easy, although too long to go into here, to establish that Plato and Plotinus by their theories laid the foundations of the system of the Doctor of Hippo.

(3) *Conclusion.* Should one contend that this explanation of Augustine is the true theory of knowledge? We do not think so, but our responsibility is to determine what Augustine thought, not to justify it. Besides, it is good to be reserved in these matters. St. Thomas speaks with respect of the system which we have attributed to Augustine: "With a certain degree of probability," are his words.[58] It is also very interesting to compare the opinions of these two great geniuses on this question. Each has written a work entitled *On the Teacher* which is the principal source. See the other passages mentioned in the notes also.[59]

3. Faith and Its Relation to Reason: Augustine the Apologist

"Augustine is the first of the Fathers who felt the need to reason out his faith and render a separate account of the preliminary problems which today we should treat in the general introduction to dogmatic theology. The Alexandrians, it is true, had raised these questions, but with them the formal and material element in faith, the primitive foundations and the elaborate deductions are all confused."[60] Thus Harnack, and in support of his contention he cites the questions of Laurentius in the *Enchiridion*.[61] We would add that the clear and concise system of the great doctor on the union of faith and reason, if it had been better understood, would have prevented the hazy subtleties of the theologians of the seventeenth century, from which the analysis of faith is today becoming disentangled with so much difficulty.

a. TWO SOURCES OF RELIGIOUS KNOWLEDGE

Augustine affirms from the beginning of his conversion the two sources of religious knowledge: reason and authority. This is the conclusion of his first work, *Against the Academics*: "No one doubts that we are driven on to learn by a double spur, authority and reason."[62] The same thesis is developed in *On Order*.[63] The necessity of believing in one authority is the very basis of *On the Advantage of Believing* in which he establishes in general that "no institution of human society can remain stable once we have decided to believe in nothing which we cannot grasp with our senses."[64] The nature of faith is clearly set forth, for example, in *Letter 147*.[65] It is not some sort of vague sentiment of the soul which adheres to a doctrine without rational motives. It is rather an intellectual adherence to truths which are certified not by an inner vision of these truths but by evidence worthy of credence: "Those things which are beyond our senses are believed if the testimony about them seems fitting."[66] Thus, according to the great doctor, the essential character of faith is that the only motive for believing be a witness, but a trustworthy witness. Science, on the other hand, sees the object in itself, in its causes or the effects closely connected with it. The freedom of adherence and the mysterious nature of the object are characteristics of Christian faith, but they do not constitute its essential structure.

b. PRIORITY OF REASON AND FAITH UNDER DIFFERENT ASPECTS

A fairly frequent résumé of Augustine's thought is voiced by Weber, who says: "Faith precedes understanding in time. To understand anything, you must first accept it. 'I believe that I may understand.'"[67] As a matter of fact, the great doctor often did affirm the priority of faith: "We are necessarily led to knowledge in two ways, by authority and reason. In time authority is first, but in reality reason precedes."[68] "We must believe before we can understand."[69] "Faith is somehow the beginning of knowledge."[70]

"We believe that we may know; we do not know that we may believe."[71] In all these passages, however, the only subject under discussion is the inner understanding of revealed truths. When considering the preparatory steps to faith no one has noted the role of reason preceding and accompanying the adherence of the mind with more preciseness and prudence than Augustine. An orderly and complete presentation of the relations between reason and faith follows.

Before any act of faith, reason has to demonstrate not the intrinsic truth of the statements of the witness, but his right to be believed on his word: "For no one believes anything unless he first thinks that it should be believed."[72] "Authority demands faith and prepares a man for reasoning. . . . On the other hand, reason does not depart from authority altogether when it considers whom it should believe."[73] "It is our task to consider what men or books we should believe that we may worship God correctly."[74] *Letter 120* studies the relationship of reason and faith and, after having proclaimed the guiding principle that "we would not even be able to believe unless we had rational souls," it explains this priority of reason: "If therefore it is reasonable that faith precede reason for the deeper truths which cannot be grasped, certainly whatever reason there was which led to this conclusion should itself precede faith."[75] But once the authority and the existence of the divine testimony have been established, it would be foolish to wait before believing until all those questions have been solved "which cannot be decided before we believe, lest life itself be terminated in unbelief."[76]

Even in the very act of faith reason retains this vision of the authority of the testimony: The mind can attain only truth, and the truth of revealed dogmas appears only in the testimony concerning them. St. Augustine never tires of repeating: "Everyone who believes, thinks; for by believing he thinks and by thinking he believes."[77] But what does the believer see? Not only the concepts, the elements of dogma,[78] but the truth of these dogmas, made known by an authorized witness, "if the testimony appears proper."[79] Augustine states this even more clearly: "For faith has eyes by which it sees that that is somehow true which it does not yet see; it certainly sees that it does not yet see what it believes."[80] (The "somehow" expresses the truth only as viewed extrinsically by the witness.) What would have been Augustine's surprise if he had been told that faith must close its eyes to the proofs for the divine testimony lest it become knowledge! Or if he had been told of that so-called faith of authority which supposedly gives its assent without regard for any motive proving the validity of the testimony, as if it were possible for the human mind to accept testimony without motives, or, what comes to the same thing, without any known motives! Or again, what would have been his surprise if told that testimony, even though expertly analyzed, could ever lead to real knowledge, that is, an intrinsic view of the object. St. Augustine, on the contrary, far from being afraid of the words "knowledge" and "vision," demanded both, provided that their object be only the testimony: "Our knowledge therefore is made up of things seen and things believed. But we ourselves are witnesses of those objects which we saw or which we now see; regarding the objects which we believe, however, we are moved to belief by other witnesses." Thus faith requires certain credentials "which, once they are seen, lead us to believe what we do not see."[81] He immediately adds that this adherence to dogmas which rests on a recognized witness worthy of credence could be called knowledge, but always remains faith because it does not see the object in itself.

For a deeper understanding of the mystery, however, faith precedes reason. As soon as the divine testimony becomes known, reason stops at the threshold of the mystery, without, however, withholding its faith until it has a better comprehension of it. It does not even demand as a condition for belief that all questions have been solved. For it is after believing that the believer will search out explanations more or less in keeping with the dogma. Augustine repeats this over and over and he loves to invoke the authority of Isaias (7:9), or rather the inexact translation of the Septuagint: "Unless you believe you shall not understand."[82] This was to be the great thesis later introduced into early Scholasticism by Anselm: faith seeking understanding.

Two sermons contain a remarkable résumé of this theory. The first is *Sermon 43* in its entirety, where the truth of the two formulas "understand that you may believe; believe that you may understand" is explained in the conclusion.[83] The other is the eighteenth sermon on Psalm 118, especially the following passage: "For although no one can believe in God unless he understands something, he is nevertheless enabled to understand more by the very faith with which he believes. For there are some things which we do not believe unless we understand and some others which we do not understand unless we believe."[84]

C. PROOF OF THE FAITH

The task of the apologist has been sketched in *On Freedom of Choice*. The principal points are to set forth the claims of the authority which is invoked and to answer objections "previously upheld against unbelievers in order that their infidelity be crushed by the weight of authority or that they be shown, as far as possible, how it is not foolish to believe such things and then how it is foolish not to believe them."[85] As a foundation for any proof Augustine lays down the cardinal principle that knowledge of divine providence must precede all else and that all proofs of revelation by miracles presuppose the existence of God and His government of the world: "For if the providence of God does not look after men's affairs there is no need to take religion seriously."[86] The great proofs on which Augustine rests the authority of Jesus Christ or of the Church in *On Faith in Things Unseen*, *The City of God*, and *On the True Religion* are already found in *On the Advantage of Believing*.[87] He mentions four proofs in particular. The first is the miracles of Christ, by which "the sick were healed and the lepers cleansed." In addition to miracles he uses prophecies as a proof.[88] The third proof is the multitude of the faithful,[89] an insufficient argument if Augustine had not also considered, along with the number of the faithful, the miraculous foundation of the Church with its note of catholicity, which he so often appealed to against the Manicheans and Donatists, and the providential miracle which alone can explain its conquest of the world.[90] The great proof, however, which seems to have impressed Augustine the most, is the holiness of Christianity incarnate in the Church, and its moral transformation of the world.[91] He was thoroughly convinced himself by the accounts of the heroism of the Apostles.[92] In *On True Religion*, after having sketched a magnificent portrait of the moral revolution which had been accomplished, he concludes that, if the great philosophers Socrates and Plato were witnesses of this today, "they would become Christians."[93] To the Bishop of Hippo as to the Fathers of the Vatican Council,[94] the Church appears as the one great proof placed within reach of all: "The house of the Lord is a mountain placed in the open."[95]

d. SOURCES OF FAITH

(1) *Three rules of faith.* In general Augustine proclaims the authority of three rules of faith: Scripture, tradition, and the teaching power of the Church. It is so clear that he sacrificed neither the Bible to oral tradition nor the Church to the Bible that Protestant critics, unable to reconcile these two factors, have here again accused Augustine of contradiction: "All those who place Scripture above the Creed can make use of the name of Augustine, just like advocates of the opposite position, for he has strengthened the trend to emphasize the Bible while at the same time encouraging those in the Church who, like Tertullian, tear down the biblicists."[96] This reproach has no foundation, for St. Augustine, when mentioning the various sources of our faith, clearly outlines their subordination and harmony.

The canonical Scriptures are an infallible norm for him: "Only to the canonical writings do I owe consent without any hesitation."[97] ("Only" is in opposition to the writings of the Fathers and the apocryphal books.)

Everything, however, is not contained in Scripture, for tradition alone has transmitted to us many of the revelations made to the Apostles, such as the baptism of infants: "There are many things which the universal Church holds, and which because of this are believed to have been commanded by the Apostles, even though they are not found in any written document."[98] This tradition of the necessity of infant baptism provides him with his favorite proof for original sin.[99] To be truly apostolic, however, tradition must be endowed with the character of universality. St. Augustine in his time formulated the rule which Vincent of Lerins was soon afterwards to develop more fully: "Whatever the universal Church holds, not because of its institution by a council but because it has always been taught, is rightly considered a matter of faith solely because handed down by the authority of the Apostles."[100] Corresponding to oral tradition is the Creed, the "rule of faith," which the interpreter of Scripture must consult as an inviolable law.[101] Augustine often wrote commentaries on the Creed;[102] Hahn has drawn from these commentaries two forms of the Creed, one used at Milan and the other in Africa, of which the most important variation is the conclusion, "eternal life through the holy Church."[103]

Above Scripture and tradition is the living authority of the Church. She alone certifies the validity of Scripture according to his celebrated statement: "I would not believe in the Gospel unless the authority of the Catholic Church ordered it."[104] She it is who transmits the Creed to us.[105] By her teaching she is the supreme norm which must be followed in the interpretation of Scripture and tradition: "The doubts of those seeking information must not go beyond the boundaries of the Catholic faith."[106] Finally, by her councils she decides all controversies.[107]

In the logical order of the proof for the faith by Augustine, the divinity of the Church, which is not proved by Scripture (there would otherwise be a vicious circle) but by the great miracles of its foundation and holiness, precedes knowledge of the Sacred Books or at least of their inspiration. Then he receives from the Catholic Church, known as divine in the essentials of its religious thought, the Creed and the inspired Scriptures which reveal to him more clearly the mission and the privileges of the Church. That is the sense of this famous passage: "There are many things which rightly keep me in the bosom of the Church: the universal consent of peoples and nations holds me, its miraculously established authority holds me . . . ,"[108] and so forth.

(2) *St. Augustine and the Bible.* It is certain that Augustine contributed to the development of the role of Scripture in the Church both by his example and his theories. Harnack did not hesitate to say that at the beginning of the fifth century Holy Scripture undoubtedly held a different place in the life of the Western Church than it did in the East. It remained more in the foreground, a fact principally due to the influence of Augustine.[109]

Augustine is one of the earliest witnesses to the complete canon of the Scriptures. He had accepted the deuterocanonical books at the very time when St. Jerome was satisfied with the doubts raised about them in the East. Moreover, as Harnack points out, Augustine's opinion became the rule for the entire West.[110] The list of canonical books which he gave in 397[111] agrees perfectly with the so-called Gelasian Canon which modern critics believe was promulgated by Pope Damasus in a council at Rome held in 374[112] and with the list sent to Exuperius of Toulouse by Pope Innocent I in 405.[113] A similar catalog with unimportant variations had previously been prepared in 393 by the Council of Hippo at which Augustine was present while only a priest.[114] This canon was ratified at Carthage in 397 and 419.[115] These councils do not presume to publish a definitive list and add that Pope Boniface must be consulted "to confirm this canon."[116] All the same Augustine knows and permits divergences among various Churches[117] and especially the doubts of the Eastern Church.[118] In his own personal opinion, however, he never wavered about the validity of the deuterocanonical books and he steadfastly defended the inspiration of the Book of Wisdom in his *City of God*.[119] He did change his ideas about the author of several books. He had attributed the Book of Wisdom to Jesus Sirach, but later changed his mind[120] without being able to name an author.[121] Rottmanner has proved that Augustine from the beginning of 409 till his death never once cited the Epistle to the Hebrews as a writing of the Apostle, although he never said anything against its Pauline origin.[122] He rejects the apocryphal writings energetically.[123]

The teaching on inspiration also owes to Augustine its exact formulation in the sense of a "strict biblicism,"[124] that is, of the divine origin and consequently absolute inerrancy of the Sacred Books "whose truth," as the Vatican Council later proclaimed, "no one doubts unless he is an infidel or irreverent person."[125] It is the Spirit of God who "speaks through the mouth of the prophets and guides the pen of the Apostles."[126] You can even say that the books of the Apostles are the writings of Jesus.[127] Every absolute statement of Scripture, even those which the author conceived without revelation, becomes a true revelation for the reader because it is guaranteed by the word of God, who inspired it. Therefore any error in the Bible is impossible.[128] If you think that you have come across a false statement it is because "either the text is incorrect or the interpreter made a mistake or you do not understand."[129] The whole of *On the Agreement of the Evangelists* and the controversy with St. Jerome on the Epistle to the Galatians (2:14 ff.) were intended to exclude not only all voluntary deception from the Bible, but every unconscious error as well.[130] Nevertheless, to grasp Augustine's theory precisely we must take careful account of the restrictions which he himself laid down. He admits that there were oversights and confusion of one name for another by the sacred writers.[131] Discourses are recorded faithfully as far as the matter and thought are concerned, but great differences of order and expression can be found among the evangelists.[132]

St. Augustine's views on the translations of the Bible were less fortunate. He considered the Septuagint as inspired. Undoubtedly he relates the legend of the seventy-two cells as a pious tradition,[133] but he insists upon the inspiration and explains the divergences between the Hebrew and Greek texts as willed by the Holy Spirit, both of them being inspired even in the sections which are wanting in one of the two.[134]

Because he recognized the authority only of the Greek text of the Old and New Testament, St. Augustine maintains complete freedom of judgment and discussion regarding the Latin translations. He generally favors the "Italian" texts because he prefers the Vetus Itala translation, but he frequently uses the old "African" texts and even on occasion the Vulgate of St. Jerome.[135]

There are just two important observations to be made concerning St. Augustine's hermeneutics. The first is that he laid down a strict law of extreme prudence for the determination of the meaning of Scripture. People should be on their guard against interpretations which are hazardous and opposed to science, for they thus make the Word of God a laughingstock to the incredulous.[136] Secondly, Augustine was the first to propound, but without absolute certitude, the theory of the plurality of literal meanings, which would have been fatal to the science of exegesis if it had prevailed. Any pious or true meaning which the reader can or wishes to understand when reading the Bible, even if the sacred author had never even thought of it, would be the meaning of Scripture because it is willed by the Holy Spirit who foresaw this future interpretation. "For my part," he says, "if I were the inspired writer, I would have wished to speak thus. . . ."[137] We are all acquainted with the discussions which this theory has caused. St. Thomas had approved it without reserve in *De potentia*,[138] but is more cautious in the *Summa*[139] where he keeps only the formula and understands it in an entirely different manner of the allegorical, moral, and spiritual meanings which are based on the single literal meaning. Augustine's opinion today has been universally abandoned.[140]

An overall judgment of Augustine's exegesis is difficult to formulate, so diverse are the aspects of his work. The most remarkable of his biblical studies pertain to several fields. In the theory of exegesis (*On Christian Doctrine*) he is generally praised. In preaching (*Commentaries on John, Discourses on the Psalms*) where he readily sought the mystical and allegorical interpretation he is unsurpassed. On some special questions (*On the Agreement of the Evangelists*) we have to admire his depth of perception. But there are almost no connected commentaries except the *Literal Commentary on Genesis* and the essays on the Epistles to Romans and Galatians. The strictly exegetical work of Augustine does not equal, then, either in scope or in scientific character, that of St. Jerome. Three circumstances contributed to this inferiority. One was an insufficient knowledge of the biblical tongues. He read Greek, but with difficulty. All that we can conclude about his knowledge of Hebrew was that he was familiar with Punic, a Semitic language related to it.[141] Secondly, the moral purpose and practical need of the hour which his eloquence aimed at carried him to indisputable abuses of the mystical sense. Finally, in his polemics the two great qualities of his genius—the ardent passion of his African temperament and the prodigious subtlety of his mind—never left him the quiet and peace necessary for an exegete, but rushed him into interpretations which did violence to the text, or were ingenious but without foundation. Thus, for example, the passage in Matthew (17:20) which attributes to Jeremias a prophecy of Zacharias is used by Augustine to show that the Holy Spirit wished thus to demonstrate the agreement or rather the identity of all the prophecies.[142] An exaggerated allegorism is likewise born of the desire to verify the agreement of the two Testaments according to the formula: "The New Testament lies hidden in the Old, and the Old is evident in the New."[143] Clausen has assembled a series of texts where Augustine's exegesis cannot be accepted.[144]

CHAPTER VIII

The Divine Nature

FOLLOWING what has been said about the lofty concepts Augustine borrowed from the Platonic theories, some of his fundamental ideas on our knowledge of the existence of God, His nature, and the Trinity must be mentioned.

I. THE EXISTENCE OF GOD

In Augustine's mind, the existence of God is one of those truths on which Providence has thrown such light that it is inescapable. No one can be completely ignorant of God: "God is hidden everywhere; He is manifest everywhere. No one can know Him as He is, but no one is permitted not to know Him."[1] Even atheists refuse to believe only because of passion, "in their hearts."[2] Moreover, there are very few of them, "a rare type of man,"[3] for it is really a kind of insanity: "That madness belongs to only a few."[4]

God is not, however, for us the object of our direct and immediate intuition. We have seen that according to St. Augustine's theory of knowledge we receive knowledge neither from an immediate contemplation of God nor from innate ideas. He describes in his commentary on Genesis how our soul, starting with the knowledge of sensible things, rises all the way to the "invisible things of God" through the illumination of the Word.[5]

Although he mentioned all the classic proofs for the existence of God, rarely is a systematic demonstration to be found in his writings. He places particular emphasis upon the consensus of the human race: "Except for a few whose human nature is too depraved, the whole human race acknowledges that God is the author of this world."[6] The ancient proof through finality and the order of the world was developed by him with an inimitable delicacy, grace, and feeling: everywhere in the beauty of nature he sees the name of the divine architect. "Noble philosophers looked and knew the Maker from His handiwork."[7] His eloquence is especially admirable when he develops the metaphysical proof of the finite and changeable world crying out for an infinite and changeless Creator. In the *Confessions* he exclaims: "I have questioned the earth . . . and the sea . . . and the depths . . . and they have answered: 'Look above us. . . . He made us.' "[8] Again, with more cogent logic: "Behold, the heavens and the earth exist. They cry out that they were made, for they are changed and undergo variation. Whatever has not been made and nevertheless exists, has nothing in it which did not exist before; this is what change and variation mean. They also cry out that they did not make themselves . . . ."[9] A profound reflection of Augustine in answer to one of the questions of Evodius in 415 should be mentioned: all our proofs show that God exists, not that He ought to exist. There are no *a priori* reasons for His existence.[10]

Augustine's outstanding proof, however, is the one developed explicitly in *On Eighty-three Different Questions*,[11] more fully in *On Freedom of Choice*,[12] and finally in the *Confessions*.[13] It rests upon the comprehension of an eternal and unchangeable truth, superior to man, and can be formulated in this manner: If the mind of man (and the angelic mind),[14] occupying the highest level in the hierarchy of beings in the universe, discovers a being more perfect, that being must be God. Now, my mind ascertains that there is an eternal and unchangeable truth above itself which it does not create, but which it contemplates. This truth is not mine nor in me because others contemplate it as well as I do and without my assistance. This truth is therefore God Himself or, if one supposes that there is a yet more elevated being, it at least leads us to this being, the source of all truth.[15] Jules Martin sees in this proof the foreshadowing of St. Anselm's argument. But he is mistaken in that, for Augustine does not conclude to the existence of God from a concept about Him. Rather, analyzing the characteristics of truth, he finds that they are inexplicable unless there is an unchangeable being behind them, the source of unchangeable truth. After 388 this idea took hold of Augustine's soul and betrayed itself in such exclamations as the following: "O God, You are the Father of truth, the Father of wisdom, the Father of the true and supreme life, the Father of happiness, the Father of the good and the beautiful, the Father of the intelligible light, the Father of our awakening and our enlightenment."[16] Basically this proof, like the others, is reducible to the famous trilogy in which God is conceived by the great doctor as the source of all being, truth, and good: "The cause of existence, the ultimate reason for the understanding, and the order of life."[17]

2. THE DIVINE NATURE

The limitations of our knowledge about God—the inability to comprehend His nature and to talk about it in human language— is one of the favorite themes of the great doctor. We have already seen that he is far from being an agnostic, but he does feel more than others the torments of the divine mystery which surrounds us. He never wearies of saying that neither our concepts nor our words can exhaust the infinite: "If you understand, it is not God."[18] "God is ineffable. We can more easily say what He is not than what He is."[19] "You can say everything about God and you have said nothing worthy of Him."[20] The truest concepts will be those which are most general, provided that we know how to clarify their vague outlines. For Augustine, God is being, the absolute being, being in its fullness and perfection, being above which, beyond which, and without which nothing at all exists.[21]

Among the attributes of God simplicity is the trait he focuses on. Since God is by His essence pure actuality of being and so cannot ever be conceived as being in potency and gradually transformed into act, He is therefore all perfection. Augustine goes so far as to regret the use of the word *substance* when speaking of the divine essence, as if it introduced a distinction between the essence of the being and its accidental qualities: "If God exists in such a way that He can be said to be a substance, something is in Him as in a subject and He is not simple."[22] Therefore he concludes: "He is properly called an essence, only improperly a substance." To exclude all appearances of metaphysical composition from the divine being, he takes delight in describing the absolute identity which does not make each one of His attributes (such as goodness, wisdom, or justice) just accidents joined to His being, but His very being itself: "Whatever He has He is. . . . Thus He possesses wisdom in such a way that He is Wisdom."[23] He also insists on the identity of these attributes among themselves.[24] Following Augustine's lead, Suarez and other theologians were to add one last aspect to the divine simplicity: even our ideas of the divine attributes are not formally distinct, but mutually compenetrate one another. We cannot conceive the divine justice without including in that infinite justice which appears as the fullness of being His infinite mercy, which is also included in that fullness.[25]

The relationship of God to time and space is explained more easily in the light of the ineffable simplicity. Eternity is such a perfect actuation of all the divine life that, no change being possible, neither yesterday nor today nor tomorrow can be distinguished. For time is not born of the revolutions of the stars as Plato thought, but of the change which is inherent in every creature: "Time is the movement of a creature from one state to another."[26] His simplicity likewise shows that God is elevated above all space, present everywhere but unextended and incommensurable.[27]

The theory of the divine knowledge is summed up by Augustine in this grand conception: In one single, unchangeable glance God contemplates every being, every truth, every possible or real object. This knowledge is an eternal intuition before which the past and the future are as real as the present, but each for that portion of time in which it really exists. God encompasses all time and therefore can know the future (whether produced freely or necessarily) as infallibly as He knows the present.[28] Today no one any longer denies that Augustine admitted the knowledge of conditioned futures (pure futuribles) in God, events which will never take place, but which would have taken place if certain conditions had been fulfilled. It would seem at first glance that these purely hypothetical objects can never be present to the divine mind, since they represent nothing in reality. But, along with the other Fathers, St. Augustine admitted this knowledge in God. Moreover, as we shall see, he made this knowledge serve as the well-spring of divine providence. When the Semipelagians misinterpreted this knowledge and thought that they found traits in it which annulled the gratuity of grace and the gift of predestination, the great doctor of grace denied such applications of this knowledge, but he always admitted the knowledge itself.[29]

3. THE TRINITY

According to Schwane, Augustine would have merited the first place among the doctors of the patristic age no less by his teaching on the Trinity than by his teaching on grace.[30] His work of fifteen books *On the Trinity* certainly synthesizes and adds the finishing touches to the most profound and exact statements which had been made about this great mystery, especially in harmonizing the divinity of the Son and the Holy Spirit—never afterwards to be questioned—with the unity of the divine being. The outstanding characteristic of his Trinitarian teaching is that it clearly manifests the progress of the Latin mind in its thought about the Trinity, a progress opposed to that of the Greek or Eastern Fathers. Father de Regnon has traced this divergence in conception between the East and West, but the reader should remember that de Regnon's admiration for the Greeks did not permit him to appreciate the full value of the progress accomplished or at least initiated by the genius of Augustine.[31] This development of the dogma is all the more remarkable because the Trinitarian teaching of Augustine as molded by Scholasticism was to direct the thought of all the Western theologians. The principles held in common by the Greek and Latin Fathers at the time when Augustine wrote were the dogma of the three persons participating fully and equally in the same divine nature and the explanation of the dogma by this axiom, implicitly formulated by the Greeks themselves: "In God everything is one where there is no distinction by relative opposition," a formula in which unity is referred to the nature and distinction to the persons.[32] Expressions in the introduction to the eighth book of *On the Trinity*, which have certainly served as a model for the author of the pseudo-Athanasian Creed (the *Quicumque*), set down this great norm: The absolute properties of the essence must be predicated in the singular: "There is one God, the good and omnipotent Trinity itself. The same is true of whatever is predicated of each of the persons in themselves and not insofar as they are related to one another. For such things are predicated of them according to essence."[33] Three traits characterize the Latin way of conceiving the Trinity and the progress brought about under the influence of the great doctor: (1) the concept of the nature before the persons; (2) the insistence on attributing all the operations *ad extra* to the entire Trinity; (3) the psychological explanation of the processions.

a. NATURE BEFORE PERSONS

In his explanation of the Trinity Augustine conceives the divine nature before the persons. His formulation of the Trinity was to read: one single divine nature subsisting in three persons. The Greeks, on the contrary, put it this way: three persons having the same nature. Up to that point the attention of the Greeks was centered directly on the persons: on the Father, conceived as God in a special manner (at first the word *Deus*, ὁ Θεός, was used only for Him), "I believe in one God, the Father"; then on the Son, born of the Father, "God of God"; and finally on the Holy Spirit, proceeding from the Father as Father and then through the Son. It was only through reflection that the Greek mind considered directly the one identical divine nature in these three persons. St. Augustine, on the other hand, foreshadowing the Latin concept which the Scholastics borrowed from him, considered the divine nature before all else and investigated this nature until he attained its complete reality in the persons. God, for him, did not directly mean the Father, but the more general notion of the Godhead, conceived concretely and personally no doubt, but not as any one person in particular. It is the God-Trinity, that is, the basic Divinity unfolding itself into three persons, Father, Son, and Holy Spirit, without succession of time or nature, but not without an order of origin.

This special character of Augustine's Trinitarian theory alone explains the novel form of the pseudo-Athanasian Creed which it inspired. All the ancient creeds,[34] even those in vogue at the time of Augustine and used by him at Milan and in Africa,[35] are drawn up according to the old idea beginning with faith in one God who is the Father and concluding with the Holy Spirit, speaking of the Trinity in no other way: "I believe in God the Father . . ." (the First Person) "and in Jesus Christ, the Son . . ." (the oldest form of the Creed).[36] "We believe in one God the Father . . . and in our one Lord, Jesus . . ." (The so-called Niceno-Constantinopolitan Creed).[37] But the *Quicumque* Creed, based on Augustinian inspiration, opens by professing faith in the God-head common to the three persons: "This is the Catholic faith, that we worship one God in the Trinity and the Trinity in unity."[38]

The doctrine is certainly the same, but it is plain that the Augustinian conception anticipates and averts objections in advance because it emphasizes the unity of nature. Never, up to his time, had the divine unity been set in relief so strongly in its relation to the three divine persons. The Greeks, accentuating the role of the persons, were constantly harassed by accusations of tritheism and consequently felt obliged to recapitulate the whole Trinity in its primal source, the Father.[39] With St. Augustine, however, the oneness of the Divinity appears immediately; later, this way of considering the question was to result in the distinction between the two treatises *De Deo Uno* and *De Deo Trino*, a distinction which the Greek view would never have inspired.[40]

The equality of the divine persons likewise shines forth with greater clarity. The ancient concept brought into prominence the role of the Father as the sole source of the Divinity and, according to the expression of St. Denis, the source of every being τῆς ὀντότητος), the source and origin of the other persons, so that the Divinity seemed to belong properly to Him alone. He is God to a supereminent degree (ὁ ἐπὶ παντῶν Θεός, ὁ τῶν ὁλῶν Θεός). Such insistence, however, carried with it the danger, for minds not too keen, of a subordination of the Son and the Holy Spirit. Therefore Augustine concentrated his attention first on the divine nature with all its absolute perfections, existing identically the same in each of the three persons. Augustine can say of this great identity that "the equality is so absolute that not only is the Father not greater than the Son . . . but neither is any one person of the Trinity less than the Trinity itself."[41]

There is, it is true, another danger. Once one has become accustomed to conceiving the Divinity independently of the three persons, will one not gradually come to conceive it as a personal God before becoming the Father, Son, and Holy Spirit, thus entailing either a fourth person in God or absorbing the three persons in a new kind of Sabellianism? The theory of Cajetan[42] and Durandus[43] which affirms a subsistence common to the three persons could never have arisen from the ancient concept, although it was a natural enough product of the Latin spirit. Augustine sensed this danger and acted to prevent it when he denied that the Divinity had any reality distinct from the reality of the divine persons.[44]

b. OPERATIONS *ad extra*

Another step forward initiated by Augustine in his Trinitarian theory is his insistence on making all the divine action *ad extra* the work of all three persons indistinctly. Only according to the special way in which each person possesses the divine nature can one attribute to each of them the role in external operations which is proper to the character of its origin: simple "appropriation" is the phrase the Latins after Augustine will use. The Greek Fathers, it is true, also affirmed this unity of operation (ἐνέργεια) in God, for it was their great proof of the unity of nature. But this was the fruit of reflection, for in their direct description of the Trinity they emphasized, on the contrary, the part of each person in the operations performed in community of action until it became almost a distinct role. Hence arose those expressions which sounded quite strange to Latin ears: "From the Father through the Son in the Holy Spirit." Hence also came some absolute assertions which seemed to reserve a proper operation exclusively to each person: only the Holy Spirit formally had descended on Pentecost, just as the Incarnation belonged solely to the Son. Hence in particular arose that popular explanation of the visible manifestations of God in the Old Testament according to which the Son alone had appeared to the ancient patriarchs. St. Augustine proclaims first that in reality the manifestations are necessarily the work of the whole Trinity, although one of the persons could occasionally be manifested in a special way.[45] The Father, he adds, can appear as well as the Son.[46] As a matter of fact, in the terrestrial Paradise it was not one person, but the Divinity, Father, Son, and Holy Spirit, which was manifested.[47] The words heard by Adam were not only spoken by the Trinity, but in the name of the Trinity, "showing the person of the same Trinity."[48] Besides, in these apparitions the Trinity ordinarily makes use of angels as messengers to manifest itself under a created form.[49] Finally, in the Incarnation itself the whole Trinity effected this wonderful union, although only the Word communicates its personality to the humanity of Christ: "The Trinity wrought that human form from the Virgin Mary, yet it is the person of the Son alone; for the invisible Trinity wrought the visible person of the Son alone."[50]

C. PSYCHOLOGICAL THEORY OF THE PROCESSIONS

Finally, Augustine laid the foundations for the psychological theory of the processions. In this conception, brought into systematic form later by Anselm and completed by St. Thomas, the mind tries to penetrate into the inner life of God and, contemplating the divine nature endowed with intellect and will, explains through these two operations the number and the nature of the processions concerning the origin of the Son and the Holy Spirit. The Son is born of the Father as the *Verbum* of the divine intellect, "after the manner of the act of understanding," St. Thomas was to say.[51] The Holy Spirit proceeds from the Father and the Son as the substantial term of their love, "a procession of love."[52] With these two processions the cycle of what can be called the divine evolution is completed because only these two operations demand a substantial term. This is the profound metaphysical study which St. Augustine inaugurated by his subtle analysis of the human soul, which he liked to see as the most beautiful image of the Trinity.

He had also sought out traces of this great mystery in other creatures, analogies sometimes arbitrary and forced, but which at least show a rare inventive power in the African doctor. The best way to summarize Augustine's views on the Trinity seems to be a table showing the principal expressions and images which represent the three persons of the Trinity:[53]

EXPRESSIONS AND IMAGES OF THE TRINITY ACCORDING TO ST. AUGUSTINE

FATHER	SON	HOLY SPIRIT
A. In God Himself		
1. Supreme being	Highest wisdom	Greatest good
2. True eternity	Eternal truth	Eternal and true charity
3. Eternity	Truth	Will
4. Eternity	Truth	Happiness
5. Eternity	Form	Use
6. Father	Image	Gift
7. Origin of things	Beauty	Delight
B. In Creatures in General		
8. Unity	Form	Order
9. Existence	Knowledge	Love of both
10. Being	Knowing	Willing
11. Being	Having form	Following law
12. Source of things	Distinction	Harmony
13. Cause of being	Cause of kind of being	Cause of goodness of being
14. Nature	Education	Practice
15. Physics	Logic	Ethics
C. In the Sensitive Part of Man		
16. Object seen	External vision	Attention of mind
17. Memory	Internal vision	Will (volition)

FATHER	SON	HOLY SPIRIT
	D. In the Spiritual Soul	
18. Being	Understanding	Life
19. Mind	Knowledge	Love
20. Memory	Understanding	Will
21. Ability	Learning	Use
22. Memory (about God)	Understanding (of God)	Love (of God)

Source of the above analogies in Augustine's works:

1. DCD XI, 28 (41, 342).
2. *Ibid.*
3. DT IV, 1, 2 (42, 887); *Ibid.*, in *Prooemium.*
4. *Ibid.*
5. DT VI, 10, 11 (42, 931).
6. *Ibid.*
7. DT VI, 10, 12 (42, 932).
8. *Ibid.*
9. DCD XI, 27 (41, 340).
10. C XIII, 11, 12 (32, 849).
11. DCD XI, 28 (41, 342).
12. DD83 18 (40, 15).
13. *Ibid.*
14. DCD XI, 25 (41, 339).
15. *Ibid.* (338).
16. DT XI, 2, 2 (42, 985).
17. DT XI, 3, 6 (42, 988).
18. DT VI, 10, 11 (42, 931).
19. DT IX, 3, 3 (42, 962–963).
20. DT X, 11, 17 (42, 982); cf. E149, 6 (33, 745).
21. DT *ibid.*
22. DT XIV, 12, 15 (42, 1048); cf. DT XIV, 2, 4 (42, 1038).

CHAPTER IX

Creation and Creatures

1. AUGUSTINIAN COSMOGONY

THE main features of creation *ex nihilo*, namely, that it is distinct from God and the work of the divine free will, have been mentioned previously in connection with the Neoplatonic tendencies of St. Augustine. There remains to be considered here his theory of the Hexaemeron, a theory which testifies to the amplitude of his views in exegesis and his originality in the very difficult problem of the creation of the world.

a. SIMULTANEOUS CREATION?

Did St. Augustine hold that the entire universe was created simultaneously? We are familiar with the gropings and hesitations of his mind when commenting on Genesis.[1] He never fully allied himself with either the allegorical school of Alexandria or the literal school of Syria; on the problems of the origin of things which haunted him unceasingly, however, he derived inspiration now from one, now from the other of these schools to form what has been termed his eclecticism. All his pondering has resulted in the following conclusions.

All systems affirming the eternity of the world, even though a created world, are in his mind contrary to reason. He does not admit the theory of St. Thomas that only faith informs us that the world had a beginning. In Book XI of the *City of God* he treats this question thoroughly and proves successively that the world cannot exist outside of time: "Certainly the world was not made in time, but together with time";[2] and that time, since it is successive of its very nature, cannot be infinite and eternal:

"Because it passes by in changeableness, time cannot be coeternal with unchangeable eternity."[3] Whether one supposes that un-numbered worlds have preceded ours or whether one admits just one world "subject to the innumerable alternations of destruction and rebirth which certain periods of the world bring about" (the Platonic system), there will always be an infinite distance between time and eternity: "They should remember that nothing is eternal which has a limit."[4] To those who ask why God did not create the world sooner, he answers: Why did He not create it else-where? "If they say the thoughts of men are foolish when they imagine that space is infinite, since there is no space outside the universe, they should be told that men are just as foolish when they picture the past ages of God's rest, since there was no time before the creation of the world."[5]

The account of the six days of creation in Genesis cannot be taken literally and in its natural meaning. After 389 Augustine excludes the sense of ordinary days.[6] Among other reasons alleged, he asks what meaning three days could have without the heavens.[7] After the creation of the sun he adds: "Whoever understands that during our night the sun is shining elsewhere . . . will look for a more refined meaning in the enumeration of such days."[8]

In reality the creative action was instantaneous and the six days of Genesis correspond to the indivisible instant when everything was created.[9] Relying on the saying of Ecclesiasticus (18:1), "He created all things at the same time," Augustine rejects the idea of any new creation by God, although admitting new intervention on His part: "After that act of creation He rested from His works, not creating anything more."[10]

Contrary to most of his contemporaries, however, he does not presume that the instantaneous act of the Creator produced an organized universe such as we see today. He distinguishes between creation properly so called and the formation or development of the world. This second action is due, at least in great part, to forces placed by the Creator in the depths of nature which have gradually and progressively passed through the various phases to which the Mosaic account gives an approximation.[11]

b. PRIMITIVE ELEMENTS AND SEEDLIKE PRINCIPLES

How does Augustine conceive the primitive elements of the world and the seedlike principles (*rationes seminales*)? At the beginning, in his theory, God created the elements of the universe in the state of a confused and nebulous mass—the word is his: "A nebulous form appears."[12] These elements, according to Aristotelian terminology, he calls matter and form, or better, formless matter. Sometimes, it is true, he seems to say that God first produced invisible matter without form and without individuation: "You made the world from formless matter, which matter You made almost nothing from nothing."[13] He explains his meaning, however, in his commentary on Genesis.[14] Matter could not have been created before all form because it could not exist before all determination. It has then a simple priority of origin without any actual pre-existence: "Matter does not exist in time before its information, but in origin."[15]

Among the elements created on the first day Augustine distinguishes two types. Some were definitely constituted in their specific natures while others existed only in germ in their preexisting causes. Thus everything was created in the beginning, but the majority of beings were only in potency and enveloped in their causes.[16] "All things," he says, "were created by God in the beginning in a kind of blending of the elements, but they cannot develop and appear until the favorable circumstances are realized."[17] Elsewhere he compares the evolution of the world as it blossomed forth from the primitive elements to the development of a seed which becomes a great tree: "Just as in the seed can be found invisibly all that which one day will make up the tree, thus the world contained in itself all that which one day will become manifest, not only the heavens with their sun, moon, and stars . . . but also, in potency and in their causes, the other beings which the sea and the earth brought forth."[18] These seedlike principles (*rationes seminales*), a term undoubtedly borrowed from the Neoplatonists[19] and to become quite famous later in the Scholastic era, are nothing else than the energy latent in the germs which are destined to develop not just during the six days of creation but during all the centuries of the history of the world.[20] Augustine multiplies examples and formulas to help people understand his thought. Thus the formless matter created by God in the beginning is called the heaven and the earth "not because it was already the heaven and the earth, but because it had the power to become such."[21] He speaks the same way about plants and animals.[22] It is remarkable also that Augustine, even when he seems so daring in his explanation, out of respect for the sacred text says that these principles of life in the world did not first bring forth a seed, grain, or egg, but on the contrary a living being which produced the seed for the future.[23]

At the risk of surprising some readers, we must add that St. Augustine extended his system to man also. How, he asks, did Adam and Eve exist from the beginning of the world? "I answer: invisibly, potentially, causally, in the way that future things which are not yet made exist."[24] Thus Adam and Eve were created from the very first day, not in their perfect reality, but "according to the productive potency scattered like a seed in the world by the word of God."[25] From this potential existence, once the time had come, "Adam had to be made from the slime of the earth, and woman from the side of man."[26] To avoid mistake in this matter the reader must take heed of two important reservations. Augustine will say that the soul could not have been enclosed in any "causal principle";[27] furthermore, God will intervene in the formation of the body of man.

C. AUGUSTINE AN EVOLUTIONIST?

The question whether Augustine is an evolutionist would be ridiculous if one meant atheistic evolution or material evolution without a soul, for Augustine makes God and the soul the very center of his entire cosmogony and anthropology. But there is a theistic evolution which could appeal to the authority of the Doctor of Hippo, and with some show of truth. For when he so absolutely denies successive creations does he not admit that the Creator has endowed matter with the power of gradual differentiation and transformation which constitutes a type of evolution?

Many have thought as much. Zahm congratulates the great doctor first for having anticipated modern science in granting nature this power of transformation and then for proclaiming that "the world is under the rule of law and that God in the government of the physical universe does not always act directly and immediately, but indirectly through the mediation of secondary causes which we call the laws and forces of nature."[28] He adds: "On this point Augustine is so explicit that it is impossible to be mistaken."[29] This interpretation, nevertheless, is completely inaccurate in both parts.

(1) Augustine did not think that transformation was possible; on the contrary, affirming the immutability of species, he makes no allowance for the possibility that "different realities could come from the same primitive principle or the same seed."[30] This evaluation in Jules Martin's penetrating study is ours also. The proof for it is clear as soon as one reads the following blanket assertion: "The elements of this corporeal world have therefore their well-defined energy and their proper qualities on which depend what each one of them can do or not do and what reality should come or not come from each one of them. . . . Thus it happens that a bean does not grow from a grain of wheat, nor wheat from a bean. A beast does not give birth to a man, or a man to a beast."[31] Thus the seedlike principles do not constitute potencies in the elements to evolve "from homogeneity to heterogeneity," as Zahm thinks,[32] but presuppose as many seeds as there are to be different species. The examples cited show that Augustine's idea of species was quite strict.

Book III of On the Trinity is especially enlightening. There is no spontaneous generation, but "the invisible seeds of all beings which come into existence are hidden in the elements of nature."[33] Thus the fish and birds were born from the sea; plants and "the first animals of each species," from the earth. Innumerable other seeds exist, dispersed throughout the universe, but dormant because of the absence of the favorable circumstances, "in virtue of which they too will spring forth and produce their species."

(2) Augustine demands the immediate intervention of God for

the formation of the universe, something different from the ordinary divine concurrence. God certainly creates no longer, but His direct action is sometimes necessary to make up for the powerlessness of cosmic energies and to bring about the full development of such and such a seed at the desired moment. Now, whether this divine influence introduces new matter into the universe (a hypothesis rejected by Augustine) or whether at various intervals it gives a new stimulus (as he insists), it is always a deficiency in natural law and recourse to a miracle.

It is true that the great doctor does not specify the instances when God must intervene in this miraculous manner. But he accepts the principle. Talking of the formation of the moon he says: "If God were said to have made anything imperfect which He afterwards would bring to completion, how could that opinion be blameworthy?"[34] He categorically affirms this miraculous intervention for the formation of the body of Eve and gives his general theory in that connection.[35] Future beings, he says, are contained in the elements in two very different ways: Some will spring necessarily from this primitive seed while others can be drawn from it if God directly intervenes. Thus the body of Eve was not so much contained in the elements as in the power of God: "It was hidden in God."[36] This formation of the body of Eve is so great a miracle that not even the angels could have accomplished it.[37] The same is true of the intervention of God to introduce the soul of Adam into his body and also, it seems, for the formation of his body: "We should believe then, if the authority of Scripture and logical reasoning do not contradict us, that man was made on the sixth day in such a way that the causal principle for the human body lay hidden in the elements of the world, but the soul itself was created and once created lay hidden in the works of God until in His good time He breathed upon it . . . and placed it in the body formed from the slime of the earth."[38]

d. RECONCILIATION WITH THE TRADITIONAL SIX DAYS

Augustine always experienced great difficulty in trying to reconcile his explanation with the six days of creation in Genesis, and it can be said that he never did arrive at a definitive interpretation which he held to the exclusion of others.

According to *On Genesis Against the Manicheans*, Moses could have had several objects in view when he wrote the account of the six days. One could have been to make the Sabbath rest a sacred thing,[39] foreseeing in it also the repose of the soul through eternity.[40] Another purpose could have been to give a prophetic image of the six ages of the world.[41] Finally, he might have wished to represent the six different phases of the moral life of our souls.[42]

In the *Incomplete Literal Commentary on Genesis* he explains it as a popular way of representing not so much the succession of the divine action as the successive phases through which the created world passed under the causality of natural causes.[43] In particular Augustine gives different meanings to the words *evening* and *morning*. In the *Commentary*, *evening* designates the imperfect and indeterminate state of formless matter, while *morning* stands for the specific determination imprinted by God on this matter.[44]

Later (after 400) he proposed another interpretation. These six days, especially the morning and the evening, represent the successive phases of cognition which the angels acquire of creatures, first as they are in God (the more perfect knowledge, the morning) and then as they are in themselves (the inferior type, the evening). This symbolism corresponds to the true meaning which the author had in view.[45]

e. CONCLUSION

Augustine presented his theory with great reserve and without condemning other interpretations, "denying no one the liberty of understanding the passage better."[46] "In ignorance we hazard a guess."[47] On the other hand, he energetically demanded freedom to defend his own system. Never perhaps was he so severe to Catholics as he was here towards those involved in contradictions because they had raised their solution to the status of a dogma —and this in the most pious and humble of his books, the *Confessions*.[48] He says in particular: "Because they are proud . . . they love their own opinion—not because it is true, but because it is their own. . . . Its source is not understanding but pride."[49]

2. ANGELOLOGY

This is one of the areas of revelation in which Augustine, influenced by Neoplatonism, could not disentangle himself from some confused notions which surprise us today.

a. NATURE OF THE ANGELS

Certainly it is not at all true, as some have thought, that Augustine stated absolutely that the angels have bodies, no matter how subtle and refined this body might be imagined. Noris has made this point perfectly clear.[50] On the other hand, it cannot be denied that Augustine remained hesitant and undecided about this question to the very end. He once states that our bodies after the resurrection will be "like the bodies of the angels."[51] In the *City of God* he says: "It is uncertain."[52]

He confesses his ignorance about the number of the angels and the hierarchy of the angelic choirs.[53] The nature of their knowledge and the power of their action are also insoluble problems for Augustine.[54] In the *City of God* he concludes after a long study that the least work of creation can no more be attributed to them than the creation of the harvest of grain and fruit can be attributed to the laborer.[55]

b. HISTORY OF THE ANGELS

The moment of their creation, Augustine says, has not been revealed to us. Nevertheless he thinks that they were created along with the material universe, or at least that they are not coeternal with God.[56] Before their fall they had received grace.[57] He asks the question whether, if they lived for some time before the fall, they (even those angels who were going to sin) enjoyed the beatitude of heaven from the beginning. Augustine does not dare to deny this outright. Did they not at least have the assurance of perpetual happiness?[58] At any rate, the fall of the demons, presuming that it did take place at the very first moment of their existence, is not the result of a nature which was created evil but of the criminal misuse of their freedom of choice.[59] Their first sin was pride, and then envy.[60] After the fall of the demons, there is no redemption for them.[61] Their prison until the end of time is the atmosphere which surrounds the earth; only then will they be shackled in hell.[62] Their intelligence, darkened by the fall, is subject to error.[63]

Magic had formerly held Augustine's interest when he was still a Manichean. After his conversion he gives an explanation of it in one of his first works.[64] Certain prodigies of paganism were accepted easily enough, but he suspects trickery in regard to the perpetual light of the temple of Venus.[65] A profound psychologist, Augustine held that our thoughts caused a modification of the brain cells or of the senses strong enough to be perceived by the keen senses of the ethereal bodies of the demons.[66] In the *Retractations* he found that he had been too apodictic,[67] but his views on the external manifestation of our most intimate thought are nonetheless intriguing. Speaking of Genesis (6:2), Augustine rejects the legendary interpretation which attributes the birth of giants to the angels.[68]

C. FUNCTIONS OF THE ANGELS

Under the influence of Neoplatonism Augustine always affirmed that an angel was put in charge of each creature of this world.[69] He even wonders whether the angels which govern the stars are not so intimately joined to them that they form living beings.[70] His vacillation about the theory of the world as an immense living being is still present in the *Retractations*.[71]

The position of Augustine on the question of the guardian angels has been described minutely in the *Dictionnaire de Théologie Catholique*.[72] We might add that, relying on Luke (16:22), he considers the angels as intermediaries who make the events of this world known to the souls of the dead in the measure which God permits.[73] In fact, the great doctor sees an intimate association between the angels and the just; one no less than the other belongs to the single city of God.[74]

Miracles, finally, are accomplished by the ministry of the angels. St. Augustine teaches positively that the manifestations of God in the Old Testament should be attributed to them.[75] He also adds two important points. The angels can work miracles by their natural powers (always with the permission or command of God). Undoubtedly in certain instances, such as the Resurrection or the formation of the body of Eve, they can only furnish preliminary assistance. But the Doctor of Hippo never supposed, as did certain great theologians, that a miracle necessarily must surpass all the angelic powers, for the miracles of the Bible would disappear immediately. The second remark is that God can use the demons as instruments of His marvels: "even by the bad angels, whether at His permission or order or compulsion."[76]

3. St. Augustine's Psychology

In the study of the soul Augustine is more successful than in his angelology, which is shot through with Neoplatonism. Here he seems to be moving in his proper sphere, for an exquisite gift of inner observation and penetrating analysis allows him to describe with striking precision the most delicate phenomena of our interior life. No one has spoken of the dignity of the soul with a more passionate admiration: "God alone is better than the soul. . . . The angel is its equal, and all the rest of the universe is below it:"[77] Nourrisson says: "Although others may have presented this truth in more logical fashion, there is no one, not even Descartes, who has established more solidly that the soul, which is known by us before the body, is known without the body and better than the body."[78] Although he discussed the great psychological problems, especially during the period after his conversion, the study of the soul is less the work of a definite period than an inseparable element of all fundamental questions. In particular, although the idea of God is the culminating point of his teaching, the knowledge of the soul is the way which leads him to the knowledge of God. Therefore his theodicy can be said to be founded on his psychology.[79] On a great number of points, even if Augustine did not originate the proofs and even if occasionally these arguments, borrowed from Plato, are more ingenious or rhetorical than solidly probative, he has at least formulated with an astounding preciseness the great spiritualist theses which in spite of some opposition were soon to serve as the inspiration for all Christian philosophy. Some of the theories of Augustinian psychology were already considered in connection with Neoplatonism and his theory of cognition; others are intimately linked to his teaching on grace.[80] Here we will only point out Augustine's position on the important questions of the nature of the soul, its union with the body, and its origin.

a. NATURE OF THE SOUL

The spirituality of the soul is one of those fundamental doctrines about which Augustine never changed his opinion after reading the Platonic writers. He was not unaware that many had their doubts,[81] but he vigorously affirmed the essential distinction between the soul and the material world.[82] In particular he says: "I make no affirmations about the soul now except that it has come from God in such a way that it is not the substance of God and that it is incorporeal, that is, that it is not a body but a spirit."[83] He did not even wish the word *body* to be used in the sense of some writers who used that term for all substantial realities; he saw in that a regrettable equivocation[84] and useless quibbling over words.[85] When Faustus of Riez and others in Marseilles said that the soul is corporeal, were they not victims of this confusion of terms?

In his demonstration of the spirituality of the soul Augustine borrows some rather inconsequential proofs from Plato; the best of all, in *On the Quantity of the Soul*, rests on intellectual knowledge of the immaterial.[86] The soul therefore is *a fortiori* simple and not made up of matter and form. Augustine likewise rejects the strange opinion proposed by Evodius[87] according to which the soul at the hour of death keeps with it an ethereal body which never leaves it, "lest it become identified with the soul of all."[88]

b. UNION OF BODY AND SOUL: THE NATURE OF MAN

Victorious over materialism, Augustine also avoided a frequent excess which changes spiritualism into an extravagant idealism. Man appears to him just as he is: neither angel nor beast, but a composite nature in which matter and spirit unite without mingling. He rejects first of all the Platonic and Origenist dichotomy which sees the soul as the whole of man with the body serving as an envelope or prison, or at least as an instrument. "Whoever wishes to separate the body from human nature is a fool," he strongly affirms in 420.[89] He recognized in the soul a natural inclination to live in a body.[90] Augustine's successive definitions of man show the evident progress that this view was making in his mind. In 388 he writes: "The soul seems to me to be a substance having rationality, which is fitted to the body to rule it."[91] The same year he also writes: "Man ... is a rational soul using a mortal and earthly body."[92] These expressions will show the effects of Platonic influence. In *On the Trinity* (400–416), however, he substitutes a more exact formula for them: "Man is a rational substance made up of soul and body,"[93] or even the traditional definition: "Man is, as the ancients said, a rational, mortal animal."[94] Thus the body is no longer a stranger to man; it is the man himself. And that is not all. Augustine goes further to restore its good standing by vindicating the worth of the body against the Manichean madness and the exaggerated contempt of the Neoplatonists. He holds that the body is good in itself and he takes pleasure in describing its beauty.[95]

The soul which is united to the body is the spiritual soul, the only one which Augustine acknowledges. He not only rejects two souls in the Manichean sense—the good spirit emanating from God and the evil and animal soul coming from the spirit of darkness—[96] but he also condemns the theory of the three components and recognizes only two elements in man, body and soul. The Bible, it is true, sometimes makes a distinction between soul and spirit, and Augustine himself says: "The complete nature of man is clearly made up of spirit, soul, and body."[97] But it is one single reality which thinks (the spirit) and which animates the body and is the principle of all physiological phenomena.[98]

This union is, moreover, so intimate and profound that the spiritual soul confers not only sensitive and vegetative life on the body, but also its very corporeal subsistence and being: "The body therefore subsists through the soul and exists by the very fact that it is animated. . . . The soul gives form to the body so that the latter is body insofar as it exists."[99]

Despite the union of body and soul there is no commingling. The soul keeps its superiority and constitutes the inner man as the body makes up the outer man.[100] The soul also keeps its proper entity; it never becomes the body, nor does the body ever become spirit. The Bishop of Hippo clearly protests against a theory which has appeared in the schools at different times, once quite recently. According to its defenders, the unity of the human composite demands some sort of fusion of the spiritual substance of the soul with the material substance of the body to form a new being which would result from the two combining elements. St. Augustine has no such understanding. He says: "The body and soul are one man, although the body and soul are not one. . . ."[101] The expression might seem a little exaggerated, but it achieves its purpose of excluding any commingling which would annihilate the perfect spirituality of the soul. This union of two beings so opposed, spirit and matter, each remaining distinct from the other although living the same life, always seemed, as we can well understand, an impenetrable mystery to the sage Doctor of Hippo.

The seat of the soul, according to him, is not any special part of the body such as the head or the heart, but the entire body. That is simply a consequence of its indivisible simplicity: "The whole soul is present in all parts at the same time, and the whole soul feels at the same time in each part."[102]

C. THE ORIGIN OF THE SOUL

The torments which this problem raised in the mind of Augustine are well known, for he returned to it repeatedly.[103] To get a

better grasp on his true viewpoint in this matter two quite different questions must be considered. The first is the origin of the
first two human souls, those of Adam and Eve, which could not
be begotten by generation. The other is the origin of the souls of
their descendants. Then his certain and final conclusions must be
separated from the problems which are not solved.

(1) *Definitive conclusions.* The soul cannot emanate from the
divine substance (a Gnostic, Manichean idea), for that would be
blasphemy against the immutability, simplicity, and holiness of
God since all the deterioration of human souls along with the
changes they undergo would be imputed to Him.[104] No soul, not
even those of Adam and Eve, could spring from the natural evolution of the universe or from the bodily seed or soul of any animal
even with divine intervention, for its spirituality would thus be
destroyed.[105] He says in one place: "Nor is the soul created in such
a way that a corporeal being or irrational animal was converted
into its nature."[106] *Letter 190* rightly treats the materialistic traducianism of Tertullian harshly: "What more perverse teaching
could be mentioned than this doctrine?"[107] The traducianism
which Augustine would favor was to be, then, entirely spiritual.
The soul, according to him, springs from the soul of its parents;
the danger lies not in threatening the immateriality of the soul but
in taking away the human personality.

Augustine treated as legendary and contrary to reason and the
testimony of consciousness any previous life in which the souls,
pure spirits, would have merited by their vice to be exiled in mortal
bodies (Platonist and Origenist fantasies).[108] All the more did he
stand in opposition to metempsychosis with its successive migrations of the same soul into different human bodies or even animals.
This becomes an even more absurd hypothesis in the Manichean
doctrine, for they teach that the soul is a portion of the divinity.[109]

Neither the soul of Adam nor those of his descendants could
have come from an immaterial substance created on the first day.
Augustine, convinced that God created everything then by at least
sowing in the universe the seeds of future beings, is led to ask himself whether the soul of Adam was also produced "causally" with

the matter of the universe. The whole of Book VII of the *Literal Commentary on Genesis* is devoted to rejecting the three possible hypotheses. One is that a seedlike principle (*ratio seminalis*) would unfold into a soul at the desired time as we are told about the body of Adam.[110] The difficulty with this theory is understanding just what this seed of a soul would be. A second hypothesis is that God would have created in the beginning an immaterial substance from which He would form in the course of time all human souls. But would this substance be active, intelligent, happy, or not?[111] Finally, God could have placed the seedlike principles of souls in the angels, who would furnish God the substance of our souls as the parents do that of our bodies. But that would seem to make our souls the sons of the angels.[112] Despite his doubts, Augustine concludes that the soul of Adam was created directly, either on the first day of the world or at the moment when it was united to the body of the first man.

As for the soul of Jesus Christ, Augustine did not solve the question. Even if generationism were admitted for the other children of Adam, this soul could have been created directly by God if its dignity demanded it or it could have descended from the soul of Adam, provided that all contagion of sin were excluded: "He cleansed His soul by assuming it to Himself so that when He came into this world He was born of the Virgin without any trace of either actual or transmitted sin."[113]

(2) *Origin of the souls of Adam's children: no solution.* Four theories on the origin of the souls of Adam's descendants seem plausible to the Doctor of Hippo; each has its difficulties. If souls come from the propagation of the parents' soul, how can personality be safeguarded? If they are created, where is the source of original sin? However, on the supposition that they are created, Augustine distinguishes three systems. Souls could be created at the moment they are united to the body, but that would do away with the rest of God on the seventh day. Or they could have been created at the beginning of the world and either successively united by God to the body for which they were destined or they could have united themselves to this body. But in these last two

instances it is hard to conceive what type of existence and activity they would have had during the long centuries of waiting.[114]

Holy Scripture, according to St. Augustine, has no decisive texts favorable to either side of the question. He examined in detail a great number of passages.[115] His indecision, as a matter of fact, was to last to the end of his life and it is incorrect to say that he condemned generationism absolutely in a letter of 418.[116] His words there are explicit, and he does not wish to give a definitive statement.[117] His later works also show his continuing doubts: "I do not dare to teach what I do not know."[118] "I have not dared to make any definite statement because I confess that I do not know."[119] In 426 he wrote in the *Retractations*: "I did not know then, and I still do not know."[120] Finally, he repeats the same confession of uncertainty in his last work: "I confess that I do not know."[121] But we may say, as Bellarmine points out, that toward the end only the difficulty of the transmission of original sin kept him from adhering to the doctrine of the creation of souls.[122]

CHAPTER X

Christology

1. IMPORTANCE OF AUGUSTINIAN CHRISTOLOGY

PART from *Letter 137* to Volusianus, Augustine did not write a special treatise on the Incarnation. In all his great works, however, in the *City of God* and *On the Trinity*, in his commentaries on St. John and the Psalms, in the *Enchiridion*, the *Christian Struggle*, the *Sermons*, and especially in the explanations of the Creed, Jesus Christ appeared at the center of his theology, of religion, and of the history of mankind. Certainly there is some exaggeration in Harnack's remark that "this contemplation of Christ was a new element and Augustine was the first after Paul and Ignatius to reintroduce it."[1] Basically, however, this observation accurately delineates one facet of the thought of the Doctor of Hippo: from the time of his conversion, Jesus Christ was the guiding light of his soul.[2] He presents Christ constantly as the truth, the life, the only way to God.[3] He calls Him the universal way for souls to be saved.[4] Even more, Augustine also considers Christ, who is the way, as the goal, the heavenly home: "The God Christ is the home where we are going; the man Christ is the way by which we are going."[5] Augustine thinks of Him whenever he speaks of revelation and authority; he often finds that developments which seem to be purely philosophical are influenced by and penetrated with the spirit of Jesus Christ. No one has more consistently emphasized the following statement which he made to Laurentius: "The certain and proper foundation of the Catholic faith is Christ."[6] In that sense also Loofs can say that he has caused Western theology and piety to give to the person of Jesus Christ the place which is proper to Him.[7] The dominant thought of the *City of God*[8] consists in showing Christ at the center of the world and the religion of Christ not merely beginning with the Gospel, but towering over all ages, past and future: "The very reality which is now called the Christian religion existed in the time of the ancients and was never absent since the beginning of the human race."[9]

The Christological teaching of St. Augustine changed less with the advance of time than his teaching on grace. In spite of several doubts at the beginning, "the basic Christology of Augustine in 391 is the seed of his later teaching on Christ."[10] The influence of his teaching on his successors will be sufficiently indicated by the fact that the famous letter of Pope St. Leo the Great to Flavian (June 13, 449) drew not only on the thought but even on the expressions of *On the Trinity*.[11]

2. The Person of Christ

On no other point of revelation is the teaching of Augustine clearer, more constant, or more logically connected. On no other point, similarly, have the Protestant critics made such sorry efforts to draw him away from orthodoxy and relegate him to either Docetism or Nestorianism. The gropings, the admissions, and the unexpected conclusions of Harnack must be read.[12] Under the pretext that, according to Augustine, the entire Trinity has wrought the Incarnation, Harnack concludes that this Father of the Church could not admit that the Word has a more intimate union with the humanity of Christ than the other persons. Moreover, Harnack concludes that, because Augustine had so steadfastly affirmed the existence of a soul in Christ against the teaching of Apollinaris, he constructed the Man-God from this soul, considered as a human person: the human person received the Word into itself and the soul, the place where it was received, is the center of the Man-God.

Thus the Word does not become flesh but is united by grace with the soul of Jesus. The same critic states even more clearly that: "According to the Bishop of Hippo the inhabitation of the divinity in Jesus Christ can be conceived on the analogy of its presence in the just man as in a temple, even though he firmly maintained that the Word was made flesh."[13] That is also the opinion of Dorner, according to Scheel, who personally, along with Feuerlein, openly adhered to the Catholic interpretation of Augustine given by Schwane.[14] It will be sufficient to make a survey of the principal arguments of the great doctor to see the evident falsity of every other explanation.

a. THE WHOLE DOGMA

The complete dogma about Christ has been explained with a clarity which permits no doubt: "The entire Christ is true man and true God, God and man. This is the Catholic faith. Whoever denies that Christ is God is a Photinian. Whoever denies that Christ is man is a Manichean. Whoever confesses that Christ is God equal to the Father and true man . . . is a Catholic."[15] "Christ is one person, God and man."[16]

b. THE SON OF MAN

When explaining this title of Jesus Christ, Augustine affirms the reality of the human nature of Christ.[17] In *On the Christian Struggle* he one by one refutes the Docetists who denied a real body to Christ,[18] the strict Apollinarianists who denied Him a soul,[19] and the mitigated Apollinarianists who admitted that Christ had a soul which was the principle of life, but a soul which lacked understanding: "They deny that He had the best part of man."[20]

The Word, along with human nature, assumed those infirmities of the flesh which do not imply sin: He was passible and mortal as we are.[21] On the other hand, the personal union with the Word, an ineffable grace and a figure of the grace of adoption which Christ was to merit for us, caused remarkable privileges to pour forth upon Christ's humanity. These included the exclusion of all taint of original sin, since Christ, as Augustine tells us, was conceived without concupiscence,[22] and absolute holiness which kept Him from all personal fault, no matter how slight:[23] "Nor was it to be feared that . . . He would sin through the free choice of His will since . . . the nature of man thus assumed by God would admit within itself no movement of an evil will."[24] How could Dorner, who quotes this text, ever conclude that the holy doctor denies the freedom of will in Christ?[25] On the contrary he affirms it here and elsewhere. For example: "Was not His will free on that account? And was it not so much the more free in proportion to the greater impossibility of His becoming the slave of sin?"[26] In particular Augustine vindicates the complete liberty of His sacrifice on the cross: "He did not leave the life of the flesh unwillingly, but because He willed it, when He willed it, and in the way He willed it."[27]

Two other privileges of the humanity of Christ are mentioned. His intellectual life was free from all our lack of knowledge and even while an infant He was preserved from the lack of consciousness natural to that age.[28] In His sensitive life, His human affections developed in admirable subjection to the dominion of His will so that He seemed in times of stress "to be troubled not through weakness of soul, but in the fullness of His power."[29]

C. THE SON OF GOD

It is impossible to doubt Augustine's mind on the divinity of Jesus Christ understood in the strictest possible sense, for there is no trace of the obscurity found in certain passages about the Trinity. The assertions of Harnack, in fact, are expressly refuted: Augustine is not a Photinian since he himself relates and refutes those ancient errors.[30] It is Christ considered in His divine personality, Augustine states, who is absolutely equal with His Father: "The Arian who does not believe that He is equal does not believe that He is the Son. If he does not believe that He is the Son, he does not believe that He is Christ."[31] Against Eunomians he says: "Whoever denies that He is like the Father denies that He is Christ."[32] Also: "They brand us with an opprobrious new name, saying that we are Homoousians."[33]

He frequently enough refuted in no uncertain terms the Nestorian interpretation put on his teaching by Harnack, who said that Augustine taught merely a moral union of the Word with Christ, an inhabitation through grace. Augustine protests twice against this error in *On the Christian Struggle* (396): "Do not listen to those who wish to see Christ only as a man and a holy person. They say that He is a man, but so holy that He is worthy to be called the Son of God."[34] Other holy persons receive the gift of wisdom; Christ received the very person of the Word: "He does not have just the gift of wisdom, but bears its very person."[35] In 426, just four or five years before the Council of Ephesus, the Gallic monk Leporius, under the guidance of Augustine, retracted such a Nestorian conception in his *Libellus emendationis*.[36]

Adoptionism, a logical consequence of Nestorianism, was likewise precluded in advance by St. Augustine. The Fathers at the Synod of Frankfurt (794) were right in invoking his authority as in the following passage: "It was becoming, then, that He baptize who is the only Son of God, not His adopted Son. For adopted sons are the servants of the only Son."[37] The same thing is found in the *Libellus* of Leporius: "Let us believe that the only Son of God, not the adoptive but the true Son, . . . has suffered according to the flesh."[38]

d. UNION OF THE WORD AND THE HUMANITY

The union of the Word and the humanity is explained on every point in perfect accord with St. Cyril of Alexandria so that no divergence can be pointed out. It is a union of two natures in one single person. Augustine sometimes uses the formula traditional in the West since the time of Tertullian: "In Christ there are two substances but one person."[39] "Let us acknowledge the twofold substance of Christ. . . . And yet both are not two, for Christ is one."[40] More frequently, however, he substitutes the more precise word *nature* for the word *substance*. If the assertion of Dorner that Augustine was the first who introduced the formula of "two natures in one person" to the West is exaggerated,[41] it is at least certain that he resolutely affirmed at all times not merely the moral unity of the two persons in Jesus Christ but the absolute unicity of one person in two natures: "The mediator appeared, uniting both natures in the unity of one person."[42]

This single person is that of the Word which, subsisting from all eternity in its divine nature, has willed to subsist in time in the human nature of Christ, appropriating it by a communication of its personality: "Christ, the invisible form of God remaining, assumed the visible form of man into the unity of His person."[43] Whatever Dorner and Scheel might say,[44] it is clear that *Christ* here (as quite commonly in Augustine) is the equivalent of *Word* or *Son*; it is the Word who has united the humanity of Christ to His person: "God assumed our nature, that is, the rational soul and body of the man Christ, . . . so that the humanity and the Word . . . are one person."[45] A familiar Augustinian formula sometimes depicts the human nature as having the person of the Word: "It has the person of Wisdom (the Word)"; more often, however, he represents the person of the Word as having the human nature: "We say that the Son of God suffered in the humanity with which He was united."[46]

The humanity of Christ, then, was not already a person when the Word was united to it, and to establish this point (and at the same time the gratuity of this union) Augustine insists on the fact that this humanity never existed apart from the Word: "From the moment that the humanity began to exist it was also God."[47] In Christ "the humanity never existed as man in such a way that it was not also the only-begotten Son of God."[48] "It was not assumed as if first created and then assumed, but was created by the very assumption."[49]

e. DISTINCTION OF NATURES

The distinction of the two natures remains intact after the union. The Protestants recognize that Augustine was not less insistent on this point than St. Athanasius or St. Ambrose.

In general the formulas of Augustine exclude all penetration of one nature into the other: "By that assumption one nature is not turned and changed into the other; the Divinity is not changed into the creature so as to cease to be Divinity nor is the creature changed into the Divinity so as to cease to be creature."[50] *Letter 219* informs us that Leporius had denied the Incarnation to safeguard the divine immutability.[51] Therefore his *Libellus emendationis* emphasizes this point: "Let no one believe that we think that the two natures are reduced to one substance in the way that metals are mixed in an alloy. For such mixing involves the corruption of each component."[52] Scheel has made a summary of a whole group of texts which exclude all change, conversion, and confusion of the divine and the human.[53] The conclusion must then be drawn that the word *mixture*, condemned by the *Libellus* though frequently enough used by Augustine,[54] indicates an intimate penetration not of the natures but of the divine person in the appropriation of the human nature.

. The divinity of the Word, therefore, does not undergo any change or diminution: "God assumed a mutable creature with His immutable majesty."[55] "Human nature came to the Word, but the Word did not come, with susceptibility of change, into the human nature."[56] In vain did Reuter seek to find in the works of the holy doctor traces of the Protestant theory of krypsis, a partial renunciation by the Word of the use of its divine attributes.[57] Other Protestants like Feuerlein and Scheel[58] answered that there could be no question regarding Christ of any kenosis or krypsis, so clearly has Augustine explained St. Paul's *exinanivit*: "How did He empty Himself? By assuming what He was not, not by losing what He was. . . . Although He was God, He appeared as man."[59]

The human nature, however, remains a created nature, limited in space, time, and activity. Thus does Augustine constantly explain the text, "The Father is greater than I," as applying to the humanity of Christ.[60] It is strange that Lutherans still cite Augustine in favor of their inconsistent Eutychianism which attributes a ubiquity and pre-existence to the humanity of Christ before its conception. Scheel maintains that *Against an Arian Sermon* attributed omnipotence to the humanity.[61] As a matter of fact, it treats solely of the power of judgment on the last day,[62] and even there excludes any pre-existence of Christ as man "because He began to exist in time."

f. PERPETUITY OF THE HYPOSTATIC UNION

There is some question whether Augustine denied the perpetuity of the hypostatic union. According to Dorner[63] and Scheel,[64] Augustine thought that the Incarnation, since it had a temporal purpose, would come to an end with the Last Judgment. They base their assertion on the passage of *On the Trinity* which reads: "And then He will no longer intercede for us, once He has handed His kingdom over to God and the Father."[65] They presume that the end of His intercession will also mark the end of His reign in heaven! It is precisely in this very passage that Augustine refutes the strange opinion of certain people that the humanity would then be absorbed in the Divinity.[66] He adds: "Let us not think that Christ will hand over His kingdom to God and the Father in such a way that He deprives Himself of it."[67]

g. COMMUNICATION OF IDIOMS

The laws of the theological terminology founded on the unity of person (the communication of idioms) were not only observed, but quite accurately formulated by Augustine: "The blessed Apostle shows that this unity of the person of Christ is so made up of each nature, the divine, that is, and the human, that each of them lends its terminology to the other—the divine to the human and the human to the divine."[68] In virtue of this unity one can say that the Son of Man descended from heaven and the Son of God was crucified. According to Harnack, the expressions "the body of God" or "God born from a woman" are quite infrequent in Augustine.[69] In answer to this, their number makes little difference. Moreover, equivalent expressions abound in his writings, such as "the body of the Word."[70] Augustine does not hesitate to repeat over and over that "God has died."[71] Again he says: "Life and the Immortal One died on the cross."[72]

h. OTHER EXPRESSIONS

The occasional inaccurate formulas of Augustine do not create any difficulty if they are examined with their attendant circumstances. Many of them were later amended or retracted, such as the change of the expression "lordly man" to "since He is certainly the Lord" to avoid confusing Christ with any person having authority.[73] Some are explained more clearly. Thus, for example, Augustine seems to say quite often that the Word unites itself to a man (therefore to a person). "Man was assumed" occurs frequently in *Sermon 214*.[74] However, in this context (Scheel notes it also[75]) the concrete word *man* is used by Augustine for the concrete and singular *humanity* to which the Word united itself. Augustine himself says: "Since the entire and only Son of God, our Lord Jesus Christ, is Word and man, or, to put it more exactly, is Word, soul, and flesh. . . ."[76] Elsewhere, if attentive consideration is given to his explanations, one soon sees that even his inaccuracies of expression are inspired by a profound understanding of the dogma envisaged under some special aspect or other. Thus he compares the humanity of Christ to an article of clothing: "He was clothed with the humanity,"[77] a formula which Abelard was to misuse in a Nestorian sense.[78] Augustine, however, tells us that the expression "He was clothed" must be understood as a substantial and intimate union, not an accidental and external one. It only means that the humanity has not changed the Word in the slightest degree, no more than the garment changes the one who wears it: "Although that assumption joined the thing assumed to Him who assumed it in an ineffable way, we must not think that God was changed, since our human words can only feebly express such lofty concepts."[79] In like manner the comparison of the hypostatic union with the union of body and soul, which is often used,[80] has for its object the affirmation of the real and not merely moral union between the Word and the humanity: "The same person is God and man . . . not through a confusion of nature but in unity of person."[81] Whereas the soul and the body are but parts of the man they constitute, the Word is wholly God and is also wholly man: "Man draws near to God and becomes one person—so that there is not a half-god as if this person were God because partly God and man because partly man—but entirely God and entirely man."[82]

3. THE WORK OF CHRIST THE SAVIOR

a. THE PROBLEM

In the interpretation of Augustine's theory on the Redemption it is easy to establish how closely the teaching on salvation is linked to that on the Savior: His soteriology depends on his soterology. Abelard, since he thought that Augustine portrayed Christ purely as a man morally united by grace to the Divinity, believed that the Redemption consisted solely in the influence of His lessons and examples. All Catholic theologians, on the contrary, having recognized the true Man-God in the writings of the holy doctor, find there also the Catholic dogma of salvation, that is, the expiation of our sins on the cross by an innocent victim substituted for the guilty human race. Until recently Calvinists and Lutherans, who believed in the divinity of Christ, admitted the same interpretation. But the recent breaches opened in the doctrine of the divinity of Christ have caused these new Nestorians to return to Abelard's theory of moral redemption. Many critics have dared to attribute their rationalistic concept to Augustine. The word *expiation* is no longer used and *substitution* makes way for the "solidarity of the human family." Christ, they say, has certainly died for us ($\dot{v}\pi\grave{\epsilon}\rho$ $\dot{\eta}\mu\hat{\omega}\nu$) because His examples of virtue are salutary for us, but He has not suffered in our place ($\dot{a}\nu\tau\grave{\iota}$ $\dot{\eta}\mu\hat{\omega}\nu$). Some, if they admit that Augustine talked of the Redemption, make fun of it and maintain that he understood a ransom paid not to God but to the devil to deliver us from his enslavement.

Harnack avoids this excess. He recognized that in Augustine "Jesus is represented to us as the mediator, the victim, and the priest through whom we are ransomed and reconciled with the

Divinity, so much so that His death, as the Church preaches, is the sure foundation of our redemption."[83] But he attempts to deprive this admission of all value by ascribing these three thoughts to Augustine: (1) Reconciliation with God is much less important than redemption from the devil. (2) The lesson of humility given by Christ surpasses by far this redemption and constitutes the true work of Christ. (3) Besides, only negative results (such as the pardon of sins) are attributed to this redemption, not a positive justification.[84]

Dr. Gottschick has combated these false interpretations.[85] Like Seeberg,[86] he recognized a true expiatory redemption in the writings of St. Augustine, adding that this concept does not seem to him to be as Christian as Seeberg thought.

b. SOLUTION OF THE PROBLEM

There is no obscurity in Augustine's soteriological teaching. Our examination of its characteristics will be limited to four points: (1) the mediator; (2) the sacrifice, the principal act of His mediation; (3) the deliverance from the devil which is consequent upon it; and (4) the moral influence of Christ.

(1) *Mediator.* In what sense does St. Augustine attribute the role of mediator to the humanity of Christ? This assertion, inspired by the First Epistle to Timothy (2:5)—a favorite text of the great doctor—causes surprise at first. In the *Confessions* he says: "He is mediator inasmuch as He is man; inasmuch as He is the Word He is not an intermediary because He is equal to God, . . ."[87] and consequently equally far removed from us: "He is not mediator because He is equal to the Father, for by this He is as far removed from us as the Father is. How can there be any mediation where there is the same degree of remoteness?"[88] Again: "Christ is the mediator between man and God not as God but as man. . . ."[89] Because of this insistence Scheel blames Augustine for sacrificing the role of the Word: must not the mediator be the Man-God so as to be between the two extremes?[90] Undoubtedly that is true, and that was Augustine's understanding. Two observations will clarify his thought.

In the first place, Augustine wishes to exclude the role of mediator from the divine nature, not from the person of the Word. Since the word *Christ* designates the person of the Word subsisting in two natures absolutely independent of one another, he asks himself which one of the two, the human or the divine, can and must perform the acts of satisfaction and expiation. Now it is clear that these acts do not fall under the purview of the divine nature. The human nature, however, does not act except as informed by the person of the Word. It is therefore the Man-God who appeases the Father and saves us. That is the exact thought of the holy doctor: "We would not have been delivered through that one mediator . . . unless He were also God."[91] This role of the Word and the humanity in the Redemption is admirably explained in *Sermon 127*: "From what He has of Himself He is the Son of God; from what He has of us He is the Son of Man. He has received the lesser part from us; He has given us the greater part. For He also died because He is the Son of Man, not because He is the Son of God. Nevertheless the Son of God died, although He died according to the flesh and not according to the Word. . . . Therefore because He died, He died of what He had of us; because we live, we live from what we have of Him."[92]

Another observation is that Augustine conceived the work of the mediator under a double aspect. His double role is to appease God in the name of humanity, and, in his divine capacity, to convert the heart of man. Now there is a profound distinction underlying these two missions of Christ. The first, the appeasing of God, is the work of the MAN-God, of the Just One par excellence. (The expression *Homo-Deus* seems to be peculiar to Augustine.[93]) The conversion of man is the work of the GOD-man. It is the love of God (before the Incarnation), coming down to us until it clothes itself with our nature, which will win us over by the sight of this self-abasement—not of the humanity, for that is ineffably exalted, but of the Word in the humanity. These two viewpoints are essential for an understanding of Augustine's teaching. In *On the Trinity* he says: "The one cleansing bath for the wicked and the proud is the blood of the Just One and the humility of God."[94]

The blood of the Just One is for expiation; the humility (the abasement of God in the humanity) is to convert our pride.

(2) *Sacrifice*. The question here is whether the Redemption was, in Augustine's eyes, an expiatory sacrifice offered by Christ to His Father by means of a substitution. The answer is so clearly, so constantly formulated in all the works of the holy doctor that some people will be surprised at a question brought up by recent critics. For Augustine as for the whole Christian Church until these latter days, the first act—and the principal act—of the mediation of Christ is the expiation of our sins and our reconciliation with God through the sacrifice of Calvary, following Ephesians (5:2): "He delivered Himself for us as an offering and sacrifice to God." [95]

(a) *Three principles*. There are three principles at the basis of this fundamental dogma. The first is the concept of sin not only as a moral imperfection of the sinner but especially as an injury of the divine right, an offense against God and an outrage to His majesty. The second principle is the theory of the satisfaction due to God, a theory developed chiefly in the teaching on penance of which it is the foundation. Lastly, there is the principle of substitution (vicarious satisfaction) in virtue of which Christ offers Himself and is accepted by His Father as a victim of the sins of the entire human race for whom He thus obtains pardon. Augustine affirms all this simultaneously without distinct analysis, but with a preciseness which leaves no room for doubt: "Christ, though guiltless, assumed our punishment that He might thus cancel our guilt and do away with our punishment." [96] He addresses the terrible reproaches of the Apostle to those who see only a moral influence in the cross: "The carnal man . . . does not perceive . . . what grace the cross of Christ bestows upon those who believe; he thinks that on the cross He acted in this way only that He might leave us . . . an example to be imitated." [97]

(b) *Scriptural sources*. Augustine finds the scriptural sources of this dogma in various texts. The first is the words of Jesus at the Last Supper: "And therefore He said, 'This is My blood which shall be shed for many unto the remission of sins.'" [98] Another source is the epistles of St. Paul, the preacher of the cross. Thus, explaining the Second Epistle to the Corinthians (5:20), he says: "He made Him who had not known sin, that is, Christ, sin for our sake, a sacrifice for sins through which we can be reconciled."[99] For Augustine the dogma was really an echo of the ancient prophecies. *On the Agreement of the Evangelists* (chap. 31) shows how Isaias (chaps. 52–54) applies to Christ, especially the words: "He was wounded for our sins . . . by His bruises we are healed."[100] Augustine adds: "He assumed our crimes, but not as one who had committed them."[101] Lastly, Augustine sees the dogma as the fulfillment of the noble figure of the paschal lamb, following St. Paul in the First Epistle to the Corinthians (1:7).[102]

When we have such precise affirmations which become more accurate as they multiply, it is inconceivable that certain critics were able to attribute the origin of this redemptive idea to St. Anselm. Since the time of Cremer's articles and the agreement of Ritschl and his followers with his contention, it has been the fashion to maintain that the Anselmian theory of satisfaction was inspired by the principles of German law.[103] The best Protestant critics, the ones furthest removed from dogmatic presuppositions,[104] have shown all the incongruous elements in an assertion which adduces the German custom of wergild as the origin for a belief long before studied by St. Augustine and even formulated earlier by such Fathers as Tertullian and Cyprian. Even more, Harnack does not hesitate to affirm that, even before St. Paul, the very earliest form of Christianity was based on the expiatory sacrifice of the dying Christ.[105]

(c) *Redemptive act.* The redemptive act of Christ is the death on the cross. For Augustine, this death is: (1) A true sacrifice: "By his death, namely by the one true sacrifice offered for us, He cleansed, abolished, and wiped out . . . whatever fault there was."[106] (2) The unique sacrifice prefigured by all the ancient sacrifices: "In all those various kinds of sacrifices is understood that one sacrifice and that single victim on the cross, our Lord."[107] (3) A sacrifice perpetuated in the sacrifice of the altar which is offered throughout the entire world according to the prophecy of Malachias: "All false sacrifices have made way for this greatest and true sacrifice."[108] (4) A sacrifice consisting essentially in the death of Christ decreed by His Father. Nowhere in Augustine, however, can one find a trace of the exaggerations of Protestant scholasticism according to which Jesus on the cross was truly cursed by His Father and suffered the very torments of hell. Gretillat rightly says that these excesses have made the theory of expiation odious.[109]

(d) *Multiple role of Jesus.* The great doctor explains the multiple role of Jesus in this sacrifice. He appears first as priest and sacrificer. Sin is wiped out "through the one sacrifice of the true mediator-priest."[110] Second, He is at the same time the victim and priest because it is He Himself who offers His life and delivers His body to the torments: "He the offerer, He also the offering."[111] And precisely because this is a free offering of Himself, the death inflicted by the tormentors is transformed into a sacrifice: Christ was offered because He willed it. "And He proceeded to the suffering of death, a voluntary death, not because He had to but because He freely chose it."[112] Augustine also refers the reader to Ephesians (5:2). Third, Augustine shows Christ victorious and triumphant: "A victor and a victim, and therefore a victor because a victim, and therefore a priest because a sacrifice, changing us from servants to sons."[113] Finally, he represents Him interceding in heaven for us, as the great high priest in the Holy of Holies.[114]

(e) *Fruits of Christ's satisfaction.* The first benefit of Christ's satisfaction is undoubtedly the forgiveness of sins,[115] the pardon of all sins, even those committed after baptism.[116] "His blood . . . has blotted out all the sins of the guilty; so great a price paid has redeemed all the captives."[117] But St. Augustine is not less insistent on the positive gifts of reconciliation with God, which he expressed in many ways: It is a grace analogous to that of Jesus Christ which is assured us,[118] an incorporation into Christ, whose members all the faithful become: "Through His blood . . . they are joined to the body of Christ."[119] It is a divine adoption, hindered until then by our faults: "The Only-begotten came to loose our sins which prevented us from being adopted by God."[120] He puts the same thought more vigorously: "When about to make men Gods, God became man."[121] How could Harnack speak of a purely negative reconciliation?

(f) *Extent of Christ's Redemption*. According to Augustine, the Redemption of Christ is universal in extent and allows no exception: "The shedding of innocent blood has blotted out all the sins of the guilty; so great a price paid has redeemed all the captives."[122] Thus all sins are expiated, even those committed after baptism, which Scheel would not include in the Redemption.[123] All the captives are ransomed, even infants who die without receiving baptism. Augustine affirms this expressly.[124] Mention must be made of Augustine's argument which closes off all loopholes to the Jansenists.[125] He reasons thus: Jesus Christ has died for all without exception. Therefore all without exception are sinners: "All therefore, without exception, were dead in sin, and for all the dead there died the only person who lived."[126] That is Augustine's mature thought. When he stated that the effects of the Redemption were restricted to the elect, he has to be understood as speaking of efficacious graces which are not given to all. Augustine's sermons can leave no doubt; Scheel and Rottmanner both noted that.[127] "The blood of your Lord, if you will it, is given for you; if you do not will it, it is not given for you. . . . This is the important point, that He gave it once and for all. The blood of Christ is salvation to those who wish it, punishment to those who refuse."[128] "The true and apostolic opinion is that Christ is the Savior of all men."[129] As for the angels, Augustine would have been afraid to favor the Origenist belief in the ultimate salvation of the demons even if he had not already left them outside the plan of the Redemption. He merely mentions that the death of Christ has reunited just men and the good angels in the single city of God, in which the elect will replace the fallen angels.[130]

(3) *Deliverance from Satan*. Has St. Augustine pictured the Redemption as a ransom paid to the devil and not to God? Like other Fathers, Augustine was accused of this idea as if the devil had acquired the right to hold humanity in slavery through sin so that the blood of Christ, instead of being offered to God, would have been the price paid to the devil. This is an odious concept,

inspired by Eastern Gnosticism, which St. Gregory Nazianzen was already stigmatizing as an injustice to God.[131] Whatever the other Fathers might have thought, however, was this Augustine's true conception of the Redemption? It is correct to admit that he himself described the enslavement by the devil, to whom men were sold: "They could sell themselves, but they could not redeem themselves."[132] He affirms that the blood of Christ has been the price of our redemption. He talks of the trap set for the devil on the cross. The body of Christ was the bait with which he was taken, and so forth.[133] But a careful examination of the meaning of these images makes it painstakingly clear that this staging is only a way of dramatizing the overthrow of the devil and our deliverance. Augustine's teaching is not only foreign to the gross conception of a ransom paid to the devil, but it gives the key to expressions used by some other Fathers. Some proofs of this follow.

Augustine never expressed the thought that Christ had dealings with the devil, that He was the mediator between man and the devil, and that His blood was offered to the devil. He acknowledges only one mediation, that between men and the Father,[134] and one redemption in the proper meaning of the term, that which redeems us from the wrath of God: "All humanity can in no way be justified and redeemed from the just wrath of God, that is, from punishment, except by faith and the sacrament of the blood of Christ."[135] The expiation of sins by the sacrifice offered to the Father is the central idea of the Redemption and of Christianity for the Doctor of Hippo, as the texts quoted above show. To pretend with Harnack that this reconciliation with God is only of secondary importance is to deprive the facts of all meaning.

In addition, our deliverance from the devil is always presented as a simple consequence of the expiation and reconciliation with God, not as the result of a ransom paid to the devil. This principle is of primary importance. Far from putting some underhanded dealings with the devil in the spotlight, Augustine everywhere shows that the devil has been vanquished precisely because God received satisfaction and forgave man: "The devil is conquered . . . by the mediator between God and men, Jesus Christ, by whom we are reconciled to God once our sins are washed away. For only by sin are men separated from God."[136]

St. Augustine's theory on the overthrow of the devil positively excludes any idea of ransom. This theory is developed in Book XIII of *On the Trinity*.[137] The whole section should be read and pondered, in particular the following principles: (1) The devil had no claim on us. What some people have considered such a claim is really just a permission from God to chastise sinners. The devil was merely the executioner, not the master. (2) No ransom was therefore due, for the remission of sins by God includes our freedom: "If therefore the commission of sins subjugated man to the devil through the just wrath of God, certainly the forgiveness of sins through the gracious reconciliation of God snatched man away from the devil."[138] (3) This pardon could be gratuitous without any reparation, but it was more becoming that the divine justice should be satisfied and that the devil lose his dominion in consequence of his injustice. This is the reason for the Passion: Jesus dies for those who are guilty; the devil is the unjust slayer of this Innocent One; he is punished and loses his dominion over his victims. "What is this justice, then, by which the devil was conquered?"—Certainly this would be the time to speak of ransom, but Augustine's answer is far different.—"What is it if not the justice of Jesus Christ? And how was he conquered? Because, although he could find nothing worthy of death in Him, he nevertheless killed Him. And therefore it is right that the sinners whom he held should be sent away free."[139] This explanation recurs again and again: "He spilled the blood of the Innocent One and was ordered to depart from the guilty."[140] "You have destroyed Him whom you ought not; return that which you were holding."[141] Still more energetically he says of the devil: "He was able to spill that blood, but he was not worthy to drink of it. And because he spilled the blood of one who was not guilty, he was ordered to return the guilty. For He spilled His blood for this purpose, that He might take away our sins. . . . Those were the bonds of the captives, but He came and bound the strong one up with the chains of His Passion."[142] The devil therefore merely takes the part of one who is vanquished and chastised. It is in this sense that the cross was a trap for him: "It was a trap set for you, and you were taken by that in which you had rejoiced."[143]

But, one might object, Augustine affirms that Jesus has ransomed us from the devil. Yes, but he says also that Jesus has ransomed us from the slavery of sin,[144] from hell,[145] and from death.[146] Does anyone suppose that He paid a ransom to sin, to death, and to hell?

(4) *Moral influence of Jesus.* According to Augustine, in what does the moral influence of Christ consist? After the forgiveness of men by God the mediator must achieve a second victory, the restoration of the hearts of men to God. Without exception, no one among the Fathers has developed the moral aspect of the Incarnation with as much insistence as Augustine. Here also we find an utterly personal sign of his teaching: his thesis on the humility of God in the Incarnation is one of his most profound conceptions. Catholic theologians have left to the mystics meditation on this aspect of the work of Christ found in St. Augustine. Protestant critics, on the contrary, especially in these latter days (many probably because the theory of expiation was less pleasing to them, but many also who wish to retain it), have made the great Augustinian thesis of the "humble Christ" crystal clear.[147] It will suffice here to give an accurate statement of the thought of the Doctor of Hippo.

In the divine plan humility is the fundamental lesson of the Incarnation. Consequently, even in his most theoretical works, Augustine unites the twofold purpose of this mystery: expiation offered to the heavenly Father and humility which was restored to its former state by the unfathomable humiliations of the Word made man. This is the characteristic of the person of Jesus Christ which left the deepest impression upon his soul as it did upon the soul of St. Paul, the apostle of the "emptied-out Christ." Harnack does not tire of returning to this idea of the "humble Christ" which he sees as the pivotal point of the Christology of the Doctor of Hippo. There is no doubt that the Incarnation is the great proof for Augustine of the love of God for us.[148] It is this love which will lead our hearts to love the humility of God, which in turn, because it is made known through such self-abasements, destroys our pride. "The ideal image of humility in grandeur," says the celebrated critic, "is what conquered Augustine. Pride is sin. Humility is the source and strength of all good. From the humiliations of Christ he drew this new sentiment which he implanted in the Church, the cult of humility."[149] That is certainly the impression which the following text of *On the Trinity* gives. Humility is presented as the great salvific mystery: "It is profitable to believe and keep implanted firmly and unshakably in the heart that the humility by which God was born of a woman and led to death by mortal hands with such insults is the medicine most apt to heal the swelling of our pride and the most sublime sacrament for loosing the bonds of sin."[150]

It is precisely because of His humility that Jesus is the way. In the *Confessions* Augustine recounts how the role of Jesus as the way of souls but only through humility was revealed to him at a time when he considered Jesus only as an outstanding man: "For I was not humble enough to embrace the humble Jesus, my Lord, nor did I know what lesson His weakness would teach me. For Your Word . . . built Himself a humble home of our clay whereby He intended to detach from themselves those who would be subjected and bring them over to Himself, healing their pride and fostering their love."[151] A little later, speaking of his former pride, he exclaims: "Where was that charity building on the foundation of the humility which is Christ Jesus?"[152] This is the ordinary theme of his Christmas sermons: "Recognize the teaching of such humility. . . . Your human pride oppresses you so much that only the divine humility can raise you up."

He attributes this humility to the Word, the divine person, and not to the humanity. God surely cannot humble Himself in His divine nature, but one cannot miss the great lesson of God consenting to be united to a created nature. God alone could have mastered this virtue. "The way to this humility springs from a different source; it comes from Christ. The way is from Him who, although He was mighty, became humble. . . . What else did He teach if not this humility? Not without reason does He say: 'I am the Way. . . .' Through such humility, therefore, we approach God."[153] Thus Augustine exalts the lesson of humility less in the life and passion of the Savior than in the fundamental fact of the Incarnation, decreed and brought to fulfillment by the Word. What a profound statement is that in which he shows Christ as conqueror because in Him God is humbly united to a human nature: "He who conquered was both man and God. He conquered thus, born of a Virgin, because He did not rule that humanity as He rules other holy men, but was humbly united to it."[154]

C. CONCLUSION

An exact résumé of the Augustinian theory on the Redemption is provided in the *Enchiridion*. Harnack comments on it as the summation of his system.[155] Let the reader judge for himself: "Since sin had created a great chasm between the human race and God, it was necessary that a mediator who alone was born, lived, and was put to death without sin should reconcile us to God even to obtaining the resurrection of the flesh into everlasting life . . ." (This is the primary purpose of the Incarnation: reparation and reconciliation with God.) ". . . in order that human pride might be rebuked and healed through the humility of God; that man might be shown how far he had departed from God; . . ." (This is the secondary end of the Incarnation: the moral influence of the humble Christ—an important task, but ranking below that of reconciliation. Once this is affirmed, there is no danger of rationalism or Abelardianism as Harnack thinks.) ". . . that the fountain of grace might be opened by the only-begotten Son of God assuming the form of a servant, a form which had no prior merits . . ." (This is the result of the redemptive work, which is not just pardon and deliverance, but sanctification through a grace like to that of the Incarnation.) ". . . that the promised resurrection of the body might also be foreshadowed in the Redeemer Himself . . ." (This is the role of the Resurrection, a guarantee of the future triumph of which we are assured by the reconciliation of Christ.) ". . . and that the devil might be conquered by the same nature which he took delight in having deceived."[156] (Thus deliverance from the devil is represented as a victory over him, achieved by human nature in consequence of its reconciliation with God. There is not a word about a ransom paid to the devil.)

4. THE MOTHER OF CHRIST IN AUGUSTINE'S WORKS

The theology of the Mother of God was in its full course of development in the fourth century as a consequence of the development of Christology. By the same principle which elevated the humanity of Christ to the level of the divinity, the mother of whom God had willed to be born became in all truth Θεοτόκος (an expression already used by Athanasius and Gregory Nazianzen); this title in its turn contained ineffable privileges. Augustine, at the admission of Protestant critics,[157] far from trying to halt this movement, contributed powerfully to its acceleration. We select some of the principal characteristics.

a. ROLE OF MARY IN THE DIVINE PLAN

The incomparable role of the Mother of God in the divine plan is set forth clearly by the great doctor. He is not content with merely affirming, even before the Council of Ephesus, her divine maternity: "God was born of a woman."[158] He proceeds to look for the reasons underlying it and states that God willed the birth of the Savior from Mary precisely in order that she might cooperate in the deliverance of humanity. Adam and Eve corrupted human nature; Jesus and Mary are to save it. Thus the cooperation of Mary in the Redemption is not only a consequence of her maternity; it is the primary intention of God. It is not just a question of honoring the two sexes; there is a more profound mystery here: "Here we draw near to a great sacrament, that life should be born to us of a woman because death came to us through a woman."[159] Likewise, he adds, the devil deserved to be conquered by both sexes.

b. PERPETUAL VIRGINITY

The perpetual virginity of Mary even in childbirth is resolutely defended against Jovinianus.[160] In his Christmas sermons he celebrates this marvel: "A virgin conceiving, a virgin bringing forth a child, . . . a perpetual virgin. Why do you marvel at these things, O man?[161] He loved to attribute the accomplishment of these marvels to Mary's faith: "She brought forth because she believed."[162]

c. IMMUNITY FROM ALL SIN

Her preservation from all sin (at least personal sin) is affirmed as an admirable privilege due to the incomparable dignity of Mary: "We must except, therefore, the holy Virgin Mary, whose name, out of honor to the Lord, I do not even wish to mention when treating of sin. For from Him we know that an abundance of grace for overcoming sin in every way was conferred on her who merited to conceive and bear Him who was without sin."[163] It should be noted that Augustine in this passage had just finished ranking among sinners the most famous just men of the Old Testament: Abel, Enoch, Abraham, Elias, . . . even St. Joseph. Harnack well understood the importance of such a great privilege, especially when it rested on such motives. "Augustine," he says, "has so vigorously proclaimed the culpability of every man including the saints that this exception in favor of Mary has gone far in granting her a place apart between Christ and Christians. Augustine uses the same expressions that he uses for Jesus to express the capacity of grace in Mary."[164] This principle must not be forgotten in the following question.

d. IMMACULATE CONCEPTION

Was the Immaculate Conception affirmed by St. Augustine? From the *Incomplete Work against Julian* it is certain that Julian thought that he could confound Augustine by opposing to him the objection that his theory of original sin condemned the Virgin Mother to be a slave of Satan. Here is the entire response of the holy doctor: "We do not subject Mary to the devil because of the condition of her birth, but the reason that we do not is that the condition [of birth] itself is canceled by the grace of rebirth."[165] A number of Catholics[166] and certain Protestants[167] see this as an affirmation of the great privilege. Others[168] do not think that the text is conclusive. Harnack says that it is not sufficient to make a certain judgment.[169] To come to some conclusion, let us compare the only two possible interpretations of this text. The first is: "No, we do not subject Mary to the devil by the law of birth, and that is so because the grace of rebirth preserved her from this unhappy law." If this meaning is admitted, Mary has never been a slave of the devil and the objection of Julian falls of its own weight. This meaning is also in perfect accord with the universal protestation of Augustine cited above: "I do not even wish to mention the Mother of the Savior when treating of sin." The second interpretation is: "We do not subject Mary to the devil because, born in sin by the general law of all birth, she has been delivered from it by the grace of rebirth." The Immaculate Conception is done away with, but what difficulties are raised! First, in place of being an answer to Julian, it is an admission of defeat. Julian carries his point that the Mother of God was a slave of the devil. Second, she is put on absolutely the same plane as all other men whose original sin has been effaced. There is not even an indication about the moment of her justification. What becomes of the special place of Mary at the side of Christ which Harnack has so rightly pointed out in Augustine's teaching? Even worse, a contradiction in the same sentence is imputed to the great doctor. The words "we do not subject" deny all servitude to the devil; immediately afterwards such a servitude would be affirmed. Augustine would say literally: "We do not subject Mary to the devil, and this because she is really his slave by birth, although she was regenerated later." The reader can decide whether this interpretation is likely. On the other hand, it should be remembered that in the same work Augustine seems to make an exception only for Jesus Christ.[170] But, if one plumbs the meaning of that text, he soon sees that Augustine is there treating only of the transmission of original sin by lawful title, a transmission which affects all those who descend from Adam by natural generation. In this sense Jesus Christ is alone exempt, for Mary is not exempt by right; she is excepted in fact, in virtue of the Redemption of Him who is exempt by right.

CHAPTER XI

Grace and Pelagianism

1. Different Interpretations of St. Augustine's System

THE part of God and man in salvation and the harmony between grace and liberty indisputably form the central core of the teaching of the Bishop of Hippo. Here is where his thought was at the same time the most personal, the most powerful, and the most contested. It was the most personal because he was the first to synthesize the great theories of the fall, grace, and freedom of choice and still more because he has offered a profound explanation to reconcile them, truly his own since no trace of it is found in his predecessors. Thus the word *Augustinian* has commonly been reserved to designate Augustine's system of grace, not his entire teaching. His thought was the most powerful on this question because, as everyone admits, he was chiefly responsible for the triumph of freedom of the will against the Manicheans and of grace against the Pelagians. His teaching in great part has been solemnly adopted by the Church, and the canons of the Council of Orange are borrowed word for word from his writings. But his doctrine is also the most contested. Just like St. Paul whose teaching he develops, he has been often quoted, and often misunderstood. Friends and enemies have exploited his teaching in the most diverse senses. Without making a detailed study here of the interpretations which have been put upon his teaching, we will mention three facts which merit attention.

At all times adversaries of freedom of the will—predestinarians, Wycliffites, Calvinists, and Jansenists—have availed themselves of the authority of Augustine.

Catholic theologians, it is true, have generally recognized that Augustine safeguarded the rights of freedom of the will, but they are strangely divided concerning the nature of this freedom and the explanation of the divine action in Augustine's writings.

In our time, we must admit, a good number of critics on all sides favor the strict interpretation which sees in Augustine a theory of divine determinism fatal to freedom of the will. Richard Simon had already tried to show in Augustine's work a revolutionary tendency introducing new dogmas irreconcilable with freedom of the will which was in open break with the traditional teaching.[1] A recent historian, H. Margival, is still more severe. He pictures Augustine as the victim of a metaphysical pessimism unconsciously drawn from Manichean doctrines: "The Oriental conception of the necessity and the eternity of evil will never find a more zealous champion than this bishop. . . . In the final analysis he was to offer no stronger opposition to the Christian Stoicism of the Breton monk Pelagius than the explanations of a delicate heart, the tale of his intimate and inevitable defeats."[2]

The learned Benedictine Dom Odilo Rottmanner concludes a penetrating analysis of Augustine's teaching on grace in this manner: In St. Augustine's teaching on predestination a disagreement between his theory and practice becomes manifest. The mildness of his practice remained unchanged, as is shown by his sermons; his theory, at first inoffensive, continually developed in the direction of an excessive rigorism and an irresistible influence of God on freedom of the will. Moreover, this endless variation prevents him from developing a complete system whose parts are logically connected.[3]

Contemporary Protestant critics, even the most sincere admirers of Augustine, are unmerciful. Although the earlier reformers invoked his authority to deny freedom of choice, their successors set themselves up as the defenders of liberty against his teaching.[4] Loofs accuses him of holding an irresistible predestination and grace which are opposed to freedom of the will, to the teaching of St. Jerome, and to popular Catholicism, which could not become accustomed to it and finally declared itself "Augustinian," although really adopting Semipelagianism.[5] Harnack sees "numerous contradictions and remnants of Manicheism" in the Augustinian theory of grace.[6] Like Loofs and many others, he was deceived by this false idea of an irresistible grace.

In reality, a purely objective study of the texts—all the texts and especially those of his later years—considered in relation to each other and in the sense indicated by Augustine (just sound historical method) lead to an entirely different conclusion. Nor is this an attempt to whitewash the exaggerations and errors of one of the Fathers, for he himself has retracted some of them and there are others which we will mention. The present problem is to discover his true thought, his genuine, complete, and logical system just as he understood it.

Despite quite noticeable exaggerations on certain points, despite difficulties which explain disagreements without taking a position, we think that the texts are sufficiently clear and the critics sufficiently impartial to propose a revision of the stricter views. Therefore we unhesitatingly affirm first, that St. Augustine has formed a true and perfectly logical system without contradictions, the basis of which did not vary since the time he became bishop if we judge by his later works; second, that in this system human liberty was affirmed until the day of his death so accurately that no trace of an irresistible and necessitating impulsion ever appears in it.

2. HISTORICAL DEVELOPMENT OF AUGUSTINE'S THOUGHT ON GRACE

a. ORIGIN OF THE PROBLEM

The problem of grace arose long before Augustine's first struggles with Pelagianism in 412—that is a fact beyond doubt today. In proportion as Augustine condemned Manicheism and resolved the problem of evil by showing the part human freedom played in it, there arose for him the problem of good under a threefold aspect: philosophical, theological, and especially Pauline.

(1) *Philosophical aspect.* The philosopher accustomed to look for the influence of God in everything must ask himself how the two sovereignties of divine government and human liberty can be reconciled. The divine foreknowledge, which the ancient philo-

sophers had denied to safeguard liberty, did not disturb him. Since God knows that I will perform such and such an action freely, the verification of His knowledge, far from destroying the independence of my act, rather demands it infallibly. The foreknowledge has no more influence on the future than memory has on the past.[7] This knowledge is not the same as the concurrence of the divine action with created activity which more commonly occupies Augustine's attention. Pelagius was to deny this concurrence as he denied all divine intervention, but this facet of the problem was destined for indirect treatment only. The aspect on which Augustine riveted his attention was the special role God plays in moral life. Virtue, holiness—are these due only to human free will? Or, if their origin must be sought in God, what becomes of freedom of choice?

(2) *Theological aspect*. The theologian's problem is further complicated by revelation which asserts Christ's mysterious and continual influence on the Christian: "Without Me you can do nothing" (John 15:5). The problem of supernatural grace was added to that of providence.

(3) *Pauline aspect*. The Pauline dogma of divine predestination, separating the elect from the reprobate as if vessels of honor and of shame were formed from the same potter's clay, adds this further question: Why was human liberty not destroyed by the fall of Adam and the gratuitous predestination of God?

This is the state of the question which faced Augustine at the beginning of his apostolate. He had already attempted a rough answer to it in the *Explanation of Some Questions from Romans* (393–396).[8]

b. ERRORS ON THE REASONS FOR HIS THEORY

According to certain Protestants, Augustine was forced to hold these strict theories of predestination and grace by his conception of the essential role of the Church.[9] The theory of original sin, giving an altogether new importance to baptism and the Church which confers it, permitted him to recruit many young people for the Church. "This consideration," says Grandgeorge, "had much influence on St. Augustine's mind and thus forced him to adopt the theory of predestination."[10]

This view is entirely false, as Loofs[11] and Reuter[12] have proved. The latter establishes that the two theories of the Church and of grace are considered independently of one another by Augustine and that he never availed himself of the doctrine of original sin to buttress his teaching on the Church. His numerous writings offer no trace of this preoccupation.

C. DIFFERENT PHASES OF AUGUSTINIAN THOUGHT: ERRORS OF THE FIRST PERIOD

In no question is the study of Augustine's works in their chronological order so important as here. Even in his own time the Semipelagians were setting his first writings against his last; St. Augustine replied: "That is true, I have seen the problem better and I have corrected myself. Since you read what I have to say, why do you not advance with me?"[13]

An exaggeration to be avoided is the affirmation that the Augustine of 412 (*On the Spirit and the Letter*) was still Pelagian, an error into which the Jansenists fell. Even before his episcopacy Augustine was formulating (in 393) his great theses on original sin, "When our nature sinned in Paradise";[14] on the mass of perdition: "We are all made from the same mass of clay, which is the mass of sin";[15] and on gratuitous predestination. The only thing to note is that before his episcopacy he had not yet understood how the first good disposition of the will, faith for example, must come from God; he attributes this beginning of salvation exclusively to freedom of choice. This could really be an opening for Semipelagianism, but not Pelagianism, as the Jansenists supposed. This single error was the inspiration of various expressions which he himself corrected later. The following are examples: (1) The call to faith is a gratuitous gift of God, but the acceptance of faith is an act of human liberty alone.[16] (2) God perceives in the mass of fallen humanity differences which justify the different graces accorded to some and not to others.[17] (3) "God will not have mercy unless an act of the will precedes."[18] —Later he was to say that every good desire was already an act of mercy on the part of God. (4) The grace of his own vocation was merely external preaching. He forgot the intimate appeal at the bottom of his heart which was able to bring about its infallible acceptance.[19] (5) Belief and desire come from ourselves alone, but doing good is the gift of grace.[20] (6) He likewise taught that faith merits justifying grace.[21] This is accurate, the *Retractations* add, provided that faith itself is recognized as a gift from God.[22]

d. SYSTEM COMPLETE IN 397: IMPORTANCE OF "VARIOUS QUESTIONS FOR SIMPLICIANUS"

Another exaggeration which must be dispelled is that Augustine's doubts continued indefinitely. According to proponents of this view, Augustine, pushed by the arguments of the Pelagians, continually restricted the scope of freedom of the will until toward the end of his life he taught an absolute predestination which annihilated freedom altogether. This is a mistake. If his teaching of predestination destroyed liberty, Augustine denied it already in 397, for at the very beginning of his episcopacy (fifteen years before the Pelagian controversy began) he formulated his system in a famous reply which has not been sufficiently studied or understood. Simplicianus, Ambrose's successor to the see of Milan, posed several questions to his old pupil. Among them, he asked Augustine about Chapter IX of the Epistle to the Romans. The reply, *On Various Questions for Simplicianus*,[23] constitutes a true key to the Augustinian system because of its accuracy, its fullness, its clarity, and especially because of the rational explanation which it gives to the dogma. It must be reread if one wishes to grasp the depth of its thought and the significance of the formulas which, though in constant use later, are rarely explained elsewhere. This assertion may be striking, but there are proofs.

In his later years Augustine refers his adversaries to this book with an insistence not often noticed. In the *Retractations*, far from making any changes, he affirms that his researches were crowned with the triumph of grace: "In the solution of this question I indeed worked hard on behalf of the freedom of choice of the human will, but the grace of God conquered."[24] In *On the Gift of Perseverance* he affirms that in the former work "before the Pelagian heresy raised its head"[25] he taught the true doctrine of grace and predestination. According to *On the Predestination of the Saints* (429), it is only in that work that the Semipelagians would have been able to find the solution of their great problem. "Let some one send them the books, then," he says. "They would have found that question explained according to the truth of the Scriptures in the first book . . . to Simplicianus, unless they did not happen to be acquainted with it. If that is the case, see to it that they become acquainted with it."[26] He even dares to attribute this solution to a divine enlightenment: "God revealed this to me as I tried to solve this question when I was writing, as I said before, to the bishop Simplicianus." Let the importance of this revelation be watered down as much as one likes, once one understands that Augustine speaks thus at the end of his life in his chief works on predestination, he cannot take a dim view of the importance of this reply to Simplicianus.

In addition, some very competent critics have grasped the importance of this book although they do not seem to have understood all its doctrine. According to Loofs the whole of the specifically Augustinian teaching on grace as it was defended later against the Pelagians and Semipelagians can be reproduced by citations from this one book to Simplicianus.[27] Loofs has given the broad outlines of this synthesis in his article. Reuter says that the Augustinian system of grace and predestination in the very labor of its formation can nowhere be detected better than in this book.[28] From this time on, the whole plan which the second form of his teaching was going to assume had been sketched out.

Among contemporary Catholic writers Abbé Turmel[29] and Abbé Jules Martin[30] have mentioned the importance of this work. "The period of exact, precise, and, one can add, definitive knowledge," says Martin, "dates from the beginning of 397."[31]

A comparison of various texts strengthens this conviction. It is not true to say that the strictest formulas were reserved for the last period of his life, for predestination nowhere assumes a more imperious form than here.[32] On the contrary, Turmel observes that several points, such as the fate of infants, are treated more kindly in later works.[33] He nevertheless concludes that there is no need of appealing to a change in his thought after 397.

3. The Pelagian System

The Pelagian system must be known if one wishes to understand the theory and terminology of Augustine. Now, while its particular errors are well known and deserve no further development here, the guiding principle from which they have issued and the very basis of the Pelagian controversy are less known.

a. DOGMATIC ERRORS OF THE PELAGIANS

Their dogmatic errors were clearly enunciated in the first condemnation pronounced at the Council of Carthage in 411.[34] Coelestius, a disciple of Pelagius bolder than his master, was accused of the following errors: (1) Adam was created mortal; whether he sinned or not, he had to die. This is a negation of the supernatural elevation of the first man. Therefore there existed neither original justice nor the preternatural privileges which flowed from it. (2) The sin of Adam injured himself alone, not the human race. This is a negation of original sin. (3) Infants today are born in the state in which Adam was before his fall. This is a combination of the first two errors. Death, concupiscence, and so forth are not the result of Adam's sin, but the original condition of humanity. (4) "Adam by his death [or by his sin] does not subject the whole human race to death; [because] Christ by His Resurrection does not give new life to the entire human race."[35] This is the basis of the great argument of Coelestius and the Pelagians for their denial of original sin. It is a fact that Christ by His Resurrection does not give anyone immortality of the body nor does He give to all life of the soul, but only to those who believe and are converted. Therefore, they conclude, Adam was the cause of bodily death for no one and of death of the soul only for those who imitate his sin, but not for all. If this were not so, Adam would have more power to destroy us than Christ had to save us. That is certainly the sense of this condemnation: the Pelagians understood death through Adam in the double sense of bodily and spiritual death and insisted on the fact that "all are not spiritually reborn in Jesus Christ."[36] The affinity of Pelagian errors with Nestorianism can be seen here. Since the first Adam had not destroyed us, the second Adam is no longer the Redeemer. The Council of Ephesus was to condemn both heresies. (5) "Infants who die without baptism enjoy eternal life, in consequence of the denial of original sin. These infants are nevertheless excluded from the kingdom of heaven, although no explanation is given how this differs from eternal life." (6) "Man can live without sin and observe the commandments easily because even before the coming of Christ men lived without sin and the Law guided them to the kingdom of heaven as well as the Gospel." This affirmation of perfection attained here below is one of the most characteristic traits of Pelagianism.

These errors are the consequences of a system. What is the guiding principle which has given rise to them?

b. FUNDAMENTAL IDEA OF PELAGIANISM

(1) *Not solely a denial of the supernatural.* The underlying idea of Pelagianism is not solely its denial of the supernatural order. In great part, it is true, Pelagianism is a naturalism which excludes supernatural elevation, divine adoption, the fall, all merit of a higher order, but which admits that the will depends on the divine government. That was the source of this formal rule of interpretation: Every time that Augustine appeals to grace against Pelagius, it is a supernatural act which is involved. Now this view of the situation and this rule are incomplete: There is no doubt that Pelagius denied all supernatural grace—whatever the Jansenists might say—and admitted only the external gifts of revelation, the law, and the example of Christ.[37] But Pelagius denied more than that. Even prescinding from the supernatural order, he exaggerated the powers of freedom of choice. And these same theo-

logians (the Jansenists) recognize that fact when they appeal to the Pelagian controversy to affirm the impossibility of observing the natural law, even in what concerns its substance, without grace.

(2) *Basic error: absolute independence of human liberty.* The foundation of the Pelagian system, then, is the absolute independence of human liberty in relationship to God and its unlimited power for good as well as for evil. The origin of this system must be sought in Stoicism, whose motto Pelagius adopted: A person asks God for riches or health but not for virtue, for that depends on oneself. St. Jerome was already pointing out this influence and he exclaimed along with Tertullian: "The philosophers, the patriarchs of the heretics."[38] He also shows that Pelagius cited the ideas of the Pythagorean Sextus under the false name of Pope Sixtus II. Augustine was fooled by this for a short time.[39] According to Pelagius, man owes existence and freedom of choice (which he calls the possibility of good) to God the Creator. This is the only gift of God and, since it is gratuitous, Pelagius calls it a grace, playing on the words. Any further influence of God on freedom of choice would destroy it.

At the Synod of Diospolis Pelagius was reproached for the following statement: "It is not freedom of choice if there is need of the help of God."[40] Coelestius, quoted by St. Jerome, said: "The will is destroyed if it needs the help of another."[41] More to the point, Pelagius stated: "If something precedes it, it is destroyed."[42] Pelagius sums up his thought in his famous distinction of the three elements of the moral life: "We localize possibility in nature, willing in freedom of choice, existence in the effect. That first one, that is, possibility, belongs properly to God who confers it on His creature; the other two, that is, willing and existence, should be referred to man because they flow from freedom of choice."[43]

The most expressive formulation of the system is that of Julian of Eclanum who proclaims the complete emancipation of the will: "The freedom of the will is that by which man is freed from God."[44] Albert Bruckner, wishing to characterize Julian's teaching, does not hesitate to approve the statement of Harnack that it is atheistic in its basic structure, whatever the personal senti-ments of Julian may have been.[45] It is at least a teaching which neglects Providence and which, therefore, as Neander points out, confines God to His eternity "whence He is a simple spectator, not a participant in the drama of the world."[46]

(3) *Did Pelagius deny concurrence?* The question is also asked whether Pelagius had likewise denied all ordinary divine con-currence. He was accused of this by Paul Orosius[47] and St. Jerome: "Hear this sacrilegious statement. If I wish, you say, to bend my finger, to move my hand, to sit, to stand, to walk, . . . is the help of God always necessary?"[48] Some great theologians thought that this accusation was well grounded.[49] The debate over this point, however, has little reference to the question at hand. It is certain that St. Augustine, the great theorist of the divine con-currence in his *Literal Commentary on Genesis*,[50] did not concen-trate on this point in his debate with the Pelagians, but rather conceded their affirmation of the concurrence.[51]

However that may be, it is an absolute rule that grace as defended by Augustine can never be identified with the concur-rence, since grace in his mind is always a gift specially granted for acts of virtue alone, a gift which distinguishes the good from the bad.

(4) *Omnipotence of free choice.* The omnipotence of freedom of choice for good was a result of its emancipation. St. Jerome accused Pelagius of daring to lay claim to the very holiness of God: "You boast a justice in men which is perfect and equal to that of God."[52] By right, Pelagius was demanding for human nature the dis-passionateness and the faultlessness of the Stoics, that is to say, an absolute dominion over all passions and an insensibility by which man is, as St. Jerome said, "either a stone or God."[53] In reality, however, Pelagius affirmed that even in the Old Testa-ment those who were called holy and just were really without sin and in a state of complete perfection which was acquired solely by their freedom of choice.[54] Augustine states: "They say . . . that there were, are, and will be people on this earth who have no sin whatever."[55]

C. CONSEQUENT RIGORISM

A dreadful rigorism was the result of this exaggeration of the powers of human liberty. Since perfection is possible for man, it is obligatory. For Pelagius, as for the Stoics, every good act is obligatory; there are no counsels, only precepts.

This important facet of the system has remained unnoticed for the most part. Some sage critics have hinted at it, however.[56] The Pelagian documents published by Caspari established this fact beyond all doubt.[57] Harnack dared to say that "according to Pelagius, every man who could have acted better than he did is going to hell."[58]

The Pelagians therefore damned for all eternity every Christian guilty of the slightest venial sin, or, to put it another way, every sin was mortal for them. For a lie, an idle word, one ceases to be just and becomes reprobate and a sinner, worthy of hell.

That was the accusation directed against Pelagius by the Fathers of the Synod of Diospolis (415) when they forced him to retract this proposition: "On the day of judgment there will be no mercy for the wicked and sinners, but they will be burned in everlasting fires." All contemporary documents are unanimous about the meaning of this proposition and the accusation made against Pelagius.[59] To forestall any subterfuge, Augustine informs us in *On Nature and Grace* (written in 415 immediately before the Council of Diospolis) that Pelagius himself made this error a basic point of his system.[60] The just and children of God are not damned; therefore they have no sin however slight, since any sin would be a cause for condemnation.

Because they were unacquainted with the system of Pelagius, many critics even in these latter days[61] attributed to the Fathers of Diospolis the error of the merciful. According to them, these Fathers reproached Pelagius for holding the Catholic doctrine about the damnation of Christians who lead an evil life. This misunderstanding is not possible today.[62] One of the works published by Caspari depicts the author of the letter *De malis doctoribus*[63] condemning people to hell for an idle word.[64]

Venial sin excludes one from the Church as well as from heaven.

According to Pelagius, the minute a person violates the slightest of the commandments he is no longer a member of the Church, a member of Christ, or a child of God. St. Augustine mentioned this error.[65] In a sermon he refutes this thesis: "The Church taken as a whole has no sin in any of its single members."[66] Specht remarks that the Pelagians defined the Church as the "society of the perfect."[67]

In particular Pelagius damns the rich who do not renounce their wealth. That was the sixth proposition condemned at the Synod of Diospolis.[68] The letter from Hilary of Sicily (about 414) denounced this wild error to Augustine.[69] This rigorism, exaggerated to a point where it became unbelievable, led astray austere souls and was a powerful force in promoting the spread of Pelagianism.

CHAPTER XII

Grace as Developed by Augustine

1. OVER-ALL VIEW OF THE DOGMAS DEFENDED BY AUGUSTINE AGAINST PELAGIUS

AUGUSTINE's theory of grace includes three sections. First, there are dogmatic elements (in direct opposition to Pelagius's conclusions rather than his principles) for which Augustine merited the official approval of the Church. Second, there are more general principles which constitute the very basis of the Augustinian system and which have not been, at least explicitly, the object of a definition. Third, there are applications of these principles to the special questions of the condition of Adam, original sin, and predestination—applications which for the most part have not been treated by the Church in her decisions.

Concerning the first category, an over-all view of the dogmas established by Augustine is provided in two important documents: the canons of the Council of Carthage (418) and the twelve truths of the Catholic faith which Augustine enumerates in his letter to Vitalis.

a. COUNCIL OF CARTHAGE

Three great dogmatic truths are summarized in the eight (or nine) canons of the Council of Africa. This council, held at Carthage in 418,[1] was confirmed by the famous *Tractoria* encyclical of Pope Zozimus.[2] Everyone knows that Augustine, the soul of this council, epitomized in these definitions the truths for which he was fighting.

(1) *Original sin.* Treating the sin of our origin, he affirms the immortality of Adam before the fall (canon 1), the transmission of sins to his descendants, the necessity for infants to be baptized

"unto the remission of sins" in the proper meaning of the term
(c. 2), and the impossibility for non-baptized infants to enter the
kingdom of heaven or even to enjoy a true happiness elsewhere
(c. 3). The authenticity of the third canon is questioned; however,
it seems to be genuine.[3] In either case, the doctrine is surely
Augustinian.[4]

(2) *Role of grace.* On the necessity and the role of grace, the
Fathers assert that justifying grace is not only the pardon of past
sins but also a help, "an aid that sins be not committed" (c. 4).
This help is not only a light which reveals the law, but the love
of the good "that we may also love and be able to act" (c. 5). The
necessity of this aid is absolute and not merely "that we may act
more easily" (c. 6).

(3) *Impeccability.* Against the impeccability and the perfection
extolled by the Pelagians, the Fathers proclaim and demonstrate
by the Scriptures that in reality Providence allows men, even the
most just, to fall into sins. Anathema is pronounced against anyone who refuses to take the saying of St. John (I John 1:8) in its
strict meaning: "If we say that we have no sin, we deceive ourselves" (c. 7). Anathema is also declared against anyone who
claims that the saints do not recite the "forgive us our sins" except
for the sake of their sinning brethren (c. 8) or that they say it
merely out of humility (c. 9).

b. LETTER TO VITALIS

The letter to Vitalis develops a fourth truth, the gratuity of
grace, in twelve rules of faith. It is an excellent résumé of Augustine's struggle against the Semipelagians.[5] After the affirmation of
original sin (article 1), he stresses the gratuity of grace and its
universal necessity for all, even for infants (a. 2), and for every
action of adults (a. 3). This gratuity is proved by the distribution
of grace: God does not give it to all, but to those whom He wills
(a. 4, 5, 6). It is explained by rejecting the theory of the Semipelagians for whom the death of infants without baptism was a
punishment for the faults which they would have committed if
they had lived longer (a. 7, 8, 10). It is confirmed by the prayers of

the Church to obtain faith for infidels and by prayers of thanksgiving for converts (a. 11, 12).

2. Three Fundamental Principles of the Augustinian System

Father Wolfsgruber maintains that the key to the whole Augustinian system lies in Augustine's assertion of these two truths: Man is free; he can do nothing without grace.[6] These two statements are undoubtedly of great value; but they only create a mystery, they do not explain it. The true key, therefore, is elsewhere, in the Augustinian explanation of the divine government of wills. This is a theory which is as original and profound as it is absolutely unknown to the most intelligent Protestant critics such as Harnack, Loofs, and so forth.

There are at the basis of the Augustinian system not two, but three fundamental principles whose precise meaning must be determined. First, God, through His grace, is the absolute master of all the determinations of the will. Second, man remains just as free under the influence of grace as he is in its absence. Third, the reconciliation of these two truths depends upon the method of the divine government.

a. FIRST PRINCIPLE

The absolute sovereignty of God over the will is opposed to the Pelagian principle of the emancipation of liberty.

(1) *Affirmation of this sovereignty.* Well before the time of Pelagius, Augustine's theology was tending to establish the all-powerful influence of God in the order of virtue as well as in the order of truth. God, the first cause, is the author of all good, of all moral perfection, of all salvation. No man is good or virtuous without the gift of God which is called grace because it is completely gratuitous. No one is saved without the special gift of final perseverance, prepared by a specially gracious predestination of God. "Without doubt God has the fullest power over the hearts of men to turn them where He pleases."[7] Freedom of choice will

not impede the divine decrees: "To will or not to will is in the power of the one who wills or does not will in such a way as not to impede the divine will and not to overcome its power."[8] The reason is evident: "He has the wills of men more under His control than they themselves have."[9] In particular, no matter how obdurate a person is, He can convert him when and as He pleases: "Who therefore would act so impiously and foolishly as to say that God cannot turn to good the evil wills of those whom He wills, when He wills, and where He wills?"[10] Likewise there is no will, no matter how exalted in holiness, which does not fall into the worst excesses without God's protection. St. Augustine asserts this even of the angels[11] and in general of every creature.[12] With great emphasis he states: "There is not a single sin which one man has committed that it would not be possible for a second man to commit, if the Ruler by whom man was made were absent."[13]

(2) *Exercise of this sovereignty.* Augustine has formulated three laws concerning the exercise of this sovereignty.

The first is that every good and salutary act without exception is the fruit of a grace, of a gift from God. Without this gift of God, there is no merit for heaven. Speaking of adults, he says: "We know that grace . . . is given to adults for each and every act."[14]

The second law, a consequence of the first, is the priority of grace over good will. Far from being merited by some sort of good desire, by faith or prayer, grace precedes and prepares everything, since good desires, faith, and prayer must come from it.[15]

The third law states that not only is Pelagian inerrancy, the preservation from all, even the slightest faults, incapable of realization for weak human beings without a special grace, but that this gift itself is a privilege so rare that it has been granted only once or twice in the history of humanity. All other men, even the saints, have had slight faults and have had to recite the "forgive us our sins."[16] In connection with this, a movement in Augustine's thought toward a sterner attitude can be ascertained. Until 415 he tolerated the statement that there are just persons without sin, provided that this perfection is attributed to the grace of God: "We can, after a fashion, bear with those who hold this opinion."[17] After 415, however, as in the Council of Carthage (418), he denied the proposition that any just person, even with the help of grace, lives without sin.[18]

The feature dominating these laws, however, is the extent of this dependence, even apart from the supernatural order.

(3) *Extent of this dependence.* Even in the natural order the dependence of every created will is so universal that no act of virtue is performed without a gift from God. "My liberty can do all things," says Pelagius. "Your liberty," responds Augustine, "attains to nothing without God. It depends on Him in everything, at every instant." That was the understanding of St. Thomas and the Scholastics of the Middle Ages, and of our time also.[19] However, to avoid a serious confusion, the remark should be made that these theologians do not say that Augustine demands supernatural grace for a single act of natural virtue (an error of Baius and the Jansenists); they merely wish to say that every act of virtue is truly a gift of God—not because the will could not perform it, but because, as a matter of fact, it would not will to act without this providential mercy. Much misunderstanding has arisen from the fact that this principle has not been grasped. In particular the great theology of the Middle Ages, which adopted it and made it one basis of its system of liberty, has not always been rightly appreciated. Many, it is true, have been dismayed by these sweeping universal statements because they did not comprehend the nature of this gift of God which leaves liberty untouched. An explanation of it will be given below.

The mind of Augustine, nevertheless, if one reads the texts without preconceptions, is indisputable. The foundation on which he rests the necessity of grace for each and every act is not the supernatural character of the meritorious act, but the universal principle that God must be the unique source of all good (as He is the source of all truth through illumination),[20] and *a fortiori* of all moral good or virtue. This important text should be pondered: "Because all goods, as we have said, whether great, moderate, or small, are from God, it follows that the good use of freedom of choice, which is virtue, is also from God and is reckoned among the great goods."[21]

The formulas stating that every good desire comes from God and that, without Him, freedom of choice is always toward evil are universal and without restriction: "No one has anything of himself except deceit and sin."[22] "When I say to you that without the help of God you do nothing, I mean nothing good, for you have the freedom of choice to act evilly without the help of God."[23] The negative formulas do not support the limitation of God's sovereignty to the supernatural order. From the fact that freedom of choice has no efficacy in the order of salvation the conclusion cannot be drawn that it can only commit sin, for all the natural virtues fall within its power. Besides, to thus limit these texts it would be necessary to admit that Augustine never talked of the weakness of the will in observing the natural law in its entirety.

In addition, Augustine has expressed himself on this subject in the most explicit manner. First, he demands this gift of God for natural virtues, which avail nothing toward heaven and are found (although rarely, it is true) among unbelievers. Polemon, a young pagan, for example, gives up intemperance: "It is the gift of God," cries Augustine, "lest I should attribute that improvement which has been wrought in him to human power and not to divine."[24] There is also the no less gripping example of King Assuerus.[25]

Second, this is also one of the principles of his polemic with Julian of Eclanum on the virtues of unbelievers. He accuses Julian not only of having exaggerated these virtues, but also of not having recognized in each of them the gift of God: "How much better it would be—if you find such delight in praising these pagans—. . . how much better it would be, I say, that you acknowledge in them these very things as gifts of God."[26] After a remarkable passage on divine Providence which ordains all moral excellence from afar, he concludes: "How much more bearable it would be if you attributed to the divine gift those virtues which you say pagans possess rather than to their own will alone, although they know nothing of this."[27]

Finally, Augustine distinguished quite explicitly the two orders of grace: the grace of the natural virtues (a simple gift of internal providence which prepares efficacious motives for the will) and the grace for salutary and supernatural acts which is given with the first preludes of faith. The latter is the grace of children (*gratia filiorum*); the former is the grace for all—even strangers (*filii concubinarum*), Augustine adds, can receive it. Speaking of death courageously suffered by a heretic, he says that it is a gift of God, but far different from the gifts reserved for Christians: "As one cannot deny that this is a gift of God, so one must understand that there are other gifts of God for the children of that free Jerusalem which is above, our mother."[28]

Because he forgot this important distinction between these two graces, Vasquez did not know how to find in Augustine supernatural actual grace before justification. Suarez, on the other hand, did not dare to give the gift of the natural virtues the title of grace for fear that an argument denying supernatural grace would be drawn from that teaching.

b. SECOND PRINCIPLE

Freedom of choice, even under the influence of efficacious grace, was always safeguarded by St. Augustine.

Everybody grants two important facts. First, St. Augustine had from the very beginning defended freedom of choice against the Manicheans so ardently that his works are an inexhaustible arsenal: "No one is worthy of shame or punishment who . . . does not do what he is not able to do. Do not shepherds in the mountains, poets in the theaters, teachers in the schools, . . . and the human race throughout the world shout that lesson?"[29] Second, in the Pelagian struggle Augustine perceived immediately the danger of compromising freedom of the will by exalting the role of grace; he wished at all costs to avert this peril while avoiding the opposite pitfalls.[30] Augustine adopts the expression of St. Jerome: "Where there is necessity, there is no reward," although Loofs accuses him of standing in opposition to the Doctor of Bethlehem.[31]

Some, however, have claimed that little by little, caught up in the logic of his ideas, he had sacrificed freedom of the will on the altar of divine determinism. But the texts are absolutely against this accusation.

(1) Augustine never retracted his principal ideas on freedom of choice; he never modified his thought on the factor which is its essential condition, that is, its complete power of choosing or determining itself. Who will dare to say that in the revision of his works he lacked clear-sightedness or sincerity on a point of such importance?

He does not blame the Pelagians for demanding the power of choice; he rather joins them in proclaiming that without it there is no responsibility, no merit, no demerit. He does blame them, however, for exaggerating this power. Julian, denying the enticements of concupiscence, conceived freedom of choice as a balance whose two scales are in perfect equilibrium: "The will is like a scale which you try to balance with equal weights on each side; it is as free to incline towards evil as it is towards good."[32] Augustine protests that this equilibrium did exist in Adam, but was upset by original sin. The will must struggle and fight against an inclination to evil, although it remains master of its choice.[33] Augustine shows clearly that freedom of choice remains, although not the same freedom which Adam enjoyed, for he had the privilege of original integrity.[34]

(2) On the contrary, there is not a single one of his later anti-Pelagian works in which Augustine does not positively proclaim the complete power of choice. True, he also states that God has the absolute power of directing this choice. But he had always stressed this divine power with equal vigor since at least 397. If, then, one claims that he denies liberty because of that, let him not say that he became a determinist just at the end of his life; the objector should maintain that Augustine had destroyed freedom of choice already in 397 in the *Questions for Simplicianus* and the following works, which nevertheless favored liberty so much that Jansenius accused them of Pelagianism. In 426, for example: "To will or not to will is in the power of the one who wills or does not will in such a way as not to impede the divine will and

not to overcome its power; for even from those who do what He does not wish He brings about what He wishes."[35] Two statements are categorical: God can convert any hardened sinner, but He will convert him while leaving him the power to refuse conversion. How? Augustine will tell us presently. In 427, among the twelve articles of faith concerning grace, this one is found: "Whoever has received the efficacious grace of faith gives his consent only with complete independence of his free will."[36] In 428–429 he writes: "Not because it is not in the choice of man's free will to believe or not to believe, but because in the elect the will is prepared by the Lord."[37]

(3) Efficacious grace works infallibly, but never by an irresistible impulse, for even under its influence the will remains master of itself. From the beginning of the Pelagian controversy (412) he had taught: "To give our consent to God's calling or to withhold it is a function of our own will."[38] He had already given the reason for this in the same work: "For God wishes that all men be saved . . . not, however, so as to take from them their free will, by the good or bad use of which they will be most righteously judged."[39] He repeats this tirelessly, for example in 415: "In doing right there is no bond of necessity."[40] Towards the end, while revising his works in 426, he was far from retracting anything which he had taught in the commentary on Romans about the freedom of faith and of good will.[41] He rather confirmed it, saying: "Both of them [faith and free will] are ours because of freedom of choice; both are nevertheless given us through the spirit of faith and charity."[42] A righteous act, even a supernatural one, is the work of man and God.

C. THIRD PRINCIPLE

The Augustinian theory on the divine influence reconciles both grace and freedom of the will.

Is there a contradiction between the two principles just stated? Harnack, Loofs, and others thought so because, according to them, Augustinian grace is an irresistible impulse. Is this, however, the true thought of the great doctor? He thought, certainly, that he had reconciled the two dogmas and was astonished that the monks of Hadrumetum had not understood him. This solution has been pointed out by older theologians and in our days by Schwane and others, but in too summary a fashion.[43] An explanation of it will justify the system of the Doctor of Hippo.

(1) *Explanation of the way grace operates.* The solution rests on three Augustinian theories and gives an equally valid explanation of the divine influence on both natural and supernatural virtues.

(a) *Theory of volitional psychology.* The will never determines itself without a motive, without the attraction of good perceived in the object: "Nothing attracts the will to action unless it is seen. What each one decides to take or leave is in his power...."[44] Now, although the will remains free in the presence of any motive, in point of fact it often makes different resolutions according to the different motives which are presented to it. There is the whole secret of the influence exercised by eloquence (the orator does nothing but present motives), by meditation, or by good reading. What power would he not have over the will who would be able to present such or such a motive for action at his pleasure? Well, that is precisely the privilege of God in virtue of the first principle.

(b) *Theory of intellectual psychology.* St. Augustine noted this truth of universal experience that man is not master of his first thoughts. He can influence the course of his reflections, but he himself cannot determine the objects, the images, and consequently the motives which are presented to his mind. "No one has power over what chances to come into his mind," he says, "but to give consent or to withhold it is in the power of one's own will."[45] But since *chance* is only a word, it is really God who determines these first perceptions of man as He pleases, either through the providential action of external causes or interiorly by the ministry of angels or even by a divine illumination sent to the soul.[46]

The divine influence on the will already seems very powerful because God is the one who attracts the will by presenting to it all the motives or inducements which His omnipotence ordains. .

However, His influence would still be uncertain without a third element.

(c) *Theory of the divine knowledge.* Not only does God send at His pleasure the illuminations and enticements which are the will's inspiration in determining itself, but He knows, even before choosing among all the illuminations of the natural and supernatural order, the answer which the will will freely make to each one of them. Thus in the divine knowledge there are for each created will indefinite series of motives which would at this moment be rejected. There are also other series which as a matter of fact (though quite freely) would entail an acceptance of the good. God could have, then, at His pleasure, wrought the salvation of Judas, if He had willed it, or allowed Peter to perish. No freedom of choice stands in opposition to His plans, although it always retains the power of destroying itself. Consequently it is God alone who, in His utter independence, determines, by the choice of this motive or this inspiration (whose future influence He knows), whether the will is to determine itself for good or for evil. Therefore a man who has done good ought to thank God because He has sent him an inspiration previously seen to be efficacious, even though that favor was refused to someone else. All the more, each of the elect owes it to the divine goodness alone for having received the series of graces which God knew to be infallibly, although quite freely, linked with final perseverance.

This theory, most assuredly, need not be accepted, for the Church has never adopted it as her own; one can ask where and how God knows the result of these graces, for Augustine always affirmed the fact and never inquired into the manner.[47] But can the thinker who created and defended this logical system until his dying day be accused of fatalism and Manicheism? This, then, was the solution which Augustine always laid down as the foundation of his system.

(2) *Proofs.* After 397 he expresses this solution with great clarity. Among other questions, Simplicianus asks him how the ninth chapter of the Epistle to the Romans, treating of the predestination of Jacob and Esau, ought to be understood.[48] Augustine

first decides that the thought of St. Paul means that every good desire comes from grace "so that no one glories in the merits of his works,"[49] and from a grace so infallible in its results that human liberty will never resist it. Then he asserts that this efficacious grace is not only necessary if we are to be able to act righteously, but also because, as a matter of fact, we would not even will to act without it: "That is why the saying of Scripture, 'There is no question of him who wills or of him who runs, but of God showing mercy,' must not be understood in this sense that without His aid we are unable to obtain what we will, but more exactly in the sense that we are not even able to will without an invitation from God."[50] This is the source of the great difficulty: How does the power to resist grace fit in with the absolute certitude of the result? Augustine's answer to this difficulty follows: There are many ways to invite a person to the faith. Since souls are differently disposed, God knows which invitation will be received favorably and which will not be so received by each person. Only they are the elect for whom God chooses an efficacious invitation, although God could convert all: "If God wished to have mercy on them, He could call them in a manner apt to move them so as to understand and follow. It is true, therefore, that many are called but few are chosen; they are chosen who are called in a fitting manner. They, however, who did not answer and did not obey their calling are not chosen because they did not follow although called. . . . Whomever He has mercy on He calls in such a way as He knows suitable for him that he not spurn the caller."[51]

Is there any trace of an irresistible grace here, or of that inevitable impulsion which has been the subject of so much discussion? And yet this is an explanation to which, in his last years, Augustine referred his adversaries. If it is understood one need not be uneasy about freedom of the will.

In 412 he reiterated this explanation in *On the Spirit and the Letter*. Every good act comes from God—but why? Because "God influences our willing and believing indirectly through our perceptions." He immediately explains the processes by which God prepares the efficacious warnings, now by His external providence, now by an interior light which presents the thought to us which will as a matter of fact save us, "whether externally through evangelical exhortations . . . or internally, where no one has power over what chances to come into his mind."[52] Even then freedom of choice remains untouched, "for to give consent or to withhold it is in the power of one's own will." That is the teaching of this work about which Augustine makes the following remark in the *Retractations*: "In this book, insofar as God helped me, I bitterly disputed against the enemies of the grace of God."[53]

In his last years, from 428 to 430, Augustine, far from forgetting this important theory, makes it the basis for all his teaching on predestination; a reading of *On the Gift of Perseverance* or *On the Predestination of the Saints* without this explanation is foredoomed to result in lack of comprehension. Without respite Augustine returns to this knowledge which precedes predestination, directs it, and insures its infallible outcome. If God did away with freedom of the will through an inevitable pressure, any necessity for the divine foreknowledge would disappear. But if the divine inspirations leave complete freedom to consent or to resist, one can see that before predestining such a grace God examines, in His foreknowledge, the effect which it will produce. Thus, speaking of efficacious grace, Augustine says: "God . . . has prepared these gifts of His . . . in His foreknowledge. Those whom He predestined, therefore, them also He called with that calling which I am not ashamed to mention often."[54] This choice of a calling foreseen to be efficacious is nothing else than predestination: "For the disposition of future works in His foreknowledge, which cannot be deceived or change, is absolute and nothing but predestination."[55] He describes this efficacious calling in the same work.[56] More briefly, he shows that God is the master of our heart and our thoughts: "Our heart and our thoughts are in His power."[57]

The same teaching appears in his last book, the *Incomplete Work against Julian*. When Julian accuses him of sacrificing freedom of choice, he always appeals to the foreknowledge of God to reconcile the two factors. He complains of those who mistake the meaning of this profound doctrine: "You must be forgiven because you err in a subject so deep. But far be it that the intention of the Almighty and All-knowing should be hindered by man. They seldom think of this important subject. . . . Admit the presence of grace: God calls one this way, another that way, each one as He deigns."[58] St. Prosper showed that he had understood his master well in replying thus to the objection that the reprobate were swept along in the grips of a fatalistic necessity: "They did not become subject to the necessity of perishing because they were not predestined, but they were not predestined precisely because it was known from their voluntary evil doing that they would be such in the future."[59]

Finally, this explanation harmonizes with the secondary theories of Augustine on the influence of grace. The first of these theories is the moral influence of victorious grace. Certainly the interior word of God to the soul (illumination and inspiration in the supernatural order) is a physical reality. But nowhere does Augustine represent it as an irresistible impulse imprinted by the stronger on the weaker. It is always an appeal, an invitation which allures and seeks to persuade.

He describes this gentle attraction under the graceful image of candy offered to a baby: "You show a green branch to a bird, and you attract it. Candy is shown to a child, and he is attracted; he is attracted by what he runs to, attracted by loving it."[60]

Another aspect of the influence of grace in St. Augustine's work is the preparation of the will. "The will is prepared by God," he says, following the translation of Proverbs 7:35 in the Septuagint. That is a consecrated formula to which he returns tirelessly. Father Rottmanner quite rightly adduces nearly thirty passages;[61] they could be multiplied. In the *Incomplete Work against Julian* alone there are eight.[62] Now Augustine always proclaims that this preparation leaves the soul master of its determination, at the same time assuring its consent: "Not because it is not in the choice of man's free will to believe or not to believe, but because in the elect the will is prepared by God."[63] Thus even after this preparation the will *can* refuse, but it will not refuse because God knows how to prepare it by the choice of His grace.

Thus is explained the important place attributed to external providence by Augustine. In a famous passage he describes this providential preservation of a pagan from sin as a grace of choice: "You were not an adulterer. . . . I ruled you for Myself; I preserved you for Myself. There was no companion lest you commit adultery; I brought it about that there was no companion. The time and place were inept; I brought it about that this was so. A companion was present, the time and place were apt, but I terrified you lest you consent. Recognize therefore the grace of Him to whom you are in debt even for what you did not commit."[64] Where is the irresistible impulse here?

In the *Confessions* St. Augustine does not tire of returning to the "marvelous and secret ways" which Providence used to convert him.[65] He reproaches Julian for not recognizing this providential action which prepares our virtues.[66] Augustine explains final perseverance, the most precious of all graces, precisely by this providential action which makes death coincide with the state of grace.[67]

In this manner an explanation can be given for the categorical statement that, when two men are equally tempted, there is no other reason why one resists the temptation while the other falls than the free choice of their wills: "Take two men who are equally disposed in body and soul. . . . If both are tried by the same temptation and one yields to it . . . while the other perseveres, . . . what is the cause of this if not their own free wills, since both had the same dispositions of body and soul?"[68]

This is the genuine Augustinian system of grace. We must now examine it to see whether it harmonizes with his explanations of original sin and predestination.

3. AUGUSTINIAN TEACHING ON ORIGINAL SIN

a. STATE OF ADAM BEFORE THE FALL

Augustine's conception of the state of Adam and his grace is a truly difficult one and the point of departure for many errors,

Jansenism among others. Baius, in fact, and his successors considered the immortality and other privileges of the state of original justice as a natural prerogative of humanity. They then concluded from this that, according to Augustine, freedom of choice had only existed in Paradise before the Fall and that it had been taken away by the sin of Adam with our nature's other endowments.[69] Here are some indications which will suffice to establish Augustine's true thought.

In answer to Pelagius, Augustine described the privileges of Adam: immortality, impassibility,[70] and integrity or preservation from all revolt of the senses.[71] Besides these gifts he attributes a miraculous knowledge to the first man[72] and a still more extraordinary gift, that of preservation from error.[73]

When he asserts the gratuitous and supernatural (*quoad modum*) character of these gifts Augustine has already refuted Baius. Thus, concerning the immortality, he states as clearly as the Greek Fathers—Athanasius, Cyril of Alexandria, or Gregory Nazianzen—that man, naturally mortal, owed his immortality to an admirable grace of the Creator: "That state was given to them from the tree of life by a marvelous grace of God."[74] "He was mortal because of the condition of his animal body, but immortal because of the gift of the Creator."[75] When, therefore, he says in these same works, speaking of the descendants of Adam, that "death . . . was justly inflicted . . . not by the law of nature but by the law of sin,"[76] theologians have understood his meaning perfectly and interpret it in this manner: Historically and in fact, only the sin of Adam has inflicted death on us because God had shielded us from the law of our nature. That is also true of the other gifts; St. Augustine recognized this when he asserted that God could have made the actual condition in which we are born like to the primitive condition of our first parents, a statement which by itself overthrows the whole system of Jansenism.[77]

The most precious gift of all, the sanctifying grace of divine adoption, was likewise conferred on Adam. Augustine announces this openly by saying that our Christian rebirth re-establishes in us the image of God which Adam had lost by his Fall[78] or by explaining that righteousness of the will was conferred on the first man by the charity of the Holy Spirit.[79] Since the supernatural character of divine adoption is such a basic point of Augustine's teaching, one is astonished that it could ever have been denied. When he proves that this adoption is an incomparable grace, he does not prove it by our present state of being sinners (the Jansenist system), but by the universal and profound reasoning that we are creatures and that this adoption divinizes us, making us partakers of the divine nature. There is a magnificent explanation of this adoption in *Against Faustus*: "We, however, . . . are creatures which He had not begotten, but made. Therefore He adopted us that He might make us brethren of Christ according to His pattern. . . . Since we were not born of Him, but created and formed, He begot us by His word and His grace that we might be His sons."[80] Again he says: "The Son of God came that . . . He might enable us who were the sons of men to become the sons of God . . . that we might become partakers of His own nature."[81]

Concerning actual grace, after having taught that Adam had received it in a very high degree,[82] Augustine develops an important difference between the grace of Adam and that of his redeemed children. The grace received by Adam conferred on him the power of perseverance ("a help without which he could not persevere"); his Christian children who in fact are saved, on the contrary, receive perseverance itself ("the help by which they persevere"). The Jansenists concluded from this that there was an essential difference between Adam's grace and ours: the grace of Adam allowed the freedom of resisting while, on the contrary, it necessarily produces its effect since the Fall. In the terrestrial Paradise the Molinist system of grace was in operation; in fallen nature, however, there is no more liberty and no more sufficient grace.

This interpretation takes into consideration neither St. Augustine's purpose in this passage nor his most explicit explanations. (1) His purpose is not to explain every grace, but especially the gift of perseverance. Comparing, then, the grace of Adam under this aspect with that of Christians who really persevere, martyrs for example, he makes the observation that Adam had received only the power of perseverance, if he so willed, while the martyr has received the efficacious grace of perseverance. (2) In his explanations, far from denying that freedom of choice is not in keeping with the grace of the redeemed, he explicitly affirms it.[83] He merely notes that we need a stronger grace than that of the terrestrial Paradise in order that our freedom of choice triumph over the rebellion from which Adam was preserved: "A greater freedom of choice is necessary against so many great temptations."[84]

b. ORIGINAL SIN

St. Augustine was not the first to maintain the existence of original sin, but he did, in the dogma of the original Fall, distinguish with more sharpness and insistence than his predecessors the punishment and the guilt—the punishment which took away from his descendants all the privileges conferred on Adam; the guilt which consists in this that the sin of Adam, the cause of this Fall, although not personally committed by his descendants, is nevertheless in a certain measure imputed to them in virtue of the moral union established by God between the head of the human family and his descendants.

To pretend that Augustine was the innovator of this doctrine and that before him the Fathers only asserted the punishment of Adam's sin without speaking of its guilt is a historical error which, in our opinion, is quite evident. Disputes can arise about the mind of this or that individual pre-Augustinian Father, but taken collectively any doubt is impossible. The Protestant Seeberg and many others announce this fact and give references to Tertullian, Commodianus, St. Cyprian, and St. Ambrose.[85] It is truly the guilt, the moral corruption, and not only the punishment and sorrow which they stress: "No one born under sin could be saved since the very heredity of our evil condition has bound him to the fault."[86] This precious text gives a yet deeper meaning to these words: "Adam lived and in him we all lived. Adam perished and in him we all perished."[87] It also explains this statement: "Before we are born we are tainted with contagion."[88] Since Augustine adduced such texts in his answer to Julian,[89] it is hard to understand that some critics today still dare to accuse him of having introduced the first notions of guilt and sin into the original Fall. Dorner himself has explicitly refuted this unbelievable assertion.[90]

The truth lies in this apt remark of Turmel (a remark too often forgotten by its author):[91] Original sin, sin though it is, has a nature essentially different from other faults; it does not require a personal will-act of Adam's descendants for them to incur responsibility for the fault of their progenitor which is morally imputed to them. The older Fathers, especially the Greeks, insisted on this penal and afflictive aspect which is the first to be noticed, while Augustine was led by the Pelagian polemic (and only by it) to place the emphasis on the moral aspect of the sin of the human race in Adam.

C. ROLE OF CONCUPISCENCE IN SIN

At first sight and to judge by the apparent wording of certain formulas, one would be tempted to state that Augustine identified original sin with concupiscence, as Turmel and many others have done.[92] But a comparison of these texts with others leads to an entirely different conclusion. According to the great doctor, concupiscence is only one of the effects of the Fall of our ancestor, although it is quite intimately connected with original sin. Here, especially, it is not a question of spinning hypotheses but of considering and harmonizing all the texts.

He himself warns us that concupiscence is original sin in the same way that ignorance or even death is, that is, in virtue of that metonymy which identifies effects with their cause. (There is this difference: concupiscence, being an inclination to sin, manifests the trait of moral imperfection which gives more reason for labeling it sin.) This is so true that the most faithful of Augustine's disciples in the Middle Ages defined original sin in terms of both ignorance and concupiscence: "Original sin is concupiscence after evil and ignorance of good."[93] But no one dares to say that, according to Augustine, ignorance is a constitutive element of original sin.

Moreover, he always vigorously upheld these two assertions: Concupiscence remains in its entirety after baptism; original sin nevertheless is totally effaced and destroyed.[94] Now, if original sin is identified with concupiscence, how can it be effaced while concupiscence remains just as it was before? One might answer that it is no longer imputed, quoting Augustine's statement: "It . . . is forgiven so . . . as to be no longer a sin."[95] These terms are understandable if concupiscence is not sin but an adjunct, an effect of sin confused with it in terminology. But if it is nothing but sin in all its reality, it is clear that the entire sin remains, except that God would not impute it to us any longer. This, however, is the very interpretation (later to become Protestant teaching) against which Augustine is protesting in this passage. He was accused of saying that baptism does not really take away this sin: "It does not take away sins, but scrapes them off."[96] He declares that this is a calumny. Yet it is claimed that in the same passage he would admit that the entire sin remains, though no longer imputable! Augustine seems, however, to come to this clear conclusion: If the nonimputation of concupiscence totally destroys the entire sin, then, since concupiscence remains, the only explanation must be that sin is not constituted by concupiscence but by the moral imputation of concupiscence.

This is precisely the explanation which Augustine gives formally and with great profundity. He explicitly distinguishes two quite different elements in concupiscence. One is the physical reality of concupiscence (the inclination towards evil); the other is the guilt of concupiscence, that is, the moral imputability of concupiscence. This latter, in other words, is our culpability in being subject to the rebellion of the senses, for it is our sin, imputed to all of us who are children of Adam for having lost the state of innocence which was destined for us in the beginning. This moral imputability of concupiscence, so often misunderstood, is therefore that share of responsibility morally imputed to each child of Adam in virtue of which God can say to him: "It is your own fault (not personally committed, but the fault of your family which has been justly visited upon you) if you are subject to a rebellion from which I wished to spare you." Thus original sin is not properly constituted by concupiscence in itself (Augustine positively declared that God could create an innocent man with concupiscence, and this at the close of his life),[97] but it consists only in this, that we are responsible for the presence of this evil within us, that is, that by our (moral) participation in the sin of Adam we are the authors of this concupiscence. As long as this moral union of our responsibility is joined to that of Adam, God will see in us, with a legitimate displeasure and hostility, this rebellion of the senses. (The same must be said of ignorance and death.) This moral voluntareity, this culpability, is by itself precisely and formally the whole essence of original sin; concupiscence, ignorance, and so forth are properly its effects. Thus, when God in baptism pardons this moral voluntareity which makes us responsible for the sin of Adam, original sin is totally forgiven. Concupiscence, however, remains, but it no longer implies guilt in us since the sin has been forgiven: "It is . . . forgiven so . . . as to be no longer a sin."[98]

Not only is there no contradiction, but rather perfect harmony with Augustine's general theory according to which every sin belongs essentially to the moral order. Consequently sin, a transgression of the divine law (committed personally or in moral union with another person), can never consist in such a purely physical element as concupiscence which is independent of our free will.

Augustine himself makes the precise application of this principle to original sin. In a passage the more authoritative because it was written at the end of his life he states that every sin is in the will, that original sin is no exception, that it actually did not exist in its physical reality except in the will of Adam, although his descendants "are implicated in his culpability," and that concupiscence is an effect.[99] (He says that it is formally a punishment.) Here is the close of the passage (which should be read all the way through): "As if the sin which we say that infants derive from Adam through their origin, that is, because implicated in his culpability and consequently subject to punishment, could be anywhere but in the will, since it was committed by the will when the divine precept was transgressed."[100] It is not possible to say that here there is question of concupiscence after baptism[101] since Augustine is explaining precisely how there can be sin in infants before baptism.

It is, moreover, beyond all controversy that, when explaining the transmission of original sin, Augustine's expressions exaggerate the role of concupiscence. Since sense pleasure ordinarily enters into human generation, he seems to say that it is the necessary condition for the transmission of the original stain which touches the flesh even before it taints the soul. This somewhat material conception of original sin was expressed quite crudely by his disciple Fulgentius[102] and adopted into early Scholasticism by Peter Lombard: "The cause of original sin lies in the manifold defects of the flesh, especially in a pollution which the body, when it is conceived, contracts from the parents in the heat of intercourse and sexual concupiscence."[103] However, a more attentive study, especially of a passage in the *Incomplete Work Against Julian*, does away with this gross interpretation.[104] There Augustine has recourse to a moral union between Adam and us similar to the solidarity which unites us to Christ the Savior: "Because they were clothed with the flesh of him who sinned in his will they contract from him the responsibility for sin . . . just as children who put on Christ . . . receive from Him a participation in justice."[105] The great doctors, St. Thomas,[106] St. Bonaventure,[107] and their successors for example, were able to surmise that the mere fact of being born a child of Adam through natural generation makes the human person responsible (in the degree set forth) for the sin of his ancestor and for his own abasement. But a slow and continuous elaboration was yet necessary, and this is one of the points in which the progress or clarification of dogma stands out most clearly.

d. DAMNATION, THE CONSEQUENCE OF ORIGINAL SIN

A more serious exaggeration made by Augustine concerns the very degree in which the sin of Adam is transmitted to his descendants, that is, the inmost nature of the damnation of the children of Adam. He is often accused of overburdening fallen humanity with terrifying anathemas. He was the first who used φύραμα in the pejorative sense of *dough* or *mass*,[108] and he calls the line of Adam a mass of slime; a mass of sin, of sins, of iniquity; a mass of wrath, of death, of damnation, of offense; a mass totally vitiated, damnable, damned.[109] But all this constitutes the dogma of the Fall, not its explanation. If there is sin, there is damnation, and that to the same degree in which there is sin; no Catholic can doubt this. But are this sin and damnation of the same nature as personal sin and the damnation which it merits? Expressions which are at first sight too severe teach us nothing about Augustine's thought; that must be sought for in his theory about the fate of infants who have died without baptism. There, despite the efforts of certain theologians and even of the great Scholastic doctors to soften his statements, his theory is really too severe, although less cruel than some have thought.

His theory is too severe, for he consigns these souls to hell and condemns them to eternal punishment there. In the beginning he hesitated or even granted the possibility of an intermediate place between heaven and hell,[110] but later his doubts are resolved and he always speaks of the punishment which they have to suffer. Even in *Letter 166*, although he confesses his embarrassment: "When the question of the punishment of infants comes up I am pressed by difficulties and hardly know what to say," he does not hesitate about the existence of such a punishment, "whither they are necessarily taken."[111]

His theory is less cruel than has been thought, for he always proclaimed the mildness of this punishment; he calls it the "gentlest punishment,"[112] the "lightest condemnation."[113] And this is not to be understood merely in comparison to the punishment of the other souls in hell, for Augustine immediately adds that he does not dare to decide whether their lot is not preferable to simple annihilation: "I do not dare to say, although I cannot determine what type of place it will be, whether it would be better for them to be annihilated than to be there."[114] Augustine is therefore less severe than Schmid believes him to be.[115] It remains certain that in his thought the damnation due to original sin alone is essentially different from that which personal sins merit. Theology has progressed since then and expressed in clearer terms the thesis that original sin deprives one solely of supernatural benefits, leaving nature intact.

c. NUMBER OF HEREDITARY SINS

Augustine did not maintain that sins other than Adam's are transmitted, although one must remember that, for him, it is not unlikely that children have the iniquities of their parents: "That infants are also bound by the sins of their parents, not only their first parents but also their own from whom they were born, is not at all unlikely."[116] Here are the limitations which he adds to this strange opinion. (1) These sins are hereditary only to the third generation, since the passages of the Old Testament on which this theory rests (Deut. 5:9) allow this reservation. (2) Although these parental sins create a true responsibility, they cannot corrupt human nature as the sin of Adam did: "Although they cannot change nature in that way, they nevertheless make one's children responsible for them unless a gratuitous grace . . . intervenes."[117] (3) These hereditary sins are so different from the sin of Adam that the latter alone requires a Redeemer.[118] Hardly any of St. Augustine's disciples borrowed this error from him; St. Gregory the Great, however, can be cited.[119]

4. AUGUSTINIAN PREDESTINATION

a. EXPLANATION OF THE PROBLEM

To understand Augustine's attitude it will be better to compare the various answers which have been made since his time to the question he raised. The problem of predestination amounts to this: Does God, in His creative decree and before any act of human liberty, determine by an immutable choice the elect and the reprobate? Must the elect during eternity thank God for having rewarded their merits or must they also thank Him for having, before any meritorious act on their part, chosen them to merit this reward? Three answers have been given to the above question.

(1) *Semipelagian answer.* The Semipelagian system decides the problem in favor of man. God predestines everyone equally to salvation and gives to all an equal measure of graces. Only the free will of man, by resisting or consenting to grace, decides whether one will be saved or lost. All special predestination, if it is not founded on the real or conditional merit of the elect, would be opposed to the justice of God and to human liberty. They go so far as to insinuate (and later theologians were to repeat this) that the number of the elect is neither determined nor certain.

(2) *Predestinarian answer.* The predestinarian system (which the Semipelagians attributed to St. Augustine and which others think is really to be found in his writings) asserts not only a preferential choice of the elect by God from all eternity (rightly understood, this is the Catholic dogma), but at the same time the predestination of the reprobate to hell and the absolute powerlessness of both classes to escape from the irresistible impulse which leads them on to either good or evil. These two assertions constitute the essential character of the predestinarianism attributed to St. Augustine by the Semipelagians and really taught by Calvin.

(3) *Catholic answer.* Midway between these two extreme opinions, the Catholic dogma, which was not fabricated but only formulated by Augustine, simultaneously asserts these two truths: The eternal choice of the elect by God is very real, very gratuitous, and constitutes the grace of graces; this decree, however, does not destroy the divine will to save all men and moreover is realized only through human freedom of choice, leaving full power to the elect to fall and to the non-elect to rise again.

b. SOLUTION OF ST. AUGUSTINE

Does this last system truly represent the thought of Augustine? Our answer will consist in an analysis of the divine decree as Augustine understood it.

(1) *Knowledge of God before the decree of predestination.* Before any divine decree to create the world the infinite knowledge of God presents to Him all the graces and different series of graces which He can prepare for each soul, along with the consent or the refusal which would follow in each circumstance —and that in millions and millions of possible combinations. Thus He sees that St. Peter, if he had received a different grace, would not have been converted and Judas, if a different divine call had sounded in his heart, would have done penance and been saved.

Our actual world, with all its history from Adam to the Last Judgment, is only one of millions and millions of worlds which God could have brought into being. Among these worlds there are some in which all would be saved, others in which all would be lost, and others in which the damned and elect are mixed. For each man in particular there is in the mind of God an unlimited number of possibilities, some of virtue and salvation, others of crime and condemnation; and God will be free, in choosing such a world and such a series of graces, to determine the future history and final destiny of each soul. This is the knowledge which, according to Augustine, precedes and enlightens the choice of God. If He had wished to save Judas "means were not lacking," for He saw the grace which would save him; He was able to choose it, but He preferred another.[120] This knowledge showing Him the different ways of saving Judas was not the knowledge of vision which beholds only future events (the conversion of Judas was never a future event), but another type of knowledge—whatever name it is given—whose object embraces the conditional responses of each free will to each call from God. Without this knowledge neither Augustine nor predestination can be understood.[121]

(2) *Tenor of the divine decree.* Faced with all these possible

worlds, God, by an absolutely free act, decides to bring this actual world into existence just as it appeared in the midst of the possible worlds with all the circumstances of its historical evolution, with all the graces which in fact have been or will be distributed until the end of the world, and finally with all the elect and reprobate who God foresaw must exist in it once He really created it. Now, according to Augustine and the Catholic faith as formulated by him, in this decree of complex unity an analysis will disclose two elements between which an essential distinction must be drawn.

The first element of this decree is the certain determination of the elect in virtue of an entirely gratuitous benevolence (before any merits) in their regard. God, in fact, in decreeing to create this world and to give this series of graces with this succession of circumstances which will lead freely but infallibly to such and such results (the despair of Judas and the repentance of Peter), decides at the same time the name, the place, and the number of all the citizens of the future Jerusalem. The following factors comprise Augustinian predestination: (1) The election according to His purpose of which Augustine spoke so frequently.[122] (2) God's immutable choice which obliges one to state: "The number of the elect is certain and will neither be increased nor decreased."[123] It is evident, in fact, that only those will be saved who God knows will wish to cooperate with the grace decreed for them. The list of the elect and the reprobate is closed, and known only to the eyes of God. Although all the elect *could* fall and the non-predestined *could* be converted, as a matter of fact none of the elect will wish to be lost and none of the reprobate will wish to yield to grace. No one will pass from one rank into the other. To say with Cassian that Judas was of the number of the elect before his fall is to deny the infallibility of God's knowledge. (3) This election is the gratuitous gift above all others which, far from being merited, is the source of all merit, the gift of gifts, in virtue of which "even man's merit is a gratuitous gift."[124] Again "grace is not due to our merit but our merit is due to grace."[125] No one could have merited this election, for God could, among the other possible worlds, have chosen one of them in which other series of graces would have led to other results. He saw a world where Peter would have remained impenitent and Judas would have been converted. It is, therefore, *prior* to any merit of Peter and any fault of Judas that God decided to give them the graces which saved Peter and not Judas. God does not wish to give paradise to anyone gratuitously; He does, however, very gratuitously give Peter the graces with which He knows that Peter will be saved. (4) It is a predestination which forces one to say that neither God nor Jesus Christ had the absolute will to save all men. God could, if He had willed, have chosen a world where all souls would be saved. "He could have saved Judas," says Augustine, "but He did not will to."[126] "He certainly could have converted the wicked. Why did He not do it? Because He did not will to. Why did He not will to? That is His own mystery."[127] (5) Predestination is the mystery of mysteries not because it interferes with freedom of choice but because there is only one response Augustine could give to this question: "Why did God, when He saw that Judas could have been saved with another grace, not give it to him?" Augustine's answer is: "O the depths . . ." (Rom. 11:33).[128]

One should notice at this point that this theory of predestination proposed by Augustine is exactly the same as the Catholic dogma which all the schools teach under this undisputed formula: Predestination taken as a whole is absolutely gratuitous (before any merits). This point is worth mentioning because many have seen in these truths only an expression of Augustine's severity. All the schools also agree in their proclamation of the second element in the divine decree.

The second element is the sincere will of God to give all men the power of saving themselves and the freedom of damning themselves. In the elect there is no irresistible impulse of grace towards paradise; in the wicked, no obduracy towards damnation. According to Augustine, God in His creative decree has explicitly excluded every set of events in which grace would take away man's liberty and every situation in which man would not have the means to resist sin. That is the essential point of the system:

by it he refutes the predestinarian heresy which has been ascribed to him. Indisputably there is absolute certainty that only the elect will wish to be saved. But to say that there is no possibility of salvation for the others is contrary to the uninterrupted teaching of Augustine in his last works as well as his early ones. A few indications will be sufficient.

In *On Genesis Against the Manicheans* he had said: "All men can be saved, if they wish it."[129] "A work of his youth!" one might say, "he changed his mind." But later, when the Pelagians made use of this passage, did he retract it? Just the opposite, for in the *Retractations* he makes this strong statement: "It is absolutely true that all men can do this, if they wish, but their will is prepared by the Lord."[130] This preparation is what he has explained to Simplicianus: "Whomever He has mercy on He calls in such a way as He knows suitable for him that he not spurn the caller."[131] In his last volume, the *Incomplete Work Against Julian*, we find the same assertion: "Man can will good, but his will is prepared by the Lord."[132] In his sermons Augustine does not only say: "Not knowing whether you are predestined, struggle as if you were," but he explicitly adds: "It depends on you to become one of the elect." An example is this: "You have received the power to take your place on the right hand of the Lord, that is, to become a son of God."[133] "It is now in your power . . . to choose which of these two [elect or reprobate] you wish to be. . . . Choose while there is time."[134]

An objection can be raised based on the Augustinian axiom proved above: "The lists of the elect and the reprobate are closed." Now, if anyone at all could pass from one rank to another, why will some not upset the divine plan? Such an objection shows that one has forgotten Augustine's famous explanation. When God made His plan "He prepared the wills"; He knew infallibly, before His choice, what would be the response of the wills of men to His graces. No one will pass from one rank into the other— not because no one could, but because no one will wish to. God knows that. Thus I cannot make God destine another series of graces for me than the one which He has determined; however, if I am not saved with these graces it will be not because I was not able, but because I did not will it.

Thus the much-disputed formula, "If you are not predestined, bring it about that you will be," must be explained. Under this form and taken in its strict meaning, Rottmanner says quite rightly that it is not Augustinian.[135] I add that it would only be an irrational paradox, since its meaning would be: "If God knows infallibly that you will be damned, make Him know the opposite." The theory contradicts itself. But this formula (although it is too paradoxical and, I repeat, should be abandoned) can be used to explain in a pointed manner the absolute possibility for each person to become one of the elect. And that, in the fullest sense, is an Augustinian dogma: "Who are the elect? You, if you wish."[136] "Are you not yet attracted? Pray that you may be."[137] "It is prepared for others. Become like others and it is prepared for you."[138]

Such are the two essential elements of Augustinian and Catholic teaching on predestination. This is the dogma common to all Catholic schools (save for the mode of reconciliation concerning which the Church allows complete freedom). Once these two points are settled, the long debates of the theologians on predestination before or after merits are far less important than many people think. We will say enough about this to make Augustine's position in this dispute clear.

(3) *The divine motives of the decree.* What is the position of Augustine in the controversy whether special predestination to heavenly glory comes before or after merits? Since the sixteenth century Thomists and Augustinians claim the Doctor of Hippo as a proponent of the strict system and some illustrious defenders of intermediary knowledge (*scientia media*) follow them, as Bellarmine[139] and Suarez.[140] Others, though not followers of that school, at least concede that St. Augustine taught their doctrine.[141] The partisans of the milder system are, nevertheless, still in the majority, and most of them think that they are faithful to the teaching of Augustine. Where is the truth?

(a) *True meaning of the problem.* Note first of all that very often the problem is poorly proposed. On the one hand, certain defenders of predestination after merits have imagined that God decides to give such a series of graces without knowing the effect which they will produce, and that only after His decree will He see the future consent or refusal which will merit heaven or hell. This shows a basic and serious misunderstanding of the dogma of the gratuitous gift made to the elect: God would wait on our decisions, which is a Semipelagian theory. On the other hand, the partisans of predestination before merits often wish to make only this simple statement: God, before knowing the conversion of Peter in the knowledge of vision, knew and willed this conversion; He decided to give the grace which would save him and the glory which he would merit through this grace. In his learned study of predestination, the Benedictine Janssens does not wish to prove, it seems, or at least he does not prove more than this one fact.[142] The three Benedictine principles which he enunciates[143] are equally true in all Catholic systems, for they present only the pure doctrine: all schools must hold it and Molina, far from denying it as many suppose, systematized the theory of intermediary knowledge only to reconcile this dogma with human liberty. According to both Molinism and Augustine, God, before knowing the final perseverance of Peter in the knowledge of vision, decides to give him this grace which He knows (through intermediary knowledge) must result in this perseverance. By that same act, therefore, He decides, before any merit on Peter's part, that Peter will merit paradise.

Here, then, is the true aspect of the problem which must be solved. When God, from all possible worlds, decreed independently of any merit to create this one with this series of determined graces and this series of meritorious acts and this series of souls freely saved or lost, was there among these three inseparably connected objects one which favorably attracted the complacency and the will of God, one whose realization was His primary intention, the purpose for which He acted? For example, God has chosen the series of graces which He infallibly saw linked to the conversion and salvation of Peter. Was this choice dictated to

God because He willed the salvation of Peter absolutely, or did He rather, while loving his salvation, have another motive for creating this world and giving this series of graces?

(b) *The two systems.* According to the partisans of predestination before merits, God, prior to this whole series of elect, has loved and willed precisely this celestial Jerusalem with the determined number of elect and the celestial hierarchy which will result from the history of our world. It is through love for these elect that He has chosen the actual series of graces and if, for example, He had foreseen that these graces would not have saved Peter or any other of the elect in this world, He was prepared to choose another series which would have been efficacious.

The thorn in this system is the reprobate. Logically one must conclude—so it seems to the adversaries—that God has chosen for them graces previously foreseen to be inefficacious precisely because they would not correspond with them. If He had foreseen that Judas would allow himself to be converted by these graces, He was prepared to choose another series which he would resist. This is a hard saying.

According to the Molinists, on the other hand, when God decided to create this world with this precise series of graces which He knew must prepare such a hierarchy of elect, He did not have the glory and salvation of these elect as His primary and absolute intention. While undoubtedly giving these graces only for salvation, He always loves in a particular way those who by their faithfulness are saved with them. And finally, He would not have changed the series of these graces if He had foreseen that Judas would be converted or that Peter would not rise again. God, in choosing this world, loves above all every manifestation of His divine attributes in the evolution of the graces given to humanity. He willed, for example, to render the divine love resplendent in Christ's acceptance of the kiss of Judas and in Jesus' affectionate look at Peter, and He would have been prepared to give these graces even if Peter had resisted and Judas yielded to such great love.

(c) *Attitude of St. Augustine.* Which of these two systems did

Augustine adopt? The text demands this reply: He chose neither of them. In his time this very subtle and basically secondary question had not yet been raised. The dogma alone was in question. Did it, or did it not, depend on God alone (without any merit of man) to choose the grace of Peter, this grace which God infallibly sees linked to his salvation, and to choose for Judas this grace which He knows must be obstinately refused, although other graces would have found Judas docile and Peter obstinate? This is the dogma which all Catholics have recognized as the true Pauline tradition.

The passages from Augustine's works *On the Predestination of the Saints* and *On the Gift of Perseverance*, according to Rott-manner's learned compilation, state this much (and that is a great deal), but they do not state and do not even attempt to state anything else. The holy doctor affirms this quite clearly: "By this preaching of predestination only that most pernicious error is overthrown whereby it is said that the grace of God is given according to our merits."[144] The remark must also be made that the great doctor knew only one predestination, that of grace, and of efficacious grace.[145]

Indirectly, however, do not Augustine's expressions favor the strict opinion? De San's exhaustive study casts serious doubts on this fact.[146]

For my part, I believe that the debate taken objectively and in itself, is well-nigh insoluble, since Augustine never imagined any further question beyond the disputed dogma. But when the most important adversaries concede that St. Augustine taught the milder system not only in 397[147] but also in 412[148] and 416,[149] and when in the next place they claim that he wavered after 418, becoming more and more strict and even adopting predestinarianism, I maintain that this thesis is absolutely contrary to the texts and the assertions of St. Augustine. (1) The earlier texts, even of 397 (*On Various Questions for Simplicianus*), are as affirmative and categorical as those of 428 or 429. Loofs and Reuter have proved that. (2) Not only did Augustine never retract his views on predestination, but he made precise references to the work of 397 even in his last days.[150] Elsewhere he presumes that his various works are in accord on this point. In 429 he stresses the agreement between the letter to Paulinus of 417, the one (quite strict) to Sixtus in 418, and his actual teaching.[151] (3) In his last works, for example *On the Predestination of the Saints* (428–429),[152] he forcefully repeats that the divine foreknowledge precedes and illumines predestination and that there is no predestination in God to sin, but only a foreknowledge of it. This is the same as saying that God, before beholding the free play of the will, does not have a formal and absolute intention of exercising His vindictive justice, of preparing and obtaining merits for reward or sins for punishment. An examination of his theory about Adam in 421 forces one to conclude that he never made greater allowances for merits: "God would have willed to preserve . . . the first man if . . . He had foreknown that man would have had a steadfast will. But because He foresaw that man was to misuse his freedom of choice. . . ."[153]

5. AUGUSTINIAN THEORIES IN APPARENT OPPOSITION TO THE ABOVE SYSTEM

The explanation of St. Augustine's system on grace would be incomplete if one did not explain the principal assertions which seem to deny freedom of choice and subject fallen man to the most absolute form of divine determinism. Most frequently these difficulties are purely verbal. Objections are fabricated from expressions taken in their actual, literal meaning. These expressions the Doctor of Hippo was using in an entirely different sense, which he himself had explicitly indicated. Briefly, for a complete understanding of his teaching, one must first make himself an Augustinian dictionary, working not from *a priori* conceptions, but according to Augustine's own indications. It is a long and difficult task, but how many prejudices would be brushed aside by it! We can give only a few examples of this here.

Was Augustine wrong in using these words in a different

meaning than they originally had? One answer might be that in his time terminology was vaguer and more inaccurate, and that the complexity of the problems inevitably opened the door to a certain obscurity of expression. But the question is not to decide whether he was wrong or right, but whether he really acted in this way. It must be stated frankly at the outset that Augustine's literary method of emphasizing his doctrine by expressions which far overreach it, resulting in troublesome paradoxes, has often obscured his teaching and caused distaste in many minds. That is the explanation of a very important and often misunderstood fact. Later theologians have more than once corrected the exaggerated formulas of the African Doctor, at the same time keeping the true thought of these expressions as he had clearly explained it. No one today, for example, would say that freedom of choice was lost through the Fall of Adam. And there is one thing more: The Church has condemned some propositions taken verbatim from Augustine, even though these were sanctioned by the Council of Orange. These condemned propositions had been used in a meaning other than that which Augustine intended.[154]

a. FIRST THEORY: FREEDOM OF CHOICE LOST THROUGH THE FALL

Augustine teaches in his later works that "man lost freedom of choice through the Fall."[155] The answer to this is easy. Augustine explains most explicitly that this liberty which was lost is not the power to choose between good and evil as one pleases (a power which we still have and without which, he says, man could not even sin). It is rather that original perfection of the will freeing it from concupiscence, which Adam had received and which, Augustine says, alone merits the beautiful name of freedom in its fullest meaning: "Who of us would say that freedom of choice was lost to the human race by the sin of the first man? Freedom indeed was lost through sin, but it was that freedom which existed in Paradise, to have full righteousness with immortality. . . . For freedom of choice has not been lost in the sinner to this extent that by it men sin, especially they who sin with delight."[156]

Besides, when these expressions are brought up the objector

forgets that they are taken not only from his later works but also from the earlier when he was very favorable to human liberty. It was in 388 that Augustine had already stated in terms which surpassed the force he was to use on later occasions: "The man who has refused to act rightly when he could loses the power when he wishes to have it."[157] Are these words of 388 compatible with human liberty? If they are not, let there be no more talk of determinism creeping in at the end of his life, for it was present through the whole of it. And if they are compatible, how can milder expressions in later works be irreconcilable with liberty?

b. SECOND THEORY: NECESSITY OF SIN IN FALLEN MAN

Augustine maintains that in fallen man there are absolutely necessary sins, a necessity of sinning. He proves this by concupiscence, which is both an inevitable sin and a source of sin.[158]

Augustine, however, is careful to explain that in this passage he does not call the faults for which we are responsible and which God can punish necessary sins, but rather the unregulated desires of the senses which are a shameful, though inculpable, decadence in formerly innocent human nature. Pelagius and Julian exalted human nature and its power to arrive at absolute perfection, dispassionateness, and sinlessness. Augustine raises an objection based on the moral deformity of these involuntary rebellions of nature; only in heaven will our freedom of choice be liberated from these disorders which later Scholasticism was to entitle material sins.[159] One may be astonished at such sweeping terminology. One may accuse Augustine's interpretation of too great subtlety in distinguishing two divine laws: the one, "You shall not follow your desires," forbidding voluntary sins, that is, consent to the desires of concupiscence; the other, "You shall not lust," condemning even indeliberate excitations, a law which is incapable of realization on this earth, but whose violation will not be personally imputed to us nor visited upon us.[160]

Once these explanations are proposed, it becomes impossible to confuse Augustine's theory with that of Baius which is condemned by the Church.[161] The resemblance is merely verbal: Baius understands that the involuntary desires of concupiscence constitute so many personal sins, "a true disobedience to the law," for each of which unbelievers and sinners will be judged and punished in hell.[162]

Therefore: (1) Leaving aside original sin which is in a class by itself (although physically inescapable for the descendants of Adam, it is voluntary only in a moral sense and that through an extension of the free choice of the head of the family), every personal sin is essentially free according to Augustine and presumes the complete power of not committing it. (2) The same thing applies to ignorance: When it does not excuse from sin the reason is that it is voluntary and culpable in itself. At the beginning (388–395) he wrote: "Faults are not imputed to you because you are in ignorance against your will, but because you neglect to seek the knowledge you do not possess. Nor is it a fault that you do not bind up your wounded members, but that you contemn Him who wishes to heal them."[163] Sin, therefore, consists in a disregard for grace. Nor can one maintain that this passage is virtually retracted in later works, for quite the contrary is true. In 415, in the heat of the Pelagian controversy, he cites this passage word for word (even separating it from the phrases which follow it)[164] and corroborates its worth in reconciling freedom of choice and grace. In 426–427 the *Retractations* change nothing in this text, although they insist on the (material) sins of concupiscence and ignorance.[165] (3) Thus St. Augustine taught to the very end that no commandment of God is impossible. His celebrated formula in *On Nature and Grace* remains the perfect expression of his thought to the very end: "Therefore God does not command impossibilities, but when He commands He counsels you to do what you can for yourself and to ask His aid in what you cannot do."[166]

C. THIRD THEORY: GOD'S GRACE IS INVINCIBLE

An Augustinian maxim which is repeated under hundreds of forms is that the grace of God is invincible; one cannot resist the will of God; one cannot stay His omnipotence. "The weakness of the human will is helped by the fact that it is unavoidably and insuperably influenced by divine grace." [167]

Here again a comprehensive understanding of Augustinian vocabulary will explain everything. If *grace* means, as in our theological language, any divine inspiration, Augustine would be a Jansenist. But the *grace* which Augustine speaks of against the Pelagians is almost always, and especially here (in *On Punishment and Grace*, which treats solely of final perseverance and of the celebrated *auxilium quo*) only efficacious grace, that which God gives knowing that it will surely meet with acceptance. Now this grace or this series of graces, although not irresistible, in fact will always be victorious. This is the infallibility of the divine success which Augustine consistently explains by remarkably accurate expressions: "No man's will resists God when He wills to give salvation. For to will or not to will is in the power of the one who wills or does not will in such a way as not to impede the divine will." [168] With this grace man does not resist, he does not hinder, he does not overcome; but he can resist, he can hinder, he can overcome because he can will not to do it. If Augustine sometimes says that man cannot resist the will of God, [169] he means that freedom of choice cannot hinder God from choosing among His graces that one which will in fact meet with acceptance.

d. FOURTH THEORY: SALVATION EFFECTED ENTIRELY BY GOD

At the end of his life Augustine attributes everything in the work of salvation to God. He seems to retract, therefore, all his earlier teaching on the role of freedom of choice. An example is this: "All is ascribed to God lest anyone grow proud." [170] Or: "Everything should be attributed to God." [171]

Again the difficulty lies in a misunderstanding of Augustinian language. "To ascribe all to God" does not deny man's action, but rather the fact that this action can accomplish nothing without grace, not even a good desire or a very short prayer. The meaning of this expression in the Augustinian theory (which is the same as the Catholic teaching here) is that each of the elect in heaven must say: "There is not a single good act in my life for which I do not owe thanks to God." In reality this theory is opposed to Augustine's early error which attributed the beginning of faith to free will. In 397 he received an understanding of the text: "What do you have that you have not received?" From then on there was no further variation in his teaching. He saw that everything comes from God. But far from denying the part of man and his merits, he asserted their importance to the very end of his life in even his most rigorous works.[172]

e. FIFTH THEORY: GRACE NOT GIVEN TO ALL MEN

Augustine did not only assert that grace was gratuitous, but also that God, at His pleasure and without injustice, absolutely refuses it to many men. For example: "We know it is not given to all men. . . . We know that those who do not receive grace are passed over by a just judgment of God."[173]

That is true, but what, according to Augustine, is the kind of grace which God refuses? It is only efficacious grace (of faith for adults, of baptism for infants). But who doubts that God does not give efficacious grace to all? This is one of the most overlooked aspects of Augustine's teaching. Against Pelagius who attributed the choice of good to freedom of will alone, Augustine wished to stress God's sovereign dominion over this determination and His influence which prepares it at His pleasure by choosing a grace whose infallible result is foreseen. It is this grace which makes us will to act; it is this which is refused or given according to the free choice of God alone. As for those who have not received this special gift, Augustine, far from depriving them of other sufficient graces, explicitly presumes the presence of these gifts when he distinguishes the different types of divine callings or appeals and when he attributes damnation to the will's resistance.

f. SIXTH THEORY: GOD WILLS TO SAVE ONLY THE ELECT

The divine will to save all men (according to I Tim. 2:4), first asserted by Augustine in 412,[174] was later modified and progressively confined to very narrow limits. He no longer admits that God wishes to save all men, but only the elect.[175]

This objection has been answered, and very learnedly, by the great theologians.[176] Basically, this problem too is a matter of vocabulary. The meaning given to the word *divine will* changed as Augustine grew older, entailing at the same time some changes in his formulas and in his exaggerated interpretations of the saying of the Apostle: "He wishes that all men be saved." The will of God can be sufficiently sincere to bestow the gift of sufficient graces without being absolute and efficacious. Having this view of the divine will in his earlier works, therefore, Augustine stated that God wishes to save all men. However, as the Pelagian controversy pressed him, he turned his attention more and more to efficacious grace which alone distinguishes the elect and, as a consequence, he came to consider God's absolute will of saving men. Now it is evident that God does not have the absolute will to save all souls. "A distinction thought up by the theologians," some one will say. Yes, as far as the words go. Basically, however, Augustine himself imposes it upon us, for in the interpretations of I Timothy 2:4: (1) he never retracted his earlier teaching; (2) he goes further and asserts that he approves all his former interpretations on the sole condition that the will of God be not frustrated (he is speaking of the absolute will here);[177] (3) he gives the example of Adam whose perseverance God did not will since he did not persevere, and immediately adds that God had, however, willed to preserve him in grace: "He also wished . . . to preserve the first man."[178] Therefore, in the very text which is used as an objection against us, Augustine preaches the doctrine of two wills in God: one a conditional will which is not realized since freedom of choice resists it; the other an efficacious will which is realized, but which does not extend to all men.

CHAPTER XIII

The Church

" AUGUSTINE merits to be called the Doctor of the Church as well as the Doctor of Grace."[1] Those are Specht's words approving the judgment of Moehler: "Whether one considers their depth of feeling or their vigorous thought, there has been nothing written on the Church since the time of St. Paul comparable to the works of St. Augustine."[2] He completed, corrected, and surpassed the beautiful pages of St. Cyprian on the divine institution of the Church, her authority, her essential notes, her mission in the economy of grace and the administration of the sacraments. The Protestant critics Dorner, Bindemann, Böhringer, and chiefly Reuter staunchly proclaim and sometimes exaggerate this role of the Doctor of Hippo. Although Harnack refuses to interpret everything in Augustine in the light of this idea, he does not hesitate to write: "This is one of the points on which Augustine especially stresses and confirms the Catholic idea. He was the first [!] to transform the authority of the Church into a religious power in the world and to present the doctrine of the Church as an embodiment of the practice of the people."[3] He is not the first, for Dorner points out that Optatus of Milevis had uttered basically the same teaching.[4] Augustine, however, has gone deeper and systematized into a complete framework the views of St. Cyprian and Optatus.

Augustine's work in this field was occasioned chiefly by the Donatist schism, the last episode of the great Montanist and Novatian controversies which had torn the Church since the second century.[5] While the East was pondering the divine and Christological problem of the Word in its various aspects, the West, probably because of its more practical mentality, was preoccupied with the moral question of sin under all its forms. The general problem of the holiness of the Church always existed: Can the sinner remain in her bosom; can he be forgiven? In Africa the problem took on a special aspect, focusing especially on the holiness of the ecclesiastical hierarchy. The Donatists, by refusing to accept the validity of ordination conferred by a bishop who had given the Scriptures to the heretics (a *traditor*), raised serious problems: Do the hierarchical powers depend on the moral dignity of the priest? How can the holiness of the Church and the unworthiness of her ministers be reconciled? To what degree is the sanctifying power of the sacraments attached to the rite itself and to the person who confers it? Finally, the schism raised another problem as a result of these controversies, the unity of the Church.[6]

1. Institution of the Church as Mother of Souls and Prolongation of the Work of Jesus Christ

a. MISSION OF THE CHURCH

Augustine very profoundly described the plan of the Savior for the salvation of humanity, a plan diametrically opposed to the individualistic concept of the Reformation. The latter in effect isolates at least in principle each member of the faithful; salvation is a personal affair between the soul and Christ; no priest, no human mediator must interfere. For the Doctor of Hippo, on the contrary, God has not left man isolated in any sphere: in the physical and intellectual life He has given him the family and society; for the supernatural life He has also prepared a family and a society for man—the Church, whose role, guaranteed by divine promises, is to give him life and to lead him to salvation. Jesus Christ was the mediator; the Church is to be the mediatrix. She is to carry on His work, or—more accurately—Jesus Christ will carry it on in her and through her. Augustine develops this theme under many forms. (1) The Church is the way of salvation: "Flee from anyone who is not a Catholic in order that forgiveness, resurrection, and eternal life may be granted you through the one, true, and holy Catholic Church."[7] (2) The Church is the supreme authority for the guidance of humanity: "The whole sum of authority and the light of reason is found in that one saving name and in His one Church, set up for the restoration and reformation of the human race."[8] (3) The Church is the true mother of souls: "The Church is a spiritual mother."[9] (4) The Church is associated with the Man-God in this maternity as Eve was with Adam.[10] (5) The Church is associated with the Divinity: "The Father is God; the mother is the Church."[11] (6) The Church is the spouse of Christ, whose holy betrothal was celebrated at the moment of the Incarnation in the bosom of Mary.[12] (7) The Church is the mystical body of Christ which was to be represented, along with His real body, under the Eucharistic symbols. (8) The Church is the true city of God, the kingdom of heaven, figured and announced on each page of the Sacred Books by the terrestrial Paradise, Noah's ark, the holy city of Jerusalem, and finally by Mary herself.[13]

b. NECESSITY OF THE CHURCH

"Outside the Church there is no salvation." Not only does Augustine approve this famous saying of St. Cyprian, but he teaches us that this was the unanimous belief even of the separated sects. "Who denies this?" he asks.[14] Another expression of Cyprian, "He will not have God as his father who does not wish to have the Church as his mother," was frequently on his pen.[15] That explains his forceful works against the Donatists in which he orders them to come back into the Church.[16] In the sermon to the people of Caesarea he exclaims: "The Donatist Church can have everything without the Catholic Church; it can have dignities, . . . sacraments, . . . songs of alleluia, . . . faith and the preaching of faith. But salvation—that can be found nowhere outside the Catholic Church."[17] The Holy Spirit who vivifies the Church does not vivify members who are separated from her.[18] Finally, our love for the Church is the measure of the indwelling of the Holy Spirit in us.[19]

C. INFLUENCE OF GOD

God's immediate influence on souls, however, is not hindered by this ordinarily indispensable role of the Church. That is an accusation of the Protestants which Augustine had foreseen. (1) In the Church, God acts ceaselessly in souls through His grace as the interior teacher and inspirer of all good.[20] (2) Outside the Church, God's hands are not tied: He can work marvels of grace without human intervention in souls who do not yet know the Church, as the case of the centurion Cornelius witnesses, who had received the Holy Spirit before being baptized.[21] God acts thus to show more clearly that it is always He and not the minister who sanctifies: "Why does it happen now this way, now that way, unless to prevent us from attributing anything to our human pride but all to divine grace and power?"[22] The conclusion is that God sometimes sanctifies without the Church and the sacraments, but never one who scorns the sacraments: "Therefore we conclude that an invisible sanctification has been offered to some and used to advantage without visible sacraments. . . . Not on that account, however, is the visible sacrament to be scorned, for one who scorns it can in no way be sanctified invisibly."[23] (3) Finally, even when the priest and the sacraments intervene, it is always God alone who gives grace and sanctifies. This is one of his favorite ideas against the Donatists who attributed grace to the holiness of the minister. "Christ heals, Christ cleanses, Christ justifies," he exclaims, ". . . and yet [the Donatist] adds that . . . I justify, I make one just."[24] What he says of the influence of the sacraments he repeats of the office of teaching: "External instruction is only a help. It warns you. But He who teaches hearts has His throne in the heavens. . . . He alone is your teacher, Christ."[25]

2. TRUE CONCEPT OF THE CHURCH, RECONCILING HER VISIBILITY AND HOLINESS

a. THE PROBLEM

The Donatist error of making the sacramental power depend on the holiness of the minister should have logically resulted in making the Church a gathering of only the just to the exclusion of every sinner. That was just the system which the bishops of that sect proposed at the conference of Carthage in 412.[26] We have pointed out that the Pelagians had far surpassed them in this respect.[27] From their teaching, however, this terrible difficulty arises: Since personal holiness cannot be verified, who is in the Church and where is the Church? If her visibility disappears there is no more society or infallible authority.

According to the Catholic concept, the Church is the society of all the baptized subject to the ecclesiastical hierarchy. Visibility is vindicated, but holiness seems to be done away with, for one can be subject to a pastor, or even be a pastor, and at the same time be a sinner.

Which of these two concepts represents Augustine's mind? To believe Harnack on this subject, Augustine's doctrine here also is a web of contradictions.[28] At various times the Church is, according to the great doctor, either the Church of heaven, "the heavenly society," of which only a pale image appears on earth, or she is the great city of God which from the beginning of the world encompasses all souls subject to God, even the angels. Again she is the communion of only those souls which actually possess holiness even if they are outside the Christian society. Finally, she is the society of the predestined alone or the assembly of the baptized in the Catholic sense. Catholic theologians have long ago reconciled these various definitions which, taken from different points of view, are neither exclusive nor contradictory.[29]

b. THE SOLUTION

The truth is that St. Augustine proposed the Catholic conception as his thesis and defended it countless times against the Donatists. The Church is the visible society of the baptized obedient to the hierarchy. Sinners are truly in the Church. Catechumens are not yet full members of the Church; public heretics are no longer members.

When he restricts the Church to only the predestined or the just, it is not a contradiction but a variation in his way of considering the problem. He then considers the Church of the future, of eternity, which will be freed from all admixture of evil. He tells us this explicitly: "Behold, what I have said is clear. Different periods of the Church must be distinguished. . . . She now contains sinners within her, but then she will have none at all."[30] In particular he often dreams of the Church as she exists in the divine foreknowledge, which already separates the goats from the sheep.[31] Again, in the Church militant itself he distinguishes two ways of belonging to her. Sinners are only materially united to her without participating in her inner life. The just in her are vivified by the Holy Spirit. Now, in comparison with the latter, the former, the dead, those whom he calls "foul members"[32] and "bad humors,"[33] do not really belong to the Church—today one would say to the soul of the Church. Likewise, in comparison with the predestined, the future reprobate who are in the Church today belong only imperfectly to the body of Christ, especially if they are really sinners as he envisages in the famous (but obscure) rule, "of the true and mixed body."[34] This is the meaning of that formula which embodies his entire doctrine on sinners: "They are not to be considered as wholly belonging to that Church."[35]

The holiness of the Church, then, will not be perfect and absolute except in heaven. Here below she has a holiness of right, of principle and efficacy, and actual holiness in a great number, although she suffers from the mingling of the tares until the day of the harvest.[36]

3. Divine Constitution of the Church

Augustine is far from conceiving the Church as a collection of equal members who one day, for the preservation of order, set up laws and administrators. It is Jesus Christ who has given the Church her constitution. Augustine sketches its salient features for us.

a. Divine Origin of the Threefold Ecclesiastical Power

The divine origin of the threefold ecclesiastical power is the basis on which everything rests. It is derived from the Church's mission as the mother of souls. To act upon these souls, a true authority is needed. Thus all Christ's power has been given by Him to the Church: "She is the one who holds and possesses all the power of her Spouse and Lord."[37] This supernatural authority has a threefold function: to teach, govern, and sanctify; or doctrinal, legislative, and sacramental power. The pastors, says Augustine, have received from Christ "sheep to be fed, that is, to be taught and ruled." With the right of teaching comes governing power, and the sacramental power comes from the fact that the pastor is the "minister, that is, the dispenser of the Gospel and the sacraments."[38]

b. AUGUSTINIAN THEORY OF CHRISTIAN PRIESTHOOD

It is a certainty that the great doctor, while casting much light on the sacrament of orders, has also shown the insurmountable barrier which separates the priest from the laity. This assertion, according to Loofs, is the pivotal point of Roman teaching about the hierarchy. The best Protestant critics, Böhringer,[39] Harnack, and others, have to admit that this concept of Augustine destroys their chimera of a universal priesthood and equal power among all the faithful.

It is Jesus Christ Himself who has instituted a priesthood, "an order of clerics,"[40] essentially distinct from the people, "the laity." The word *hierarchy* is not found in Augustine; the reality it stands for is asserted clearly, however. The sacred powers of teaching, forgiving, and so forth have not been given to the community, but only to the Apostles and their successors to use for the community. To the Apostles alone is entrusted the authority, the "governing of the Church."[41]

The hierarchical powers are not conferred by the will of the multitude but by ordination, which consecrates the minister and separates him from the laity forever. "Augustine is the first," says Harnack, "to give us a doctrine of the sacrament of orders, but he did nothing more than assemble elements contained in ancient practice."[42] Dorner recognizes that Optatus of Milevis had already expressed the same thoughts.[43] These are the principal assertions:

(1) Orders is a true sacrament. (2) It consecrates the priest as baptism consecrates the Christian: "Each of them [baptism and ordination] is a sacrament and each is given to man through a consecration; the one when he is baptized, the other when he is ordained. Therefore it is illicit to repeat these sacraments in the Catholic Church."[44] (3) It marks the priest with an indelible character. If the cleric should be deposed, the sacrament still remains with him forever: "The sacrament of orders remains in those ordained. If a person is removed from his office for some fault he is not deprived of the Lord's sacrament once it has been conferred, although it remains for judgment."[45] (4) Only the priest can offer sacrifice: "We offer sacrifice; you are not permitted."[46]

There have been futile attempts to find contradictions in the great doctor on this point also. He probably recognizes a general priesthood in all the faithful, and applies to them the "kingly priesthood" of St. Peter (I Pet. 2:9) and the saying of the Apocalypse (20:6), "priests of God and Christ,"[47] but, as Harnack admits,[48] he takes care to explain that true priesthood is reserved to the bishops and priests, "who are properly called priests in the Church." The faithful are called priests only because baptism and confirmation have made them members of Christ, the pontiff of the new law.[49]

C. ORGANIZATION OF THE HIERARCHY

St. Augustine mentioned the various degrees of the sacred ministry. In different places he enumerates the various orders of porter,[50] reader,[51] acolyte,[52] and subdeacon.[53] The three major orders which Optatus of Milevis called the three priesthoods, the diaconate, the priesthood, and the episcopate, are often mentioned. He also speaks of metropolitans[54] and primates: "the primate, the bishop of the first see, the eldest."[55]

The essential superiority of the episcopacy over the priesthood was recognized by Augustine. In his work *On Heresies* he mentions the error of Aerius who had denied this.[56] This passage should clear up a statement in a letter to St. Jerome in which an expression of humility could be misinterpreted.[57]

Finally, at the summit of the hierarchy, he proclaimed the primacy of the Bishop of Rome and recognized the monarchical character of government established by Jesus Christ in His Church. Attempts have been made to make Augustine an episcopalian who would admit the equality of all the bishops and not recognize a sovereign authority either in St. Peter or his successors.[58] The further charge is made that he maintained that the Bishop of Rome is only the representative, the symbol of the unity of the Church, not the principle of a true sovereign authority.[59] Explicit passages, however, and the whole conduct of the Bishop of Hippo[60] give the lie to these assertions.[61] Augustine affirms the primacy of Peter among the Apostles with a clarity which dispels all doubt. The comparison between St. Cyprian and St. Peter must be read: In martyrdom they are equal, but what a preeminence of dignity in Peter "in whom the primacy of the Apostles shone forth with such excelling grace. . . . For who does not know that that primacy over the apostolate is to be preferred to any other bishopric?"[62] Peter represented the Church when he received the keys, not in this sense that the power was handed over to the community, as some still claim,[63] but as the head of a people representing this people: "The Apostle Peter, because of the primacy of his apostolate, personified this Church, symbolizing her generality."[64]

d. PRIMACY OF THE ROMAN PONTIFF

Here again St. Augustine is a peerless witness of this dogma. The transmission of Peter's primacy to his successors, the Roman Pontiffs, is an incontestable doctrine in his writings. Unfortunately, discussion of it would take us too far afield. The authors treat it well.[65] We therefore give only some fundamental notions. (1) The uninterrupted succession of the Bishops of Rome, the successors of Peter to whom the Lord entrusted all His flock, is what keeps Augustine in the Christian faith: "The succession of bishops, beginning from the very chair of the Apostle Peter to whom the Lord . . . entrusted His flocks to be fed down to the present episcopate is what keeps me in the Church."[66] (2) The Roman episcopate appears as the center of the unity and the proof of the true apostolicity of the entire Church, for it is to Peter as a representative of the entire Church that Jesus said: "On this rock . . ."[67] (3) The Church of Rome is the rock unconquerable by the gates of hell. In his *Psalm Against the Donatists* we read:

Enumerate the priests from the very chair of Peter

And in that succession of Fathers see who succeeded whom.

That is the rock which the gates of hell shall not conquer.[68]

(4) The primacy of the Apostolic See has always been fixed at Rome: ". . . the Roman Church, in which the primacy of the Apostolic See always flourished."[69] "And for this reason, St. Cyprian, finding himself in communion with Rome, was not disturbed when condemned by a council of seventy bishops."[70]

4. Doctrinal Role of the Church

a. INFALLIBLE TEACHING POWER OF THE CHURCH

The infallible teaching power of the Church appears as a basic truth in Augustine. (1) We have already seen that the Church is, through the miracles which surround her, the guarantee and proof of Christianity.[71] He even places her above Scripture and Tradition in the sense that she is the supreme rule of interpretation for both of them.[72] In the Church, and particularly in the Roman Church, resides "the summit of authority, whose supremacy only the height of impiety or the rashness of arrogance denies."[73] (2) Infallibility is the divine prerogative of her teaching. Augustine assures us with St. Paul (I Tim. 3:15) that in the divine plan "she is the predestined column and bulwark of truth."[74] She is the impregnable rampart of truth; heresies issue from her bosom, but the gates of hell shall never prevail against her.[75] To attack her is an error: "The authority of mother Church and the established canon of truth are so endowed that whoever bucks against this strong and unbreakable wall will himself be smashed to pieces."[76] (5) The source of this infallibility is the permanent assistance of

Christ who governs the Church through His Holy Spirit: "The Head stationed in heaven . . . governs His body."[77] Thus no new heretic can overrun her, "since the Head rules and helps His whole body."[78] Without this indwelling of the Lord nothing would preserve her from error: "Unless the Lord were living in the Church at this very moment, the most studied speculations would end up in errors of all sorts."[79] Thus the condemnation of Pelagius was pronounced "with the help of the Savior who watches over His Church."[80]

b. COUNCILS

The councils are the primary agency of this infallible teaching power. The Protestant critics claim that St. Augustine was never able to point out a certain subject for the infallibility of the Church. They should study his theory of the councils better. In general he distinguishes particular councils "which are convoked in individual regions or provinces" from universal councils "which are called into plenary session from the whole Christian world."[81] Midway between these two he ranks the plenary councils of a vast country, for example, the "plenary council of all of Africa" at Hippo in 393. Now in his mind the decision of a truly universal council is infallible. He gives the following proofs. (1) He told the Pelagians that one could engage in controversy before a council; to do so afterwards would overthrow the foundations of the Church.[82] (2) He likewise recognizes with the Donatists the legitimate hesitation of holy bishops "until in a plenary council of the whole world that which was piously believed was solidly established to the removal of all doubts."[83] What council is it which defined this pious belief in the validity of heretical baptism? That is a difficult problem to decide. Augustine reverts to this question time and time again and even says that this council was held before he was born, "after the suffering of Cyprian before we were born."[84] Is it the Council of Nicea in 325 or that of Arles in 314?[85] The fact which is important is that this decision cut off forever all possibility of doubt for the holy doctor.[86] (3) An objection is drawn from his well-known statement: "Earlier plenary councils are often corrected by later ones."[87] The Protestant critics have not noted that these plenary councils cannot be ecumenical. The word *often* is a proof of that. Had there been a great number of universal councils? Was there a single example of a council of this type which was corrected by a later council? Moreover, the word *corrected* can well mean changes in the matter of discipline and not of faith.

C. INFALLIBILITY OF THE POPE

The infallibility of the pope clearly stands out both from the teaching and from the very conduct of the Bishop of Hippo. To illustrate this we present some characteristics of the correspondence exchanged with Rome during the struggle against Pelagius. (1) The collective letters of Augustine and his associates to Innocent I[88] in the name of the Council of Milevis in 417[89] and of Augustine and some other bishops[90] attest the primacy of the Bishop of Rome. In the first we read: It is a duty to have recourse to the "Apostolic See" and to its pastoral ministry. God especially directs the pope in his counsels: "He deigns to direct you in your deliberations and to hear your prayers."[91] The pope's authority is confirmed by Holy Scripture.[92] (2) After Innocent I had asserted in his reply the doctrinal primacy of Rome,[93] Augustine approved this reply.[94] (3) He accuses Julian of Eclanum of not having listened to Pope Innocent whose replies could not betray the ancient doctrine of the Church.[95] (4) Finally, according to Augustine, the reply of the pope settles all debate. It is therefore irreformable and infallible. If the formula, "Rome has spoken, the case is closed," is not found in so many words in Augustine, the exact equivalent is found in one of his sermons: "Concerning this case [Pelagianism] the reports of two councils were sent to the Apostolic See. From there replies came; the case is closed. Would also that the error were ended."[96] Thus the Roman episcopate is the Apostolic See par excellence; councils are subject to its judgment and have no validity without its approval. Once Rome has spoken all dispute is settled without reference to the consent of the Church.

5. ECCLESIASTICAL GOVERNMENT OF SOULS

St. Augustine includes under this subject the legislative and coercive power. The existence of this legislative power, which he calls the "ruling of the Church,"[97] is not doubtful in his mind. On the one side are the "lords by whom the Church is now governed,"[98] on the other is the multitude to be governed, "the people to be ruled."[99] The right of government demands the strict duty of obedience in these subjects and Augustine repeats often: "The care belongs to us; obedience, to you."[100]

A certain coercive power is, according to Augustine, consequent upon the power of the keys: "The Church has received with the keys the right to bind and to loose. If anyone spurns her reprimands and her corrections, he becomes, as the Lord said, as a pagan and a publican."[101] As for the exercise of this right, the holy doctor describes the sanctions of his times in these terms: "By correction, degradation, excommunication, and other licit and ordinary checks which take place daily, keeping the unity of peace, in the Church."[102]

In particular it is interesting to see Augustine describing the two excommunications which later came to be known as the greater and the lesser. The latter, of a penitential nature, deprives a person of certain advantages without breaking off his union with the Church: "For we do not separate from the people of God those whom we lower by degradation or excommunication to a more humble place for doing penance."[103] The other excommunication, on the contrary, radical and complete, entirely cuts off "incurable members."[104] "This excommunication produces the same effect in the Church that the ancient law accomplished by the punishment of death."[105] Augustine still consoles those who are victims of unjust excommunication. Let them obey and then "they pass the test more than if they had remained within."[106] "The Father seeing in secret, crowns them in secret."[107]

The account of Augustine's opinions on the use of force against heretics has been related in the history of his life.[108]

CHAPTER XIV

The Sacraments

I. SANCTIFYING POWER OF THE CHURCH THROUGH THE SACRAMENTS

In Augustine's thought the basic idea is that the sacraments are the inner bond which attaches Christ's children to Him and their mother. They are the treasure of graces which the Savior has entrusted to the Church as her own good and as the instruments of her influence on souls.

a. NOTION OF SACRAMENT

The notion of sacrament in St. Augustine does not yet have that precision which it was to attain in the thirteenth century. He was, however, the first to disentangle the scattered elements. He conceived a sacrament first as a "sacred sign"[1] and then as a social bond, a means of union among the members of the Church: "The Lord . . . collected a society of new people by sacraments which are few in number, easy of observance, and excelling in significance."[2] This sacramental sign is immediately determined. It is a rite commemorative of the past, signifying "a sacred gift which we ought to receive."[3] Undoubtedly this gift to be received is grace; this grace is produced by the rite in virtue of its institution by Christ, independently of any personal merit of the minister. But these ideas, developed here and there, are nowhere synthesized as the essential notes of every sacrament. Thus Augustine will use this title of many things which are not sacraments according to our use of the term, such as instruction in the Creed, for instance, or the Lord's Prayer.[4] He speaks of the sacrament of exorcism.[5] Nevertheless, the Protestant critics still propose the following as Augustine's definition of sacrament: "A sacrament is a material sign of a spiritual object, instituted by Jesus Christ but naturally apt to designate that object through which God communicates His grace to those who make use of it under certain conditions."[6]

b. INTRINSIC EFFICACY

The intrinsic efficacy of the sacraments was studied on the occasion of the Donatist schism. The general dogma on which Donatists and Catholics were in agreement asserts the sanctifying influence of the sacraments. This feature is, according to Augustine, the distinctive character of the sacraments of the new law as compared to those of the old. The former prophesied grace, ours confer it.[7]

The problem raised by the Donatists was the determination of the special influence of the sacred rite and of the human instrument in the conferring of grace. According to them, ordination conferred by one who had handed the Scriptures over to the heretics (a *traditor*) could not be valid. How could he who does not have the Holy Spirit give Him to others? Logically they had to conclude that every minister in the state of sin loses his sacramental powers. The Reformation was to raise the same problem, but with the emphasis shifted to the subject: Is it the sacrament which sanctifies, or only the faith of him who receives it? Considered under this double aspect, Augustine's works against the Donatists[8] constitute some sort of defense of this dogma by their rational, though incomplete, explanation of the role of these three elements: rite, minister, and subject.

A sacrament is valid in spite of the unworthiness of the minister, even if he is a *traditor* or a heretic. This is the same as saying that the minister does not lose his powers of orders because of his sins. The fundamental reason for this teaching is based on the Augustinian theory of the Church. The true minister of the sacraments is not this individual, not even this consecrated person, but the Church, the spouse of Christ who sends the priest, and ultimately Christ Himself who works always in the Church and through the Church. Even when the minister is separated from her by heresy or schism he represents this Church with whose character he is marked by ordination or baptism. Thus it is the Church, it is the dove who baptizes, even when the sacrament is given by a heretical vulture.[9] It is the spouse of Christ who brings them forth "both in her own womb and in the wombs of her servants, by virtue of the same sacraments as if by virtue of the seed of her husband."[10] Again, it is Jesus Christ Himself who baptizes, as Augustine preaches so often. Or finally it is the Holy Spirit who acts.[11] Therefore, to the axiomatic phrase of the Donatists, "the moral state of the minister must be taken into consideration," Augustine answers: "Do not think about the person conferring, but what is conferred."[12]

Does this valid baptism conferred by a heretic give grace? Augustine often denies it, but he is always presuming the bad disposition of the subject "inasmuch as he consents to the wickedness . . . of the heretics."[13]

The theory of the reviviscence of the sacraments has grown from this whole teaching: When the person baptized by a heretic returns to the Church with the desired dispositions, the sacrament produces its effect which was previously hindered by the sin of the subject.[14]

In conclusion, therefore, Augustine really taught the efficacy of the sacraments in the very manner which Scholasticism and later the Church signified by the formula *ex opere operato*: "Baptism benefits for salvation those who use it well not because of the merits of those who administer it nor because of the merits of them to whom it is administered, but because of its own holiness and truth on account of Him by whom it was instituted."[15]

C. THE SACRAMENTAL CHARACTER

According to Reuter "Augustine is the first of the doctors who introduced the term *character* into the theory of baptism and ordination. Although he never joined the adjective *indelible* to it, its meaning is found in the most authentic interpretation of Augustinism."[16] Augustine, however, did not fabricate this doctrine, but merely explained the assertions of his predecessors that neither baptism nor the power of orders is lost by schism or apostasy and that these two sacraments cannot be repeated. The reason for this is, Augustine says, that they imprint on the soul an irremovable mark which he compares to the military standard then in use.[17] This character remains always with the baptized person.[18] Augustine has therefore clearly distinguished two totally different effects of these two sacraments: the grace of the Holy Spirit, which is conferred only on well-disposed souls; and the character, which is always imprinted if the baptism was correctly administered.[19] The inability to lose the power of orders and the validity of ordinations conferred by heretics gave rise to heated controversies in the tenth and eleventh centuries, the basis of which was always Augustine's authority. Peter Damien relied upon him to uphold the validity of these ordinations, as did the monk of Constance, Bernold, against Cardinal Humbert.[20]

d. NUMBER OF THE SACRAMENTS

The notion of sacrament was still too vague for Augustine to have thought of an exact enumeration. Therefore he is satisfied to tell us that they are less numerous, more simple, and more deeply significant than those of the Old Testament.[21] In a letter he names baptism, the Eucharist, "and other such things as are prescribed in the canonical Scriptures."[22] In a sermon he states more precisely "baptism, the Eucharist, and the other holy sacraments."[23] These two assertions alone suffice to refute the thesis of Hahn that St. Augustine knew only two sacraments. Moreover, for the ultimate solution of the question the word *sacrament* should not serve as a guide, but the basic doctrine and especially the efficacy attributed to a rite. Now, in comparing various texts of Augustine, one arrives at this conclusion: Of our seven sacraments, six are described by Augustine with truly sacramental characteristics. All of these six receive the name of sacrament (in slightly different senses) or are enumerated with the true sacraments. Baptism is explained through entire books; orders has been mentioned; the Eucharist, penance, and marriage will be studied separately.

Confirmation is quite clearly described. First of all, Augustine puts it on the same level with baptism and the Eucharist among the sacraments of infants: "The sacrament of chrism . . . is holy in the line of visible signs, like baptism itself."[24] He then describes its supernatural efficacy in being a gift of the Holy Spirit: "The spiritual anointing is the Holy Spirit Himself, whose sacrament consists in a visible anointing."[25] Christian fortitude is the grace proper to this rite and justifies the name which later was given it.[26]

Only extreme unction does not seem to be described by Augustine. At least the texts alleged in the *Confessio* of Torres are all apocryphal, and those of Cupetioli treat of confirmation. Nevertheless, in the *Mirror of Scripture* he relates, along with other precepts drawn from the Epistle of St. James, the famous passage (5:14): "Is anyone sick? . . ."

2. THE EUCHARIST AND THE REAL PRESENCE

It is a unanimous conviction among the Protestant critics, according to Loofs, that "the greatest doctor of Western Catholicism took almost the same position as Berengarius, Wyclif, and Calvin in his teaching on the Eucharist."[27] Harnack shares this opinion,[28] but he is far from being as certain about it and discloses a real difficulty even though he says that no single text of Augustine is absolutely decisive in favor of the real presence. Certain contemporary Catholics apparently have some misgivings.[29] In reality, and even the Protestants agree, there are two series of texts in Augustine which seem irreconcilable at first glance. Expressions in favor of the real presence abound—all Augustinian language is shot through with this idea—but other texts, gathered by Loofs, Dorner, and others, of which Catholic scholars have always been aware,[30] seem to assert a figurative presence. Three elements must be considered in the solution of this problem.

a. UNCONTESTED FACTS

Certain uncontested facts make the Protestant interpretation of Augustine's teaching impossible.

In all the great doctor's writings there is not a word—not a single one—which hints at the slightest divergence of opinion from his contemporaries or predecessors on this subject of such importance. He always claims that his teaching is that of the entire Church. In addition, the doctrine of the real presence of Christ in the Eucharist was so clearly predominant in the Greek and Latin Church at that time as to defy any other interpretation: it was the soul of the whole liturgy. Loofs himself admits that Tertullian was a witness of "the realistic conception of the Eucharist by the Church in Africa."[31] One must then assert that Augustine either had no comprehension of the clear thought of the great doctors—Chrysostom, Cyprian, Hilary, and the rest— or that he separated himself from them without ever examining or criticizing their teaching! Who would believe this?

In particular, St. Ambrose expressed belief not only in the real presence[32] but also in what Loofs terms the realist-dynamist concept of the transubstantiation. (The text is so clear that Loofs in desperation denies its authenticity.) Since Augustine ordinarily speaks of the Eucharist as Ambrose, his venerated teacher "who planted and watered me,"[33] and since he never indicates a divergence of opinion on this point, he must have understood the expressions of Ambrose in the same sense.

None of his contemporaries or his successors, none of his adversaries (and many there were, rabid and perspicacious partisans of the Donatists and Pelagians) has ever pointed out any discrepancies in Augustine's Eucharistic teaching. Nevertheless, the works *On Christian Doctrine* and *On Catechizing the Unlearned*, the source of the suspect passages, were available to all of them. Finally, the disciples of Augustine, Caesarius of Arles and Gregory the Great for example, were all defenders of the real presence.

In conclusion, a fact vouched for by Augustine with a noteworthy insistence is the Eucharistic arcanum, the secret faithfully kept from the catechumens concerning this mystery: "We should not mention this now because of the catechumens."[34] One has to admit that, if the Lord's Supper is a simple symbolic ceremony, this mystery is still difficult to explain. In that case, forgiveness of sins by the Church would have an entirely different importance.

b. THEORIES DEMANDING THE REAL PRESENCE

The texts in favor of this dogma are quite numerous and sometimes so clear that some Protestants admit that they cannot find an explanation for them. Here is what Loofs proposes. Augustine's language, he admits, is absolutely realistic. He also admits that his expressions have had their part in keeping later theologians from a symbolic explanation. But Augustine, according to him, understood them in a figurative sense because in certain passages he himself asserted that the Eucharist is a sign. Consequently the first texts are of little value in revealing the inner thought of the holy doctor. The learned critic, it seems, never examines these expressions, taken in their figurative sense, to see whether they would not often stand in flagrant contradiction to their context. We leave aside now numerous passages in which the Eucharistic bread and the Body of the Savior are identified. Let us cite some passages where not only Augustine's words, already quite meaningful, but his theories and reasoning processes absolutely demand the real presence. Without this presence the following theories are absolutely inexplicable.

(1) *Adoration of the Eucharist.* The adoration of the Eucharist, justified by Augustine because it is the Body of Christ, is the first of these theories. The passage from one of his sermons on the Psalms is justly famous. Augustine reading in the Psalms: "Adore the footstool of His feet," is troubled, for it is idolatry to adore the earth. Then he straightway finds the solution. The body of Christ was taken from the earth in the womb of Mary and this body is what we adore in the Eucharist. In this case, then, the earth can be adored without impiety: "In doubt I turn to Christ and find how the earth can be adored without impiety. . . . Flesh is from the earth and He received flesh from the flesh of Mary; He walked here in the very flesh and gave that flesh to us to eat for our salvation; but no one eats that flesh without first adoring it. Thus we have found how such a footstool of our Lord's may be adored. Not only do we not sin by adoring, but we sin by not adoring." [35] Truly now, if Augustine does not admit that the

body of Christ is really in the Eucharist, does not his reasoning collapse, bereft of all meaning? Furthermore, what a parallelism of expression! We adore the same flesh which He had received from Mary, which He possessed in the course of His life—and that is what we eat.

"Augustinian subtlety," one might object. But this precise passage was inspired by, even modeled upon, the clear commentary of Ambrose which has caused such anguish to Protestant authors: "Therefore by *footstool* the earth is understood, and by *earth* the body of Christ which we today also adore in mysteries and which the Apostles adored . . . in the Lord Jesus."[36] (It is the *same* body, adored by the Apostles, adored on the altar!) After this agreement of thought, how can any opposition be set up between the beliefs of Ambrose and Augustine?

(2) *Miracle of Jesus at the Supper.* In his commentary on the Psalms Augustine assures us that the expression "and he was carried in his own hands," unintelligible of David or any other mere mortal, is fulfilled to the letter in Christ: "For Christ was carried in His own hands when, commending to us His own body, He said: 'This is My Body (Matt. 26:26).' For He carried it in His own hands."[37] Take away the real presence, and how does Christ carry Himself in His own hands? "Metaphorically," would be the reply, for the sign has received its name from the thing signified. But then what becomes of the marvel for which Christ is exalted here, namely, that "no one carries himself in his own hands"? Any man can do that much. Another thing to note is that he insists on this marvel, for he returns to it again: "When He was commending His very body and blood. . . ."[38]

(3) *Miraculous transformation of bread in the consecration.* With Harnack[39] and Dorner[40] Protestants say that St. Augustine never spoke of transubstantiation. When this passage is quoted: "Not all bread but only that receiving the blessing of Christ becomes the Body of Christ,"[41] they reply that it is merely a moral transformation as in the other sacraments. They have a similar explanation for this text: "He becomes present through a certain consecration, but He is not born."[42]

Here is another theory which is significant for the real presence. In Book III of *On the Trinity* the Bishop of Hippo explains the interventions and the miraculous manifestations of the divine omnipotence. Now not only does he cite the mysterious consecration of the Eucharistic elements, but he makes that the great miracle beside which the other miracles of God are not too surprising. Man has been able to manufacture this bread and wine, but the operation of the Holy Spirit is needed to change them into such a great sacrament: "After it is transformed by the hands of men into that visible species, it is sanctified so as to become so great a sacrament only through the invisible operation of the Spirit of God. . . . What wonder also if in the creation of heaven and earth . . . God works the visible things which He wills in order to manifest Himself in them . . . without His very substance appearing?"[43] This, certainly, is a good peculiar to the Eucharist. If there were question solely of a figurative presence, what purpose would this invisible operation of the Holy Spirit serve? Why would it be enumerated among the great works of God? Why would he make a point of insisting on this mystery a second time[44] when treating of the great miracles worked by God and His angels, hailing it as a great mystery about whose origin and explanation the catechumens are in ignorance? Without the real presence this whole passage is inexplicable.

(4) *Unworthy Communions*. The Communion of the unworthy would also be inexplicable for St. Augustine if there were no real presence. In the symbolic system sinners undoubtedly receive the sacrament, the sign, but they do not eat the Body of Christ since this would be to participate in the virtue of the sacrament, in the union with Christ from which the sinner is excluded. Now the holy doctor teaches that the sinner receives the Eucharist validly, that "he eats the Body of Christ and drinks His Blood"[45] without receiving the grace of the sacrament. In Catholic teaching nothing is clearer. But if Augustine rejects the real presence, what does the sinner receive, what does he eat above and beyond the sign? Harnack quite faithfully records: "That which the unworthy receive—and according to Augustine they receive the sacrament

validly—remains a complete mystery. But I cannot subscribe to Dorner's statement that there is no evidence in Augustine that unbelievers partake of the real Body and Blood of Christ."[46]

(5) *Eucharistic sacrifice.* Especially of moment is the fact that Augustine's teaching on the Eucharistic sacrifice would be inexplicable. The evidence here is of unequalled richness: It is always Christ Himself who is at once the victim and the priest offering Himself to His Father at the same time He is offered by the minister at the altar. Thus in her dying moments Monica asked that she be remembered at the altar "where she knew the victim was dispensed by which the handwriting is blotted out."[47] This is the very victim who has saved us. Augustine adds that the "sacrifice of our redemption"[48] was celebrated near the body of Monica.

Every time that he speaks of this sacrifice which is commemorative of the one on the cross, he repeats that it is the offering of the Body of Christ, a sacrosanct offering, and so forth—incomprehensible bombast if there is merely a question of a figurative ceremony: "Christians celebrate the memory of this sacrifice [of the cross] in the sacred offering and partaking of the Body and Blood of the Lord."[49] He remarks of the fatted calf killed on the return of the prodigal son: "That calf is offered to the Father in the Body and Blood of the Lord and it nourishes the whole house."[50] Harnack claimed that Augustine never spoke of the Body of Christ offered anew to the Father by the priest. What does that text mean then? And there are many others. In one of his sermons it is "the priest who offers the sacrifice."[51] But there is an even more significant thought in Augustine. In Book XVII of the *City of God* he is not content to say that the new Eucharistic sacrifice, which takes the place of all the ancient immolations, is offered by Jesus Christ Himself, and that the victim is His Body and His Blood: ". . . the priest Himself, the mediator of the New Testament according to the order of Melchisedech, enables us to partake of His Body and Blood."[52] It is for this sacrifice of the altar, he adds, that His body was formed in the Incarnation, in order that He could offer it to His Father on the altar and give it to those who believe in Him: "Therefore we also recognize that saying of the same mediator speaking through the prophet: 'Sacrifice and oblation You would not, but a body You have fitted to me' (Ps. 39:7), because His Body is offered and administered to the participants in place of all those sacrifices and oblations."[53] Thus the Body which is offered as a victim and distributed to the communicants is the same body with which the Word was united in the Incarnation. In fact, He assumed it precisely for this purpose. That is an idea dear to Augustine, and he develops it again in his commentary on the Psalms.[54] It is incredible that Dorner has persisted in holding that in this passage the Body of Christ means the Church, His mystical body.[55] The Church would thus be the body formed for Christ in the womb of Mary, the body offered to the Father and distributed to partakers of the Eucharist!

(6) *Applications*. Finally, the applications of this teaching about the Eucharist which Augustine loves to make would be unintelligible, as also the conclusions which he formulates. See how he proves to an unchaste person that Holy Communion imposes on him an obligation to virtue: "You already know your dignity, you already know where you are approaching, what you are eating, what you are drinking—even more, Whom you are eating and Whom you are drinking. Restrain yourself, therefore, from fornication."[56] Without speaking of the little efficacy this argument would have if the Eucharist were only a figure, one cannot imagine how, if Christ is not present, the speaker could have been able to correct himself the way he did: "You know Whom you are eating and Whom you are drinking." Could a Sacramentarian express himself in this manner? Likewise, could he, with St. Augustine, compare the blood of Christ to the blood of Abel crying to heaven for vengeance and say that the Blood of Christ received in Holy Communion cries out thus to His Father? "The blood of Christ has a loud voice on earth when the answering 'Amen' of those who believe in Him comes from all nations. This is the clear voice of Christ's blood, since the voice of the faithful redeemed by His blood is the voice of the blood itself."[57]

Certain formulas, it must be confessed, are difficult and startling (not as startling, however, as the preceding passages ought to be to adversaries of the real presence). To write them off simply as a matter of endless contradiction would be far too simple a solution. To reconcile all he has said it is sufficient, or so it seems to us, to penetrate deeper into the mind of the great doctor and to recast our concepts of these matters in the mold of the thought of Augustine's time. The obscurities have their origin in the different aspects of the Eucharistic mystery; the controversial texts, studied in the context where they are found, often provide a remarkable confirmation of Catholic dogma. We reduce the principal objections to three theories whose full import does not always seem to have been grasped.

(1) *Signs and figures in the Eucharist.* For Augustine, it is said, the Eucharist is a figure of the Body of Christ. In his commentary on the Psalms he says that at the Supper "He entrusted and handed over to His disciples the figure of His Body and Blood." [58] A general theory is given in *Letter 98*: The sacramental signs, he says, because of their resemblance with the realities which they represent, receive the names of these realities. Thus, although Christ was really immolated only once, we say that He is immolated daily. Thus again "as in one way the sacrament of the Body of Christ is the Body of Christ so the sacrament of faith is the faith." [59] (The baptism of infants allows us to say that they have the faith.) No other text, says Loofs, is so enlightening as this one. The only one at all approaching it is from *On Catechizing the Unlearned*. [60]

In explanation of Augustine's position we can say that these expressions are natural if one stops to consider two factors: (1) The Eucharist, in the Catholic view, is distinguished from the other sacraments by the grace it produces. In addition, it is composed of a double element: the one invisible, the body of Jesus Christ; the other, the only visible and sensible one, the bread, or that which remains of the bread, the accidents which take its place and preserve its appearances. Now this bread—or, as we say today, these species—is truly, in the full meaning of the term, a sign of the Body of Christ and not that Body. The species represent this Body which our eyes do not see and which only faith discovers. (2) On the other hand, Augustine attributes the word *sacrament* only to the visible and palpable element (any invisible element is the reality or the power of the sacrament). While today the term *sacrament* or *Blessed Sacrament* evokes the idea of the Body of Christ, in the fourth century these words properly signified the appearances of the bread, that which was improperly called bread or the nature of bread. It should not be surprising then if Augustine says that the sacrament of the Eucharist (the sensible element, the accidents) is a figure of the Body of Christ, since that is strictly the truth. This terminology is quite reasonable on other grounds also. Do our adversaries know that theologians are still disputing whether the Body of Christ constitutes, in the strict meaning of the term, the very essence of the sacrament? It is also necessary to point out to the less educated reader that we do not see, we do not touch, we do not break the Body of Christ but only the sign of that Body which is mysteriously present. These reflections apply also to our eating of it.

(2) *Spiritual eating*. According to this opinion, Augustine admitted only a figurative eating; the famous passage from *On Christian Doctrine* is adduced as a proof. The precept "Unless you shall eat. . . .," taken literally, would command a heinous crime: "Therefore it is a figure ordering us to communicate in the Lord's passion and to rest sweetly and usefully in the thought that His flesh was crucified and wounded for us."[61] Another well-known text is also used: "You are not about to eat this Body which you see. . . . I have entrusted a sacrament to you; spiritually understood, it will give you life. Although of necessity it must be celebrated visibly, it must still be understood invisibly."[62] The twenty-sixth and twenty-seventh treatises of the *Commentary on St. John's Gospel* can also be cited.

An explanation of these texts consists solely in grasping Augustine's true thought. As above, he was considering the sign of the

Body of Christ or the sensible sacrament, so here also he envisages the eating, that is, the reception or the action of the faithful making them like Christ, as fulfilling the great law "Unless you shall eat. . . ." Now, Augustine's reply is quite Catholic and quite correct in its three assertions: (1) There is no material, carnal eating in the sense of the coarse Capharnaites: "They understood that saying foolishly . . . and thought that the Lord was about to cut some particles from His own body."[63] He mentions this same error and refutes it in other passages also.[64] (2) He demands a spiritual eating,[65] a partaking by the heart, not by the teeth,[66] in such interior acts as faith and the remembrance of Christ who died for us. Today the Church uses the same expressions to indicate the dispositions required of the faithful for a fruitful reception of Christ. (3) Finally, Augustine terms this eating "figurative" quite rightly in view of his meaning and terminology. For, it must be noted, he does not say that the presence of Christ is only a figure; it is the eating of Christ which is called figurative, and rightly so. For if Christ is really present, if the reception of His Body in us is real, if the eating of the species is also real, then the eating of the Body of Christ by our bodily organs is only figurative. The Body of Christ, indeed, is shielded from all that real action which is called eating. It is not ground by the teeth nor altered nor assimilated. Only the species are touched. That is the teaching which the great doctor was attempting to instill in his people. The Church still speaks to the faithful in the same language that Augustine used: "Why do you prepare your teeth? Prepare your souls, for it is only in your soul that Christ assimilates Himself to you." Thus, just as above the Body of Christ was really present through a sign (the species), so this Body is really received, not merely figuratively, through a real eating of the species and a figurative eating of the sacred Body which can be neither changed nor assimilated.

One might object that this spiritual eating of Augustine excludes all real reception of Christ. This is a gratuitous and false interpretation. First, it is contrary to the text. Augustine is rejecting only a material eating, a dividing up of Christ. The real reception of Christ in the Blessed Sacrament is nowhere repudiated. The whole exterior rite, with the consecration and its effects known by the faithful, is explicitly required: "It must necessarily be celebrated visibly. . . ." Second, such an interpretation is contrary to the purpose of the holy doctor. He is preoccupied only with rejecting any division of the Body of Christ, with explaining how "He is not consumed in bitefuls." [67] In a sermon he shows this same preoccupation: "Do you think that I [Christ] am about to divide into parts this body which you see, that I am about to cut up My body and give it to you?" [68] Augustine replies not by denying that one receives Christ, but by stating, on the contrary, that He gives us His Body and Blood for nourishment: "He gave us the salutary food of His Body and Blood." [69] The integrity of His body, however, is safeguarded by this spiritual eating: "And He quickly solved the great question about His integrity. . . . Let them eat life, let them drink life . . . His life still remains entire. . . . If anything is visibly consumed in the sacrament, in very truth it is spiritually eaten and spiritually drunk." [70] Third, such an interpretation is contrary to the context, since the principal text used as an objection [71] proclaims the obligation of adoring the Eucharistic Body of Christ. [72] Finally, it is contrary to the principle (so often enunciated by Augustine) of infant Communion. He placed such insistence on this that many have thought that he believed the reception of the Eucharist indispensable for salvation according to the law "Unless you shall eat. . . ." But what type of eating could he suppose in infants? Only material? That is useless. Spiritual through faith? That is impossible for them. He admitted then a spiritual eating through the real presence of Christ.

(3) *The Eucharist as a figure of the Church, the mystical body of Christ.* One of the most conclusive texts against the real presence, according to his adversaries, is *Sermon 272* in which the Eucharistic bread and wine represent only the faithful: "If therefore you wish to understand the body of Christ, hear the words of the Apostle, 'You are the body of Christ' (I Cor. 12:27). If therefore you are the body and members of Christ, your mystery is placed on the Lord's table; you receive your mystery [your

symbolic image]. . . . For you hear 'the body of Christ' and you answer 'Amen.' Be a member of the body of Christ, that your amen may be sincere."[73] Going on to show that the unity of the Church made up of the multitude of brethren is like that of the bread formed from a great number of grains, Augustine concludes: "He consecrated the mystery of our peace and unity on His table."[74] Thus, according to St. Augustine, the Body of Christ in the Eucharist is not His real body but His mystical body, the Church. Dorner and Loofs thought that this argument was unanswerable and even a Catholic journal was dismayed by it.[75]

By way of explanation, Augustine's concept of the Eucharist as the great bond of the Church and of the Eucharistic symbols as the image of her unity is not only in keeping with his thought but, we dare to say, one of the dominant ideas in his Eucharistic theory. He returns to it constantly, in his sermons to neophytes for example.[76] Starting with these two ideas, namely, that the Church is the true mystical body of Christ, the body to which one must belong to participate in His life, and secondly, that the partaking of His Body and Blood in the Eucharist makes one a member of the Savior, one with Him, he envisages this mystery as the sacrament of perfect incorporation of the faithful into Christ and His Church. "O sacrament of unity! O bond of charity!" he exclaims.[77] He borrowed from St. Cyprian the symbolism of the bread and wine formed from numerous grains of wheat and grapes crushed and melted together into a oneness. This is a theory as beautiful as it is ancient in the Church. But far from being an objection against the real presence, it is an admirable confirmation of it.

The symbol of the Church, in fact, is used by Augustine only as a secondary, mystical meaning for the expression *Body of Christ*. He always presupposes the primary, literal meaning which denotes the real body of Jesus Christ. One could dispute above in the first of the two series of texts whether Augustine understood that the body of Christ was *present* or only *represented* in the Eucharistic bread. To pretend, however, that the expression "This is My Body" and all the Eucharistic texts literally and exclusively designate, according to Augustine, only the mystical body of Christ and in no way point to His real body is absolutely contrary to the evidence. All the texts already cited, even those alleged by Loofs and Dorner, are in clear opposition to such an interpretation which would put these words in Augustine's mouth: The body of Christ born of Mary which is adored in the Eucharist is the Church; the bread come down from heaven which we eat is the Church;[78] the victim of Calvary who offers Himself on the altar is again the Church; the blood given in the sacrament before being shed on the cross[79] is not the blood of Christ, but always the Church. It would even be necessary to attribute this whole teaching to St. Paul also whose words "one bread, one body" (I Cor. 10:17) inspired the whole theory of the Bishop of Hippo.

The truth is that for St. Augustine as for St. Paul the Eucharist and the formulas which express it encompass a double mystery. First there is the mystery of the real Body and Blood of Jesus Christ given under the symbols of bread and wine and the incorporation of the faithful to Christ Himself who becomes, by the sacramental power, a principle of divine life. Second, there is the mystery of the mystical body of Christ, the Church, and the incorporation of the faithful into the unity of this mystical body. This second symbol, far from excluding the first meaning, essentially presupposes and flows from it as a logical symbolic consequence. This is true for Paul and for Augustine. The faithful, when they receive the sacraments and especially when they "eat" the real Body of Christ, are incorporated into Him and derive their life from Him. It is precisely because of this that they form, in their multitude, one sole mystical body, the Church. St. Augustine has explicitly anticipated our arguments. In *Sermon 227*, wishing to develop against the Donatists his favorite thesis of the unity of the Church figured in the Eucharist, he begins by asserting the literal meaning, the partaking of the Body and Blood of Christ, that Blood which was shed for our sins. See how he talks to the neophytes who had made their Communion Easter night: "The bread which you see on the altar, sanctified by the word of

God, is the Body of Christ. The chalice, that is, the contents of the chalice, sanctified by the word of God, is the Blood of Christ. Through those objects our Lord wishes to entrust us with His Body and Blood which He shed for us unto the remission of sins."[80] Thus far, certainly, this Body and Blood shed for us is not the Church but the real body of the Savior. That is the primary and literal meaning of the Eucharist. Immediately he shifts over to the figurative meaning, the unity of the Church: "If you have received worthily, you are what you have received. For the Apostle says: 'One bread, one body.' Thus he explained the sacrament of the Lord's table. . . . In that bread you are given an example how you ought to love unity. For is that bread made of one grain?"[81] If you have received the Body and Blood of Christ worthily, you are already that which you have received (that is, members of Christ, Christ Himself). That is not all. The same sermon discovers this symbol of the Church in two other sacraments: "You were the grains of wheat," he says in substance. "You had to be ground by exorcisms, kneaded by the water of baptism, and baked by the fire of the Holy Spirit typified in the chrism (confirmation) to become this mysterious bread which you are." Would anyone say that baptism and confirmation are solely symbols of the unity of the Church?

3. Penance

The principal points of Augustinian teaching on what Harnack calls "the problem proper to the Latin Church"[82] are presented here. In fact, while the East was divided over the person of Christ, the West was chiefly torn by the various forms of Novatianism and asked itself how the Church should treat sinners. To understand Augustine's theory of penance we must here suppose the clear demarcation he made between mortal sins (*letalia, crimina*) which condemn one to hell and venial sins which are compatible with grace. More details about the moral theology of Augustine will be given in the next chapter.[83]

a. FUNDAMENTAL NOTION

Augustine's fundamental notion is the famous distinction of the three penances, so different in their nature and object.[84] We take the concise formulation of this distinction from one of his sermons.[85] The first penance is baptism, a remedy for all sins: "Baptism was instituted for all sins."[86] The second is the daily penance of prayer (especially the Lord's Prayer: "Forgive us our sins") for venial sins or for the failings of each day: "Prayer was instituted for venial sins without which we cannot live . . . ; we are cleansed once by baptism, we are cleansed daily by prayer."[87] Elsewhere he adds corporal and spiritual fasting and almsgiving, especially the pardoning of injustices, to the list: "Sin is expiated by the sacrifices of merciful works."[88] There is question here only of venial sins in the present meaning of the word, that is, sins which do not merit hell: "There is question of the daily, slight, and venial sins without which this life cannot be lived" in opposition to offences in punishment for which the guilty "will not possess the kingdom of God."[89] The third type of penance is the "great penance" by which the Church imparts forgiveness of grave faults: "Those whom you see doing penance have committed grave crimes, either adultery or some other hideous deed. Therefore they do penance. For if these were slight sins, daily prayer would have sufficed to blot them out."[90]

b. POWER OF THE KEYS

In this third type of penance he asserts not only a true sacramental power of forgiving sins before God to which one must have recourse for grave faults, but also the extension of this power to all offences without exception. The time of rigorism was definitely over.

This doctrine is perfectly expressed in the *Enchiridion*. He is treating of true forgiveness before God "so that those whose sins are forgiven may gain eternal life" and not only of reconciliation in the external forum "that satisfaction may be made to the Church."[91] This forgiveness is granted to every fault, "for any crime, however great."[92] The necessity of having recourse to the power of the keys is clearly indicated by these words: "For outside the Church sins are not forgiven. For she received as her very own the pledge of the Holy Spirit (II Cor. 1:22) without whom no sins are forgiven."[93] In the same work the denial of the power of the keys, if it lasts until death, is called the unforgivable sin "against the Holy Spirit."[94]

Sermon 352 gives this résumé of the entire teaching on penance. It is the Church which has received the power of bringing the spiritual Lazarus, "a dead man hidden and rotting," back to life in virtue of these words: "Release him" (John 11:39–44).[95] This power is universal, for the foolhardy ones who wished to make exception for certain faults "have been separated from the Church and declared heretics."[96] Finally, there is no other means of forgiveness offered us: "Grave and deadly sins . . . are forgiven by the keys of the Church."[97] "The Church received . . . the keys . . . in the person of Peter, that is, the power of binding and loosing sins."[98] It is absolutely incomprehensible that Charles Lea dared to attribute to the Doctor of Hippo a denial of the sacramental power of the keys.[99]

C. MATTER OF SACRAMENTAL PENANCE

What sins are subject to this sacramental penance? The constant assertion of Augustine exempts venial sins, which are effaced by the virtue of penance and by works which the latter inspires (fasting, almsgiving, prayer).[100] It is beyond all doubt that confessions of devotion were not common, a fact which explains why, according to the remark of Rottmanner (a remark which has wrongly caused scandal in many),[101] there is no record that St. Augustine ever received the sacrament of penance from the time of his baptism until his death. This observation applies to the other holy Fathers also. General confession (contained, for example, in the recitation of "forgive us our sins")[102] was sufficient: "We also, the bishops, when assisting at the altar, strike our breasts with the whole congregation."[103] The humble explanation of episcopal penance in *Sermon 56* ought to be read.[104] Augustine, speaking on the Our Father, has said that we are all trespassers before God because of our sins: "Perhaps you will ask me: 'You also?' And I answer, 'I also.' 'What? You also, holy bishops, you are sinners?' 'We also are sinners.' 'You also! No, it is impossible; do not calumniate yourselves like that.' 'I do not calumniate myself at all; I speak the truth: we are sinners.' " [105] And he indicates remedies for these faults of daily life: prayer and almsgiving—not confession.

Mortal sins, on the contrary, those which exclude one from the kingdom of heaven according to the First Epistle to the Corinthians 6:9–10, are all submitted by Augustine to sacramental penance with the use of the power of the keys. This stands out clearly from the proof given for the distinction of two types of penances after baptism.[106] Only "slight, momentary, daily sins" are wiped out by interior penance, by prayer. Other sins are not forgiven "except to those who having given due satisfaction obtain forgiveness for their crimes." [107] We recall that he excepts only venial sins "without which this life cannot be lived" from ecclesiastical penance.[108] Likewise "grave and deadly" sins must be submitted to the keys; only "light and minute sins which cannot be avoided" are excepted.[109]

One question remains. Does Augustine subject all mortal sins to public penance or only certain offences of exceptional gravity? The question is as difficult as it is important.

In one series of texts, Augustine mentions only two classes of sins, venial and mortal, and seems to assign all mortal sins to public (*laboriosa*) penance.[110] Thus he distinguishes only venial sins "without which this life cannot be lived" and mortal sins, all of which necessitate exclusion from the Eucharist: "For which you must be separated from the Body of Christ." [111] Since all mortal sins deprive one of Holy Communion, some distinguished critics conclude that they are all subject to public penance.[112]

But it is not less certain that in other places Augustine, in addition to venial sins which are wiped out by prayer, quite clearly distinguished two kinds of mortal sins, one of which is subject to the excommunication of public penance while the other is healed "by some medicinal correction" even without exclusion from the Eucharist: "Unless there were some sins so grave that they must also be punished by excommunication [public penance] . . . ; unless there were sins which are not healed by that humbling penance which is given to those who are penitents in the Church, but only by some medicinal correction, the Lord Himself would not have said: 'Correct him between you and him alone. If he listens to you, you have gained your brother.' "[113] Whatever meaning one wishes to attach to these remedies and this ecclesiastical correction, it is certain that there is question of mortal sin. (Venial sins are reserved to a third series of texts. Besides, in other places the words "you have gained your brother" indicate a grave fault.) It is also certain that this mortal sin is subject to some sort of private penance which is not public penance.[114]

His famous *Sermon 351 On Penance* distinguishes more explicitly two kinds of mortal sins. Only notorious scandals are subject to public penance. The orator is speaking of the sinner: "Let him come to the bishops. . . . If his sin is not only a grave evil to himself but also a great scandal to others—and the bishop thinks that it will benefit the Church—let him receive from the dispenser of the sacraments the amount of his satisfaction . . . so that he does not appear averse to doing public penance."[115] If, therefore, the authenticity of this sermon is admitted,[116] one must avow that the minister of the sacrament does not condemn all sinners to public penance. An interpolation does not seem likely, for other texts could be cited in addition.[117] A clearer affirmation is made in yet another work: "It is probably possible to judge who should not be compelled to undergo a painful and grievous penance even though they confess sins."[118] (These *sins* do not seem to be venial sins, since venial sins do not have to be confessed.)

To reconcile these two series of texts, it is sufficient to admit that everyone guilty of mortal faults must submit himself to (private) confession, the first act of ecclesiastical penance. The minister then imposes "the treatment of complete penance" with public satisfaction for certain graver faults and "private satisfaction" for lesser faults.[119]

d. METHOD OF ADMINISTRATION

The first act is the confession of the guilty person. All Augustine's texts, far from presuming a public confession, fit in better with private, auricular confession.[120] Loofs proves that the confession was secret by this statement: "We do not betray ourselves publicly, but we accuse ourselves in secret."[121]

The minister is, according to Augustine, "those who preside over the Church."[122] *Sermon 351* names the "prelates" and a little later the "dispensers of the sacraments."[123] These, then, are the bishops (very numerous in Africa) and perhaps those who were delegated to this ministry.

The role of the minister after the confession consists in pronouncing the "judgment of guilt" of which a Gelasian decree speaks.[124] He decided whether or not there was need for public penance[125] and how long this penance should last.[126] St. Augustine does not describe the imposition of this penance, but he calls it, along with the other Fathers, the "act of penance." He informs us that this ceremony formed part of the administration of the sacrament of penance since, even in the perilous dangers of an epidemic, the faithful came in haste, some to ask for baptism or reconciliation, others for the "act of penance."[127]

The different degrees and practices of public penance are but vaguely indicated. It is sorrowful, humiliating, and deprives one of the Eucharistic table: ". . . a graver penance by which those who are properly called penitents in the Church are removed from participation in the Sacrament of the Altar."[128] These words confirm the distinction mentioned above between the two types of penance. According to the *Enchiridion* "the space of time is not to be so much considered as the amount of grief."[129]

e. SOLEMN RECONCILIATION

Solemn reconciliation concluded the penance. We know that the faithful regarded this as necessary.[130] The thirty-second canon of the Third Council of Carthage (August, 397), at the beginning of Augustine's episcopacy, forbids priests to reconcile penitents without consulting the bishop except in a case of necessity in his absence.[131]

f. THE FATE OF A RELAPSED PERSON

First of all, the holy bishop preaches, with the other Fathers, that solemn penance cannot be repeated: "Once in the Church ... lest cheap medicine be less useful to those who are sick."[132] But it is difficult to determine the condition of those who relapsed, that is, those who after a first reconciliation had again fallen into grave sins. Augustine asserts very clearly that they can certainly obtain forgiveness from God if they have true sorrow for their sins: "Who, however, would dare to say to God: 'Why do You forgive them again?' "[133] To deny this doctrine is to make such sinners prey of all the vices which follow in the wake of despair. He had even said on one occasion that God grants them "the bountiful gifts of life and salvation."[134] It seems then that the African Church observed the decree of Pope Siricius (385) which permitted relapsed persons to assist at prayers, but forbade them to receive Communion save in danger of death.[135]

g. PENANCE: A SACRAMENT?

Is penance a sacrament for St. Augustine? Whatever his language may indicate, the forgiveness granted by the Church indisputably possesses in his teaching all the characteristics which present terminology attributes to the sacraments. Specht[136] rightly accuses Dorner[137] of having here also denied the sacramental character of penance and even the role of judge so clearly given to the priest by the great doctor.[138] Harnack has rightly noted this last fact;[139] he even pretends that Augustine is the first [?] who has laid the basis for the sacramental theory of penance by his assertion that the grace produced is different from that of baptism. Harnack adds that in the fourth century penance was ordinarily joined with baptism "as if they were the two important sacraments."[140]

But is it not true, as is said so often, that Augustine never called penance a sacrament? In the following passage he explicitly enumerates it among the sacraments and likens it to baptism, confirmation, and the Eucharist: "If therefore the saying of the Gospel, 'God does not hear the sinner' (John 9:31), means that the sacraments cannot be celebrated by a sinner, how does He hear a murderer praying either over the water of baptism, or over the oil of confirmation, or over the Eucharist, or over the heads of those on whom his hands are placed? All these actions are validly performed even by murderers. . . ."[141] This imposition of hands is truly a sacrament; the terminology is explicit; the discussion and reasoning demand it. He is speaking of those sacraments which a heretic can confer validly, since even a murderer can dispense them. But what sacrament? Confirmation? No, it is already named in the list. Orders? No, for in the same work he says that this imposition can be repeated: "The imposition of hands, unlike baptism, can be repeated."[142] Penance is the only one left. As a matter of fact, Augustine asserts that this rite concerns the forgiveness of sins: "If the imposition of hands were not applied to one coming from heresy, he would be as it were judged to be wholly blameless."[143]

This last text raises the very complex question of the imposition of hands on converted heretics. Is this action to be understood as "confirmation" as the Greeks practiced it? Or is it a non-sacramental rite, likened to confirmation?[144]

4. MARRIAGE

The doctrine concerning this sacrament, developed in many special treatises,[145] owes great progress to Augustine. He laid its foundation on the general principle of the three goods, which also mark its three great elements: The end of marriage or children, the law of marriage or the mutual fidelity of the spouses, and the sacramental meaning, that is, the indissoluble bond between Christian spouses which is a figure of the union of Jesus Christ with His Church.

The sacramental character of marriage was recognized by

Augustine. Let it be noted, however, that we do not base the proof for this on the fact that he gives it the title of sacrament. This term is as vague in the holy doctor's writings as it was in the text of St. Paul (Eph. 5:32) which he followed. We can say with Vasquez, Mullendorf, and others that St. Augustine did not apply this term to marriage in the same sense that he did to baptism, the Eucharist, and orders in which there is a special consecration of a material element. On the other hand, however, we believe with Schanz[146] that the term has an exalted meaning here, since St. Augustine really attributes to marriage two characteristics which make it a true sacrament in the modern sense of the word. First, there is the institution by Jesus Christ Himself of this remarkable symbolic representation of His union with the Church.[147] Second, grace is conferred in virtue of this sacramental institution. That is the consequence of the great Augustinian theory that every sacrament of the New Testament confers the grace which it signifies. Now, this signification is here a fact of singular importance; it is the source of holiness for Christian marriage and elevates it above all natural marriages: "For the people of God, however, this good is also in the holiness of the sacrament."[148] Notice the precise delineation of Augustine's thought in this remarkable passage. The marriage of Christians is elevated to the holiness of a religious sign. Then, in order that it represent Christ and His Church exactly, it must be absolutely indissoluble, stricter even than natural marriage which could have been dissolved by divorce. Marriage, once it became a sacrament, by its very meaning denotes an indestructible nuptial bond as long as the spouses live. Finally, this bond is what Augustine properly calls the reality of the sacrament.[149] It is compared to the character of baptism and the character of orders.[150]

The indissolubility of marriage found a staunch defender in Augustine. He makes it a natural property of natural marriage, although God could have allowed exceptions as the Pauline privilege witnesses.[151] In Christian marriage, however, indissolubility is an essential property because it forms the reality of the sacrament. Thus neither adultery nor actual separation nor sterility nor even apostasy can dissolve this bond. Only the death of one of the spouses will sunder it.[152] After these sweeping pronouncements of 419, it is not surprising that shortly afterwards he wrote the work *On Adulterous Marriages*[153] to condemn the dissolution of the marriage bond because of fornication. He had already rejected this point in 396;[154] the surprising thing is that between these two dates (in 412) he could have expressed a doubt on this point: "So that in this case as far as I can see, one might be pardonably mistaken."[155] These words were not retracted.[156] His last opinion, however, ought to be followed. The hesitations of the *Retractations*, "a very difficult question,"[157] do not seem to concern the basic problem in question, but the circumstances and nature of this fornication.

Perpetual virginity is not incompatible with marriage, according to Augustine, because the use of marriage is not necessary to establish the bond, which is the essential element of the contract and the sacrament. Thus he recognized a true marriage between the Blessed Virgin and St. Joseph.[158]

CHAPTER XV

St. Augustine's Moral Theology: The Doctor of Charity

WHEN the German critics recently envisaged Augustine as the inspirer of Christian piety it was not at all a sign of disdain for his dogmatic labors, but a profound observation on the character of his genius and work. His genius, as we shall see later, lies chiefly in the feeling which accompanies the contemplation of the truth. True knowledge, for him, is only that wisdom (*sapientia*) which is relished by the heart as it enlightens the mind. Philosophy is nothing else but piety. That is a principle to which he continually returns: "The wisdom of man is piety."[1] Thus his works are characterized by the practical stamp and the deep impress of Christian life which he infuses into souls. He considers contemplation of mysteries as a means to union with God: "It is good to adhere to God."

The point the critics have grasped to a lesser degree is that no one has been better able than Augustine to show the indissoluble bond by which moral theology is linked to dogma. In his voluminous works everything is treated dogmatically so that it is difficult to set apart any writings of a strictly moral nature.[2] But he knew how to embody practical suggestions for the life of the soul in all these dogmatic treatises. Our discussion here will be limited to the foundations of moral, the fundamental law of charity, particular laws, and the degrees of moral perfection.

1. Foundations of Moral Theology

The foundations of moral theology, according to St. Augustine, can be reduced to three principles: First, the purpose of life is found only in God, the Supreme Good; second, moral good and obligation; third, merit and good works, the complement of faith.

a. PURPOSE OF LIFE

The end of man and the purpose of his life are found only in God, the Supreme Good. Since moral theology is the science of the laws of the will or of the free development of life, the fundamental problem which attracted Augustine at first was the final goal toward which all the energies of our soul tend. Where is the end of our being? Where is that good whose possession will result in our perfection and put an end to all our strivings and inclinations, satisfying our desires forever in a blissful repose? This end, of course, is God Himself, who therefore appears under a new aspect, as the First and Supreme Cause. As Creator He was the source of all being and the ontological order; as the Supreme Good He is the source of all volition and the principle of all conscious activity. The whole of moral, either implicitly or explicitly, will consist in directing our free choice towards God. This is the first foundation of moral science which Augustine developed from the very beginning.[3] Later this thought dominates and penetrates the warp and woof of the *Confessions*.[4] He returns to it in *On the Trinity*[5] and the *City of God*.[6] It also appears in other works.[7] The general progress of his thought will be outlined.

His point of departure is an undeniable psychological fact: the innate (therefore given by the Creator), irresistible yearning of our soul for happiness. The soul wishes to exist, to be good, that is, to attain to the full blossoming of its life in peace and happiness. This tendency is the principle of all our desires, even in the case of suicide.[8] No one can escape this thirst after happiness. No one can even dispute its existence; all the controversy centers around its object.[9] The Augustinian conception of moral theology is frankly eudaemonistic. Happiness is conceived as the end of life precisely because the soul searches for it with an irresistible drive. There is an optimism in this view essential to all logical spirituality. Augustine could never pretend that this happiness was a chimera and that nature, a cruel stepmother, plays a barbaric game by deluding us with yearnings impossible of fulfillment. And no one can accuse this theory of covering over a refined Epicureanism, much inferior to Stoicism. Augustine has already replied to this objection.[10] His theory of charity, to be given presently, will reconcile our desire for happiness with the purest love of the good.

A second Augustinian principle identifies happiness with God Himself. Starting with the Platonic truth that good is identified with being and that evil is only a lack or negation of being, he establishes the fact that perfect and absolute Good will exist only where there is complete Being without limits—consequently, immutable and eternal Being. Every creature, however, is a mixture of being and nothingness: "And I looked at the things beneath You and I saw that they were neither pure being nor absolute nothingness."[11] God alone, then, is the perfect good, the "chief good, the good of all goods, the good whence all goods come, the good without which nothing is good, and the good which is good for other things."[12] Thus God, our true happiness, must be the only object of our yearnings: "God is the summation of all goods. . . . We must not linger here below nor seek elsewhere; the first is dangerous, the other useless."[13] The great, the only fundamental law of moral theology is to attach ourselves to God. Augustine time and time again borrows the formulation of this law from Psalm 62:9: "It is good for me to adhere to God. He is complete goodness. Do you wish more? I grieve at your wishes. Brethren, what more do you wish? There is nothing better than to adhere to God."[14]

The celebrated theory of Book I of *On Christian Doctrine* was a consequence of the above.[15] God alone can be loved for His own sake, Him alone can we fully enjoy. Created goods must only be used, for they are but means by which we go to God.[16] This formula, borrowed from Augustine by Peter Lombard,[17] was to be the first maxim developed at the beginning of all the Summas.[18]

But the enjoyment of God who beatifies the soul is reserved for the future life.[19] Here below only one thing is possible, the struggle to unite ourselves to Him by knowledge and love: "We cannot adhere to God except by love, affection, and charity."[20] All Christian morality is summed up then in the victory of charity, or the love of God to the contempt of self, over greed, the love of self to the contempt of God.

People[21] have been astonished to learn that Augustine scoffed at the confused teachings of antiquity on the nature of the Sovereign Good and that he declared that, with the exception of Plato, no ancient philosopher knew how to penetrate the mystery of life. The reason for this is that, in his opinion, the most beautiful sayings of the different schools on good and obligation were tainted with an irremediable vice, a forgetfulness of God and the worship due to Him. Only Plato had made virtue depend directly on the Supreme Good, on God, and had thereby divinized the science of moral.

b. GOOD AND OBLIGATION

Only two topics, little appreciated in these days, will be mentioned in this connection since Augustine did not make an extensive exploration of this field from the standpoint of natural reason. The revealed law was enough for him.

(1) *Absolute nature of good and evil*. The absolute nature of good and evil was admirably taught in Book II of *On Christian Doctrine*.[22] The great doctor proves that there is an immutable justice, independent of the customs of peoples.[23] In addition, as Weber mentions,[24] he goes beyond the divine will to find the source of good and evil. Thus lying is not evil because God has prohibited it, but He prohibited it because it is contrary to the eternal justice, the norm of rectitude.[25] This is the profound meaning of the famous definition of eternal law as prescribing what is already determined by the divine intelligence and the order of beings: "The eternal law is the divine mind or the will of God commanding the observance of the natural law and forbidding any disruption of it."[26]

(2) *Source of obligation*. Just because a thing is good does not mean that it imposes an obligation. In fact, Augustine distinguishes, with the Gospel, precepts and counsels. Since there is a

supererogatory perfection over and above the obligatory virtues, it is quite clear that every good is not of obligation. Obligation entails a debt, therefore it is due to someone. Consequently the Doctor of Hippo conceives every duty as imposed by the sovereign rule of God. The order of the world belongs to God who has the right to have it respected. Thus every sin is conceived as an injustice in relation to God: "Sin is the will to keep or seek what justice forbids."[27] St. Augustine loves to develop this point. Sin is a violation of the divine rights at least in the sense that it degrades the soul, the dwelling of God, and destroys the order of the world. In a very beautiful sermon he says: You are intemperate. Who has the right to accuse you? Certainly no man, "but God . . . nevertheless accuses you, since He demands of you the integrity of His temple and the purity of His dwelling."[28] Likewise: "You offend Him with your mischief; when you injure yourself you injure Him, for you do injury to His grace, to His dwelling place."[29] Augustine does not tire of returning to this idea.[30] Obligation, then, begins at the point where man's will, overturning the essential or natural order of creation, injures the domain of the Creator by debasing it. Man is not obliged to aspire to the highest perfection, but he is obliged not to destroy the work and property of God.

C. MERIT AND THE NECESSITY OF GOOD WORKS

Here especially, if we can believe the Protestant critics, is where the Catholic character of Augustinian teaching stands out. This teaching, moreover, is eminently moral in character. How was Protestantism able to break the indissoluble bond which natural morality had established between duty and salvation and to posit the uselessness of virtue as the basis of its new Gospel? It could do this only by relinquishing all claim to the authority of Augustine on this point. "In his writings," says Bindemann, "the relations of works with faith are vigorously asserted in the Catholic sense. There he treats both merits and the invocation of the saints."[31] It will be sufficient then to mention the three principles which Augustine placed in opposition to the Protestant conception.

(1) *Nature of salvific faith.* Neander had pretended to find in the Bishop of Hippo the Protestant idea of faith, the assurance of one's own justification by Christ. But Dorner, following Wiggers, proves quite well that Augustine demands an intellectual adherence to revealed truths.[32]

(2) *Necessity of works.* Not only did Augustine never admit the Protestant theory of salvation by faith alone, as Harnack concedes,[33] but he rejected it repeatedly. The only faith which justifies is that which operates through charity.[34] Or again, without works faith will save no one.[35] He also reconciles St. Paul (Rom. 3:28) with St. James (2:20) this way: The former asserts the uselessness of works before faith while St. James is underlining the need of works after faith.[36]

(3) *Good works are meritorious for the believer.* This point is one which must forever stand in irreducible opposition to anyone who would attribute to Augustine a deterministic fatalism. The idea of merit presupposes, as a matter of fact (by the nature of things and according to the teaching constantly proposed by the great doctor), responsibility of the agent, freedom of choice, and dominion over one's actions.[37] Now he always asserted the merits of the just, though he maintained at the same time that these merits were due to a gratuitous gift: "Whoever enumerates his true merits, what is he enumerating except Your gifts?"[38] Loofs concludes that this theory of merit was an open invitation to Semipelagianism.[39] That is evidently wrong, however, since the very first merit is also due to grace. It would have been more correct to conclude that people were deluded when they attribute to Augustine the idea of a necessitating grace, absolutely incompatible with merit.

2. FUNDAMENTAL LAW OF CHARITY

None of the Fathers has made this characteristic of the law of Christ, "the law of love," stand out more clearly than Augustine.

The *Enchiridion* reduced the whole of moral theology to charity just as it synthesized all dogmas in faith: "The purpose of every precept, therefore, is charity, that is, every precept is referred to charity.[40] As early as the writings of *On the Morals of the Catholic Church* (389) he saw only different forms of a single charity in all the virtues.[41] This basic concept appears under different guises. There are, for instance, the two loves which constitute the two cities in the *City of God*: "Two loves built two cities: love of self to the contempt of God built the earthly city; love of God to the contempt of self the heavenly."[42] Likewise "Scripture gives no other precept than charity."[43] The role given to charity by Augustine, however, has been strangely interpreted. It is necessary to restore its correct meaning by disentangling it from various errors.

a. IS CHARITY THE ONLY VIRTUE?

Baius and the Jansenists concluded that any affections of the soul besides Christian or supernatural charity towards God are mundane and culpable desires. But they failed to understand Augustine. In hundreds of places he informs us that charity is not always the love of God, a theological virtue, but also the love of the good, of virtue, of order. It is true that the good comes from God as its principle and tends towards Him as its objective end; it is also true that love of the good finds its highest act and fulfillment in the formal love of God, but St. Augustine never wished to restrict the field of virtue to this last act: "What is desire of the good if not charity?"[44] He recognizes and admires other less noble and more human virtues, even merely natural virtues: "The human love by which one loves his wife is licit. . . . It is human, but, as I said, it is licit."[45] He even adds that this love is obligatory and proclaims that it is found among pagans.[46] He also states: "Charity is also known as good will."[47]

b. IS THEOLOGICAL CHARITY REQUIRED FOR AN UPRIGHT ACT?

Certain Augustinian theologians have contended that a positive and formal influence of the motive of theological charity is needed for an act to be upright or even meritorious. Such was Louis

Habert, led into this exaggerated position by Augustine's insistence in demanding that every act of love elicited by our will be directed to its last end, to God: "Without this love of the Creator no one can use any creature well."[48] "All these precepts of love, that is, of charity are such great commands that, if a man acts without charity, none of the actions which he thinks he has done well are really good."[49]

But God is the source of all law, all order, and all honesty according to the holy doctor. Therefore, as soon as the will acts under the impulse of any virtue, it implicitly and objectively relates everything to God, even though it does not explicitly think of Him. St. Augustine's theory is not that one must always love God explicitly to love the good, but that one must love the good so as never to lose the love of God. Therefore he sings the praises of each virtue taken by itself. In a sermon he explains and completes the famous theory on the cardinal virtues which he first formulated earlier.[50]

C. DOES AUGUSTINIAN TEACHING LEAD TO QUIETISM?

Is the teaching of Augustine on the pure love of God a quietist doctrine? Does he confuse charity with the desire to possess God? The quietists have triumphantly cited the expressions of Augustine which demand a pure love of God devoid of all self-interest, the love of a wife who loves her husband for himself and not for the advantages which he provides: "Let us, therefore, brethren, love God purely and chastely. The heart is not pure if it worships God for reward."[51] Is this not to condemn or at least to exclude any reflection by the soul on its own happiness?

The theory of Augustine, in reality, is the very opposite of quietism. He forbids the desire of any good distinct from God, of any happiness centered in an object other than God. Even in the text quoted he orders us to love God, our reward and our happiness. Just previous to those words he gives this beautiful theory. The pagans, he says, were expecting from God the goods of the earth, flocks and harvests. Now, God leaves these goods to His enemies.[52] "What therefore? Will we not receive a reward for our worship of God? Certainly, the very God whom we worship. He will be our reward because we will see Him as He is." [53] To desire the fruition of God is a pure love, the love of the spouse. [54]

He also defends against all onslaughts the desire of this eternal, divine recompense: "Pay attention, brethren, to what is for sale. God tells you that what He has is for sale. Buy it. What does He have for sale? 'I have repose to offer; buy it with your labor.' " [55]

Augustine likewise approves the fear of hell even when it is fear of punishment alone without being the filial fear of losing God: "What is pious fear? It is fear lest you lose these goods." [56] This passage admirably explains why he condemns in the same context the fear of the person who is still attached to evil. [57] Augustine's thought on the efficacy of attrition has been studied by the theologians, recently by de San. [58]

d. DOES CHARITY INCLUDE THE LOVE OF BENEVOLENCE?

The desire to possess God, according to St. Augustine, plays a big part in charity. From this fact springs an interpretation of his teaching diametrically opposed to the preceding. Charity is done away with, says the quietist, as soon as the soul loves with the desire of possession. Such love is a culpable egoism, at least in an incipient degree. In opposition to this, according to Bolgeni and his disciples, Augustine preached nothing but selfish love, the desire of God in order to possess Him. Charity becomes a mere chimera, says Bolgeni's new school, if it seeks to love God for Himself without seeing Him as the happiness which is the culmination of our desires. Pure love of God is an unnatural striving, for every will, made for the good, always seeks in everything that good which must be its own good. Thus Augustine would have had no knowledge of what the theologians, following St. Thomas, call the love of benevolence, the love of God considered in Himself because of His infinite perfections without any consideration of our own happiness. True charity would be the love which seeks one's happiness not in the largess of the beloved, but in the community of life and affection: "A charity which desires to see and enjoy."[59] "For if God is man's chief good . . . it then follows that, since to seek the chief good is to live rightly, there is no other way to live rightly than to love God with your whole heart, your whole soul, and your whole mind."[60] To desire God is to love God, according to this profound statement: "To love God for His own sake means this: to hope for God from God."[61] "Love Him for His own sake; desire from Him only Himself."[62]

We confess that these expressions and numerous others apparently favor this theory, but in reality the teaching of the Bishop of Hippo protests against this narrow interpretation. He teaches, it is true, that the will could not love God if God were not its sole and true Good, that is, its God, the source and end of its being. It is also true that he often presents to us as the object of our love, God, the supreme happiness of man. But this is owing to his profound conception of the relations between the soul and God. For him everything in the world has come from an act of love of God the Creator. Everything must return to God, the last end, by an act of created love. That is the meaning of his famous statement: "He is not worshipped except by love."[63] "We go [to God] not by walking but by loving."[64] Now to direct this movement of return to God, Augustine had to present God and the divine perfections in their relationship with the soul which has the obligation of seeking Him. God appears to the soul then as the end, the goal, the repose, the beatitude: "You made us for Yourself. . . ." But the principles of the Augustinian theory must not be forgotten. On the one hand, God is our beatitude because He is God; to love Him as the source of our happiness is to love and glorify all His infinite perfections. That is the underlying meaning of this statement: "If [the chief good] is nothing else but God . . ., what lover of God can be prevented from loving himself."[65] On the other hand, God is the last end of all things, of our final happiness as well as of our virtue on earth, and our happiness itself must tend to glorify Him. That is the deeper meaning of the Augustinian formulas about God, the end of everything, whom one can enjoy but not use. In the elect the joy of possessing God would cease to exist if this joy egoistically terminated in itself and did not return to God as a most beautiful canticle to His glory. The following represents Augustine's view. Although we separate in our mind the happiness of the elect and the glory of God, these two things really form one admirable unity for Augustine. When he demanded that we love God, the source of our happiness, he did not forget that this happiness, to exist at all, must be related like everything else to Him who is the last end of all beings: "I call charity that movement of the soul which aims at the enjoyment of God for His own sake, and the enjoyment of oneself and one's neighbor for God's sake." [66] Leibniz's statement, made when he was seeking to reconcile Bossuet and Fénelon, is verified in the happiness of the elect. "To love," he said, "is to find one's happiness in the well-being of another." [67] The elect are happy because of the well-being of God, because of the glory of God, and in particular because their happiness is a new manifestation of this divine glory.

3. PARTICULAR LAWS OF MORAL THEOLOGY

a. DOUBTFUL CONSCIENCE

A passage from *Against the Academics* is often cited as being in opposition to the theory of probabilism, [68] but wrongly, for this text only refutes the system of the Academy and proves that one cannot commit murder and adultery just because some men see no wrong in them. The passage does not treat the present question. Augustine was rather favorable to probabilism in a letter. [69] Speaking of the attendants at the worship of idols, he permits them, in case of doubt, to avail themselves of their liberty.

b. INDIVIDUAL MORAL PRINCIPLES

Augustine seems rather harsh in his decisions. Thus in the letter just cited he does not allow one to slay an unjust aggressor to save one's possessions or even one's life. [70] He correctly reprobated all lies, even lies of convenience. [71] He cleared the cult of the saints and angels of all accusations of idolatry. There is no clearer statement than his refutation of Faustus: "The Christian people celebrates the memory of the martyrs to stir up imitation of them, to be associated with their merits and helped by their prayers. Nevertheless, we offer sacrifice to none of the martyrs, but to the God of the martyrs Himself, although we offer it in memory of them."[72] Prayer for the departed is solemnly inculcated.[73] There is the immortal page of the *Confessions* where he asks that prayers and the Eucharistic sacrifice be offered for his mother.[74] These practices, in fact, along with almsgiving, are the principal means of offering solace to the dead.[75] And always he adds that only they will be thus consoled who during their lives had merited that the prayers of the Church be applied to them.

C. SOCIAL MORAL PRINCIPLES

Augustine proclaims the eminently social character of man and distinguishes the three societies to which he belongs: the family (*domus*), the state (*civitas*), and humanity.[76] The brotherhood of man, celebrated by the pagans themselves, draws men closer together because of "their hope for the same celestial reward."[77]

In the family he proclaims the Christian emancipation of women. True, the wife is subject to the authority of her husband[78] but she now has the same matrimonial rights as he.[79]

In civil society the right to private property is derived from the divine right, since all wealth is a means provided by God for fulfilling our destiny. In society the exercise of this right is sanctioned by human right or by civil law. That is all that Augustine was trying to say in a poorly understood passage of his commentary on John.[80] It is inconceivable that writers like Barbeyrac, the translator of Puffendorf, and Nourrisson,[81] following Wyclif on this point,[82] attributed to him an abominable theocratic communism according to which the Christian who believes in God would be the sole subject of property rights while the unbeliever or sinner would lose all rights. They refer to this passage: "Everything, therefore, which is possessed in bad faith belongs to another; he who uses a thing wrongly possesses it in bad faith."[83] But the very next lines of this text clearly indicate that we have here one of the African Doctor's frequent oratorical exaggerations and even, we might say, a poor pun centering on the double meaning of *male possidere*. Augustine adds that we must be satisfied with civil laws which allow the wicked to have their property. Besides, he explicitly teaches in all his works that God gives earthly goods to the wicked as He does to the good: "He gives this to the good and the bad."[84] "Lest these things be considered evil they are given to the good; lest they be considered the great or the chief goods they are given to the bad."[85]

In reference to slavery Augustine, without preaching its abolition for which the customs of the time would not have been prepared, declares it contrary to the primitive nature of man and adds that "it is not work which degrades the slave, but sin."[86] He demands that slaves be treated with mildness as members of the human family. He approves their emancipation;[87] he calls them to the true nobility of monastic life.[88]

In the delicate question of the authority of the prince and the obedience due to civil laws, Cunningham rightly admires Augustine's wisdom and moderation.[89] The learned doctor insists upon the great law of justice for societies: "Without it, what would the great empires be but teeming broods of robbers?"[90] The prince ought to govern for the public good.[91] No law can oblige if it is not derived from the eternal law.[92] The good of society is the chief good to such an extent that he permits, if the public good demands it, a change in the established government and the overthrow of an unjust and oppressive democracy to establish an aristocratic or monarchical power.[93] A soldier does not have to inquire whether a war is unjust but should obey.[94]

In regard to the relationship between Church and state, Augustine states that wherever the laws respect the rights of conscience, the Church or the heavenly city is not concerned about diversities in customs, laws, or institutions. She suppresses nothing, she destroys nothing; on the contrary, she preserves such a social order and conforms to it.[95] But while Augustine asserts the rights of the civil authority in its own sphere, he also maintains freedom of conscience against a prince who invades the realm of faith: "To pretend that Christian liberty frees one from obedience to the prince is an error; but the error is yet greater if one thinks that one's faith could ever be subject to a civil magistrate."[96]

4. DIFFERENT DEGREES OF CHRISTIAN MORAL PERFECTION

a. HIERARCHY OF MERITS AND DEMERITS

In general, Augustine establishes a moral hierarchy of merits and demerits. In the fourth century Stoic ideas had infected certain minds and, following the lead of Jovinianus, many more or less freely denied all inequality in good as in evil. Man is either virtuous or criminal, but it is impossible to lay down various degrees of wrong-doing or of virtue. This teaching would be hard to believe if Protestants and many rationalists did not still maintain this paradoxical position today. Now it is to the credit of St. Augustine that he has, with more precision than his predecessors, explained in all its different aspects what Harnack calls "the scale" of virtue and vice.[97] This learned critic quite rightly remarked that this is one of the salient points of "his Catholicism" and he accurately enumerates the four principal aspects of the question, all of which show the absolute opposition of the Protestant system to that of Augustine.

(1) The distinction between precepts and counsels—the former cannot be violated without sin while the counsels are only a work of supererogation—has been clearly explained in the *Confessions* in reference to Matthew 19:21: "If you wish to be perfect";[98] in *On Holy Virginity*, commenting on the First Epistle to the Corinthians 7:25: "I have no command from the Lord";[99] and in *Letter 157* where he refutes the Pelagian error imposing voluntary poverty as a precept.[100] In *On the Labor of the Monks* the religious state is called "a higher grade of holiness."[101]

(2) A clearer and more precise distinction between mortal and venial sin is also due to the labors of the Bishop of Hippo. Until his time a general vagueness surrounds this subject even in the best authors. They often give the title of venial to sins which are really very serious but which the Church forgives before the hour of

death. One author was to say later: "Some sins are mortal and become venial when submitted to the sacrament of penance."[102] Augustine, however, drew up quite clearly a line of absolute demarcation between venial and mortal sins according as they merit eternal fires or not. Thus, treating of the Acts of the Apostles in the *Mirror of Scripture*, he refutes the lingering error which limited mortal sins to the three canonical crimes and adds: "That all other sins which separate one from the kingdom of God besides these three are not mortal is . . . a foolish statement. Neither robbers nor greedy men nor drunken men nor blasphemers nor the rapacious will possess the kingdom of God."[103] Thus we see that Augustine considered mortal sins (*letalia, mortifera, crimina*) in the meaning and extent of modern theology.

Venial sins, on the other hand (he also calls them slight, daily) are compatible with grace, holiness, and the right to heaven. They are the faults of each day whose forgiveness is obtained by prayer whereas mortal sins demand reconciliation by the Church: "There are venial sins without which we cannot live."[104] Venial sins are represented by the wood and straw in the edifice built upon the foundation of Christ (I Cor. 3:15).[105] Finally, venial sins are those slight faults which even the most holy never succeed in avoiding; when, in fact, Augustine maintains against the Pelagians that every man sins, he is treating only of venial sin.[106]

The examples which he gives of these slight failings show the agreement of his thought with the present teaching of theology: "Sometimes he laughed a little immoderately or joked for the sake of relaxation. . . ."[107] To this theory of venial sin is attached the teaching on purgatory, which was especially developed by St. Augustine.[108]

(3) In the just, there is, then, a scale of degrees of perfection as there is a hierarchy of wickedness in sinners. Augustine's famous formula sums this up: "Incipient charity is incipient justice; advanced charity is advanced justice; outstanding charity is outstanding justice; perfect charity is perfect justice."[109]

(4) This is the reason why Augustine teaches that in heaven there is a hierarchy of glory corresponding to the hierarchy of

merits and likewise in hell punishments which are proportioned to the crimes: "In happiness one will outshine another and in sorrow one will find it somewhat more tolerable than another."[110]

b. RELIGIOUS LIFE

In particular, the teaching of the perfect life and the religious state is marked in Augustine with a wise, moderate, and practical asceticism. In his enthusiastic eulogies of virginity,[111] while exalting the superiority of perfect continence, he always upholds the holiness of marriage: "We prefer virginity to marriage not as a good to an evil, but as the better to the good."[112] His rule is eminently practical; the same characteristic stands out in his theory of the works of the monks.[113] He stands in sharp contrast to Eastern ideas; the active genius of the Roman West here modifies with felicitous results the concept of the monastic life and prepares those great orders of Western monks whose influence was to be so profound in all arenas of intellectual and civilizing activity. In Augustine's works are found a defense and an explanation for the vows in general,[114] for the religious profession in general,[115] for monastic obedience,[116] and for evangelical poverty.[117] In *Sermon 356* he appears as the apostle of this last virtue among his clergy.[118] But here also he guards against the excesses of Pelagian rigorism which forbids any earthly wealth; possessing goods is not evil for a Christian, but using them for evil.[119] "Root out your pride; then riches will not hurt you."[120]

c. MYSTICAL THEOLOGY

Without making a detailed study of his theory on the three phases of the spiritual life, we cannot omit all mention of this important fact. It was Augustine's role, by infusing Christian vitality into the Neoplatonic theories on the purification of the soul, to introduce into Western asceticism, even before the time of the pseudo-Areopagite, the whole collection of images and formulas which still nourish our ascetical literature. Thus mystical theology owes to him the distinction of the three great stages in the ascent of our soul to God which are called the purgative, illuminative, and unitive ways or lives.

The dominant idea is one of a necessary progress in the striving of the soul to contemplate God and become united with Him. Just as Augustine himself in the *Confessions*,[121] so we must climb the ascents of the heart and sing the canticle of degrees. These degrees can be distinguished in various ways. In *On the Quantity of the Soul* Augustine, joining Aristotle's division of our faculties to Plato's method of elevating the soul to the contemplation of the beautiful, distinguished seven activities of the soul or seven degrees which it must surmount.[122]

He describes them with an exquisite charm, summarizing them in these terms:[123] (1) life; (2) feeling (sensitive life); (3) art (that is, thought or the intellectual life); (4) virtue (or moral striving for purification); (5) tranquillity (calm of the mastered passions); (6) entrance (*ingressio*: this obscure word denotes the gaze of the purified soul fixed on God, seeking to penetrate into the sanctuary of the Divinity); (7) contemplation (which is abiding in God). He also expresses these degrees under another form: (1) from the body; (2) through the body; (3) around the body; (4) to oneself; (5) in oneself; (6) to God; (7) with God.[124]

More often, however, he omits the first, more philosophical degrees and reduces the ascent of the soul to the three operations which today constitute the three ways of purification, illumination, and union or contemplation.[125]

Purification, in the mind of the Platonists, consisted in separating the soul from everything corporeal. The body was essentially a defilement and prison of the soul and had to be excluded from the future life.[126] In the more Christian outlook of Augustine, however, purification of the heart means the destruction of the love of all other things except the soul and God, the elevation above everything changeable and perishable.[127]

Illumination directly signifies the increase of light and the increasingly clear view of the Supreme Beauty which accompany the intense striving to fix the gaze of the soul on God. Indirectly and as a result, however, illumination is an increasingly intimate relationship of our soul with God through the virtues, especially the three theological virtues. This typically Platonic connection between light and virtue surprises us today. Augustine explains it in a profound passage of the *Soliloquies*: "The vision of the soul is reason. But because it does not follow that everyone who looks sees, correct and perfect vision, that is, one which results in sight, is called virtue. For virtue is correct or perfect reason."[128] He goes on to show the role of faith, hope, and charity in fixing the gaze of the soul on the divine light. From this it becomes clearer why baptism, because it crowns our purification with the light of faith, is called illumination.

Union with God, "the Father of Truth,"[129] becomes more and more intimate in the light of contemplation: "It is as though the soul were dwelling in God. Then what transports, what enjoyment of the chief and only true Good! What breath of tranquil calm and eternity! What can I say of these things? These are the marvels which great souls have declared, insofar as they thought fitting to speak of them, great and incomparable souls who, we believe, have contemplated and now contemplate these things."[130] The account of the ineffable conversation between Augustine and Monica at Ostia gives us both the theory and a perfectly charming example of this sublime state.[131]

Recently the influence exercised by Augustine has been compared to that of pseudo-Dionysius the Areopagite. Ritschl was the first to express the idea that the pseudo-Areopagite in the East and Augustine in the West had exercised a parallel influence. Each of them left the imprint of ecclesiasticism, pertaining to cult in the case of Dionysius, to moral in Augustine.[132] Harnack has this to say about such an estimate.[133] Both of them, far from modifying the Catholicism of the people, submitted to forces which were at work before their time in the two Churches. Let us add that, just considering the area of mystical theology, Augustine enjoys the threefold superiority of Western genius over pseudo-Dionysius: First, the superiority of a certain and unequivocal doctrine. In the description of the divine union he clearly safeguards the distinction of the soul and God, whereas occasionally one fears in the

Eastern author, as in Plotinus, that the soul will be absorbed in the pure oneness that is God. Second, the superiority of precision and clarity. He does not compound bombastic terms and pretentious language which obfuscate his thought in vague generalities. Third, a more profoundly moral character, as Harnack notes.[134] For Augustine, the ascetical life must be a spiritual life and a striving after virtue. He does not allow it to be absorbed by the external practices of a purely material asceticism or by the sort of mystical reveries which prepare the way for the follies of quietism.

CHAPTER XVI

Eschatology

1. ORIGENISM AND MILLENARIANISM

I<small>N</small> the description of our future destiny (a question about which several important points were still very obscure in the fourth century) St. Augustine's merit is to have avoided the double pitfall of the systems of Origen and the millenarians.

a. ORIGENISM

Origenism, after having disturbed the whole of Christian teaching by its bizarre anthropology, that is, by its theory that souls are spirits which have sinned in previous existences and are exiled in the body, likewise overturned the economy of the world to come with its novel ideas on a multiplicity of successive existences, the quality of resurrected bodies, the nature of future punishments, and especially its theory that eternal punishment is replaced by a final restoration which would bring about the primordial equality in happiness granted to all, angels and devils. The whole doctrine was a collection of monstrous errors. Augustine, firmer on this point than St. Jerome and other Fathers, was never misled by these dreams. He condemns them collectively,[1] warning us that "the Church has rightly rejected them."[2] This is probably an allusion to the letters of Pope Anastasius I against Rufinus and Origen (400–401), letters addressed to Simplicianus, Bishop of Milan,[3] and John of Jerusalem.[4]

b. MILLENARIANISM

In regard to the millenarianist dreams of a second coming of Christ who would reign on earth with the just, his attitude was less clear at the beginning. Certainly he always rejected the ridiculous tales of a gross and carnal chiliasm, as he himself notes in the *City of God*.[5] He adds, however, that he found a certain fascination at first in the spiritual kingdom or the Sabbatarianism of a thousand years which he recognized in the Apocalypse (chap. 20). As a matter of fact an indication of this is found in one of his sermons: "The Lord will reign on earth with his saints. . . ."[6] But he was not slow to repudiate this error. Consequently, from then on the kingdom of Christ and the first resurrection of the Apocalypse meant for him the actual period from the Ascension to the Last Judgment, a period during which Christ reigns with the Church on earth and with the just happily awaiting the resurrection.[7]

2. THE LOT OF SOULS FROM DEATH TO JUDGMENT

a. THE PROBLEM

This is one of the questions where it is most difficult to pinpoint the thought of the holy doctor. In the fourth century millenarian ideas had thrown a considerable amount of obscurity on this question in the minds of men. For the chiliasts, such as St. Justin, Irenaeus, and Tertullian, this time between death and the resurrection was not a period of happiness for the just, but one of waiting for the earthly kingdom which they were to share with Christ. Many were convinced that the souls of the saints remained in a special place (the bosom of Abraham, an infernal limbo, paradise) until the judgment. This conviction was accompanied by a great deal of uncertainty about the condition of such souls. Some Fathers even seem to have denied them happiness. St. Ambrose, Augustine's teacher, (despite certain texts influenced by IV Esdras, chap. 7) represents the saints in heaven mingling with the angelic choirs.[8] St. Augustine himself did not entirely escape all uncertainty. Thus Pope John XXII and the Anglican Thomas Burnet who tried to revive his error[9] claimed that, according to Augustine, the souls of the just (at least, Burnet says, if we except the martyrs) do not enjoy the vision of God until the resurrection.

Mabillon is very partial to this opinion.[10] Petavius[11] and Gener[12] think that Augustine was undecided. Turmel asserts that he had kept alive "the belief in the postponement of punishment until after the resurrection."[13] "According to St. Augustine," he says, "the soul deprived of its body has only a blunted sensibility and is incapable of keen joy or suffering."[14] This last interpretation, we are going to see, is absolutely against the texts. We must realize with Muratori[15] and Schwane[16] that there is a certain vagueness in the ideas of St. Augustine, especially concerning the place where these souls live. But his system as explained in the light of numerous texts leaves no doubt about the happiness of these souls because of the vision of God.

b. AUGUSTINIAN SYSTEM

Immediately after death the eternal destiny is fixed. Guilty souls are enclosed in a place of torture; the just in regions of repose and happiness.

All of this, as everyone admits, is indisputable. In the interval which separates death from the resurrection, he writes in 428, "according to what they did . . . souls are either tortured or find rest."[17] The same thought appears in 421 in the *Enchiridion*. This period, he says, "contains souls in hidden places of rest or anguish as each one merits."[18] Again in 415 he proposes the same idea with an explanation of this rest which is a true happiness: "All souls have different fates when they leave this world. The good have joy; the bad, torments. But when the resurrection occurs, the joy of the good will be greater and the torments of the bad worse since they will then be tormented in the body."[19] This joy is still better expressed: "The soul is either borne to that place of punishments or to that other place where we find not corporal punishments, but quiet and joy."[20] In a sermon he says: "Forgive and then death will come as a father instead of as a judge. Instead of a tormentor, it will come as an angel to carry you to the bosom of Abraham. Instead of taking you to prison, it will lead you to paradise."[21] This fact alone excludes all blunted knowledge, all drowsiness of the soul, although the word *sleep* is used in the very passage where it is said: "The good have joy."[22] When Augustine refers the retribution for our works to the Last Judgment, there can only be question of a more solemn, public, and more complete retribution. (*Ultimate retribution* is his own expression.)[23] It only remains to determine whether the damned already suffer the infernal fires, whether the elect already enjoy the vision of God.

The reprobate suffer the fires of hell from the time of their death. Not one of the texts alleged by Turmel excludes this fire and there are many which explicitly state that the fire does exist. Thus, talking of the evil rich man "plunged in flames" Augustine asserts that this is the state of the wicked after death: "The burial place of hell, the depth of punishments which gnaws at the proud . . . after this life."[24] *Sermon 280* describes the future tortures, but adds that "even now the one thirsts in hell for a drop of water from the finger of the beggar while the other is happily resting in the bosom of Abraham."[25] Again he speaks of "the torments of hell"[26] and the "ungodly rich man in the torments of hell."[27]

St. Augustine very often asserts that the souls of the saints enjoy the beatific vision at the present moment. In reference to all the saints, when describing the happiness of those who have finished their pilgrimage here below, he says: "Not such a place is that home of ours, Jerusalem, where all are good. . . . There all the just and holy enjoy the Word of God without reading. . . . For what is written for us in books they perceive through the face of God! O great home of ours."[28] In Augustine's commentary on John the good thief is shown to be blessed by the presence of Christ as God even before the Resurrection of the Savior: "The soul of the thief . . . already blessed by the gift of Him . . . was able to be with Him in paradise that same day."[29] The *Confessions* describe the happiness of Nebridius in the bosom of Abraham: "He no longer puts his ear to my mouth, but his spiritual mouth to Your fountain and drinks, as much as he can, of wisdom according to his desire, happy without bounds."[30] It is in God that Nebridius thinks of Augustine: "Nor do I think that he is so inebriated by that potion that he is forgetful of me, since You, Lord, whom he drinks, are mindful of me."[31] Thus he drinks the very Divinity, he becomes intoxicated with this source of eternal wisdom and happiness. Elsewhere he asserts, speaking of the martyr St. Stephen but applying the teaching to all the saints, that they are with Christ, enjoying unspeakable pleasure: "Where, then, did Jesus receive the soul of Stephen? In what haven, in what heaven of heavens? . . . Hear Jesus Himself: 'Father, I wish that where I am, there they also be with Me.' To be where Christ is! What mind can grasp that!"[32] Another text, or rather a theory, removes all doubt by its very strangeness. The happiness of the souls of the just after death is, in Augustine's mind, a truth so certain that he extends it to the just of the Old Testament even before the Passion. The false conclusion he draws from this idea is that Jesus Christ, after His Passion, descended into the hell of the damned and not into the limbo of the just. Why? Because, he says, the just in limbo already enjoy the beatifying presence of the Godhead and he can see no reason for Jesus to visit them: "I have not yet been able to find what advantage His visit would have been for the just in the bosom of Abraham, since I think that He never withdrew the beatifying presence of His divinity from them."[33] He confirms this thought by the promise to the good thief and draws this bold conclusion: "Therefore at that time He was already in paradise and the bosom of Abraham through His beatifying presence and in hell through His judicial powers."[34]

Speaking of the vision of God for the martyrs in particular, his assertions are so clear that Burnet himself acknowledged it. Augustine depicts the martyrs seated at the eternal banquet where Christ Himself nourishes them with His divinity: "There is a great banquet where the viands are the Lord of the table Himself. No one else feeds the banqueters of himself, but Christ the Lord does this; He is the host; He, the food and drink. . . . O happy ones. . . . They have completed their sorrows and received their rewards."[35]

In another place he speaks of their happiness with God: "O happy abode! Faith knows it. . . . Where, then, are these saints? In a place of rest, there where everything is good. What more do you seek? You do not know the place; think of their merit!

Wherever they are, they are with God."[36] They are also with Christ and rejoice in Him: "They have passed from this world to the Father. They sought Christ by their confession; they obtained Him by their death."[37] Even more, these souls are not only with Christ but they reign with Him. This kingdom is the lot of all who die in the Lord according to the word of the Apocalypse, 14:13: "Although they do not yet have their bodies, their souls already reign with Him."[38] But why does the Apocalypse speak only of the martyrs? Augustine's reply is very important, for it shows that a distinction cannot be set up between the martyrs and the rest of the saints: "The martyrs are the only ones mentioned because to them especially this kingdom belongs; they especially rule after death. But it is the lot of all and the other departed souls must be included in it."[39]

St. Augustine sometimes makes the bosom of Abraham and paradise abodes distinct from the angelic heaven.[40] Elsewhere he seems to think this is only a difference in terminology and says that the true abode of the souls of the just is God: "God is our abode after this life."[41] In any case paradise and the bosom of Abraham are a place of happiness, one of the numerous mansions of heaven.[42]

At the resurrection the punishments and rewards of souls will be, according to Augustine, much more substantially increased than later theologians were ever to teach. Here, we believe, is where his theory differs essentially from the common teaching. It seems that there had been some obscurity in his mind on the different manners of seeing God face to face, for he doubts, not that the just see Him, but that they see Him "as the angels do." That is the meaning of two famous passages.[43] "Eternal life with the angels" is not conferred until after the resurrection. Thus, for him, the rewards and punishments before the Last Judgment are only a shadow and "like a dream" in relation to the future realities. This comparison is explicitly enunciated in a sermon where nevertheless the present happiness of the saints is magnificently extolled: "With what joy do they now partake of the spiritual banquet!"[44] This happiness, however, is only a part of the pro-

mised beatitude, "a small particle."[45] The same comparison of
the dream appears in another sermon: "Such as dreams are."[46] It
is important to note that this increase in happiness is sometimes
attributed to the return of the body. Thus he asserts that the just
souls cannot at the present time, like the angels, see the Divinity,
"whether because of another hidden cause, or because they have
a natural appetite to care for the body which keeps them back
somewhat, as long as the body is not joined to them, from striving
with their whole attention toward the summit of heaven."[47] This
reasoning did not convince later theologians.

3. PURGATORY

St. Augustine is the first of the Fathers, Hofmann states, who
formulated in a really precise way the teaching on purgatory hinted
at in the earlier Fathers, for example, in the "cleansing fire" ($\pi\hat{v}\rho$
$\kappa\alpha\theta\alpha\rho\sigma\iota\kappa\acute{o}\nu$) of St. Basil and St. Gregory of Nyssa.[48] But here again
certain critics have cast obscurity on the thought of the great doc-
tor. According to Turmel he did not assert the existence of purgatory; toward the end of his life he was merely on the verge of
conceding its existence. The question of its existence, however,
has been confused with doubts about the nature of that state.

a. EXISTENCE OF PURGATORY

The existence of purgatory is absolutely certain in Augustine's
writings, just as in those of his teacher St. Ambrose who distinguishes so clearly the fire of purgatory from that of hell.[49] It is
without the slightest hesitation that Augustine says in the *City of
God*: "But some undergo temporal punishment in this life only,
some after death, and some both now and then, but all these
suffer before the last and most terrible judgment."[50] Again, he
decides without a trace of doubt that the Last Judgment brings
purgatory to an end.[51] More precisely yet, he asserts that these
punishments suffered by the souls of the departed will obtain for
them, at the judgment, mercy "that they be not sent into ever-

lasting fire."[52] He says that the slothful soul will suffer after death "either the fire of purgation or eternal punishment."[53] He is not less precise in his commentary on the Psalms. He asks God to purify him in this life that he will not have to suffer after death the purifying fire (*emendatorio igne*). He explicitly distinguishes two kinds of fire, one which tortures the damned and one of expiation for the just: "He will correct those who will be saved by means of fire."[54]

In addition, the teaching of a period of expiation after death is closely linked to that of prayers for the departed which Augustine taught so often.[55] "Do You forgive her her debts," he says of his mother.[56] "There is contained here," he says in a sermon, "a certain, indubitable truth, transmitted by the Fathers and confirmed by the practice of the universal Church, that prayer obtains from God a more merciful treatment for the departed in expiation of their faults."[57] He proves this by the commemoration of the departed at the Eucharistic sacrifice. Among the errors of Aerius he mentions one condemning prayer for the departed: "Nor is it to be denied that the souls of the departed are solaced by the prayer of their living friends."[58] One does not solace a person unless he is suffering. Finally, all the explanations which we are about to record on the nature of this expiation necessarily suppose its existence.

b. NATURE OF THE PUNISHMENT

The nature of the punishments of purgatory is, on the contrary, quite obscure and puzzling for the great doctor. The punishment of material fire, so certain in hell, is here only a probability toward which he is inclined. He often explained the phrase "as if by fire" of St. Paul (I Cor. 3:15).[59] It is likely that he always understood by this a cleansing fire for slight faults. But what is this fire? Sometimes it is the fire of trials and punishments in this life,[60] sometimes it is death itself with its pains.[61] Occasionally it is even the fire of the Last Judgment which completes the purification of some souls: "They will be cleansed by the fires of the Last Judgment."[62] Finally, between death and judgment there is perhaps a real fire which seems to be like that of hell.[63] Augustine's doubts centered upon this fire: "I do not refute their arguments because they may be true."[64] How could anyone, in fact, admit that he doubts about the existence of expiation when he asserts it so categorically, and that twice in the same work? Likewise the doubt expressed in the *Enchiridion*[65] concerns only the fire, "some sort of cleansing fire," because further on he energetically states that these souls suffer.[66] Because of the uncertainty of Augustine and other Fathers about the *fire* of purgatory, the Church, as Bellarmine observes,[67] has not made any pronouncement on the subject.

c. INTENSITY OF THE PUNISHMENT

Augustine unhesitatingly destroys any illusion about the intensity of these punishments and asserts that they surpass all the sufferings of this earth. Because the Apostle said: "He will be saved," this fire has been scorned. But be on your guard: "Although surely saved through fire, that fire will nevertheless be more grievous than anything man can suffer in this life. And you know how much the evil have suffered and can suffer."[68]

d. SUBJECTS OF THIS PUNISHMENT

The souls subject to this purification are those who must still expiate for their sins, although they are in the grace of God. He often repeated this in his commentaries on the text "as if by fire." In the *Enchiridion* he states again that only those souls are solaced by the prayers of the Church who have merited during their life to be aided by the prayers of the living.[69] He explicitly mentions that baptized infants who have died before committing any personal sins are delivered not only from hell but from purgatory also: "Not only is such an infant not destined for eternal punishment, but it does not even suffer any cleansing torments after death."[70]

e. TERMINUS OF PURGATORY

After the Last Judgment purgatory will exist no longer. The final sentence recognizes only the elect and the reprobate.[71] But

Augustine, we recall, would not be loath to admit with other Fathers—St. Hilary, for example—the purification of certain souls at the very moment of judgment according to the sayings of Malachias (3:1–6) and Isaias (4:4): "It seems more clear that some souls in that judgment shall suffer some kind of cleansing punishments."[72]

4. THE FINAL RESURRECTION

The resurrection appears in his treatises, letters, and sermons as one of the Christian dogmas which then was a vivid preoccupation of people's minds and gave scope for sometimes strange and even coarse questions.[73] *Sermons 361* and *362* form with the *Enchiridion* and the *City of God* a complete treatise on the truth and explanation of this dogma.[74]

Faith in the resurrection is defended against the attacks of the pagans throughout *Sermon 361*. Augustine says that it is the dogma most violently attacked;[75] the immortality of the soul has its proponents among the pagans, but the resurrection is accepted by no one: "On no other subject is the faith contradicted as violently, as stubbornly, as strenuously, and as argumentatively."[76] He relies for his defense of the dogma on the Resurrection of Jesus Christ, on the miracle of the world's faith,[77] and on the creation and also the marvels of nature, no less mysterious than the Resurrection.[78]

For the resurrected body to be the same as it was in life, it is sufficient that the same material elements come together to form it, even if they are distributed in a different manner: "A statue recast in the same mold remains identical to itself, although the particles are in different places."[79]

The universality of the resurrection allows no exception among the dead.[80] Every human being, even if he never saw the light of day, will be reborn to this life.[81] But will all die? Will there not be an exception made for those alive on the last day? Augustine remains doubtful about this because of St. Paul's text (I Thess.

4:14–16), but he is inclined to think that all men are condemned to death by original sin: "I would like to hear what the more learned say on this topic."[82] The "living and the dead" of the Creed can refer to the saints and the wicked, or again to those living at the moment of the final cataclysm.[83]

Incorruptibility will be given to the body of the reprobate also in order that the fire may not consume them.[84] Only the body of the just will be glorified. This is not the ethereal body of the Origenists but the same body born of the earth, now transformed and immortal.[85] This earthly flesh itself, he says in a sermon, will become heavenly and angelic.[86] Another sermon described its incomparable beauty,[87] still another its marvelous agility.[88]

5. The Last Judgment

Two replies of Augustine to Hesychius, Bishop of Salona in Dalmatia, complete the doctrine explained in detail in Book XX of the *City of God*.[89] The reality of this solemn judgment is proved by the testimony of the prophets, of the Apocalypse, and especially of our Lord.[90] It is in His humanity that Jesus Christ is constituted the supreme judge of men.[91] Thus it is this humanity which will show itself to all, the reprobate and the elect; only to the elect will His divinity be revealed.[92]

The manifestation of faults will be accomplished by a sudden illumination of consciences through the power of God. This is the book of life.[93]

Augustine's prudence in regard to the date of the end of the world was noted by Ittameyer.[94] He is far from participating in the chimerical hopes of many of his contemporaries. He confesses his ignorance and does not think that any prophetic gift permits the calculation of this time. In a letter he joins St. Jerome in condemning the rashness of such calculations and adds: "I choose to confess my cautious ignorance rather than profess a false knowledge."[95] In a further reply he concludes that one who dares to assert the nearness of the judgment "speaks hopefully, but is deceived more dangerously."[96] At any rate the preaching of the Gospel in the entire world must come first.[97]

6. Hell

St. Augustine is not the originator of the teaching of an ever-lasting hell, as has been sometimes said, but he has investigated with an astounding patience all the systems which deny it, especially in the *City of God* where he sets forth all the positions he could think of against this doctrine.[98]

a. ETERNITY OF HELL

He proves the eternity of hell against Origen, relying on the saying of Christ (Matt. 25:41–46).[99] In a letter to Deogratias he adds some considerations from reason.[100] The *Enchiridion* refutes the false mercy of the Origenists, who saw the assertions of Scripture as a threat rather than a true statement: "These words are more terrifying than true."[101]

b. HELL IN THE CHRISTIAN CONCEPT

From the doctrinal viewpoint, the error of the merciful which granted final salvation to some after a more or less lengthy period of expiation was often expounded and refuted by Augustine.[102] In Book XXI of the *City of God* he enumerates its subtleties which assure salvation in turn either to all the damned (chap. 18, 29), to all the baptized (19, 25), to only those baptized Catholics despite a subsequent apostasy (20, 25), to Catholics who persevere in the faith despite their sins (21, 26), or only to the faithful who had given alms. The Doctor of Hippo refutes all these as opposed to the teaching of five Apostles: Paul, Peter, John, James, and Jude.[103] In particular, almsgiving and the intercession of the saints can bring it about that a soul not merit hell. They can do nothing, however, about bringing the soul back once it has fallen.[104]

From the historical viewpoint, was this error of the merciful as predominant and universal in the fourth century as Turmel claims?[105] Was it St. Augustine who, by his intransigent teaching, finally succeeded in imposing the dogma of the everlasting punishment of sinners? Such an assertion would go against the evidence of the texts and the facts. The strongest argument rested upon the strange misunderstanding which we have pointed out in reference to the Fathers of the Synod of Diospolis.[106] This error was wrongly attributed to them, for they had repudiated it and Pelagius together. St. Augustine besides asserts that the number holding it is relatively small. In the *Enchiridion* he says that "this was said by some."[107] When he says later: "In vain therefore some, nay a great number,"[108] that last phrase must not be understood, at the risk of contradiction, except in the absolute sense of a *great number* and not in the relative sense of the *greatest number*. Finally, the holy doctor, without yet condemning this error as heretical, rightly thought that it was contrary to divine faith: "Those who believe this and are yet Catholics. . . ."[109] In the reply to Dulcitius which leans towards this opinion he adds: "I also would wish that it were thus, but I must yield to the clear meaning of Scripture."[110]

C. DELIVERANCE OF THE DAMNED

Were the damned delivered at the descent of Christ into hell? This problem, arising from the First Epistle of St. Peter, 3:18–21, had a vivid fascination for Augustine. Had Jesus Christ really preached the faith to damned unbelievers and saved them? He asserts this clearly enough in the *Literal Commentary on Genesis*.[111] Interrogated by Evodius on this subject, he confesses his perplexity.[112] Afterwards he regards it as certain that our Lord truly descended into the hell of the damned and not into the limbo of the just.[113] In that case, whom did He save? Unbelievers at the time of Noah? Why only those? All unbelievers? This would be consoling, but what are the consequences? Unbelievers after the time of Christ could hope for the same salvation.[114] His conclusion therefore was that Christ delivered those "whom He willed."[115] Perhaps, he adds, the whole passage is simply allegorical.[116]

d. MITIGATION OF PUNISHMENT

In the *Enchiridion* Augustine asserts that prayers for the damned do not avail to solace them although they do console the living: "Prayers for the very wicked, although they are no help to the dead, are some sort of consolation for the living."[117] Faure concludes rightly from this that Augustine in the following quotation did not teach nor personally admit any mitigation of the sufferings of hell. He tolerates, nevertheless, a doctrine very similar to it, namely, that these punishments are periodically lessened: "Let them think, if it pleases them, that the punishments of the damned are lessened somewhat at certain intervals."[118] But he is very careful to add that this opinion has no other foundation than a human compassion and that in any case the eternity of punishment is beyond dispute.[119] The same discretion is shown in the *City of God* in reference to a similar opinion on the divine mercy in regard to the damned, "which indeed I do not favor just because I do not reject it."[120] He had just recalled that the Church never prays for the damned "nor does she now pray for infidels and the ungodly departed."[121] St. John Chrysostom had asserted this mitigation of the infernal punishments which has found one or two other champions, even Peter Lombard.[122] Since the severe censure of St. Thomas,[123] however, this belief has fallen into discredit.[124]

e. REALITY OF MATERIAL FIRE

St. Augustine is both quite affirmative and quite moderate about the reality of the material fire. He is affirmative, for he condemns the Origenist interpretation which admitted a metaphorical and spiritual fire, remorse, and so forth.[125] He even finds in the union of the soul and body a reason for admitting that corporal fire could affect the fallen angels themselves "in whatever wonderful but true manner."[126] He is moderate, for he allows the reader freedom to choose for himself since the teaching was not then fully developed.[127] In any case, this fire is not of the same intensity for all.[128]

7. HEAVEN AND THE VISION OF GOD

The angels and the elect of humanity form one single heavenly city and they enjoy together the ineffable happiness which has its source in the vision of God.[129] Do the eyes of the glorified body share in this vision? That was a problem much discussed in those days and many were in favor of it. We today are surprised at the hesitations of Augustine, even more when we see that his doubts began and grew stronger as he grew older. In the beginning he denied absolutely that our bodily eyes share in the sight of God. In 408 in a letter to Italica he rejects a corporal vision with extreme severity; he even calls it a folly (*dementiam*).[130] Even the glorified eyes of the Savior cannot see the Father.

Later his denial was softened. Toward 413 a letter to Paulinus (really a treatise on the vision of God) again condemns this error, but with more indulgence.[131] A letter to the bishop Fortunatianus excuses and softens his earlier statements even further.[132] The letter of 415 to Evodius, who had asked him about this subject, is of the same nature.[133] In a sermon he allows a certain freedom provided that no injury is done the infinite spirituality of God: "Let us not try to put God in a place."[134]

Finally, towards 426, he has real doubts and attempts a reconciliation in the *City of God*: "Is it not possible, is it not very likely that the risen, when they are contemplating with their transfigured bodily eyes the new heavens and the new earth, should clearly discover God present everywhere and governing everything just as from watching the movements and the actions of life in men we discover life itself? . . ."[135] All that is very vague, just as the two imaginary suppositions to justify the sight of a spiritual being by a material organ. The first is the hypothesis of such a transformation that the glorified eye would no longer be a bodily eye, but a spiritualized eye, that is, because it would no longer be an eye. The second imagines that God is seen simultaneously in creatures and in Himself: "In order that He may be seen in the spirit by each one of us in ourselves, that He may be seen by another in himself, that He may be seen in Himself, that He may be seen in the new heaven and earth."[136] According to the *Retractations*, this is his last word on the subject.[137] Posterity has not understood him. Philosophers like Nourrisson[138] have accused him of abandoning the clear distinction he had established with Plato between the sensible and the intelligible. His earlier opinion has prevailed in the schools and in the Church.

CHAPTER XVII

The Characteristic Genius of
St. Augustine

CRITICS have often inquired into Augustine's dominant quality, that trait which better characterizes his work and explains his fascinating influence on posterity. At different times they have considered various aspects of this great genius. Some were struck chiefly by the profundity and originality of his concepts. Augustine is for them the great sower of ideas on which the minds of the future were to live. Others, with Jungmann and Stöckl, have praised him because of the marvelous harmony of all the superior qualities of his mind, or again because of the universality and extent of his teaching. "In the great African doctor," says Father Zahm, "we seem to find united Plato's powerful and penetrating dialectic, Aristotle's profound scientific concepts, Origen's knowledge and pliant mind, the charm and eloquence of Basil and Chrysostom. Whether he is considered as a philosopher, as a theologian, or as an exegete . . . he is always remarkable and the uncontested teacher of all the ages."[1] Schaff admires especially "the rare union of the speculative talent of the Greeks with the eminently practical spirit of the Latin Church, a union which in him alone is realized in so eminent a degree."[2]

In all these judgments there is a great deal of truth, but the dominant characteristic of Augustine's genius and the true secret of his influence, in our opinion, must be sought in his heart, in his heart which penetrates the lofty speculations of his soaring mind and brings them to life with a white-hot feeling. Basically this is the general and traditional estimation which we are enunciating, since the heart has always been used as a symbol for Augustine, as the sun is for St. Thomas. Bougard interprets this symbol in the following manner: "Never had a man united in the same soul such inflexibly rigorous logic with such tenderness of heart."[3] This is also the opinion of Harnack, Böhringer, Nourrisson, and Storz. A short analysis of Augustine's love of truth will give us the key to his work and influence.

1. CHARACTERISTICS OF AUGUSTINE'S PASSION FOR TRUTH

a. FUSION OF INTELLECTUALISM AND MYSTICISM

The admirable fusion of a profound intellectualism with an enlightened mysticism is, then, the characteristic trait of Augustine. Truth for him is not just a sight to be looked at; it is a good which must be made one's own. We must love and live from truth. "O truth, truth! How intimately even then the marrow of my soul was sighing for you."[4] Augustine's genius is the marvelous gift of being able to embrace truth with every fiber of his soul—not with the heart alone, for the heart does not think; nor with the mind alone, for the mind grasps only truth which is abstract and already half dead. Augustine seeks the living truth. Even though he combats certain Platonic ideas, he still partakes of the rich heritage of Plato rather than of Aristotle. Probably for this reason he belongs to all times because he is in touch with all souls. But he is especially a modern, for doctrine in his pages is not the cold light of the schools; it is pulsating and permeated with personal feeling. Religion is not just a simple theory; Christianity is not merely a series of dogmas. It is also a life, as we would say today, or more exactly, a source of life.

Let no one be fooled by this, however. Augustine is not a sentimentalist, a pure mystic; the heart alone does not explain his power. If the dry and cold intellectualism of the metaphysicians gives way in him to an impassioned vision of truth, this vision is the basis for everything. He never knew that ethereal mysticism of our times which allows itself to be deluded by a vague and pointless sentimentalism. For him, emotion is deep, living, and alluring precisely because it is born of a firm, certain, and precise dogmatism which desires to know what it loves and why it loves. Christianity is a life, but life in the eternal and immutable truth. If no other Father has put his heart into his writings as much as Augustine, neither has any other likewise fastened the gaze of a clearer and more profound mind upon truth.

b. THE TRUTH IS GOD

The truth which gripped Augustine is God Himself. He did not, in fact, fall in love with that curiosity which loves only knowledge of truth, for it is truth itself which he desires to possess and live from—not such or such a truth, but the only and total truth in which all the basic problems of the world are resolved. He seeks the Being, the True, the Good which encompasses and explains everything, that is, he seeks God. He endlessly yearns for "God, that is, the truth . . . which is grasped by the intellect and the inner mind, the truth which always remains."[5] "The true philosopher is the lover of God,"[6] he exclaims. Thus all his teaching is essentially theological.[7] But Augustine's God is not the cold and abstract God who is the object of the interminable analyses of Scholasticism. It is the living God whom he seeks. He loves each one of His attributes, even the most abstract, as a reflection of the divine life in its relationships with our soul. He has a passionate desire for eternity, because for him the eternity of God is divine thought and divine love hovering watchfully over time, the cradle which was to hold our lives, even before time began. For Augustine, God Himself is the fatherland of our soul. This fact explains the celebrated dialogue: " 'What do you desire to know?' 'God and the soul.' 'Nothing more?' 'No, absolutely nothing.' "[8]

Other Fathers exalted the majesty and power of the Creator. Augustine is the first to be allured by the beauty of God: "I was snatched to You because of Your beauty."[9] On this subject no one has ever written pages so on fire. This beauty "ever old, ever new" inspires the rapturous elevations of the *Soliloquies* and the passionate cries of the *Confessions*. "I then saw in my spirit, O God, Your invisible beauties in the visible things which You have drawn from nothing."[10] Once having enjoyed this sight, his soul keeps for life a remembrance inflamed with love: "Returning to my ordinary occupations I brought nothing but a loving memory."[11] To other minds the sight of the world reveals the existence of God. Augustine, however, in that sublime appeal to all creatures, asks them about beauty. Their reply is an invitation to love: "But both the heaven and the earth and all things which are in them, behold on every side they tell me to love You."[12] "And to ask them," he adds, "I had only to look at them. Their beauty was their reply."[13]

C. COMMUNICATIVE TENDERNESS

Augustine's passion is not characterized by violence, but by a communicative tenderness. Tertullian also, with his fiery African temperament, had a passionate desire for truth. Besides the fact, however, that his horizon was otherwise hemmed in, his passion was a tyrannical thing which tried to impose the yoke of violence. Due to a lack of moderation, his feelings led him astray most grievously. Augustine's soul is just as ardent, but ardent with a love shot through with a tenderness for God and souls. He is so exquisitely delicate that from time to time he feels and makes us feel the most intimate emotions. This is the cause of the irresistible effect of the *Confessions*.

A Protestant thinker, Feuerlein, has highlighted (with exaggerations, it is true, and allowing the marvelous power of Augustine's intellect to remain in the background) Augustine's exquisite sensitivity which he calls the "feminine elements" of his genius. "There is something more than chance or accident," he says, "in the exceptional role which was allotted to his mother Monica in his intellectual development. This is the note which essentially distinguishes him from Luther, of whom it could be said: 'He is all man.' "[14] Schlosser is not afraid to say that there is more true poetry in Augustine's works than in all the writings of the Greek Fathers.[15] It is beyond dispute that no other thinker has been the cause of so many tears nor of tears so holy.

2. This Characteristic Genius an Explanation of Augustine's Doctrinal Work

Christian dogmas are not considered speculatively in themselves as much as in their relations with the soul and the great duties of Christian life. This is the only explanation of his division of theology—at first sight so strange—in the *Enchiridion*. He reduces all Christian doctrine to the three theological virtues. He does this because he is considering the different activities of the soul in the mysteries by which it must live. Likewise he is quite brief in the exposition of the divine mysteries, though he develops extensively the anthropological dogmas of sin and grace. The starting point of these investigations in all his early works is, as Eucken well notes,[16] essentially human and psychological. It is happiness: it is the thought motivating the "You made us for Yourself and our heart is restless. . . ." of the *Confessions*.[17] It is the same everywhere. In the Trinity, abbreviating the subtleties of the Greek Fathers, he contemplates by preference the inner life of the Divinity as a movement of the Being who is first all-powerful, then knowledge, and finally love. In the Incarnation he devotes more time to the moral aspect, to the triumph of humility.[18]

This is also the source, in Augustine's work, of a characteristic till then unknown: the vibrant personality which discloses itself everywhere. He inaugurated that type of literature in which the author's individuality reveals itself in the most abstract subject matter. "In his writings," to quote Eucken again, "the evolution of thought is to a pre-eminent degree the expression of his personality. Even his personal life makes itself known directly without any intermediate agent."[19] The *Confessions* are an inimitable example of this. Harnack, in this regard, admires the African doctor's exquisite gift for psychological observation and his captivating facility for portraying these intimate observations.[20] This talent is seen by Harnack as the secret both of his originality and his grandeur.

It is this characteristic also which distinguishes Augustine from other doctors and endows him with his own proper qualities. Ambrose, with his entirely Roman spirit, is also attracted by the practical aspect of questions but he never soared as high nor touched the heart as deeply as his disciple of Milan. Jerome is the more learned exegete, better equipped for scripture study. His style is also purer; despite his impetuous spirit, however, the solitary of Bethlehem is less penetrating, less warm, and less attractive than his correspondent of Hippo. Athanasius is as subtle in his metaphysical analysis of dogma but he does not arouse the heart and get hold of the entire soul as the African doctor does. In the Eastern Church Origen has played a role of innovator comparable to Augustine in the West, but his influence, infelicitous on more than one count, took place rather in the sphere of speculative understanding whereas Augustine, through his gifts of the heart, extended his influence far beyond the ordinary world of the theologians. Bossuet, he who most of all men of genius resembles Augustine in his loftiness and universality, is superior to him in the artistry and polish of his works but lacks this alluring tenderness of soul. If Augustine is less thunder-striking, he is more appealing and gently subjugates the spirit.

3. Universal Influence on Subsequent Generations

Augustine's universal influence on subsequent generations is due to the union of the gifts of heart and mind. A speculative genius alone has no direct influence on the multitude. The Christian world, outside of professional theologians, does not read St. Thomas Aquinas. On the other hand, without a precise and definite view of dogma, mysticism would soon fall into ruin as soon as the mind awoke and discovered the emptiness of metaphors. This is the fate of the misty pietism which is found in all ages whether they know Christ or not, whether they are indoctrinated by Schleiermacher, Sabatier, or their disciples. But every soul has access to Augustine's genius which is in love with light and warm with love. The entire Church, the teachers and the faithful, were to allow themselves to be imbued with his thoughts and his feelings. More than any other critic, Harnack admires and describes this influence which Augustine exercises over the entire life of the Christian people. If Thomas Aquinas is the doctor of the schools, Augustine is, for Harnack, the inspirer, the restorer of Christian piety. If Thomas inspires the canons of the Council of Trent, Augustine, besides having molded Thomas himself, inspires the inner life of the Church; he is the soul of all the great reforms which have taken place in her bosom. The Protestant critic shows how Catholics and Protestants live on the piety of Augustine: "Augustine breathed forth the feeling of the mystery of sin which is consoled by hope with a greater depth of emotion and with more exquisite phrases than had been known before his time. Even more, through these intimate confidences he has surely reached millions of souls, he has exactly described their interior state, he has traced such a living and irresistible picture of hope that the things he experienced himself have been relived time and time again in the course of the intervening 1500 years. To these very times the interior and vital piety as well as the method of expressing it in Catholicism are essentially Augustinian. The soul is entirely penetrated with his feelings. People think as he did and rethink his thoughts. The same can be said of many Protestants, and not the worst among them."[21] In like manner even those for whom dogma is only a relic from the past proclaim that the influence of Augustine will always survive: "The Augustine who should live forever," says Böhringer, "is neither the theologian nor the Father of the Church nor the champion of ecclesiastical battles. The religious genius of Augustine is the thing that is immortal."[22]

This true emotion is also the disguise which conceals certain defects from the reader or makes him forget them. "Augustine never could have exercised," says Eucken, "all the influence which he has unless the highest degree of sincerity had reigned at the bottom of his soul in spite of his rhetorical exaggerations."[23] Frequent repetitions are likewise excused because they are the expression of a deep sentiment: "Despite all the repetitions there is felt in his writings the spontaneous pouring out of a highly-gifted spirit and a pious heart.'[24]

But Augustine's deep feelings are also, it must be admitted, the source of exaggerations and sometimes errors which create a real danger to the inattentive or badly disposed reader. Certain theologians, in their love for St. Augustine, desired to justify and admire his every statement, to proclaim him infallible. Nothing could do more damage to this glory than these excesses. The reaction mentioned above[25] has its origin in this fact. We must then recognize that sometimes his passion for truth riveted his attention too fixedly on only one side of a complicated question. This was the source of unqualified formulas which were too absolute, false in appearance sometimes in one sense and sometimes in another. "The oratorical temperament which he possessed to such an eminent degree," says Becker very well, "the degree of elevation which was becoming his rich imagination and his ardent soul are not the safest gifts for the speculations of philosophy."[26] The great doctors of the Middle Ages had well remarked: "His expression is stronger than his meaning."[27] This is the origin of the pretended contradictions which are attributed to him and the errors which the predestinarians of all times lay at his doorstep. The role of the more reserved spirits of Scholasticism also becomes clear. Thomas Aquinas was a necessary corrective for the Doctor of Hippo. He is less noble, less original, and especially less vibrant. But the calm, didactic method of his intellectualism permits him to correct, through a severe criticism, Augustine's exaggerations, and to give his terminology more accuracy and precision, and to prepare, in brief, the dictionary thanks to which the African doctor can be read without danger.

The Protestant Schaff has written: "The great genius of the African Church . . . from whom the Middle Ages and the Reformation have received an equally powerful impulse, although in such opposite directions, has not yet completed the work assigned him by Providence. He is still a connecting link between the two opposed sections of the Church in the West, Catholicism and Protestantism, and he encourages hope that a time will come when the discords of the past will be forgotten in the sweet agreement of perfect knowledge and perfect love."[28] May that dream come true!

Part Four

INFLUENCE

CHAPTER XVIII

Authority of St. Augustine

THERE is no question of examining here the problem of the authority of the Fathers of the Church. We presuppose the general principles. But Augustine's unparalleled role as the great doctor of the Church and especially the exceptional approbations which the Holy See has lavished on his teaching, particularly concerning the problems of grace, seem to have endowed his writings with an official authority, the meaning and extent of which it is essential to determine.

I. OFFICIAL DOCUMENTS ESTABLISHING THE AUTHORITY OF ST. AUGUSTINE

a. LETTER OF ST. CELESTINE I

(1) *Occasion of the letter.* The occasion of this letter to the bishops of Gaul in 431 is indicated by Celestine. Prosper and Hilary, those two laymen whose zeal he praises (the same two who had informed the Bishop of Hippo of the Semipelagian opposition to his teaching), came to Rome and informed the pope of the trouble caused among souls by presumptuous priests who raise rash problems, "disputing in public about questions not taught in the schools." In a reply sent to Prosper and Hilary for the bishops of Gaul the pope urges them to impose silence on those priests who attack teachers whose disciples they had never been. The silence of the bishops looks very much like connivance on their part. Therefore "let novelty cease its attack, if such is the case, on the ancient customs. . . ."[1] It is clear that the one under discussion is Augustine, who was persecuted even after his death. The pope clearly proves this by the following eulogy which was to become the norm

regulating the respect due to the Bishop of Hippo, a norm which nevertheless was tempered by the reservations contained in a document accompanying the letter. This document was to cause considerable controversy also.

(2) Text of the letter
(a) Eulogy of Augustine in the letter of Celestine

Augustinum, sanctae recordationis virum, pro vita sua atque meritis in nostra communione semper habuimus, nec unquam hunc sinistrae suspicionis saltem rumor aspersit: quem tantae scientiae olim fuisse meminimus, ut inter magistros optimos etiam ante a meis semper decessoribus haberetur. Bene ergo de eo omnes in commune senserunt, utpote qui utique cunctis et amori fuerit et honori. Unde resistatur talibus quos male crescere videmus.[2]

Augustine, whose life and merits have remained in holy memory, was always in communion with us; never did even the shadow of malicious suspicion fall upon him. So great was his knowledge, as we well recall, that my predecessors always ranked him among the masters. Thus in general everyone held him in high esteem as a man who reflected love and honor on all. Thrust back, then, the scheming of those men whom we see growing in evil.

(b) Restriction in the CHAPTERS which accompany the letter

Profundiores vero difficilioresque partes incurrentium quaestionum, quas latius pertractarunt qui haereticis restiterunt, sicut non audemus contemnere, ita non necesse habemus adstruere; quia ad confitendum gratiam Dei, cujus operi ac dignationi nihil penitus subtrahendum est, satis

As for the more profound and difficult questions which these controversies have raised, questions fully developed by the authors who have fought against the heretics, we certainly do not have the rashness to make light of them, yet we do not consider it necessary to add anything. In fact, to admit

sufficere credimus, quidquid secundum praedictas regulas apostolicae sedis nos scripta docuerunt: ut prorsus non opinemur catholicum quod apparuerit praefixis sententiis esse contrarium.[3]

the grace of God whose influence and mercy must not be minimized, it suffices to hold fast to the doctrine which, according to the preceding regulation of the Apostolic See, their writings have taught us. Thus we regard whatever appears to be contrary to the decisions above as entirely opposed to the Catholic faith.

In the older citations of this text by theologians the words *Augustine and others* are inserted in place of the word *authors*.[4] This is merely a gloss which has slipped into the text.

(3) *Origin and authority of the* CHAPTERS. There can be no doubt about the authenticity of Celestine's letter. Prosper of Aquitaine summarizes it in these words which sufficiently indicate its contents: "Through this man [Celestine] the freedom of derogatory speech was taken away from those among the Gauls who found fault with the writings of Augustine of holy memory when, persuaded by the advice of his counsellors [a reference to the proceedings of Prosper and Hilary] and praising the piety of the books which displeased those in error, he showed by his sacred eloquence what authority must be given to those writings."[5] He then cites the entire passage on St. Augustine. But what is the source of the ten *Chapters*[6] which are appended to the final formula of the letter with a special introduction of their own? Their origin is not certain. Baronius, Suarez, and Sirmond established long ago that the *Chapters* do not constitute part of Celestine's letter; they do not even come from his hand. There is no indication in the letter that they are to follow. The expressions used, moreover, in referring to previous decisions of earlier popes are not the sort that a Roman Pontiff would use when speaking of his predecessors. In addition, they are of later date than the letter of Celestine, for Prosper in the passage just quoted makes no men-

tion of them and admits that the Semipelagians can still be pardoned. Although Vasquez, Petavius, and recently Hergenröther[7] and Faure still believed in their authenticity, the debate seems closed. Who, then, compiled these *Chapters*? Was it St. Leo when he was deacon, as Paschasius Quesnel thought, or was it rather, as Dom Coustant asserts, St. Prosper himself who, to put an end to the opposition against the latter works of St. Augustine, would have drawn up this list of propositions and asked Pope St. Sixtus III (432–440) to approve it?

Whoever the author is, their authority is not contested. These *Chapters* have always been regarded, at least since the sixth century, as a document officially expressing the faith of the Church. Pope St. Hormisdas alludes to them in a letter of August 13, 520, to the bishop Possessor as a certain formulation of the Catholic faith: "The *Chapters* are kept in ecclesiastical libraries."[8] At the same time, in 520, the deacon Peter and his companions, writing to the African bishops exiled in Sardinia, cite them along with Celestine's letter.[9] These *Chapters* were joined with the letter of Celestine in all the collections of official documents "with the wish and approbation of the Apostolic See," according to the Benedictines who edited the letters of Celestine.[10] Suarez rightly adds that these *Chapters* are in most part extracts from the councils of Africa or from papal decisions against the Pelagians.

b. LETTER OF POPE ST. GELASIUS I

Pope St. Gelasius I in his letter to the bishops of Picenum (November 1, 493), after a refutation of Pelagianism, energetically reprehends, among other abuses, the negligence of the bishops in repressing the attacks of the Semipelagians against St. Jerome and St. Augustine: "A still greater abuse is growing, namely, that in the sight and presence of the bishops a dying fly, as it is written (Eccles. 10:1), spoiling the sweetness of the ointment, attempts to cast aspersions on Jerome and Augustine of happy memory, those two lights of the teachers of the Church."[11]

C. LETTER OF POPE ST. HORMISDAS

Possessor, a bishop in Africa who had fled from Constantinople, finding the minds of men around him troubled and disturbed by the writings of Faustus of Riez, consults the pope on this subject. The letter was received by the pope July 18, 520.[12] Hormisdas gave the following reply on August 13, 520, to the two questions asked.[13] First, speaking of the special question of Faustus, he says that his works have no authority in the Church or (according to the usual formula) "I have not accepted him." This is an allusion to the so-called Gelasian decree whose fifth part[14] places the writings of Faustus among the apocrypha (books of heretics or people under suspicion).[15] On the general question of grace, Hormisdas refers Possessor to Augustine, to the *Chapters*, and to St. Paul in these terms:

De arbitrio tamen libero et gratia Dei, quod romana (hoc est catholica) sequatur et asseveret Ecclesia, licet in variis libris beati Augustini, et maxime ad Hilarium et Prosperum, possit cognosci, tamen in scriniis ecclesiasticis expressa capitula continentur, quae, si tibi desunt et necessaria creditis, destinabimus; quanquam qui diligenter Apostoli dicta considerat, quid sequi debeat evidenter cognoscat.[16]

One can come to know what the Roman Church, that is, the Catholic Church, teaches about freedom of choice and the grace of God in the various works of blessed Augustine, principally those which he addressed to Prosper and Hilary. This teaching is also formulated in the *Chapters* which are kept in ecclesiastical libraries. If you do not have a copy and judge them necessary, we will send them to you, although anyone who considers carefully the words of the Apostle will know clearly what he must hold.

There are two observations on this important text. First, the pope does not assert that it is easy to decide questions on grace with only the works of Augustine nor that it is sufficient to consult them alone. If it were necessary to decide everything by the writings of Augustine, Petavius says well, why would the pope refer to the decisions collected by the Church and to St. Paul himself?[17] Second, the works addressed to Prosper and Hilary are the two books *On Predestination* and *On Perseverance*. The primary purpose of these works is not to explain the manner of predestination, but to establish the absolute gratuity of grace against the Semipelagians: "You see . . . with what evidence this grace is defended, in opposition to which human merits are extolled as though man first gives something that he may receive in return."[18]

d. POPE BONIFACE II

Pope Boniface II and the Fathers of the Council of Orange (530–531) sanction the special authority of St. Augustine. The canons of the Council of Orange (530) which were sent from Rome by Pope Felix IV to the bishops of Gaul do not name, it is true, the Doctor of Hippo, but it is clear that they are taken from his works. As for Pope Boniface II, the successor of Felix IV, in the letter approving the synod (January 25, 531) he asserts that "many Fathers, above all Bishop Augustine of happy memory,"[19] have transmitted the teaching on grace.

e. POPE JOHN II

Pope John II, in his letter to various senators against the Nestorians (534), cites, before the other Fathers, St. Augustine "whose doctrine, according to the statutes of my predecessors, the Roman Church follows and preserves."[20] There is in this letter an assertion of the traditional veneration of the Holy See for the teaching of Augustine.

f. LATER TESTIMONY

The eulogies of Augustine by following popes are numerous, but they are less official and precise.[21] Adrian I (772–795), for example, calls him "the principal Father and the best Doctor."[22] More recent pontiffs have professed the same veneration. Marcelli quotes the meaningful words of Alexander VII to the Academy of Louvain: "May you always desire to follow the unshaken and safe dogmas of Augustine and Thomas."[23] He also quotes statements of Clement X, Innocent XII, Clement XI, and so forth.

The most significant document of the modern era is the order given by Clement VIII to the consultors of the Congregation *De Auxiliis* to guide themselves in the affair of Molinism according to the teaching of St. Augustine: "I have decided to conduct this whole dispute according to the norm of Augustine's teaching on grace," he says in his discourse of March 20, 1602, to the first solemn convocation held in his presence. He gives three reasons: Augustine has vanquished the Pelagians; he has omitted nothing concerning questions under discussion today; the popes have always asserted the authority of his teaching.[24]

In the light of these documents which come from such high sources and are so eloquent in St. Augustine's cause, a problem is raised: Has the Church therefore approved and adopted the entire teaching of St. Augustine, at least in the field of grace? Is it never permissible to deviate from him?

Three answers have been given to this question. For some, the authority of Augustine in this matter is absolute, irrefutable, and without exception. For others, these eulogies are vague formulas leaving full liberty. But the great number of theologians, taking a moderate position between these two extremes, recognize a real normative authority in St. Augustine, although hemmed in with reservations and wise delimitations.

2. EXAGGERATED INTERPRETATION OF AUGUSTINE'S AUTHORITY

a. EXPLANATION

According to this school, every word of the great doctor on grace and freedom of the will is a rule of faith from which one must never deviate. All the adversaries of freedom of choice have leaned on Augustine and exalted him above everyone else. The Jansenists did not even flinch when making this extraordinary assertion: A single phrase from Augustine must be preferred to the most solemn decisions of the Church. Jansenius himself laid the foundations of this absurd theory throughout the introduction to the second volume of his *Augustinus*. Some of the chapter titles read: "The evangelical, apostolic teaching of Augustine, unsurpassed in authority, on the grace of God, written in the name of the whole Church with the silent consent of all other authors." "Augustine has determined the limits of true theological knowledge by his own teaching." He ends the book with this statement: "There is but one Augustine, the image of all, in place of all, and above all." It would be better, Jansenius adds, to drop from theology everything that does not have its source in Augustine.[25] His practice certainly corresponds to his theory. He finds in Augustine the propositions of Baius condemned by the pope, for example, the fifty-third. What does he do? He hesitates—so he says—but finally, out of respect for the popes who have so often praised Augustine, he maintains that the proposition was condemned not as false (because it is Augustine's), but because it was "disturbing the peace."[26] "What about the proposition which the Apostolic See has proscribed? I confess that I cling to it. But what about the teaching of Augustine? . . ."[27] The disciples imitated their master. There is nothing more common than to find the following reasoning among them. The condemned propositions of Baius are St. Augustine's. That is enough to reassure us. In 1677, the Jansenist Havermans was not afraid to act as spokesman for the faction. It is he who formulated the thirtieth proposition condemned by Alexander XII (December 7, 1690): "Whatever doctrine one finds clearly rooted in Augustine can be held and taught without regard for any Apostolic Bull."[28]

All Catholic theologians have avoided this excessive view. Many, however, have on occasion exaggerated the importance of the papal eulogies and maintained that all of Augustine's opinions concerning the vast problems of grace were canonized by the Church. Dr. Koch in his study on the topic mentioned this excess particularly in regard to Noris who goes so far as to forbid one to discover any obscurities in Augustine.[29] He relates that during the

controversies *De Auxiliis* the Molinists were accused of not accept-
ing this principle in its full rigor. "Any teaching of Augustine on
grace or predestination," said Diego Alvarez, "must be considered
as a dogma of the Catholic Church."[30] In a letter to an Augustinian religious Barthelemi de Los Rios we read "this utterance of
an old man": "Whoever thinks that Augustine should be reprehended for anything he said convicts himself of heresy by his very
statement."[31] Among Molinistic propositions which were accused
of falsehood in another document the twenty-second reads as
follows: "It is not right to say that whatever Augustine asserted
and did not retract must necessarily be held by all."[32] The twentieth proposition granted that Augustine's works contain some
inaccurate phrases which must be avoided. According to the
authors we are discussing, however, this is the capital crime of
irreverence, just as though St. Thomas had not had even stronger
things to say on this subject.[33] Noris, Koch adds, wished to defend
everything and have everyone admire all of Augustine's writings.
In our days Muttermuller and others still regard all Augustine's
theories on grace as defined truths.

b. CRITICISM

This system is evidently inadmissible, since it is incorrect to
maintain that the Church has always adopted all of Augustine's
explanations on the complicated questions of grace.

The condemnation of Havermans' proposition by Alexander
VIII already establishes one limitation: Every decision of the
Church must be preferred to the statements of Augustine. The
reason for this is plain, for the Church has the gift of divine assistance; Augustine did not enjoy it.

The very wording of the pontifical approbations does not imply
this blanket approval. None of these eulogies is a positive sanction
of the system without reserve. They are rather general eulogies of
his works and teaching. Sometimes these eulogies are directed to
him and other Fathers together, none of whom are thought to be
infallible. Sometimes they are just a simple defense against attacks.

Since no examination was made of the tremendous work of Augustine, how could it have been approved in all its parts?

The *Chapters* of Celestine explicitly place reservations on the profound and difficult questions. This is an important point too often passed over in silence by certain theologians. Whoever may have drawn up these *Chapters*, the popes, by sanctioning them, likewise sanctioned this wise reservation. This restriction implicitly affects all subsequent approbations since the most formal, as that of John II, are granted "according to the degrees of my predecessors."

But what are these profound questions which are passed over and left open? According to Quesnel[34] who relies on the words of St. Augustine,[35] there would be question of the objections raised by the Pelagians: How does St. Augustine's theory of concupiscence square with the dignity of marriage? How does the predominant role of grace agree with the eulogies given to the saints, to freedom of choice, to the law? Does original sin demand a traducianism in respect to the origin of souls? We, however, believe this restriction covers a much broader field than the one indicated by these questions. We are not hesitant to state that these reserved questions encompass all the subtle problems discussed during the Pelagian controversy which the councils and the sovereign pontiffs did not wish to treat. Such are, for example, the manner in which grace is efficacious, the state of pure nature, the detailed explanation of predestination, of the distribution of grace, and so forth. In a word, the popes have approved the teaching of Augustine in relation to all the dogmatic points defined under his influence. They have not approved his opinions in relation to the subtle problems which these definitions do not touch. That is why we distinguished above[36] the dogmas defended by Augustine from what, in our opinion, comprises his system. Noris, quite embarrassed by the reservations which condemn his exaggerations, has thought up a strange theory. This famous last paragraph of Celestine's letter gives us absolutely no choice. Its author certainly intends to impose the solution of Augustine on all questions; for the present, however, he thinks it useless to formulate the canons.[37] This explanation overlooks the words of the very text: "We certainly do not have the rashness to make light of them, yet we do not consider it necessary to add anything." One does not speak this way of opinions which he wishes to impose.

The decision of Clement VIII relative to the Congregation *De Auxiliis* has not extended the authority of Augustine further than the letter of Celestine. Molina was accused of Semipelagianism. It was natural to check to see whether his teaching was in harmony with the dogmatic assertions of the great adversary of Semipelagianism. In the *Scriptum Clementis VIII* sent to the congregation as a directive rule none of the fifteen theses under which are grouped all the texts can be reduced to a purely dogmatic question already defined against the Semipelagians.[38] No formula, taken literally in its Augustinian meaning, decides the questions disputed by the Thomists and the Molinists, the explanation of the infallible efficacy of grace. Even the fifth thesis, which appears dangerous to the Molinists, leaves the question of the mode of influence untouched. The decision of Clement VIII's successor, Paul V, proves this well enough. Not only does he allow freedom to the two schools, but in a decree written in his own hand and destined for the ambassador of Spain who was urging the pope to decide the question, he returns again to the famous reserve clause of the *Chapters*: "The Council of Trent," he says, "has wisely set to one side, after the example of Celestine, the subtle and complicated questions on the manner of the divine influence."[39]

A brief of Innocent XII (February 16, 1674) to the Academy of Louvain summarizes and confirms our interpretation of the *Chapters*. The Academy had asked the pope to declare that the Augustinian ideas of grace efficacious in itself and of predestination before any merits (interpreted according to the mind of the *Lovanienses*), since they had not been disapproved by the condemnation of Jansenius, must be maintained until a new decision of the Holy See. Innocent XII refused and replied by citing the last paragraph of the *Chapters*.

The popes, finally, have sanctioned the liberty of departing from Augustine's thought in non-defined questions about grace by a

most solemn act. There is no doubt that the great doctor condemned infants who have died without baptism to sensible
punishment. As a consequence it seems that proponents of a milder
theory should be reprehended. As a matter of fact, Pius VI, in the
famous condemnation of the Synod of Pistoia in the Bull
Auctorem Fidei (August 28, 1794), has sustained the benign
opinion and declared that it was free of Pelagianism.[40]

Such was also the feeling of the great theologians of all schools.
They have always recognized the limitations of Augustine's
authority and have sometimes, however reluctantly, departed from
his thought. The famous author of *De locis theologicis*, Melchior
Cano, did not exempt Augustine from those human weaknesses
which are found in the most illustrious of doctors.[41] Likewise, in
reference to predestination, Bañez, attributing to St. Augustine an
antecedent reprobation of the damned because of original sin,
refutes the opinion quite severely and is not afraid to say: "If
therefore Blessed Augustine had averted to the evil consequences
of this opinion, he would never have stated that original sin alone
is the universal cause of the reprobation of all the damned."[42]
Noris makes some vain attempts to attenuate the importance of
this passage.[43] The moderate conclusions of Suarez must be read
also.[44]

In addition, the Church and the theologians, in determining
these wise limits of Augustine's authority, were following the
counsels of Augustine himself. Denzinger[45] and Koch[46] have shown
quite well that nothing is more anti-Augustinian than to claim
that every word of Augustine is to be accepted as a rule of faith.
Augustine himself energetically protests: "In all my writings I
desire not only a pious reader but also a free censor. . . . I do not
desire that my writings be obeyed as though they were the canonical Scriptures."[47] He does not weary of returning to this subject,
especially in the introduction to the books of *On the Trinity* and
in his *Letters*: "My writings constitute no sort of canonical
authority."[48] The following is his own practical rule in regard
to the other Fathers. He writes to St. Jerome that apart from
Scripture "I so read others that, no matter how much they are

famed for holiness and learning, I do not think anything true because they thought it so but rather because they have been able to persuade me either by means of the canonical authors or through a probable reasoning process which does not depart from the truth. I do not imagine that you, dear brother, think otherwise."[49] "I want my readers to be as critical of me as I am when reading what others have written."[50]

3. CRITICISM OF THE EXAGGERATED INTERPRETATION; THE RESPECT DUE TO THE AUTHORITY OF AUGUSTINE

a. EXPLANATION

In opposition to the preceding theologians and perhaps as a reaction, other authors have thought that the pontifical approbations were only vague formulas without practical consequences. Thus Launoy, Richard Simon, and recently Margival have not hesitated to insist that St. Augustine was mistaken not only on secondary points, but on the very heart of the problem. The Bishop of Hippo, they say, is an innovator; breaking with the tradition of the Fathers who preceded him, he introduced predestinarianism into the Church.[51]

b. CRITICISM

It has been shown above that these assertions, from the historical point of view, are contrary to the texts of Augustine.[52] Here we must add that they are in contradiction with the teaching of the Church. To claim that St. Augustine not only innovated, but that he introduced false innovations into the Church by changing her faith (that was certainly Richard Simon's intention in some passages on original sin) is to accuse the Church of having erred and changed her belief. We do not have to investigate this here, for this teaching is the denial of the whole of Christianity. This is what irritated Bossuet and explains the sometimes exaggerated statements by which he defended the Church and St. Augustine.[53]

Other critics, however, accuse Augustine of predestinarian or Jansenist errors by showing that the Church, far from adopting them, has proscribed them. This system does not seem acceptable even with the restrictions laid upon it. The papal documents, if they have any meaning, mean at least that the Bishop of Hippo is orthodox, that he has not sacrificed freedom of choice to the sovereignty of God. One can admit certain exaggerated formulas ("His expression is stronger than his meaning."),[54] certain obscurities, certain uncertainties, certain hesitations, and certain overly severe personal opinions on some points (such as the fate of infants), but to find in his works the theories of Calvin is to say that the Church for fifteen centuries has adopted as a guide an adversary of the faith.

4. CONCLUSION

The conclusion is already contained, it seems to us, in the distinction formulated in the letter of St. Celestine I and the restriction which accompanies it. On the one hand, in the important questions which constitute the faith of the Church in the matter of freedom of the will and grace, the Doctor of Hippo is really and truly the authorized witness of tradition against the Pelagian and Semipelagian errors as St. Athanasius was against Arius and St. Cyril against Nestorius.[55] Thus the existence of original sin, the absolute necessity of grace at least for every salutary act, the gratuity of the gift of God which precedes all merits of man because it must cause them, the predilection of God for the elect to whom He gives graces previously seen to be efficacious, and with all that the freedom of man and responsibility for his faults —all these are points which the Church not only accepts from Augustine, but admires and recommends in his teaching. Witnesses of this are the canons of the Second Council of Orange.

On the other hand, the more subtle explanations of secondary problems which concern rather the manner than the fact are left by the Church, for the moment at least, to the prudent study of theologians. Thomassin claims freedom of discussion on pre-destination before or after merits.[56] Bossuet himself, the zealous defender of Augustine's authority, correctly asserts that this great doctor has not even treated this subtle question debated in the schools.[57] Thus true Augustinism, freed from accessory ideas, will remain intact in its fundamental principles and will accept new developments and new lights with the progress of the teachers and councils of the Church.

Abbreviations

Standard abbreviations are used throughout the notes except for the following. Numbers within a parenthesis, (42, 504–572), refer to the volume and column numbers of Migne's *Patrologiae latinae*. An alphabetical list of the symbols used to designate the various works of Augustine follows:

AC	*Ad Catholicos epistola de unitate ecclesiae*
AD	*Ad Donatistas post collationem*
AJ	*Annotationes in Job*
B	*Breviculus collationis cum Donatistis*
C	*Confessiones*
CA	*Contra academicos*
CAL	*Contra adversarium Legis et Prophetarum*
CAM	*Contra Adimantum Manichaei discipulum*
CC	*Contra Cresconium grammaticum partis Donati*
CD	*Contra duas epistolas Pelagianorum ad Bonifacium Papam*
CEM	*Contra epistolam Manichaei quam vocant Fundamenti*
CEP	*Contra epistolam Parmeniani*
CF	*Contra Faustum Manichaeum*
CG	*Contra Gaudentium Thamugadensem episcopum Donatistarum*
CJ	*Contra Julianum haeresis Pelagianorum defensorem*
CLP	*Contra litteras Petiliani Donatistae*
CMA	*Contra Maximinum Arianorum episcopum*
CML	*Contra mendacium ad Consentium*
CP	*Contra Priscillianistas et Origenistas*
CS	*Contra Secundinum Manichaeum*
CSA	*Contra sermonem quemdam Arianorum*
Col	*Collatio cum Maximino Arianorum episcopo*
DA	*De actis cum Felice Manichaeo*
DAC	*De agone christiano*
DAO	*De anima et eius origine*
DB	*De baptismo contra Donatistas*
DBe	*De beata vita*
DBC	*De bono conjugali*
DBV	*De bono viduitatis*

DCa	*De catechizandis rudibus*
DCD	*De civitate Dei*
DCF	*Disputatio contra Fortunatum*
DCj	*De conjugiis adulterinis*
DCns	*De consensu Evangelistarum*
DCnt	*De continentia*
DCG	*De correptione et gratia ad Valentinum*
DCM	*De cura pro mortuis gerenda*
DD7	*De diversis quaestionibus* VII *ad Simplicianum*
DD83	*De diversis quaestionibus* LXXXIII
DDD	*De divinatione daemonum*
DDoC	*De doctrina christiana*
DDoP	*De dono perseverantiae ad Prosperum et Hilarium*
DDu	*De duabus animabus contra Manichaeos*
DFO	*De fide et operibus*
DFS	*De fide et symbolo*
DFV	*De fide rerum quae non videntur*
DGnI	*De Genesi ad litteram liber imperfectus*
DGnL	*De Genesi ad litteram libri* XII
DGnM	*De Genesi contra Manichaeos*
DGsE	*De gestis cum Emerito Donatistarum episcopo Caesareae*
DGsP	*De gestis Pelagii*
DGr	*De grammatica*
DGrC	*De gratia Christi et peccato originali*
DGrL	*De gratia et libero arbitrio ad Valentinum*
DH	*De haeresibus ad Quodvultdeum*
DI	*De immortalitate animae*
DLA	*De libero arbitrio*
DMa	*De magistro*
DMe	*De mendacio*
DME	*De moribus ecclesiae Catholicae et de moribus Manichaeorum*
DMu	*De musica*
DNB	*De natura boni contra Manichaeos*
DNG	*De natura et gratia contra Pelagium*
DNu	*De nuptiis et concupiscentia*
DOD	*De octo Dulcitii quaestionibus*
DOM	*De opere monachorum*
DOR	*De ordine*
DP	*De patientia*

DPB	*De peccatorum meritis et remissione et de baptismo parvulorum*
DPJ	*De perfectione justitiae hominis*
DPS	*De praedestinatione sanctorum ad Prosperum et Hilarium*
DQ	*De quantitate animae*
DS	*De sancta virginitate*
DSD	*De sermone Domini in monte*
DSL	*De spiritu et littera*
DSy	*De symbolo*
DT	*De Trinitate*
DUB	*De unico baptismo contra Petilianum*
DUC	*De utilitate credendi*
DVR	*De vera religione*
E	*Epistolae* (E28 = *Epistola* 28)
En	*Enchiridion ad Laurentium de fide, spe, charitate*
EnP	*Enarrationes in Psalmos*
ER	*Epistola ad Romanos inchoata expositio*
ExG	*Expositio Epistolae ad Galatas*
ExR	*Expositio quarumdam propositionum ex Epistola ad Romanos*
J	*In Epistolam Joannis ad Parthos tractatus* X
JE	*In Joannis Evangelium tractatus* CXXIV
LH	*Locutiones in Heptateuchum*
OJ	*Opus imperfectum contra Julianum*
PD	*Psalmus contra partem Donati*
QE	*Quaestiones Evangeliorum ex Matthaeo et Luca*
QH	*Quaestiones in Heptateuchum*
R	*Retractationes*
S	*Sermones* (S17 = *Sermo* 17)
SC	*Sermo ad Caesareensis ecclesiae plebem*
SO	*Soliloquia*
SS	*Speculum de Scriptura sacra*
T	*Tractatus adversus Judaeos*

NOTES

Notes

CHAPTER I. ABERRATIONS AND CONVERSION

1. Paul Orosius, *Liber apologeticus*, I, 1 (31, 1175).
2. C I, 11, 17 (32, 668).
3. *Ibid.*, 9, 14 (32, 667).
4. *Ibid.*
5. C III, 4, 8 (32, 686). Text corrected according to the Vienna *Corpus*. (CSEL, XXXIII, 49–50).
6. C I, 11, 17 (32, 668).
7. C VI, 16, 26 (32, 732).
8. C VIII, 7, 17 (32, 757).
9. C III, 3, 6 (32, 685).
10. C II, 9, 17 (32, 682).
11. Loofs, "Augustin," *Realencyclopädie für protestantische Theologie und Kirche*, ed. Herzog, 3rd ed., Leipzig, 1897, II, 268.
12. C III, 4, 7 (32, 685).
13. DME II, 19, 68 (32, 1374).
14. DUC I, 2 (42, 66).
15. C III, 6, 10 (32, 686–687).
16. Augustine later mentioned this fact in a sermon to his people. See S51, 5, 6 (38, 336).
17. C IV, 15, 24 (32, 703); V, 10, 20 (715–716); VII, 3, 4 (735).
18. C V, 10, 18 (32, 714).
19. DDoP 20, 53 (45, 1026).
20. CA I, 1, 3 (32, 907).
21. C IV, 4–5, 7–10 (32, 696–697).
22. Possidius, *Vita S. Augustini Episcopi*, I (32, 35).
23. C III, 11, 19 (32, 691).
24. *Ibid.*, 12, 21 (32, 693).
25. C IV, 16, 30 (32, 705).
26. *Ibid.*, 15, 27 (32, 704).
27. CLP III, 17, 20 (43, 357).
28. C IV, 2, 3 (32, 694).
29. *Ibid.*, 3, 5 (32, 695).
30. C VII, 6, 10 (32, 739).
31. DUC I, 2 (42, 66–67).
32. DME II, 18–20, 65–75 (32, 1372–1378).
33. C V, 11, 21 (32, 716); DUC I, 7 (42, 69).

34. DCF I, 6 (42, 114–115); E79 (33, 272).
35. C V, 3–6, 3–11 (32, 707–710).
36. The *Eversores* were a band of student cutups. See C V, 8, 14 (32, 712).
37. C V, 14, 25 (32, 718). Cf. V, 7, 13 (711).
38. *Ibid.*
39. C VII, 1, 1 (32, 733).
40. *Ibid.*, 10, 16 (32, 742).
41. *Ibid.*, 12, 18 (32, 743).
42. *Ibid.*, 20, 26 (32, 746–747). Cf. VII, 1, 1 (733).
43. *Ibid.*, 9, 13 (32, 740).
44. C VI, 14, 24 (32, 731).
45. *Ibid.*, 11, 19–20 (32, 729).
46. C VII, 20–21, 26–27 (32, 746–748).
47. *Ibid.*, 18, 24 (32, 745).
48. C VIII, 2, 3 (32, 750).
49. *Ibid.*, 12, 29–30 (32, 762).

CHAPTER II.   CONVERSION TO EPISCOPATE

1. E26 (33, 105–108).
2. DOR I, 3, 6–8 (32, 981).
3. CA I, 2, 6 (32, 909).
4. DOR II, 20, 52 (32, 1019).
5. Adolf Harnack, *Monasticism* and *The Confessions of St. Augustine*, trans. E. Kellet and F. Marseille, London, 1901, p. 141.
6. Loofs, "Augustin," *Realencyclopädie für prot. Theol. und Kirche*, II, 268.
7. L. Gourdon, *Essai sur la conversion de saint Augustin*, Cahors, 1900, pp. 45–50.
8. *Ibid.*, p. 83.
9. Wörter, *Die Geistesentwickelung des hl. Augustinus bis zu seiner Taufe*, Paderborn, 1892, p. 64.
10. C IX, 4, 7 (32, 766).
11. CA III, 20, 43 (32, 957).
12. *Ibid.*
13. CA II, 2, 5 (32, 921).
14. *Ibid.* (922).
15. *Ibid.*
16. DOR II, 5, 16 (32, 1002).
17. DOR I, 10, 29 (32, 991).
18. *Ibid.*

19. *Ibid.*
20. DOR I, 11, 31 (32, 992).
21. *Ibid.*, 32 (32, 994).
22. DOR I, 8, 25 (32, 989).
23. SO I, 1, 3 (32, 871).
24. *Ibid.*, 5 (872).
25. DOR I, 10, 29 (32, 991).
26. SO I, 1, 5 (32, 872).
27. G. Boissier, "La conversion de saint Augustin," *La fin du paganisme*, Paris, 1891, I, 376.
28. Gourdon, *Essai*, p. 49.
29. C VII, 20, 26 (32, 746–747).
30. DBe I, 1, 3 (32, 960–961).
31. DOR I, 5, 13 (32, 984).
32. *Ibid.*, 10, 29 (32, 991).
33. SO I, 10, 17 (32, 878).
34. C IX, 6, 14 (32, 769).
35. Cf. Dom Morin, *Revue bénédictine*, 1894, pp. 49–77.
36. C IX, 11–13, 27–37 (32, 775–780).
37. Here occurred the miraculous cure of Innocentius. Cf. DCD XXII, 8, 3 (41, 763).
38. E126, 7 (33, 480); E157, 39 (692).
39. E17, 5 (33, 85).
40. S355, 2 (39, 1569); E126, 7 (33, 480).
41. St. Jerome writes that the custom is deplorable. *Epistola*, 102, 7 (22, 534).
42. DCF (42, 111–130).
43. Possidius, *Vita*, VII (32, 39).
44. (40, 181–196).
45. E22 (33, 90–94).
46. Hefele, *Histoire des conciles*, II, 88.
47. E29 (33, 114–120).

CHAPTER III.   THE EPISCOPATE

1. Possidius, *Vita*, VIII (32, 40).
2. Rottmanner, *Historisches Jahrbuch*, 1898, p. 894.
3. E32 (33, 125–129).
4. S355, 6 (39, 1572); S356, 14 (1580).
5. Possidius, XI (32, 42).
6. *Ibid.*, XXII (51).

7. CEM II–III, 2–3 (42, 174–175).

8. DA (42, 519–552).

9. A *traditor* was one who had handed over the Scriptures to the state police during the recent persecution under Diocletian.

10. These men were also known as *montenses,* "mountaineers," and *campitae,* "plainsmen."

11. Nathanael Bonwetsch, "Donatismus," *Realencyclopädie für prot. Theol. und Kirche,* IV, 796.

12. Hefele, II, 89; Mansi, III, 924.

13. See the reproaches in CLP I, 19, 21 (43, 255).

14. E44 (33, 173–180).

15. E49 (33, 189–191).

16. E51 (33, 191–194).

17. Hefele, II, 127; Mansi, III, 771–774. These are Canons 66–69 of the *Codex Ecclesiae Africanae.*

18. Hefele, II, 155; Mansi, III, 791–794; CC III, 45 (42, 523).

19. E88, 7 (33, 306); E76 (263–266).

20. CC III, 46, 50 (43, 523).

21. *Ibid.,* 51 (43, 524).

22. *Ibid.,* 43, 47 (43, 521).

23. Possidius, *Vita,* XII (32, 43).

24. R II, 5 (32, 632).

25. Hefele, II, 155; Mansi, III, 1159.

26. E88, 7 (33, 306); E185, 25 (804).

27. E88 (33, 302–309). Read this letter for a catalog of facts to enable you to make an impartial judgment of the conduct of the Catholics. Cf. E89 (309–313), which was written to Festus to ask for the support of the laws.

28. E93 (33, 321–347) treats thoroughly the question of punishing the heretics. Also E97 (357–359); E105 (396–404). Cf. the correspondence with Nectarius, a pagan, on an analogous subject, E90, E91, E103, E104 (313–318, 386–395).

29. E100 (33, 366–367). Cf. CC III, 50, 55 (43, 526).

30. E128 (33, 487–490).

31. B (43, 613–650).

32. E144 (33, 591–592).

33. E134 (33, 510–512).

34. E185 (33, 792–815). See Jules Martin, *Saint Augustin,* Paris, 1901, pp. 373–388, for an excellent study on the tolerance shown in the works of the holy doctor.

35. SC (43, 689–698); DGsE (698–706).

36. Cf. E204 (33, 939–942); CG (43, 706–752).

37. Cf. DDoP XX, 53 (45, 1026).

38. DGsP, XXII, 46 (44, 346).

39. E146 (33, 596).

40. DGsP XXVI, 51 (44, 349).

41. Cf. Marius Mercator, *Commonitorium super nomine Coelestii*, I, 1 (48, 69); *Liber subnotationum in verba Juliani*, Pref., 5 (48, 114); Mansi, IV, 290; Hefele, II, 170; DGrC II, 2-4, 2-4 (44, 386-388).

42. DGsP XXII-XXIII, 46-47 (44, 346-347).

43. St. Jerome, *Epistola* 143 (22, 1181).

44. Cf. E175 (33, 758-762); Mansi, IV, 321-324.

45. See the synodal letter to Innocent, E176 (33, 762-764); Mansi, IV, 334-336.

46. E177 (33, 754-772); Mansi, IV, 337-344.

47. Philippus Jaffé, *Regesta Pontificum Romanorum*, ed. Wm. Wattenbach, Leipzig, 1885, nn. 321-323; Mansi, III, 1071-1080; E181-183 (33, 779-788).

48. E178 (33, 772-773).

49. DGrC I, nn. 32, 35, 36; II, nn. 19, 24 (44, 376-378; 394-396). The passage is summarized (45, 1715-1716).

50. (48, 497-505). Cf. (45, 1718).

51. (45, 1719-1723).

52. Mansi, IV, 376-378; DGrC II, 6-7, 7-8 (44, 388-389); CD II, 3, 5 (573-575); *Libellus Paulini diaconi* sent to the pope by the accuser of Pelagius (45, 1724-1725).

53. (45, 1725-1726); Jaffé, *Regesta*, n. 342.

54. The number is given by Photius (45, 1730).

55. Canon numbers 108-127 in Mansi, III, 810-823. Cf. Denzinger, *Enchiridion symbolorum*, 26th ed., Freiburg, 1947, 101-108.

56. Hefele, II, 184-185.

57. Jaffé, *Regesta*, ann. 418, n. 342a.

58. Cf. J. Hergenröther, *Handbuch der allegemeinen Kirchenges-chichte*, Freiburg im Breisgau, 1879, I, 295. Jaffé, *Regesta*, n. 343.

59. E190, 23 (33, 865-866); Prosper, *Liber contra Collatorem*, nn. 15, 57 (45, 1730-1731).

60. Prosper, *ibid.*, 15 (45, 1731).

61. E191 (33, 867-868); E194 (874-891).

62. DGrC II, 7, 8 (44, 389).

63. E202 (33, 928-929).

64. E201 (33, 927).

65. Cf. The decree of Constantius, father of Valentinianus, in the year 421 (45, 1750).

66. (45, 1732-1736).

67. OJ I, nn. 1, 2, 6, 9, 27, 32, 66; III, nn. 10, 165 (45, 1051–1085; 1251; 1316). Cf. chap. 9, pp. 148–151 for comments on Augustine's traducianism.

68. Marius Mercator *Liber subnotationum* (48, 109–172). Cf. (45, 1737–1740).

69. Mansi, IV, 518; Cassian, *De Incarnatione*, I, 4 (50, 23–24); Tillemont, *Mémoires*, Paris, 1710, XIII, 883–885.

70. E194 (33, 874–891).

71. E214, E215, and the reply of Valentinus, E216 (33, 968–978).

72. E217 (33, 978–989).

73. Cassian, the famous abbot of Saint Victor, was at their head. Cf. *Collationes*, XIII, 9–18 (49, 914–946), which were composed before 426.

74. E225, E226 (33, 1002–1012).

75. E213 (33, 966–968) gives the official account of this election.

76. Col (42, 709–742); CMA (42, 743–814); S140 (38, 773–775).

77. CSA (42, 693–708).

78. E220 (33, 992–997).

79. Rottmanner, *Historisches Jahrbuch*, p. 897.

CHAPTER IV.   WRITINGS OF ST. AUGUSTINE

1. Tillemont, *Mémoires*, vol. XIII; Dom Remy Ceillier, *Histoire générale des auteurs sacrés et ecclésiastiques*, Paris, 1744, vol. XI.

2. See appendix, p. 401.

3. *Confessionum* (32, 659–868). Cf. R II, 6, 1–2 (32, 632).

4. C I, 1, 1 (32, 659–661); IX, 6, 14 (32, 769); XI, 1, 1 (32, 809).

5. R II, 6, 1 (32, 632).

6. C I, 1, 1 (32, 661).

7. *Retractationum* (32, 583–656).

8. Tillemont, *Mémoires*, XIII, 1040.

9. E224, 2 (33, 1001).

10. *Epistolae* (33, 61–1162).

11. (33, 751–752; 789–792; 929–938).

12. Ebert, *Histoire de la littérature du moyen âge*, Paris, 1883, I, 270.

13. (33, 1173–1177).

14. Joseph Fessler, *Institutiones patrologiae*, 2nd ed. Jungmann, Innsbruck, 1890–1896, II, 380–384.

15. R, Prologue (32, 585–586).

16. E26 (33, 103–107).

17. Wörter, *Die Geistesentwickelung des h. Augustin*, pp. 75–210. Cf. D. Ohlmann, *De S. Augustini dialogis in Cassiciaco scriptis*, Strasbourg, 1897. (Inaugural dissertation).

18. *Contra academicos* (32, 905–958). Cf. R I, 1, 1–4 (32, 585–587).

19. *Be beata vita* (32, 959–976). Cf. R I, 2 (32, 588).

20. DCD XVIII, 54, 1 (41, 620).

21. R I, 2 (32, 588).

22. *De ordine* (32, 977–1020). Cf. R I, 3, 1–3 (32, 588–589).

23. *Soliloquiorum* (32, 869–904). Cf. R I, 4, 1–4 (32, 589–590).

24. *Soliloquiorum animae ad Deum* (40, 863–898).

25. *Meditationum* (40, 901–942).

26. See the article on Anselm, DTC, I, 1340.

27. *Manuale* (40, 951–968).

28. *De immortalitate animae* (32, 1021–1034). Cf. R I, 5, 1–3 (32, 590–591).

29. R I, 5, 1 (32, 590).

30. *De quantitate animae* (32, 1035–1080). Cf. R I, 8, 1–3 (32, 594).

31. *De magistro* (32, 1193–1220). Cf. R I, 12 (32, 602).

32. C IX, 6, 14 (32, 769).

33. See below, pages 109–114. Cf. the question *De magistro* of St. Thomas which was inspired by this work in *De Ver.*, q. 11. (*Truth*, Chicago, 1953, II, 77). Also W. Ott, *Über die Schrift des h. Augustinus De magistro*, Hechingen, 1898.

34. *De grammatica liber* (32, 1385–1408).

35. *Principia dialecticae* (32, 1409–1420).

36. *Categoriae decem ex Aristotele decerptae* (32, 1419–1440).

37. *Principia rhetorices* (32, 1439–1448).

38. *Historisches Jahrbuch*, 1898, p. 894. Cf. Teuffel, *Geschichte der römische Literatur*, 5th ed., p. 1133. Huemer maintains the same point. "Der Grammatiker Augustinus," *Zeitschrift für österreichische Gymnasien*, 1886, IV, 256.

39. *De musica* (32, 1081–1194). Cf. R I, 11, 1–4 (32, 600–602).

40. E101, 3 (33, 369).

41. *De civitate Dei contra paganos* (41, 13–804). Cf. R II, 43, 1–2 (32, 647–648).

42. E136–138 (33, 514–535).

43. G. von Hertling makes a good point when he shows that "civitas" is here used in a new meaning, *Augustin*, Mainz, 1902, p. 100.

44. R II, 43, 1 (32, 648).

45. *De vera religione* (34, 121–172). Cf. R I, 13, 1–9 (32, 602–605).

46. E162, 2 (33, 705).

47. *De utilitate credendi ad Honoratum* (42, 65–92). Cf. R I, 14, 1–6 (32, 605–608).

48. *De fide rerum quae non videntur* (40, 171–180).

49. E231, 7 (33, 1026).

50. *De divinatione daemonum* (40, 581–592). Cf. R II, 30 (32, 643).

51. *Sex quaestiones contra paganos* or *Epistola 102* (33, 370–386). Cf. R II, 31 (32, 643).

52. *Epistola 118 ad Dioscorum* (33, 432–449).

53. *Tractatus adversus judaeos* (42, 51–64).

54. *De haeresibus* (42, 21–50).

55. *De moribus Ecclesiae catholicae et de moribus manichaeorum* (32, 1309–1378). Cf. R I, 7, 1–6 (32, 591–594).

56. *De duabus animabus* (42, 93–112).

57. *Acta seu disputatio contra Fortunatum manichaeum* (42, 111–129). Cf. R I, 16, 1–2 (32, 612).

58. *Contra Adimantum manichaei discipulum* (42, 129–172). Cf. R I, 22, 1–4 (32, 618–620).

59. R I, 22, 1 (32, 619).

60. *Contra epistolam manichaei quam vocant Fundamenti* (42, 173–206). Cf. R II, 2 (32, 631).

61. *De libero arbitrio* (32, 1221–1310). Cf. R I, 9, 1–6 (32, 595–599).

62. R I, 9, 3–6 (32, 595–599); DNG 67, 80–81 (44, 286–288); DDoP 11–12, 26–30 (45, 1008–1011).

63. *Contra Faustum manichaeum* (42, 207–518). Cf. R II, 7, 1–3 (32, 632–633).

64. CF I, 1 (42, 207).

65. C V, 3–6, 3–11 (32, 707–711).

66. Fessler, *Institutiones*, II, 295.

67. *De actis cum Felice manichaeo* (42, 519–552). Cf. R II, 8 (32, 633–634).

68. *De natura boni contra manichaeos* (42, 551–572). Cf. R II, 9 (32, 634).

69. *Contra Secundinum manichaeum* (42, 577–602). Cf. R II, 10 (32, 634).

70. The letter of Secundinus is given in Migne (42, 571–578).

71. R II, 10 (32, 634).

72. *Ad Orosium contra priscillianistas et origenistas* (42, 669–678). Cf. R II, 44 (32, 648–649).

73. (42, 665–670).

74. E237, 3 (33, 1035).

75. E166 *De origine animae hominis* (33, 720–733); R II, 45 (32, 619).

76. *Contra adversarium Legis et Prophetarum* (42, 603–666). Cf. R II, 58 (32, 654).

77. For more on the Manichean controversy, the following can also be consulted: DVR; DUC; DGnM; C; E 79, 236; EnP 140; S 1, 2, 12, 153, 192, 237.

78. *Psalmus contra partem Donati* (43, 23–32). Cf. R I, 20 (32, 617).

79. For a literary study of this *Psalm*, see William Meyer, *Anfang und Ursprung der lateinische und griechischen rhythmischen Dichtung.*

80. *Contra epistolam Parmeniani* (43, 33–108).

81. CEP I, 8–14, 13–21 (43, 43–50); III, 6, 29 (43, 105–108).

82. *De baptismo contra donatistas* (43, 107–244). Cf. R II, 18 (32, 637–638).

83. Cf. these other passages referring to Cyprian: CC I, 32, 38 (43, 465–466); II, 31–38, 39–49 (43, 439–496); DUB 13–16, 22–26 (43, 605–609).

84. *Contra litteras Petiliani donatistae* (43, 245–388). Cf. R II, 25 (32, 640–641).

85. CLP I, 18, 20 (43, 254); II, 14–23, 31–55 (267–279); 39–43, 92–102 (292–295); 73–101, 163–233 (309–339); III, 39, 45 (371).

86. *Ad catholicos epistola contra donatistas* or *De unitate Ecclesiae* (43, 391–446).

87. *Indiculus librorum tractatuum et epistolarum S. Augustini*, chap. 3 (46, 8).

88. Mansi IX, 261–262.

89. R II, 25 (32, 640–641).

90. (43, 389–390).

91. *Contra Cresconium grammaticum partis Donati* (43, 445–594). Cf. R II, 26 (32, 641).

92. CC III, 47, 51 (43, 524–525); R II, 26 (32, 641).

93. *De unico baptismo contra Petilianum ad Constantinum* (43, 595–614). Cf. R II, 34 (32, 644–645).

94. *Epistola 108 ad Macrobium* (33, 405–418).

95. *Breviculus collationis cum donatistis* (43, 613–650). Cf. R II, 39 (32, 646).

96. *Ad donatistas post collationem* (43, 651–690). Cf. R II, 40 (32, 646–647).

97. (33, 577–583).

98. *Sermo ad Caesareensis Ecclesiae plebem Emerito praesente habitus* (43, 689–698).

99. *De gestis cum Emerito Caesareensi donatistarum episcopo* (43, 697–706). Cf. R II, 51 (32, 650).

100. *Contra Gaudentium donatistarum episcopum* (43, 707–752). Cf. R II, 59 (32, 654).

101. Cf. E204 (33, 939–942).

The following *Letters* also treat of the Donatist controversy: E 23, 33–35, 43, 44, 49, 51–53, 56–58, 61, 66, 70, 76, 86–89, 93, 97, 100, 105–108, 111, 112, 128, 129, 133, 134, 139, 141, 142, 144, 173, 185, 204 (PL 33).

See also JE 4–6, 9–23, J 1–4 (PL 35). EnP 10, 25 (II), 30 (III), 32 (III), 33 (II), 35, 36 (II, III), 39, 54, 57, 85, 95, 98, 101, 119, 124, 132, 145, 147, 149 (PL 36–37). S 10, 46, 47, 88, 90, 99, 129, 138, 146, 265, 266, 268, 269, 292, 357–360 (PL 38–39).

102. Cf. Garnier, ed. of Mercator, VI, 2, "De scriptis ab Augustino adversus pelagianos" (48, 546–566).

103. *De peccatorum meritis et remissione et de baptismo parvulorum ad Marcellinum* (44, 109–200). Cf. R II, 33 (32, 644). This book is often cited, even by Augustine, under the title of *De baptismo parvulorum*. See, for instance, E139, 3 (33, 536). Sometimes it is called simply *Liber ad Marcellinum*.

104. *De spiritu et littera* (44, 201–246). Cf. R II, 37 (33, 645–646).

105. Cf. DCF XV, 8 (42, 312); OJ II, 157 (45, 1208).

106. *De natura et gratia ad Timasium et Jacobum* (44, 247–290). Cf. R II, 42 (32, 647).

107. See the letter thanking Augustine from Timasius and James: E168 (33, 741–742).

108. *De perfectione justitiae hominis* (44, 291–318).

109. *De gestis Pelagii* (44, 319–360). Cf. R II, 47 (32, 649).

110. *Epistola 186 ad Paulinum* (33, 815–832).

111. *Epistola 188 ad Julianam* (33, 848–854).

112. (61, 633–638).

113. (48, 554).

114. *De gratia Christi et de peccato originali contra Pelagium et Coelestium* (44, 359–410). Cf. R II, 50 (32, 650).

115. CJ IV, 8, 47 (44, 762).

116. *Epistola 194 ad Sixtum romanum presbyterum (et postea Pontificem)* (33, 874–891).

117. *De anima et ejus origine* (44, 475–548). Cf. R II, 56 (32, 653).

118. *De nuptiis et concupiscentia ad Valerium comitem* (44, 413–474). Cf. R II, 53 (32, 651).

119. *Contra duas epistolas pelagianorum ad Bonifacium romanae Ecclesiae episcopum* (44, 549–638). Cf. R II, 61 (32, 655).

120. OJ I, 18 (45, 1057).

121. *Contra Julianum haeresis pelagianae defensorem* (44, 641–874). Cf. R II, 62 (32, 655).

122. *Opus imperfectum contra secundam Juliani responsionem* (45, 1049–1608).

123. DNu II, 2, 2 (44, 437).

124. *De gratia et libero arbitrio ad Valentinum et cum illo monachos* (44, 881–912). Cf. R II, 66 (32, 656).

125. E214, which explains the letter to Sixtus, and E215 (33, 968–974).

126. E216 (33, 974–978).

127. *De correptione et gratia ad eumdem Valentinum et cum illo monachos adrumetinos* (44, 915–946). Cf. R II, 67 (32, 656).

128. DCG 7, 11 (44, 923).

129. A. Arnauld has written a *Synopsis analytica* of this work which was printed as a preface to the work in a few copies of the Benedictine edition, but which was subsequently suppressed because of its Jansenistic leanings.

130. *Epistola 217 ad Vitalem carthaginensem* (33, 978–989).

131. *De praedestinatione sanctorum ad Prosperum et Hilarium* (44, 959–992).

132. *De dono perseverantiae ad Prosperum et Hilarium* (45, 993–1034).

133. E225, 226 (44, 947–960, quoted from 33, 1002–1012).

134. *Contra sermonen arianorum* (42, 683–708). Cf. R II, 52 (32, 650–651).

135. *Collatio cum Maximino arianorum episcopo* (42, 709–742).

136. *Contra Maximinum haereticum arianorum episcopum* (42, 743–814).

137. Col (42, 724–740).

138. Other writings against Arianism are the following: S 52, 118, 126, 135, 139, 140, 183, 341 (PL 38–39); JE 17, 18, 20, 27, 36, 37, 49, 59, 71 (PL 35); E 171, 238–242 (PL 33).

139. *De doctrina christiana* (34, 15–122).

140. Books I to III, chap. 36.

141. *De Genesi contra manichaeos* (34, 173–220). Cf. R I, 10, 1–3 (32, 599–600).

142. *De Genesi ad litteram liber imperfectus* (34, 219–246). Cf. R I, 18 (32, 613–614).

143. R I, 18 (32, 613).

144. *De Genesi ad litteram libri duodecim* (34, 245–486). Cf. R II, 24, 1–2 (32, 640).

145. R II, 24, 1 (32, 640).

146. *Locutionum in Heptateuchum* (34, 485-546). Cf. R II, 54 (32, 651).

147. *Quaestionum in Heptateuchum* (34, 547-824). Cf. R II, 55, 1-3 (32, 651-653).

148. *Annotationum in Job* (34, 825-886). Cf. R II, 13 (32, 635).

149. R II, 13 (32, 635).

150. *Enarrationes in Psalmos* (36, 67-1028; 37, 1033-1968).

151. *De consensu Evangelistarum* (34, 1041-1230). Cf. R II, 16 (32, 636-637).

152. Clausen, *Augustinus, sac. scripturae interpres,* Copenhagen, 1827, pp. 107-115.

153. *Quaestionum Evangeliorum* (35, 1321-1364). Cf. R II, 12 (32, 634-635).

154. *De sermone Domini in monte* (34, 1229-1308).

155. *In Joannis Evangelium* (35, 1379-1976).

156. *In epistolam Joannis ad Parthos* (35, 1977-2062).

157. *Expositio quarumdam propositionum ex epistola ad Romanos* (35, 2063-2088). Cf. R I, 23, 1-4 (32, 620-622).

158. Augustine recognized his early uncertainty on the doctrine and presented a corrected version in DPS, 3-4, 7-8 (44, 964-966).

159. *Epistolae ad Romanos inchoata expositio* (35, 2087-2106).

160. This matter is also taken up in S71 (38, 445-467) and in En 83 (40, 272).

161. *Epistolae ad Galatas expositionis* (35, 2105-2148). Cf. R I, 24, 1-2 (32, 622-623).

162. Augustine's intention was to omit nothing. Cf. R I, 24, 1 (32, 622).

163. *De scriptura sacra speculum* (34, 887-1040).

164. The *Speculum* was published by Cl. Menard at Paris in 1654. The critics have proved its authenticity through the testimony of Possidius and the excerpts from Eugyppius. The only change was the substitution of the Vulgate text (except for some passages) for the Vetus Itala version of the Scriptures which Augustine used almost exclusively. Tommasi has published a separate edition of it, Rome, 1679.

An analogous work with the title *Liber de divinis Scripturis sive speculum* has gone through the following editions: (1) The Oratorian Vignier in his *Supplementum operum S. Augustini,* 1654, I, 515-564, following a manuscript of Theodulfus of Orleans which was only an abridgement of the complete work. In addition, the manuscript was very poorly reproduced by Vignier. (2) Cardinal Mai in his *Nova PP. Bibliotheca,* Ib, using the Codex Sessorianus which gives the best text of the complete work, followed the Itala. (3) Weihrich, soon after the first *Speculum* appeared (CSEL XII, 287–700), following the text of the Sessorianus. In a note he gives the complete text of the abridgement of Theodulfus, according to the two manuscripts Aniciensis (Le Puy) and Mesmianus (n. 9380 at Paris).

This *Liber* differs from the preceding *Speculum* in that it lists the texts methodically, to make a doctrinal summary of them. Although Vignier, Mai, and recently Leopold Delisle have viewed the *Liber* as the true *Speculum* of St. Augustine, it is certainly apocryphal and the *Speculum* given by the Benedictines in their text is the only one which corresponds to the testimony of Possidius. Cf. Weihrich at the beginning of his edition and Leopold Delisle, *Bibliothèque de l'Ecole des chartres*, 1884, pp. 478–487.

165. *De fide et symbolo* (40, 181–196). Cf. R I, 17 (32, 612–613).

166. *De agone christiano* (40, 289–310). Cf. R II, 3 (32, 631).

167. R II, 3 (32, 631).

168. *Enchiridion ad Laurentium sive de fide spe et charitate* (40, 231–290). Cf. R II, 58 (32, 655).

169. *De diversis quaestionibus* LXXXIII (40, 11–100). Cf. R I, 26 (32, 624–630).

170. Fessler gives an analytic index, *Institutiones*, II, 365.

171. *De diversis quaestionibus ad Simplicianum* (40, 101–148). Cf. R II, 1, 1–2 (32, 629–631).

172. Cf. C VIII, 1–2, 1–5 (32, 747–751) for Augustine's relation to Simplicianus.

173. Cf. R II, 1, 1 (32, 629); DPS 4, 8 (40, 965–966). For an analysis of this book see Loofs, *Realencyclopädie für prot. Theol. und Kirche*, II, 279 ff.; Franzelin, *De Deo Uno*, thesis 57, p. 579; also the chapter on grace in this book, pp. 200–201.

174. *De octo Dulcitii quaestionibus* (40, 147–170). Cf. R II 65 (32, 656).

175. R II, 65 (32, 656).

176. *De Trinitate* (42, 819–1098). Cf. R II, 15, 1–3 (32, 635–636).

177. R II, 15, 1 (32, 635–636).

178. E169 (33, 742–748) and E174 (33, 757–758), which is the preface to the work.

John Stilting S.J., *Acta sanctorum Augusti*, Antwerp, 1743, VI, n. 125, p. 235, proves that the encounter of Augustine with the angel under the guise of an infant who was trying to drain the sea is a legend without any foundation.

179. *Epistola 120 ad Consentium de Trinitate* (33, 452–462).

180. *De fide et operibus* (40, 197–230). Cf. R II, 38 (32, 646).

181. The unsubstantiated charge has often been made that this work

was directed against St. Jerome, *In Isaiam* 66, 24 (24, 677).On this point En 67–117 (40, 263–287) can be compared with J. B. Faure, *Annotationes super Enchiridion*, 2nd ed., Naples, 1847, pp. 139–144.

182. *De mendacio* (40, 487–518). Cf. R I, 27 (32, 630).

183. *Contra mendacium ad Consentium* (40, 517–548). Cf. R II, 60 (32, 654).

184. *De continentia* (40, 349–372).

185. *De bono conjugali* (40, 373–396). Cf. R II, 22, 1–2 (32, 639–640).

186. *De sancta virginitate* (40, 397–428). Cf. R II, 23 (32, 640).

187. *De bono viduitatis seu epistola ad Julianam viduam* (40, 431–450).

188. *De conjugiis adulterinis ad Pollentium* (40, 451–486). Cf. R II, 57 (32, 653).

189. *De patientia* (40, 611–626).

190. E231, 7 (33, 1026).

191. *De cura pro mortuis gerenda ad Paulinum* (40, 591–610). Cf. R II, 64 (32, 655–656).

192. Compare this work with S172–173 (38, 935–939). Also A. Frantz, *Das Gebet für die Todten . . . nach den Schriften des Augustinus,* Nordhausen, 1857.

193. *De opere monachorum* (40, 547–582). Cf. R II, 21 (32, 638–639).

194. Le Camus, Bishop of Belley, treats this work and included commentaries on it in *Saint Augustin, De l'ouvrage des moines*, Rouen, 1633.

195. See page 60.

196. DDoC IV, 4, 6 (34, 91).

197. DDoC IV, 5, 7 (34, 91–92).

198. DDoC IV, 6, 9–10 (34, 92–93).

199. *De catechizandis rudibus* (40, 309–348). Cf. R II, 14 (32, 635).

200. *Sermones* (38, 23–1484; 39, 1493–2354).

201. See pp. 61–62.

202. See pp. 62–63.

203. Cf. S32, 1, 1 (38, 196).

204. *Epistola Secundini manichaei ad Augustinum* (42, 574).

205. Rottmanner, *Historisches Jahrbuch*, 1898, p. 894.

206. *Epistola ad Demetriadem* (33, 1099–1120).

207. E188 (33, 848–854).

208. DGrC I, 22, 23 (44, 371).

209. DGrC I, 37, 40 (44, 378–379).

210. *In Cant.*, I (91, 1075).

211. *Regula secunda clericis* (32, 1449–1452).

212. *Epistola consolatoria ad Probum* (33, 1175–1176).

213. (33, 1095–1098).

214. (33, 1120–1153).

215. *Epistola Cyrilli ad Augustinum*, 4 (33, 1132).

216. *De spiritu et anima* (40, 779–832).

217. Stöckl, *Geschichte der Philosophie des Mittelalters*, Mainz, 1864, I, 389.

218. *Tractatus adversus quinque haereses seu contra quinque hostium genera* (42, 1101–1116).

219. *Sermo de symbolo contra judaeos paganos et arianos* (42, 1117–1130).

220. *Dialogus de altercatione Ecclesiae et Synagogae* (42, 1131–1140).

221. (42, 1131).

222. *De fide contra manichaeos* (42, 1139–1154).

223. *Commonitorium quomodo sit agendum cum manichaeis qui convertuntur* (42, 1153–1156).

224. Cf. the earlier and more developed Graeco-Latin formula edited by Galland in PG I, 1462–1474.

225. *Sermo de Rusticiano subdiacono a donatistis rebaptizato et in diaconum ordinato* (43, 753–758).

226. (43, 752).

227. Adolph Harnack, *History of Dogma*, trans. from the third German ed. by James Millar, London, 1898, V, 141.

228. *Contra Fulgentium donatistam* (43, 763–774).

229. *Liber testimoniorum fidei contra donatistas*, published by Dom Pitra in *Analecta sacra et classica*, Paris, 1888, I, 147–158.

230. This is the conjecture of Dom Cabrol, *Révue des questions historiques*, 1890, XLVII, 232–243.

231. *Hypomnesticon contra pelagianos et coelestianos* (45, 1611–1664).

232. *Liber de tribus epistolis*, 35 (121, 1044–1045).

233. *De praedestinatione*, 14 (115, 1199–1200).

234. Garnier, *Opera Mercatoris*, VI, 4 (48, 572–586); L. Raab, *Disquisitio historica de libris Hypognosticon*, Altdorf, 1735.

235. *De praedestinatione et gratia* (45, 1665–1678).

236. *De praedestinatione Dei libellus* (45, 1677–1680).

237. *Collatio beati Augustini cum Pascentio ariano . . . praesente Laurentio judice* (33, 1156–1162).

238. (33, 1153–1156); cf. E238 (33, 1038–1049).

239. *Contra Felicianum arianum de unitate Trinitatis* (42, 1157–1172).

240. *De trinitate et unitate Dei* (42, 1193–1200).

241. *De mirabilibus sacrae Scripturae* (35, 2149–2200).

242. *S.T.*, III, 45, 3 *ad* 2.

243. There is a reference to Ireland in the work itself, II, 4 (35, 2176).

244. *De benedictionibus Jacob patriarchae* (35, 2199–2206).

245. *Quaestiones Veteris et Novi Testamenti* (35, 2213–2416).

246. The Benedictines list some of the strange doctrines proposed in this work (35, 2205–2206).

247. See the index (35, 2207–2214).

248. (48, 314–315).

249. They cite the source of various sections throughout the work (35, 2207–2415).

250. Consult A. Harnack, *Abhandlungen Al. von Öttingen gewidmet*, Munich, 1898, pp. 54–93.

251. *Quaestionum septemdecim in Evangelium secundum Matthaeum* (35, 1365–1376).

252. Cf. Ceillier, *Histoire*, XI, a. 4 q. 7, n. 2, p. 398.

253. *Psalterium* (40, 1135–1138).

254. *Cantici Magnificat expositio* (40, 1137–1142).

255. *De fide ad Petrum sive de regula verae fidei* (40, 753–780).

256. *De ecclesiasticis dogmatibus* (42, 1213–1222).

257. *De incarnatione Verbi ad Januarium* (42, 1175–1194).

258. *De essentia divinitatis* (42, 1199–1208).

259. *De unitate sanctae Trinitatis* (42, 1207–1212).

260. *Quaestiones de Trinitate et de Genesi* (42, 1171–1176).

261. *Dialogus quaestionum LXV sub titulo Orosii percontantis et Augustini respondentis* (40, 733–752).

262. *Viginti unius sententiarum sive quaestionum* (40, 725–732).

263. *De Antichristo* (40, 1131–1134).

264. *De assumptione beatae Mariae virginis* (40, 1141–1148).

265. *De vita christiana* (40, 1031–1046).

266. Tillemont, *Mémoires*, XV, 15–17.

267. *Briefe und Abhandlungen*, Christiana, 1890, p. 361.

268. *De vera et falsa poenitentia ad Christi devotam* (40, 1113–1130).

269. Cf. the complicated (and erroneous) casuistry in n. 27 (40, 1123–1124).

270. *Liber exhortationis*, vulgo *De salutaribus documentis ad quemdam comitem* (40, 1047–1078).

271. *De cognitione verae vitae* (40, 1005–1032).

272. *De amicitia* (40, 831–844).

273. *De vita eremetica ad sororem* (32, 1451–1474).

274. *Speculum* (40, 967–984).

275. *Speculum peccatoris* (40, 983–992).

276. *De diligendo Deo* (40, 847–864).

277. *Soliloquia; Meditationes; Manuale* (40, 863–968).

278. See page 43.

279. *De triplici habitaculo* (40, 991–998).

280. *De contritione cordis* (40, 943–950).

281. *Scala paradisi* (40, 998–1004).

282. *De septem vitiis et septem donis* (40, 1089–1092).

283. *De conflictu vitiorum et virtutum* (40, 1091–1106).

284. *De duodecim abusionum gradibus* (40, 1079–1088).

285. *De sobrietate et castitate* (40, 1105–1112).

286. *De visitatione infirmorum* (40, 1147–1158).

287. See (39, 1735–2354).

288. *Sermones ad fratres in eremo commorantes* (40, 1235–1358).

289. Except for the two authentic sermons, S355–356.

290. (40, 1159–1230).

291. *De consolatione mortuorum* (40, 1159–1168).

292. *De rectitudine catholicae conversationis* (40, 1169–1190).

293. (40, 626–723).

294. *De symbolo sermones ad catechumenos* (40, 626–668).

295. Compare them with the authentic sermons S212–215 (38, 1058–1076).

296. *Bibliotek der Symbole*, 3rd ed., p. 60.

297. See page 70.

298. Their Latin titles are: *De disciplina christiana* (40, 669–678); *De cantico novo* (677–686); *De quarta feria* (685–694); *De cataclysmo* (693–700); *De tempore barbarico* (699–708).

299. S351 (39, 1535–1549).

300. Cf. Schnönemann (47, 34); Cave, *Scriptorum ecclesiasticorum historia litteraria* . . . , saec. V, Basle, 1741.

301. *De apto et pulchro.* Cf. C IV, 13–15, 20–27 (32, 701–704).

302. Cf. R I, 6 (32, 591).

303. *Contra partem Donati libri duo.* R II, 5 (32, 632).

304. *Contra quod attulit Centurius a donatistis liber unus.* R II, 19 (32, 638).

305. *Probationum et testimoniorum contra donatistas liber unus.* R II, 27 (32, 641–642).

306. *Contra donatistam nescio quem liber unus.* R II, 28 (32, 642).

307. *Admonitio donatistarum de Maximianistis liber unus.* R II, 29 (32, 642).

308. *De Maximianistis contra donatistas liber unus.* R II, 35 (32, 645).

309. *Ad Emeritum donatistarum episcopum post collationem liber unus.* R II, 46 (32, 649).

310. Cf. *Indiculus* (46, 7–8).

311. *Adversus Primianum donatistarum Carthaginensium episcopum commonitorium.*

312. *De traditione in persecutionibus et de falso baptismo contra donatistas libri tres.*

313. *De baptismo contra eosdem.*

314. *Contra Hilarum liber.* R II, 11 (32, 634). *Responsio ad objecta Hilarii.* Both Hilarius and Hilarus are found.

315. *Expositio epistolae Jacobi ad duodecim tribus.* R II, 32 (32, 643–644).

316. *Exhortatio ad paganos; De sacrificiis spiritualibus contra manichaeos; De die Domini secundum Sophoniam prophetam contra manichaeos; De charitate.*

CHAPTER V. AUGUSTINE'S UNEXCELLED TEACHING ROLE

1. This is the title of a study by E. Feuerlein, "Über die Stellung Augustins in der Kirchen- und Kulturgeschichte," *Historische Zeitschrift*, Sybel, 1869, XXII, 270–313.

2. H. Reuter, *Augustinische Studien*, Gotha, 1887, p. 479.

3. Harnack, *History of Dogma*, V, 104.

4. Stilting, *Acta Sanctorum Augusti*, VI, 359–361.

5. *Epistola* CXLI *ad Augustinum* (22, 1180).

6. The last section of this book is devoted to the question of Augustine's authority in the Church. See chapter 18.

7. *Epistola* CCXXIX *ad S. Bernardum*, 13 (182, 405).

8. Erasmus, in the preface of his edition of Augustine, Basel, 1543.

9. *Bibliotheca sancta*, Cologne, 1576, p. 220.

10. Bossuet, *Défense de la tradition*, IV, chap. 16, ed. Lebel, V, 240.

11. *Ibid.*, IX, chap. 14, V, 501.

12. Bossuet, *Sermon pour la vêture d'une postulante bernardine.*

13. Stöckl, *Geschichte der christliche Philosophie zur Zeit der Kirchenväter*, Mainz, 1891, p. 365.

14. Harnack, *History of Dogma*, V, 95.

15. Philip Schaff, *Saint Augustin*, 1886, pp. 99–101.

16. *Ibid.*, 101–102.

17. Bindemann, *Der heilige Augustin*, Berlin, 1844–1869.

18. Kurtz, *Histoire de l'Eglise*, 9th ed., 1885.

19. Schaff, *Augustin*, p. 27.

20. Rudolf Eucken, *Die Lebensanschauungen der grossen Denker*, 4th ed., Leipzig, 1902, p. 210.

21. Harnack, *History of Dogma*, V, 61–234.

22. Harnack, *Monasticism*, p. 123.

23. Adolf Harnack, *What Is Christianity?*, trans. by Thomas Saunders, New York, 1904.

24. Friedrich Böhringer, "Aurelius Augustin," in *Die Kirche und ihre Zeugen*, 2nd ed., Stuttgart, 1877–1878.

25. Cf. Harnack, *History of Dogma*, V, 95–102.

26. Eucken, *Lebensanschauungen*, p. 210.

27. Schaff, *Augustin*, p. 97.

28. This is the central theme of Augustinian theology in the opinion of Reuter who wrote about it in his *Augustinische Studien*. Harnack thinks this the most scholarly of recent works on Augustine.

29. Thus Bonifas, *Histoire des dogmes*, Paris, 1886, I, 21, 78; Haag, *Histoire des dogmes chrétiennes*, I, 476.

30. See the article "Athanase (Symbole de saint)," DTC, I, 2184–2186.

31. Cf. Dom Morin, *Révue d'histoire et de littérature réligieuses*, 1902, pp. 147–149.

32. Bonifas, *Histoire des dogmes*, I, 21.

33. Thus Harnack, *History of Dogma*, V, 109; Sell, *Aus der Geschichte der Christentum*, 1888, p. 43.

34. Eucken, *Lebensanschauungen*, p. 244.

35. C VII, 19, 25 (32, 746).

36. Harnack, *History of Dogma*, V, 130.

37. One passage is DLA I, 2, 5 (32, 1224).

38. DPB II, 17, 27 (44, 168); DCG 11, 30 (44, 934).

39. Fénelon, *Lettres sur divers sujets de métaphysique et de réligion*, lettre IV, *Œuvres*, ed. Lebel, 1820, I, 393.

40. It was drawn up by the Oratorian ontologist, André Martin, *S. Augustini philosophia*, 2nd ed., Paris, 1863.

41. Eucken, *Lebensanschauungen*, p. 223.

42. Böhringer, "Augustinus," p. 414. See also J. A. Dorner, *Augustinus, sein theologisches System und seine religios-philosophische Anschauung*, Berlin, 1873, p. 324.

43. Schaff, *Augustin*, p. 100.

44. Cf. *Concordia, Libri symbolici*, etc., ed. Berlin, 1857, reproducing the edition of 1584, p. 17.

45. *Apologia confessionis*, a. 4, *ibid.*, pp. 64–65, 80, 92.

46. Reuter, *Augustinische Studien*, p. 497.

47. *Ibid.*, p. 511.

48. Schaff, *Augustin*, p. 98.

49. Dorner, "Augustine," in *Religious Encyclopaedia*, Edinburgh, 1883, I, 176.

50. Harnack, *What Is Christianity?* p. 251.

51. *Ibid.*, p. 261.

52. Harnack, *History of Dogma*, V, 77.

53. *Ibid.*, 88.

54. Schaff, *Augustin*, p. 98.

55. Quoted by Schaff, *Augustin*, p. 102.

56. Friedrich Loofs, *Leitfaden zum Studien der Dogmengeschichte*, 3rd ed., Halle, 1893, p. 196.

57. Thus, for instance, Reuter, *Aug. Studien*, p. 514.

58. Harnack, *History of Dogma*, V, 101–104.

CHAPTER VI. NEOPLATONIC INFLUENCES

1. This influence has been recognized by Bestmann, who was accused of denying it in his thesis, *Qua ratione Augustinus notiones philosophiae graecae ad dogmata anthropologica describenda adhibuerit*, Erlangen, 1877.

2. M. Grandgeorge, *Saint Augustin et le néoplatonisme*, Paris, 1896, pp. 70–84, 117–147.

3. C VII, 9, 13–15; 20–21, 26–27 (32, 740–742; 746–748). Cf. CA III, 18, 41 (32, 956); E 118, 20–34 (33, 441–449); DVR IV, 7 (34, 126) where he says, "With only a few changes, they would be Christians." DCD VIII, 1, 4–5, 10 (41, 225, 227–231, 234–235).

4. DOR II, 20, 53 (32, 1020).

5. R I, 3, 3 (32, 589).

6. Grandgeorge, *Augustin*, p. 31.

7. DCD VIII, 12 (41, 236–237).

8. DCD X, 31 (41, 311–312). In DCD X, 30 (41, 309–311) he compares Plato's teaching with that of Porphyry.

9. DBe 1, 4 (32, 961).

10. Cf. C VIII, 2, 3 (32, 749–750).

11. Grandgeorge, *Augustin*, p. 41.

12. DCD VIII, 12 (41, 237).

13. CA III, 20, 43 (32, 957).

14. *Ibid.*

15. Grandgeorge, *Augustin*, p. 155.

16. Dorner, *Augustinus*, p. 326.

17. R II, 4, 2 (32, 632).

18. DDoC II, 28, 43 (34, 56).

19. C VII, 20, 26 (32, 746–747).
20. DCD XXII, 28 (41, 795).
21. R I, 3, 2 (32, 588–589).
22. C VII, 9, 13–14 (32, 740–741).
23. JE 2, 4 (35, 1390). Cf. DCD X, 3, 1 (41, 280).
24. QH II, 25 (34, 604).
25. DCD X, 29, 1 (41, 307).
26. DCD X, 23 (41, 300).
27. R I, 3, 2 (32, 588).
28. DOR I, 11, 32 (32, 993).
29. DCD VIII, 2 (41, 225–226); DT 14, 1, 3 (42, 1037–1038).
30. DOR II, 17, 47 (32, 1017).
31. This is the theme of the entire work *On the Happy Life*, cf. DBe, 1 (32, 959). Also DCD XVIII, 41, 1 (41, 600–601).
32. DBe 1, 4 (32, 961); CA II, 2, 5 (32, 921–922).
33. SO I, 3, 8 (32, 873–874); CA III, 11, 24–26 (32, 946–948); DMa 12, 39 (32, 1216–1217); Jules Martin, *Augustin*, pp. 1–6.
34. Cf. C VII, 10, 16 (32, 742); DT X, 7, 9–10 (42, 978–979); VIII, 2, 3 (42, 948–949); DGnL XII, 36, 69 (34, 484).
35. DQ 33, 70–76 (32, 1073–1077).
36. DOR II, 19, 49–51 (32, 1018–1019); DI 4, 5–6 (32, 1023–1024); DLA II, 8–10, 20–29 (32, 1251–1257). Cf. André Martin, *S. Augustini Philosophia*, part II, chap. 2.
37. DCD VIII, 6 (41, 231).
38. DT VI, 6, 8 (42, 928–929): "That substance is simple in its multiplicity." Cf. JE 23, 9 (35, 1587–1588); DCD XI, 10, 1–2 (41, 325–326); DT I, 1, 2 (42, 820–821). See Grandegeorge, *Augustin*, pp. 59–68.
39. DD83 46, 2 (40, 30–31).
40. DMa treats of this (32, 1193–1220).
41. See pp. 109–114.
42. DCD VIII, 9–10 (41, 233–235).
43. DCD VIII, 10, 2 (41, 235).
44. *Ibid.*
45. C VII, 12–13, 18–19 (32, 743–744).
46. *Ibid.* Cf. Plotinus, *Enneads*, III, 2, 7 (Emile Bréhier, *Plotin Ennéades*, Paris, 1925, III, 33).
47. DLA III, 9, 24–28 (32, 1282–1285); *Enneads* III, 2, 5 (Bréhier, III, 31); DOR II, 4, 11–13 (32, 999–1001); *Enneads* III, 2, 11 (Bréhier, III, 35).
48. DLA III, 1, 1–3 (32, 1269–1272); *Enneads* III, 2, 7 (Bréhier, III, 33); En 23 (40, 244).
49. See pp. 138–139.

50. C VII, 20, 26 (32, 746).

51. Cf. DBe (32, 960–976).

52. DCD VIII, 5 (41, 229).

53. DCD X, 19, 2 (41, 308–309).

54. C VII, 9, 14 (32, 740–741).

55. DCD IX, 16 (41, 269).

56. E 118, 17 and passim (33, 440 ff.). This entire letter addressed to the pagan Dioscorus summarizes Augustine's impressions of the various philosophical schools.

57. C VII, 21, 27 (32, 747–748).

58. DCD XII, 22, 24, 26 (41, 371–376); II, 7 (41, 52–53).

59. DVR 7, 13 (34, 128–129); DGnL IX, 15, 26 (34, 403–404).

60. DVR 18, 35 (34, 137); CS 4 (42, 580–581); DA II, 18 (42, 547–548); DCF I, 13 (42, 117).

61. CP 2, 2 (42, 669–671); 8, 9 (42, 674).

62. DCD X, 31 (41, 311–312).

63. DCD XI, 4–6 (41, 319–322); XII, 15–20 (41, 363–372).

64. DCD XI, 16 (41, 365).

65. DCD XII, 15, 2 (41, 364–365).

66. Loesche, *De Augustino plotinizante*, Jena, 1880, p. 55.

67. R I, 15, 1 (32, 608); I, 11, 4 (32, 601–602); DCD VII, 23, 1–2 (41, 211–213); IV, 12 (41, 123). Grandgeorge recognized this fact also, *Augustin*, p. 111.

68. DCD X, 30 (41, 309–311).

69. DCD XII, 26 (41, 375–376); XIV, 5 (41, 408–409); DAO I, 12, 15 (44, 482–483); I, 19, 32–34 (44, 493–494).

70. DVR 1, 1 (34, 121–123); cf. DVR 5, 8–9 (34, 126–127); DCD X, 1, 1 (41, 277); VIII, 10–12 (41, 234–237); DCns I, 7–8, 12–13 (34, 1047–1049).

71. CA III, 17, 37 (32, 954).

72. R I, 1, 4 (32, 587).

73. DCD II, 14, 2 (41, 59).

74. R I, 2 (32, 588).

75. SO I, 1, 2 (32, 870).

76. R I, 4, 2 (32, 589–590).

77. R I, 4, 3 (32, 590) and especially I, 14, 2 (32, 606).

78. R I, 11, 4 (32, 601–602).

79. R I, 15, 7 (32, 610–611). Cf. DDu 13, 20 (42, 108–109).

80. DMu VI, 14, 44 (32, 1186); DI 15, 24 (32, 1033).

81. R I, 11, 4 (32, 601–602). Cf. DCns I, 23, 35 (34, 1057–1058); DGnI 4, 16–17 (34, 226–227).

82. DGnL X, 7, 12 (34, 413).

83. SO II, 20, 35 (32, 902–904); DQ 20, 34 (32, 1054–1055).

84. R I, 4, 4 (32, 590); I, 8, 2 (32, 594); DT XII, 15, 24 (42, 1011–1012); DCD X, 30 (41, 309–311); E 164, 7, 20 (33, 717).

85. DQ 32, 69 (32, 1073); E 158, 5 (33, 695). The possibility of only one soul is refuted in DLA II, 9, 27 (32, 1255); II, 7, 16 (32, 1249).

86. SO I, 14, 24 (32, 882). Cf. R I, 4, 3 (32, 590).

87. DFS 10, 23 (40, 193–194). Cf. R I, 17 (32, 612–613). An analogous idea is proposed in DMu VI, 4, 7 (32, 1166–1167), but withdrawn in R I, 11, 2 (32, 601). The question is treated fully in DCD XII, 26 (41, 375–376); XIII, 16, 19 (41, 387–389; 392–393).

88. DME II, 7, 9 (32, 1349).

89. R I, 7, 6 (32, 593–594). Cf. DCD XII, 13 (41, 360–362).

CHAPTER VII.   RELIGIOUS KNOWLEDGE

1. CA III, 10, 23 (32, 946).
2. *Ibid.*, 11, 25 (32, 947).
3. DLA II, 8, 21 (32, 1252).
4. CA III, 13, 29 (32, 949).
5. Cf. CA III, 11, 25–26 (32, 946–947).
6. DVR 39, 73 (34, 154–155).
7. DLA II, 3, 7 (32, 1243).
8. En 20, 7 (40, 243).
9. DT X, 10, 14 (42, 981).
10. SO I, 6, 12 (32, 875). Cf. DGnL IV, 32, 49 (34, 316).
11. Jules Martin, *Augustin*, p. 28, commenting on DUC 8, 20 (42, 79).
12. DQ 14, 24 (32, 1049).
13. DVR 10, 20 (34, 131).
14. DME I, 1, 1 (32, 1311).
15. E 140, 19, 48 (33, 558).
16. DOR II, 19, 61 (32, 1019).
17. DVR 4, 7 (34, 126).
18. CA II, 3, 8 (32, 923).
19. DME I, 17, 31 (32, 1324).
20. Cf. DME II, 2, 4 (32, 1346) where he shows that some seek not the truth but objections against it.
21. CF XXII, 52 (42, 433).
22. SO I, 1, 3 (32, 870).
23. DUC 16, 34 (42, 90).
24. DT I, 1, 3 (42, 821).
25. C VI, 4, 6 (32, 722).

26. DOR II, 18, 47 (32, 1017).
27. DCD X, 29, 2 (41, 308).
28. DAO IV, 11, 15 (44, 533).
29. E 159, 2 (33, 699).
30. See page 104.
31. SO I, 8, 15 (32, 877). Cf. I, 1, 3 (32, 870); I, 13, 23 (32, 881-882).
32. E 13, 4 (33, 78).
33. DGnL XII, 31, 59 (34, 479).
34. DPB I, 25, 38 (44, 130).
35. DCD X, 2 (41, 279).
36. DT XII, 15, 24 (42, 1011); R I, 8, 2 (32, 594).
37. André Martin, *S. Augustini philosophia*, part II, chaps. 19–54, pp. 176–277.
38. Jules Martin, *Augustin*, I 51 ff.
39. See pp. 102–103.
40. DGnL, XII, 27–28, 55–56 (34, 477–478); 34, 67 (34, 483).
41. DT II, 16, 27 (42, 862); JE 3, 17 (35, 1403); CMA II, 12, 2 (42, 768).
42. DT XIV, 15, 21 (42, 1052).
43. EnP 4, 8 (36, 81).
44. DOR II, 8, 25 (32, 1006).
45. *S. T.*, I, q. 84, a. 5; q. 88, a. 3.
46. Zigliara, *Della luce intellettuale*, Rome, 1874, I, chaps. 11–13; Lepidi, *De ontologismo*, Louvain, 1874, pp. 192–225; Franzelin, *De Deo uno*, Rome, 1870, pp. 140–148.
47. Cf. *De veritate*, q. 10 (*Truth*, II, 3–76).
48. Suarez, *De anima*, IV, 8, 4, Paris, 1856, VI, 741.
49. See the very interesting Franciscan publication, *De humanae cognitionis ratione anecdota quaedam s. Bonaventurae et nonnullorum ipsius discipulorum*, Quaracchi, 1883, especially pp. 34–45.
50. Cf. Lepidi, *De ontologismo*, pp. 218–219.
51. St. Thomas, *De spiritualibus creaturis*, n. 10, *Utrum spiritus agens sit unus omnium hominum, Quaest. disputatae*, Paris, 1889, XIV, 49–54.
52. DGnL XII, 30, 58 (34, 479).
53. E 120, 2 (33, 453).
57. SO I, 8, 15 (32, 877).
55. DT XII, 15, 24 (42, 1011).
56. DCD VIII, 10, 2 (41, 235). See page 100.
57. DT XIV, 12, 15 (42, 1048).
58. St. Thomas, *In II Sent.*, d. 17, q. 2, a. 1, Paris, 1873, VIII, 221.

59. Compare SO I, 6, 12 (32, 875) with *S. T.*, I–II, q. 109, a. 1, ad 2; DMa 11-12 (32, 1215-1218) with *In II Sent.*, d. 28, q. 1, a. 5, ad 3; C X, 10, 17 (32, 786), DGnL XII, 16, 33 (34, 467) with *De veritate*, q. 10, a. 6, ad 5; DT XII, 2, 2 (42, 999) with *De veritate*, q. 10, a. 6, ad 6; C XII, 25, 35 (32, 840), DVR 36, 66 (34, 151) with *Quodlibetales*, X, q. 4, a. 7, ad 1.

60. Harnack, *History of Dogma*, V, 105.

61. En 4 (40, 232).

62. CA III, 20, 43 (32, 957).

63. DOR II, 9, 26 (32, 1007).

64. DUC 12, 26 (42, 84).

65. E 147, 2-3, 7-8 (33, 599-600).

66. E 147, 2, 7 (33, 599).

67. Weber, *Histoire de la philosophie européenne*, 4th ed., p. 168.

68. DOR II, 9, 26 (32, 1007).

69. DT VIII, 5, 8 (42, 952).

70. DT IX, 1, 1 (42, 961).

71. JE 40, 8, 9 (35, 1690).

72. DPS 2, 5 (44, 962-963).

73. DVR 24, 45 (34, 141).

74. DVR 25, 46 (34, 142).

75. E 120, 1, 3 (33, 453).

76. E 102, 38 (33, 386).

77. DPS 2, 5 (44, 963).

78. Cf. DT VIII, 5, 7 (42, 952).

79. Cf. E 147, 2, 7 (33, 599).

80. E 120, 2, 8 (33, 456).

81. E 147, 3, 8 (33, 600).

82. DLA II, 2, 6 (32, 1243); E 120, 1, 3 (33, 453).

83. S 43, 7, 9 (38, 258).

84. EnP 118, sermon 18, especially n. 3 (37, 1552).

85. DLA III, 21, 60 (32, 1301).

86. DUC 16, 34 (42, 89); C VI, 5, 7-8 (32, 722-723).

87. DUC 16, 34 (42, 89).

88. See S 43, 4, 5 (38, 256), which develops II Pet., 1:8.

89. DUC 16, 34 (42, 89). Cf. E 118, 5, 32 (33, 447).

90. See S 43, 5, 6 (38, 256-257).

91. Cf. DME in its entirety (32, 1309-1378); DUC 17, 35 (42, 90). See also pp. 47-48.

92. See page 17.

93. DVR 3-4, 3-7 (34, 123-126).

94. *Constitutio dogmatica de fide catholica*, c. III.

95. Cf. J I, 13 (35, 1988).

96. Harnack, *History of Dogma*, V, 99.

97. DNG 61, 71 (44, 282).

98. DB V, 23, 31 (43, 192). Cf. DB II, 7, 12 (43, 133); IV, 6, 8 (43, 159); E 56, 1, 1 (33, 200).

99. CJ VI, 5, 13 (44, 830).

100. DB IV, 24, 31 (43, 174).

101. Cf. DDoC III, 2, 2 (34, 65).

102. DAC 13–33, 14–35 (40, 299–309); En 9–113, 3–29 (40, 235–285); S I *ad catechumenos* (40, 627–637); S 212–215 (38, 1058–1076).

103. Hahn, *Bibliothek der Symbole*, 3rd ed., pp. 38, 58.

104. CEM 5, 6 (42, 176). Cf. CF XXII, 79 (42, 452); XXVIII, 2 (42, 485).

105. DDoC III, 2, 2 (34, 65).

106. DDoC III, 27, 38 (34, 80); DGnI 1, 1 (34, 221).

107. DB II, 4, 5 (43, 129).

108. CEM 4, 5 (42, 175).

109. Harnack, *History of Dogma*, V, 98–99.

110. *Ibid.*, 98.

111. DDoC II, 8, 13 (34, 41).

112. Thiel, *Epistolae romanorum pontificum*, p. 56; Jaffé, *Regesta*, nn. 40, 91.

113. (20, 501).

114. Mansi, III, 924, canon 36.

115. Mansi, III, 891, canon 47; IV, 430, canon 29.

116. Mansi, III, 891.

117. DDoC II, 8, 12 (34, 40).

118. DCD XVII, 20, 1 (41, 554).

119. DCD XVIII, 36 (41, 596).

120. R II, 4, 2 (32, 631).

121. See SS (34, 947).

122. O. Rottmanner, "Saint Augustine sur l'auteur de l'Epitre aux Hébreux," *Revue bénédictine*, July, 1901. Cf. DPB I, 27, 50 (44, 137). Certain people even deny that the Epistle to the Hebrews is inspired.

123. DCD XV, 23, 4 (41, 470); XVIII, 38 (41, 598); CF XI, 2 (42, 245).

124. Harnack, *History of Dogma*, V, 98.

125. DGnL VII, 28, 42 (34, 371).

126. DDoC II, 6, 7–8 (34, 38–39); III, 27, 38 (34, 80); C VII, 21, 27 (32, 747); XIII, 29, 44 (32, 864); DCD XVIII, 43 (41, 604).

127. DCns I, 35, 54 (34, 1070).

128. E 82, 1, 3 (33, 277); 3, 24 (33, 286).

129. CF XI, 5 (42, 249). Cf. E 82, 1, 3 (33, 277).

130. DCnS (34, 1041–1230). See also E 93, 10, 35–36 (33, 339); DGnL V, 8, 23 (34, 329); JE 112, 1 (35, 1930).

131. DCns III, 7, 30 (34, 1175).

132. DCns II, 12, 27–29 (34, 1090–1091).

133. DCD XVIII, 42 (41, 603); DDoC II, 15, 22 (34, 46); EnP 87, 10 (37, 1116).

134. DCD XVIII, 43 (41, 604).

135. Rönsch, "Die lateinischen Bibelübersetzungen im christlichen Afrika zur Zeit des Augustinus," *Zeitschrift für die historische Theologie*, 1867, pp. 606 ff.; 1870, pp. 91 ff.; Douais, "Saint Augustin et la Bible," *Revue biblique*, 1893, 62–81, 351–377; Burkitt, "The Old Latin and Itala," *Texts and Studies*, Cambridge, 1896, IV, 55–78; P. Monceaux, *Histoire littéraire de l'Afrique chrétienne*, Paris, 1901, I, 138–154.

136. DGnL I, 19–21, especially n. 39 (34, 260–262).

137. C XII, 31, 42 (32, 844); DDoC III, 27, 38 (34, 80).

138. St. Thomas, *De potentia*, q. 4, a. 1, Paris, 1889, XIII, 118.

139. *S. T.*, I, q. 1, a. 10.

140. Cf. Patrizzi, *De interpretatione Scripturae*, Rome, 1844, pp. 15–54; J. T. Beelen, *Dissertatio theologica qua sententiam vulgo receptam esse sacrae Scripturae multiplicem interdum sensum litteralem, nullo fundamento satis firmo niti demonstrare conatur*, Louvain, 1845, especially pp. 40–48.

141. Schanz and Rottmanner, *Theologische Quartalschrift*, 1895, LXXVII, 269–276.

142. DCns III, 7, 30 (34, 1175).

143. QH II, 73 (34, 623).

144. Clausen, *Augustinus*, pp. 167–207, 252–267.

CHAPTER VIII. THE DIVINE NATURE

1. EnP 74, 9 (36, 952).

2. EnP 13, 2 (36, 141).

3. EnP 52, 2 (36, 613).

4. S 69, 2, 3 (38, 441).

5. DGnL IV, 32, 49 (34, 316–317).

6. JE 106, 4 (35, 1910).

7. S 141, 2, 2 (38, 776).

8. C X, 6, 9 (32, 783).

9. C XI, 4, 6 (32, 811).

10. E 142, 2 (33, 705). Cf. E 160, 1–3 (33, 701–702). Augustine also refers Evodius to DVR 31, 58 (34, 147–148).

11. DD83 54 (40, 38).

12. DLA II, 3–15, 7–40 (32, 1243–1263).

13. C VII, 10, 16 (32, 742).

14. R I 26 (32, 627).

15. Cf. DLA II, 3–14, nn. 7–12, 13–14, 15–38 (32, 1243–1261). Jules Martin, *Augustin*, pp. 101–188.

16. SO I, 1, 2 (32, 870).

17. DCD VIII, 4 (41, 228–229).

18. S 117, 3, 5 (38, 663). Cf. *Ibid.*, n. 7.

19. EnP 85, 12 (37, 1090).

20. JE 13, 5 (35, 1495).

21. SO I, 1, 3–4 (32, 870–871).

22. DT VII, 5, 10 (42, 942).

23. JE 48, 10, 6 (35, 1743).

24. DT XV, 5, 7–8 (42, 1061–1062). Cf. DT V, 10, 11 (42, 918); VI, 7, 8–9 (42, 929); S 341, 6, 8 (39, 1498); DCD XI, 10, 2 (41, 326).

25. Cf. Suarez, *De Deo*, X, chaps. 10–14; Zigliara, *La luce intellettuale*, II, 101.

26. DGnL V, 5, 12 (34, 325). Cf. DGnM II, 2, 3 (34, 175); C XI, 21, 27 (32, 819).

27. E 137, 2, 8 (33, 519).

28. Cf. DLA III, 2–4, 4–10 (32, 1272–1276); DCD XI, 22 (41, 334).

29. Cf. DPS 9, 17 (44, 973); DDoP 9, 23 (44, 1005–1006). See also pp. 213 ff.

30. Schwane, *Histoire des dogmes*, II, 265.

31. De Regnon, *Etudes de théologie positive*, pp. 300–429.

32. Cf. DT V, 5–6, 6–7 (42, 913–915); VIII, 1 (42, 947).

33. DT VIII, 1 (42, 947).

34. Denzinger, *Enchiridion Symbolorum*, nn. 1–13.

35. Hahn, *Bibliothek der Symbole*, nn. 33–47.

36. Denzinger, *Enchiridion Symbolorum*, nn. 1–13.

37. Hahn, *Bibliothek der Symbole*, nn. 143–145.

38. Denzinger, *Enchiridion Symbolorum*, n. 39.

39. Cf. the words of Pope St. Dionysius to St. Dionysius of Alexandria quoted by St. Athanasius, *De decretis Nicaenae synodi*, 26, *P. G.*, XXV, 464.

40. Cf. DT VII, especially chaps. 4–6 (42, 939–946).

41. DT VIII, 1 (42, 947).

42. Cajetan, *In Summam S. Thomae*, III, q. 3, a. 2; I, q. 39, a. 4.

43. Durandus, *In III Sent.*, d. 1, q. 2, n. 7.

44. See page 65.

45. DT II, 17, 32 (42, 866).
46. DT II, 17-18, 32-33 (42, 866-867); 10, 17-18 (42, 855 856).
47. DT II, 9-10, 16-17 (42, 855-856).
48. DT II, 10, 18 (42, 857).
49. DT III, 11, 27 (42, 886).
50. DT II, 10, 18 (42, 857).
51. *S. T.*, I, q. 27, a. 2.
52. *Ibid.*, a. 3.
53. The table is based, with some modifications and corrections, on that of K. Scipio, *Des Aurelius Augustinus Metaphysik*, Leipzig, 1886, pp. 66-67.

CHAPTER IX. CREATION AND CREATURES

1. See page 61, nn. 67-70.
2. DCD XI, 6 (41, 322).
3. DCD XII, 15, 2 (41, 364).
4. DCD XII, 12 (41, 359).
5. DCD XI, 5 (41, 321).
6. DGnM I, 23, 41 (34, 193).
7. DGnI 12, 36 (34, 235).
8. DGnI 13, 43 (34, 237).
9. DCD XI, 9 (41, 324).
10. DGnL V, 4, 10 (34, 325). Cf. DGnL I, 10, 18 (34, 253); DGnL 7, 28 (34, 231); DCD XI, 9 (41, 324).
11. C XII, 8, 8 (32, 829); DGnL VI, IX (34, 339-356, 393-408).
12. DGnL I, 12, 27 (34, 256).
13. C XII, 8, 8 (32, 829). Cf. DGnM I, 5, 8 (34, 177); DGnI 3, 10 (34, 224).
14. DGnL I, 15, 29 (34, 257).
15. DGnL II, 11, 24 (34, 272); V, 5, 13 (34, 326).
16. DGnL VII, 28, 41 (34, 371).
17. DT III, 9, 16 (42, 877).
18. DGnL V, 23, 45 (34, 338).
19. Grandgeorge, *Augustin*, p. 114.
20. DGnL IX, 17, 32 (34, 406).
21. DGnM I, 7, 11 (34, 178).
22. DGnL V, 4, 11 (34, 325).
23. *Ibid.*, 4, 9 (34, 324); DT III, 8, 13 (42, 876).
24. DGnL VI, 6, 10 (34, 343).
25. *Ibid.*, 5, 8 (34, 342).
26. *Ibid.*

27. See pp. 149–150.
28. Zahm, *Bible, science et foi*, Paris, 1894, pp. 58–66.
29. *Ibid.*, 66.
30. Jules Martin, *Augustin*, p. 314.
31. DGnL IX, 17, 32 (34, 406).
32. Zahm, *L'évolution et le dogme*, Paris, 1897, p. 124.
33. DT III, 8, 13 (42, 875).
34. DGnL II, 15, 30 (34, 276).
35. DGnL IX, 17, 31–32 (34, 405–406).
36. *Ibid.*, 31 (34, 406).
37. *Ibid.*, 15, 26–28 (34, 403–404).
38. DGnL VII, 24, 35 (34, 368).
39. DGnM I, 22, 33 (34, 189).
40. *Ibid.*, 34 (34, 189).
41. *Ibid.*, 23, 35–41 (34, 190–193).
42. *Ibid.*, 24, 43 (34, 194).
43. DGnI 7, 28 (34, 231). Cf. DGnL V, 5, 14 (34, 326).
44. DGnI 15, 51 (34, 240). Cf. DGnM II, 3, 4 (34, 197).
45. DGnL IV, 26–30, 43–47 (34, 314–316); V, 5, 15 (34, 326). Cf. DCD XI, 7 (41, 322).
46. DGnL V, 1, 1 (34, 321). Cf. DGnL I, 20–21, 40–41 (34, 261–262).
47. DGnL V, 8, 23 (34, 329).
48. C XII, 14–25, 17–35 (32, 832–840), especially n. 34.
49. *Ibid.*, 34 (32, 840).
50. Noris, *Vindiciae augustinianae*, chap. 4, n. 1 (47, 688).
51. EnP 85, 17 (37, 1094).
52. DCD XV, 23, 1 (41, 468). Cf. DCD XXI, 10, 1 (41, 724).
53. En 58 (40, 259); CP 11, 14 (42, 678).
54. DCD XII, 24–27 (41, 373–376).
55. *Ibid.*, 24 (41, 374).
56. *Ibid.*, 15, 3 (41, 365).
57. *Ibid.*, 9 (41, 356).
58. DGnL XI, 26, 33 (34, 443); DCG 10, 27 (44, 932).
59. DGnL XI, 23, 30 (34, 441).
60. *Ibid.*, 14, 18 (34, 436).
61. JE 110, 7 (35, 1924).
62. DCD XI, 33 (41, 346).
63. DCD IX, 22 (41, 274).
64. DD83 79, 1 (40, 91).
65. DCD XXI, 6, 1 (41, 717).
66. DDD 5, 9 (40, 586); CA I, 7, 20 (32, 916).
67. R II, 30 (32, 643).

68. DCD XV, 23, 1 (41, 468).

69. DD83 79, 1 (40, 90).

70. DGnL II, 18, 38 (34, 279-280).

71. R I, 11, 4 (32, 602).

72. See "Angélologie," DTC, I, 1218.

73. DCM 15, 18 (40, 605-606).

74. DCD XII, 1, 1 (41, 349); 9, 2 (41, 357).

75. DT III, 10, 21 (42, 881).

76. *Ibid.*

77. DQ 34, 78 (32, 1078).

78. Jean Felix Nourrisson, *La philosophie de saint Augustin*, 2nd ed., Paris, 1866, II, 312.

79. *Ibid.*, II, 321.

80. See pp. 198-204.

81. E 164, 2, 4 (33, 721-722).

82. DGnL VII, 12-22, 18-33 (34, 362-367).

83. *Ibid.*, 28, 43 (34, 372). Cf. DAO IV, 13, 19 (44, 535); DNB 1 (42, 552).

84. DGnL VII, 15, 21 (34, 363).

85. E 164, 2, 4 (33, 722).

86. DQ 13, 22 (32, 1047); 27-29, 52-58 (32, 1065-1068). Cf. DI 6, 10 (32, 1025).

87. E 158, 6 (33, 695).

88. *Ibid.*, 5 (33, 695). Cf. E 159, 1 (33, 699); E 162, 3 (33, 705).

89. DAO IV, 2, 3 (44, 525). Cf. DVR 36, 56 (34, 151).

90. DGnL VII, 27, 38 (34, 369).

91. DQ 13, 22 (32, 1048).

92. DME I, 27, 52 (32, 1332).

93. DT XV, 7, 11 (42, 1065).

94. *Ibid.*

95. DCnt 9, 22-23 (40, 364).

96. Cf. DDu in its entirety (42, 93-112); R I, 15, 1 (32, 608).

97. DAO IV, 2, 3 (44, 525). Cf. DGnM II, 8, 11 (34, 202).

98. Cf. DAO IV, 13, 19 (44, 535); 22, 36 (44, 544); II, 2, 2 (44, 495); DD83 7 (40, 13); DT XIV, 16, 22 (42, 1053).

99. DI 15, 24 (32, 1033). Cf. 16, 25 (32, 1034).

100. Cf. DT IV, 3, 5 (42, 890); CF XXIV, 2 (42, 475).

101. E 238, 2, 12 (33, 1042).

102. DI 16, 25 (32, 1034).

103. DLA III, 20, 55-58 (32, 1297-1299) (388-395 a.d.); DGnL X entire (34, 407-428) (401-415 a.d.); E 164, 7, 20 (33, 717); E 166, 1-9, 1-28 (33, 720-733) (both in 415); E 190, 1-6, 1-26 (33, 857-866) (418

a.d.); CD III, 10, 26 (44, 608) (420 a.d.); CJ V, 4, 17 (44, 794) (421 a.d.); OJ II, 178 (45, 1219); IV, 104 (45, 1400) (both in 429–430).

104. DGnL VII, 3–4, 4–6 (34, 357–358); E 140, 3, 7 (33, 541); E 166, 3, 7 (33, 723); DAO II, 3, 6 (44, 497–498). The last is quite precise.

105. DGnL VII, 9–16, 12–22 (34, 360–363); 23, 34 (34, 368).

106. DGnL VII, 28, 43 (34, 372). Cf. DH 81 (42, 45).

107. E 190, 4, 14 (33, 861).

108. Cf. E 164, 7, 20 (33, 717); E 166, 9, 27 (33, 732); E 190, 1, 4 (33, 858).

109. DH 46 (42, 35–38); DGnL VII, 9–12, 14–19 (34, 360–362).

110. DGnL VII, 22, 32 (34, 366).

111. *Ibid.*, 6–8, 9–11 (34, 358–360).

112. *Ibid.*, 23, 34 (34, 368).

113. E 164, 7, 19 (33, 717).

114. Cf. DLA III, 21, 59 (32, 1299); E 163, 6–7 (33, 587–588); E 166, 3, 7 (33, 723). See also the letter of St. Jerome which is favorable to the creation of souls, E 165, 1, 1 (33, 718).

115. A complete listing can be found in Cupetioli, Angelus, *Theologia moralis et contemplativa S. Augustini*, Venice, 1737, I, 188–195.

116. E 190, 5, 18 (33, 863).

117. *Ibid.*, nn. 2, 4, 14–16, 21 (33, 857–864).

118. DAO I, 16, 26 (44, 489) (420 a.d.).

119. DAO IV, 2, 2 (44, 524).

120. R I, 1, 3 (32, 587). Cf. R II, 45 (32, 649); 56 (32, 653).

121. OJ II, 178 (45, 1219).

122. Bellarmine, *De amissione gratiae*, IV, chap. 11.

CHAPTER X.   CHRISTOLOGY

1. Harnack, *History of Dogma*, V, 127–128.

2. Cf. C VII, 18, 24 (32, 745). See page 6.

3. DCD IX, 15 (41, 268).

4. DCD X, 32, 1 (41, 312).

5. S 123, 3 (38, 685).

6. En 5 (40, 233).

7. Loofs, *Leitfaden*, p. 221.

8. Reuter points this out, *Aug. Studien*, p. 80.

9. R I, 13, 3 (32, 603). Cf. DCD XVIII, 47 (41, 609); En 118 (40, 287).

10. This is the conclusion of a patient historical study of the Christology of Augustine by the Protestant Scheel, *Die Anschauung Augustins über Christi Person und Werk*, Leipzig, 1901, p. 391.

11. Dorner, *Augustinus*, pp. 105–106, makes an interesting comparison of Leo's letter, E 28 (54, 775) with Books I and II of *On the Trinity*.

12. Harnack, *History of Dogma*, V, 128–129.

13. *Ibid.*, IV, 183.

14. Scheel, *Anschauung Augustins*, p. 225.

15. S 92, 3, 3 (38, 573).

16. En 36 (40, 250).

17. DCns II, 1, 2 (34, 1071).

18. DAC 18, 20 (40, 300).

19. *Ibid.*, 21, 23 (40, 302). Cf. the error of Alypius at Milan, C VII, 19, 25 (32, 746).

20. DAC 19, 21 (40, 301). Cf. E 187, 2, 4 (33, 833); S 67, 7 (38, 436).

21. DPB II, 29, 48 (44, 180).

22. En 34 (40, 249); 41 (40, 252); DT XIII, 18, 23 (42, 1032).

23. En 36 (40, 250); DT XIII, 18, 23 (42, 1032).

24. DCG 11, 30 (44, 934).

25. Dorner, *Augustinus*, p. 103.

26. DPS 15, 30 (44, 982).

27. DT IV, 13, 16 (42, 898). Cf. S 152, 9 (38, 824); JE 119, 6 (35, 1952).

28. DPB II, 29, 48 (44, 180).

29. JE 60, 5 (35, 1799), but see this whole sermon.

30. C VII, 19, 25 (32, 746). See pp. 89–90.

31. S 183, 4, 5 (38, 990).

32. *Ibid.*, 6 (38, 990).

33. CSA 36, 34 (42, 707).

34. DAC 17, 19 (40, 300).

35. *Ibid.*, 20, 22 (40, 302).

36. Cf. Mansi, IV, 519–527; Hahn, *Bibliothek der Symbole*, p. 299.

37. JE 7, 1, 4 (35, 1439).

38. Hahn, *Bibliothek der Symbole*, p. 301. Cf. S 183, 4, 5 (38, 990).

39. S 130, 3 (38, 727).

40. JE 78, 3 (35, 1836).

41. Reuter, *Aug. Studien*, p. 220.

42. E 137, 3, 9 (33, 519).

43. CMA I, 19 (42, 757).

44. Scheel, *Anschauung Augustins*, p. 226.

45. DCG 11, 30 (44, 934).

46. DAC 23, 25 (40, 304). It is quite difficult to find a good transla-

tion for the Latin verb here: "Filium Dei dicimus passum in homine quem portabat." Cf. DD83 65 (40, 60): "Hominem quem Sapientia gestabat."

47. DT XIII, 17, 22 (42, 1031).
48. OJ I, 138 (45, 1137).
49. CSA 8, 6 (42, 688).
50. DT I, 7, 14 (42, 829).
51. E 219, 1 (33, 991).
52. Mansi, IV, 522.
53. Scheel, *Anschauung Augustins*, p. 184–186.
54. Cf. E 137, 3, 11 (33, 520).
55. DAC 10, 11 (40, 297).
56. E 169, 2, 7 (33, 745).
57. Reuter, *Aug. Studien*, p. 212.
58. Scheel, *Anschauung Augustins*, p. 50.
59. S 92, 3, 3 (38, 573).
60. En 35 (40, 250); DT I, 7, 14 (42, 828).
61. Scheel, *Anschauung Augustins*, p. 266–267.
62. CSA 11, 9 (42, 691).
63. Dorner, *Augustinus*, p. 101.
64. Scheel, *Anschauung Augustins*, p. 268.
65. DT I, 10, 21 (42, 835).
66. *Ibid.*, 8, 15 (42, 829).
67. *Ibid.*, 16 (42, 830).
68. CSA 8, 6 (42, 688).
69. Harnack, *History of Dogma*, IV, 184.
70. JE 110, 5 (35, 1923). Cf. Scheel, *Anschauung Augustins*, p. 265.
71. For example, E 169, 2, 8 (33, 746); S 130, 4 (38, 728); S 220 (38, 1089); EnP 102, 6 (37, 1321); EnP 147, 16 (37, 1925).
72. S 214, 7 (38, 1069).
73. R I, 19, 8 (32, 616).
74. S 214, 6 (38, 1069).
75. Scheel, *Anschauung Augustins*, p. 100.
76. Cf. DT IV, 21, 31 (42, 910).
77. DD83, 73, 2 (40, 85).
78. See DTC, I, 47; I, 414.
79. DD83, 73, 2 (40, 85).
80. For example, S 186, 1 (38, 999).
81. *Ibid.*
82. S 293, 7 (38, 1332).
83. Harnack, *History of Dogma*, V, 131.
84. *Ibid.*, 130–134, 204–205.

85. A. Gottschick, "Augustins Anschauung von der Erloser-wirkungen Christi," *Zeitschrift für Theologie und Kirche*, 1901, 97–213.

86. Seeberg, *Lehrbuch der Dogmengeschichte*, Erlangen, 1895, I, 304.

87. C X, 43, 68 (32, 808).

88. DGrC II, 28, 33 (44, 402). Cf. DCD IX, 15, 2 (41, 269); S 293, 7 (38, 1332).

89. EnP 103, 8 (37, 1384).

90. Scheel, *Anschauung Augustins*, p. 318–319.

91. En 108, 28 (40, 282).

92. S 127, 9 (38, 710).

93. Harnack is the one who mentions that Augustine was the first to use it, *History of Dogma*, V, 205.

94. DT IV, 2, 4 (42, 889).

95. Cf. S 152, 9 (38, 824).

96. CF XIV, 4 (42, 297).

97. JE 98, 3 (35, 1881–1882). Cf. JE 79, 2 (35, 1838).

98. DPB II, 30, 49 (44, 181).

99. En 41, 13 (40, 253).

100. DCns I, 31, 47 (34, 1065). Cf. EnP 68, 9–10 (36, 848–849).

101. EnP 44, 7 (36, 498). Cf. EnP 31, 18 (36, 270).

102. Cf. DDoC II, 41, 62 (34, 64); EnP 39, 13 (36, 443).

103. Cremer, *Studien und Kritik*, pp. 7 ff.

104. Loofs, *Leitfaden*, p. 273; Harnack, *History of Dogma*, VI, 62–67.

105. Harnack, *What Is Christianity?*, p. 159–165.

106. DT IV, 13, 17 (42, 899). Cf. DT IV, 14, 19 (42, 901) for the four elements of this sacrifice.

107. EnP 74, 12 (36, 955).

108. DCD X, 20 (41, 298).

109. Gretillat, *Dogmatique*, IV, 298.

110. DGnL X, 14, 25 (34, 419).

111. DCD X, 20 (41, 298). Cf. DT IV, 14, 19 (42, 901).

112. S 152, 9 (38, 824).

113. C X, 43, 69 (32, 808).

114. CEP II, 7–8 (43, 59).

115. CF XIX, 7 (42, 352).

116. Scheel denied this, *Anschauung Augustins*, p. 313.

117. EnP 129, 3 (37, 1697).

118. DPB 26, 39 (44, 131).

119. JE 53, 6 (35, 1771). Cf. S 30, 2 (38, 188).

120. JE 2, 13 (35, 1394).

121. S 192, 1, 1 (38, 1012).
122. EnP 129, 3 (37, 1697).
123. Scheel, *Anschauung Augustins*, p. 313.
124. CJ III, 25, 58 (44, 732).
125. CJ VI, 4, 8 (44, 825); OJ II, 175 (45, 1217).
126. DCD XX, 6, 1 (41, 665).
127. Scheel, *Anschauung Augustins*, p. 455.
128. S 344, 4 (39, 1515).
129. S 292, 4 (38, 1322). Cf. J. B. Faure, his notes on chapter 47 of the *Enchiridion*; Stentrup, *De Verbo incarnato, Soteriologia*, I, 387–416.
130. En 61–62 (40, 260–261).
131. Gregory Nazianzen, *Oratio* XLV, 22, *P. G.*, XXXVI, 654.
132. EnP 95, 5 (37, 1231).
133. Cf. S 263, 1 (38, 1210); S 134, 5, 6 (38, 745).
134. Cf. En 108 (40, 282); DPS 8, 15 (44, 971).
135. DNG 2, 2 (44, 249).
136. DCD X, 22 (41, 300). Cf. DT IV, 13, 17 (42, 899); DPB II, 30, 49 (44, 180); JE 53, 6 (35, 1771); S 363, 2 (39, 1635).
137. DT XIII, 12, 16 (42, 1026).
138. *Ibid.*
139. *Ibid.*, 14, 18 (42, 1027–1028).
140. S 130, 2 (38, 726).
141. S 134, 5, 6 (38, 745).
142. S 130, 2 (38, 726).
143. S 134, 5, 6 (38, 745).
144. S 30, 1, 1 (30, 188).
145. S 344, 4 (39, 1515).
146. DNG 24, 26 (44, 260).
147. Cf. Harnack, *History of Dogma*, V, 131; Scheel, *Anschauung Augustins*, p. 345–440.
148. See especially DCa, 4, 7–8 (40, 314–315).
149. Harnack, *History of Dogma*, V, 132.
150. DT VIII, 5, 7 (42, 952).
151. C VII, 18, 24 (32, 745). Cf. C VII, 19–20, 25–26 (32, 746–747).
152. C VII, 20, 26 (32, 747).
153. EnP 31, 18 (36, 270).
154. DT XIII, 18, 23 (42, 1033). Cf. EnP 8, 11 (36, 114); EnP 18, 15 (36, 163); E 205, 11 (33, 946); DGrC II, 40, 46 (44, 409).
155. Harnack, *History of Dogma*, V, 205.
156. En 108 (40, 282).
157. Harnack, *History of Dogma*, V, 235.

158. DT VIII, 5, 7 (42, 952). Cf. DGnI 1, 4 (34, 221); S 186, 1 (38, 999).

159. DAC 22, 24 (40, 303).

160. E 137, 2, 8 (33, 519); E 162, 6 (33, 707); OJ IV, 122 (45, 1418)—Julian and Augustine agree on this point.

161. S186, 1, 1 (38, 999).

162. S 215, 4 (38, 1074).

163. DNG 36, 42 (44, 267).

164. Harnack, *History of Dogma*, V, 235.

165. OJ IV, 122 (45, 1418). The Latin of this crucial and difficult text follows: "Non transcribimus diabolo Mariam conditione nascendi, sed ideo quia ipsa conditio solvitur gratia renascendi."

166. Schwane, *Dogmengeschichte*, II, 691.

167. Schaff, *Augustin*, 98. See pp. 93-94.

168. Rottmanner, *Historisches Jahrbuch*, 1898, p. 895.

169. Harnack, *History of Dogma*, V, 235.

170. OJ VI, 22 (45, 1555).

CHAPTER XI. GRACE AND PELAGIANISM

1. Richard Simon, *Histoire critique des commentateurs du Nouveau Testament*, Rotterdam, 1693.

2. H. Margival, *Revue d'histoire et de littérature religieuses*, 1889, IV, 447.

3. Dom Odilo Rottmanner, *Der Augustinismus*, Munich, 1892, p. 29.

4. Cf. Haag, *Histoire des dogmes chrétiens*, I, 207-213.

5. Loofs, *Dogmengeschichte*, 3rd ed., Halle, 1893, pp. 237, 244.

6. Harnack, *History of Dogma*, V, 217, 219-220.

7. DCD V, 9, 1-4 (41, 148-152); DLA III, 3, 6-8 (32, 1273-1275); JE 53, 4 (35, 1776).

8. ExR 55, 60, 61, 62 (35, 2076-2080); DD83 66, 1 (40, 61).

9. Baur, *Die christliche Kirche vom Anfang*, 1859, p. 143; Dorner, *Augustinus*, p. 257; Holtzmann, *Historische Zeitschrift*, Sybel, 1879, p. 132.

10. Grandgeorge, *Augustin*, p. 136.

11. Loofs, "Augustinus," *Realencyclopädie für prot. Theol. und Kirche*, II, 278.

12. Reuter, *Aug. Studien*, p. 46.

13. Cf. DPS 4, 8 (44, 966).

14. DD83 68, 3 (40, 71).

15. *Ibid.*

16. *Ibid.* Cf. R I, 26 (32, 628).

17. DD83 68, 4 (40, 72).

18. *Ibid.*, 5 (40, 73).

19. Cf. DPS 3, 7 (44, 964).

20. ExR 55, 60, 61 (35, 2076–2080). Cf. R I, 23, 1–2 (32, 621).

21. ExR 60, 62 (35, 2080).

22. R I, 23, 4 (32, 622).

23. DD7 1, 2 (40, 110–128).

24. R II, 1 (32, 629).

25. DDoP 21, 55 (45, 1027).

26. DPS 4, 8 (44, 966).

27. Loofs, "Augustinus," *Realencyclopädie für prot. Theol. und Kirche*, II, 279–280.

28. Reuter, *Aug. Studien*, p. 10.

29. Turmel, *Revue d'histoire et de littérature religieuses*, 1900, p. 392.

30. Jules Martin, *Augustin*, pp. xix, 193.

31. *Ibid.*

32. DD7 1, 2, 12–13 (40, 117–118).

33. Turmel, *Revue*, p. 211.

34. See Mercator, *Commonitorium*, 1 (48, 69–70), and more fully in *Liber subnotationum* (48, 114–115). Cf. Mansi, IV, 289–292.

35. The words in brackets are variant readings borrowed from the edition of the *Commonitorium* by Baluze, Mansi, IV, 293, and from the *Liber subnotationum* of Mercator (48, 115). The sense is the same without them, but not so clear.

36. See the speech of Pelagius cited by Mercator in connection with the *Commonitorium* (48, 88–89); Mansi, IV, 295.

37. Cf. DGrC 7–10, 8–11 (44, 364–366) and the admissions of Julian in OJ I, 94 (45, 1111).

38. Jerome, E 133, 2 (22, 1148).

39. *Ibid.*, 3. Cf. RII, 42 (32, 647).

40. DGsP 18, 42 (44, 345). Cf. E 186, 9, 32 (33, 827).

41. Jerome, E 133, 5 (22, 1154).

42. OJ V, 41 (45, 1477).

43. DGrC I, 4, 5 (44, 362).

44. OJ I, 78 (45, 1102).

45. Albert Bruckner, *Julian von Eclanum*, Leipzig, 1897, p. 176.

46. Neander, *Kirchengeschichte*, IV, 1135.

47. Orosius, *De arbitrii libertate*, 19 (31, 1188).

48. Jerome, E 133, 7 (22, 1155). Cf. nn. 5–6.

49. Bellarmine, *De gratia et libero arbitrio*, IV; Suarez, *Prolegomena*, V (*De gratia*), chap. 4, Paris, VII, 235; Suarez, *De praedestinatione Dei*, II, chap. 17, I, 455; Tanner, *De gratia*, q. 3, d. 3, nn. 65–68, II, 1202;

Arriaga, *De gratia*, d. 43 n. 3; Maurus, *De gratia*, VII, q. 68, n. 25; Scheeben, *La dogmatique*, n. 131, III, n. 35. Ernst, *Die Werke und Tugenden der Ungläubigen nach Augustin*, p. 233.

50. DGnL IX, 15, 28 (34, 404); V, 20, 40 (34, 335); E 205, 3, 17 (33, 948).

51. DNu II, 4, 12 (44, 443); CJ V, 15, 53 (44, 814). Cf. OJ III, 144 (45, 1305).

52. Jerome, E 133, 10 (22, 1158).

53. *Ibid.*, col. 1151.

54. Cf. DPB III, 1, 1 (44, 185).

55. *Ibid.*, 13, 23 (44, 200); E 176, 2 (33, 763); E 177, 18 (33, 772). The first letter is from the Fathers of the Council of Milevis to Pope Innocent; the second is from Augustine and five bishops to the same pope.

56. Tillemont, *Mémoires*, XV, 15-17; XIII, 126. Noel Alexandre, *Historia ecclesiastica*, saeculo quinto, chap. 3, n. 14, Venice, 1778, V. 28.

57. Caspari, *Briefe, Abhandlungen und Predigten*, Christiania, 1890.

58. Harnack, *History of Dogma*, V, 196.

59. Orosius, *De arbitrii libertate*, 16-18; 21-22 (31, 1185, 1187, 1191); Jerome, *Dialogus adversus pelagianos*, I, 28 (23, 544); especially DGsP 3, 9-10 (44, 325).

60. DNG 35, 40-41 (44, 266).

61. Turmel, "Eschatologie au quatrième siècle," *Revue d'histoire et de littérature religieuses*, 1900, V, 52.

62. Cf. J. Schiesl, *Der objective Unterschied zwischen Tod und lässlicher Sünde*, Augsburg, 1891, n. 9, "Die Lehre des Pelagius," pp. 25-29; *Bulletin de littérature ecclésiastique*, Toulouse, 1901, pp. 101-119.

63. Caspari, *Briefe*, chaps. 12-15, pp. 89-99.

64. Cf. *ibid.*, pp. 119-120.

65. DH 87 (42, 48).

66. S 181, 2-4, 2-6 (38, 980-982). Cf. DGsP 18, 42 (44, 345); E 186, 9, 32-33 (33, 828); Caspari, *Briefe*, p. 5.

67. Specht, *Die Lehre von der Kirche nach dem hl. Augustin*, Paderborn, 1892, p. 64.

68. E 186, 9, 33 (33, 828-829).

69. E 156 (33, 674). See Augustine's answer to Hilary, E 157, especially nn. 23-39 (33, 686-682). Also Caspari, *Briefe*, pp. 25-67.

CHAPTER XII.   GRACE AS DEVELOPED BY AUGUSTINE

1. See page 31.
2. Jaffé, *Regesta*, nn. 342-343; *P. L.*, XX, 693; XLV, 1730. The

decrees of the council are found in Mansi, IV, 326–329; also *P. L.*, XLV, 1728–1730; Denzinger, *Enchiridion Symbolorum*, nn. 101–108.

3. Hergenröther, *Kirchengeschichte*, II, n. 112.

4. Cf. DAO II, 12, 17 (44, 505).

5. E 217, 5, 16 (33, 984).

6. Wolfsgruber, *Augustinus*, Paderborn, 1898, p. 824.

7. DCG 14, 45 (44, 943).

8. *Ibid.*, 43 (44, 942).

9. *Ibid.*, 45 (44, 944). Cf. DPS 8, 13 (44, 970–971); DGrL 20, 41 (44, 906).

10. En 98 (40, 277). Cf. En 95 (40, 275); 103 (40, 280); DD7 I, 14 (40, 119).

11. DCD XII, 9, 1 (41, 356).

12. CMA II, 12, 2 (42, 768).

13. S 99, 6, 6 (38, 598).

14. E 217, 5, 16 (33, 984). Cf. canons 3–5 of the Council of Carthage, 418, Mansi, IV, 327–328.

15. DPS 17, 34 (44, 985–986).

16. Cf. E 177, 18 (33, 772); DPB II, 10–16, 12–25 (44, 158–167); DPJ 7, 16 (44, 299); CD IV, 10, 27 (44, 629); S 181, 2–6 (38, 980–983). Cf. Alticozzi, *Summa augustiniana*, Rome, 1755, IV, 145.

17. E 157, 2, 4 (33, 675). Cf. DSL 35, 63 (44, 242); DPJ 21, 44 (44, 316–317).

18. Cf. canon 113, Mansi, III, 814.

19. Vasquez, *In* I–II, d. 190; Torres, *Tractatus de gratia*, d. 4, dub. 3, ad. 12; Suarez, *De gratia*, I, 11–13 (with an important reservation on the use of the word *grace*: Suarez proclaims the kindness of God for every natural act; he does not want it to be called a grace); Esparza, *De gratia*, q. 45.

20. See pp. 112–114.

21. R I, 9, 6 (32, 598).

22. JE 5, 1 (35, 1414). Cf. canon 22 of the Second Council of Orange, Denzinger, *Enchiridion Symbolorum*, n. 195.

23. S 156, 11, 12 (38, 856).

24. E 144, 2 (33, 591)

25. Cf. DGrC 24, 25 (44, 372).

26. CJ IV, 3, 16 (44, 744).

27. *Ibid.* (44, 745).

28. DP 27, 25 (40, 624).

29. DDu 11, 15 (42, 105). Cf. DLA in its entirety (32, 1221–1310); CF XXII, 98 (42, 466).

30. Cf. DPB II, 18, 28 (44, 168).

31. DNG 45, 78 (44, 286). Cf. DGrC I, 47, 52 (44, 383).

32. OJ III, 117 (45, 1297).

33. Cf. E 86, 10, 34 (33, 829); 36 (33, 830); OJ III, 110 (45, 1294); V, 48 (45, 1484).

34. OJ VI, 11 (45, 1520).

35. DCG 14, 43 (44, 942). Cf. DGrC I, 47, 52 (44, 383).

36. E 217, 5, 16 (33, 985).

37. DPS 5, 10 (44, 968).

38. DSL 34, 60 (44, 240).

39. DSL 33, 58 (44, 238).

40. DNG 65, 78 (44, 286).

41. ExR 61 (35, 2072).

42. R I, 23, 2 (32, 621).

43. Schwane, *Dogmengeschichte*, II, 129; Hergenröther, *Kirchengeschichte*, II, n. 117; Wolfsgruber, *Augustinus*, pp. 825–830.

44. DLA III, 25, 74 (32, 1307).

45. DSL 34, 60 (44, 240).

46. Cf. the very characteristic passage in DGnL IX, 14, 25 (34, 403).

47. Molinism, in trying to answer this question, is thus distinguished from Augustinism.

48. DD7 I, 2 (40, 111).

49. DD7 I, 2, 2 (40, 111).

50. *Ibid.*, 12 (40, 118).

51. *Ibid.*, 13 (40, 118).

52. DSL 34, 60 (44, 240).

53. R II, 37 (32, 646).

54. DDoP 17, 41 (45, 1018–1019).

55. *Ibid.*

56. *Ibid.*, 14, 35 (45, 1014).

57. *Ibid.*, 8, 20 (45, 1004). Cf. DPS 10, 19 (44, 974–975).

58. OJ I, 93 (45, 1109).

59. Prosper of Aquitaine, *Responsiones ad capitula calumniantium Gallorum*, obj. 3 (45, 1834).

60. JE 26, 5 (35, 1609). The same image is used in S 131, 2, 2 (38, 730); E 217, 2, 5 (33, 980); DCG 14, 45 (44, 943).

61. Rottmanner, *Der Augustinismus*, p. 24.

62. OJ I, 95 (45, 1112); 134 (1134–1135); II, 6 (1144); III, 1 (1247–1249); 7 (1250); 13 (1252–1253); VI, 34 (1588); 41 (1606).

63. DPS 5, 10 (44, 968).

64. S 99, 6, 6 (38, 598).

65. C IV, 4, 7 (32, 696); V, 6–8, 11–14 (32, 710–712); VI, 12, 22 (32, 730); VIII, 2, 4 (32, 750).

66. CJ IV, 3, 16 (44, 744–745).

67. DDoP 9, 22 (45, 1005).

68. DCD XII, 6 (41, 354).

69. Cf. articles "Baius," DTC II, 38–111; "Jansénisme," DTC VIII, 318–529.

70. DCD XIV, 10 (41, 417); 26 (41, 434).

71. *Ibid.*, 9–11 (41, 413–418); 18 (41, 425); DGnL XI, 1, 1 (34, 429).

72. OJ V, 1 (45, 1432).

73. DLA III, 18, 52 (32, 1296).

74. DCD XIII, 20 (41, 394).

75. DGnL VI, 25, 36 (34, 354). Cf. DPB I, 3, 3 (44, 110–111).

76. DCD XIII, 14 (41, 387).

77. DLA III, 20, 56 (32, 1298). The statement made there, far from having been retracted as Jansenius claimed, is explicitly confirmed in R I, 9, 6 (32, 598).

78. DGnL VI, 24, 35 (34, 253); 27, 38 (34, 355).

79. DCG 11, 31 (44, 935). Cf. DGrC I, 21, 22 (44, 370).

80. CF III, 3 (42, 215).

81. E 140, 4, 10 (33, 541–542).

82. DCG 11, 29 (44, 933).

83. See page 58, n. 59.

84. DCG 12, 35 (44, 937).

85. Seeberg, *Lehrbuch der Dogmengeschichte*, I, 256.

86. Ambrose, *Enarrationes in psalmos*, 38, 29 (14, 1103).

87. Ambrose, *In Lucam*, VII, 234 (15, 1852).

88. *Ambrose, Apologia Davidis*, 11, 56 (14, 914). Cf. Tertullian, *De carne Christi*, 17 (2, 827). See also the texts of Cyprian quoted by Turmel, who accuses Augustine of having innovated on this point, *Revue d'histoire et de littérature religieuses*, 1901, pp. 19–20.

89. CJ I, 3–7, 5–35 (44, 644–666).

90. Dorner, *Augustinus*, p. 146.

91. Turmel, *Revue d'histoire*, 1901, pp. 30–31.

92. Turmel, *Revue d'histoire*, 1902, pp. 510–533.

93. *Summa sententiarum*, III, 11 (176, 107), falsely attributed to Hugh of St. Victor.

94. He protests when the Pelagians accused him of not affirming this destruction, CD I, 13, 27 (44, 563).

95. *Ibid.*

96. CD I, 13, 26 (44, 562).

97. R I, 9, 6 (32, 598).

98. Cf. CJ VI, 17, 51 (44, 852–853); DNu I, 32, 54 (44, 468).

99. R I, 15, 2 (32, 608).

100. *Ibid.*

101. See Turmel, *Revue d'histoire,* 1902, p. 531.

102. Fulgentius, *De fide ad Petrum,* 2, 16 (40, 758).

103. Peter Lombard, *II sententiarum,* d. 30, c. 9 and especially d. 31, c. 6.

104. OJ VI, 22 (45, 1552–1554).

105. *Ibid.*

106. Thomas, *In* II *sententiarum,* d. 31, q. 1, a. 1, Paris, VIII, 422.

107. Bonaventure, *In* II *sententiarum,* d. 31, a. 2, q. 1, Quarrachi, II, 748.

108. Petavius notes this, *Dogmatica theologia,* X, 1, 8–9.

109. Cf. the exact citations in Rottmanner, *Der Augustinismus,* p. 8.

110. DLA III, 23 (32, 1303).

111. E 166, 6, 16 (33, 727). Cf. DDoP 12, 30 (45, 1010); S 294, 4, 3 (38, 1337), a very severe statement; OJ III, 199 (45, 1333).

112. En 93 (40, 275).

113. CJ V, 11, 44 (44, 809).

114. *Ibid.*

115. Schmid, *Quaestiones selectae ex theologia dogmatica,* Paderborn, 1891, p. 255.

116. En 46–47, 13 (40, 254–255).

117. *Ibid.*

118. En 48, 14 (40, 255).

119. Gregory the Great, *Moralia,* XV, 51, 57 (75, 1110).

120. Cf. the texts cited above in this chapter, notes 8–10; also Rottmanner, *Der Augustinismus,* p. 22. An example is the following: "Far be it that the intention of the Almighty and All-knowing should be hindered by man." OJ I, 93 (45, 1109).

121. Wolfsgruber, *Augustin,* p. 828.

122. DCG 9, 23 (44, 929–930); DPS 16–18, 32–37 (44, 983–987); DDoP 9, 21 (45, 1004).

123. DCG 13, 39 (44, 940).

124. E 186, 10 (33, 820).

125. S 169, 2, 3 (38, 917).

126. DNG 7, 8 (44, 251).

127. DGnL XI, 10, 13 (34, 434).

128. DSL 34, 60 (44, 241); DCG 8, 17–19 (44, 926–927).

129. DGnM I, 3, 6 (34, 176).

130. R I, 10, 2 (32, 599).

131. DD7 I, 2, 13 (40, 118).

132. OJ II, 6 (45, 1144).

133. EnP 120, 11 (37, 1614).

134. EnP 36, sermon 1, 1 (36, 356).

135. Rottmanner, *Der Augustinismus*, p. 29.

136. EnP 73, 5 (36, 933).

137. JE 26, 6, 2 (35, 1607).

138. EnP 126, 4 (37, 1670). Cf. the collection of texts in Rottmanner, *Der Augustinismus*.

139. Bellarmine, *De gratia et libero arbitrio*, II, 15.

140. Suarez, *De Deo*, I, 13; *De auxiliis*, III, 16–17.

141. Petavius, *De Deo*, IX, 6.

142. L. Janssens, *Praelectiones de Deo uno*, Rome, 1899, II, 399–500.

143. *Ibid.*, p. 475.

144. DDoP 17, 42 (45, 1019).

145. Cf. DPS 10, 19 (44, 974); DDoP nn. 15, 34, 41, 53 (45, 1002, 1015, 1018, 1026).

146. De San, *Tractatus de Deo uno*, II, 136–214. Cf. pp. 36, 54.

147. DD7 I, 2, 6 (40, 115).

148. DSL 33, 58 (44, 238).

149. JE 12, 12 (35, 1490); 33, 5–8 (35, 1649–1651).

150. See pp. 183–184.

151. DDoP 21, 55 (45, 1027).

152. DPS 10, 19 (44, 975).

153. En 104, 28 (40, 281). Cf. Fessler, *Institutiones patrologiae*, II, 346–349; Alticozzi, *Summa augustiniana*, I, q. 7; VI, q. 2; Faure, notes on chap. 98 of the *Enchiridion*; Franzelin, *De Deo uno*, theses 56–58.

154. Compare canon 22 of the Council of Orange, Denzinger, n. 195, with the condemnation of proposition 27 of Baius, *ibid.*, n. 1027.

155. Cf. DCG 12, 37 (44, 939); OJ I, 47 (45, 1067–1068); II, 17 (45, 1148); VI, 11 (45, 1520); 21 (45, 1549). The *Chapters* of Celestine, of undoubted Augustinian inspiration, say that man has lost his "natural possibility." Denzinger, n. 130.

156. CD I, 2, 5 (44, 552). Cf. CD III, 8, 24 (44, 607); IV, 3 (44, 611). See the reflections of Julian on the text quoted, OJ I, 94 (45, 1110–1111).

157. DLA III, 18, 52 (32, 1296).

158. Cf. DPJ 1–3 (44, 291–295).

159. CD I, 10, 19 (44, 560); 17, 35 (44, 566); II, 2, 2 (44, 572); CJ IV, 11, 57 (44, 765).

160. DSL 36, 65 (44, 244); DPJ 2–7 (44, 293–298); DNG 62, 72 (44, 283); DNu I, 23–29, 25–32 (44, 428–432); CJ V, 3, 9–13 (44, 788–791). Cf. Alticozzi, *Summa augustiniana*, I, q. 5, a. 4, pp. 178–183; Faure, notes on chaps. 15 and 81 of the *Enchiridion*.

161. Baius, propositions 46, 50, 51, 75, 76, Denzinger, *Enchiridion*, nn. 1046, 1050, 1051, 1075, 1076.

162. Cf. Ernst, *Zeitschrift für katholische Theologie*, 1895, p. 191.

163. DLA III, 19, 53 (32, 1297).

164. DNG 67, 81 (44, 287).

165. R I, 9, 6 (32, 598).

166. DNG 43, 50 (44, 271). Cf. DNG 69, 83 (44, 288).

167. DCG 12, 38 (44, 940).

168. DCG 14, 43 (44, 942).

169. *Ibid.*, 45 (44, 943).

170. DPS 7, 12 (44, 970). See the references which Rottmanner has selected, *Der Augustinismus*, p. 25.

171. En 32, 9 (40, 248). Cf. DPS 16, 32 (44, 983); DDoP 13, 33 (45, 1012); 19, 50 (45, 1025); 6, 12 (45, 1000).

172. For example, DDoP 2, 4 (45, 996); E 194, 3, 6 (33, 876); E 217, 8, 28 (33, 988); especially R I, 23, 2–3 (32, 621): "Both are our own, . . . and yet both are given us."

173. E 217, 5, 16 (33, 984).

174. DSL 33, 58 (44, 238).

175. See, in 421, CJ IV, 7, 42 (44, 759); En 103 (40, 280); in 426, DCG 15, 47 (44, 945); in 428, DPS 8, 14 (44, 971).

176. Thomas, *Summa theologica*, I, q. 19, a. 6, ad 1; *In I ad Timotheum*, II, lect. 1; Alticozzi, *Summa augustiniana*, I, q. 1, a. 5; Faure, notes on the *Enchiridion*, chap. 103, p. 195.

177. En 103 (40, 281).

178. En 104 (40, 281).

CHAPTER XIII.   THE CHURCH

1. Specht, *Die Einheit der Kirche*, 1884, p. 1.

2. Moehler, *Dogmatik*, p. 351.

3. Harnack, *History of Dogma*, V, 77.

4. Dorner, *Augustinus*, p. 88 ff.

5. See page 24.

6. For a more complete exposition of Augustine's teaching on the Church we refer the reader to the works cited in the bibliography, especially that of Specht. [See also S.J. Grabowski, *The Church*, St. Louis, 1957. Tr. note.]

7. S 215, 9 (38, 1076).

8. E 118, 5, 33 (33, 448).

9. E 34, 3 (33, 132).

10. S 22, 10, 10 (38, 154).

11. S 126, 8, 8 (38, 1081).

12. J 2, 2 (35, 1990); S 12 (collection of Denis), 2 (46, 853).

13. See Specht, *Die Lehre von der Kirche nach dem h. Augustin,* pp. 9–26.

14. DB IV, 17, 24 (43, 170).

15. CLP III, 9, 10 (43, 353).

16. See E 141, written by Augustine on behalf of the bishops of Numidia, 5 (33, 579).

17. SC 6 (43, 695).

18. E 185, 11, 50 (33, 815).

19. JE 32, 8 (35, 1646).

20. See pp. 100–101, 192–196.

21. CEP II, 15, 34 (43, 76). Cf. S 99, 11–12, 11–12 (38, 601–602); S 266, 4–7 (38, 1226–1229).

22. S 269, 2 (38, 1236).

23. QH III, 84 (34, 713).

24. S 292, 6 (38, 1324).

25. J 3, 13 (35, 2004).

26. B III, 8, 10 (43, 629).

27. See pp. 188–189.

28. Harnack, *History of Dogma,* V, 163.

29. See Bellarmine, *De Ecclesia,* III, chap. 9; Stapleton, *Principia fidei,* I, 1, 8; Alticozzi, *Summa aug.,* III, 23–48; Palmieri, *De Romano Pontifice,* p. 59.

30. AD 9, 12 (43, 659). Cf. S 223, 2 (38, 1092); S 47, 5, 6 (38, 298).

31. Cf. DDoC III, 32, 45 (34, 82); DB V, 27, 38 (43, 196); IV, 3, 4 (43, 156).

32. JE 26, 13 (35, 1613).

33. J 3, 4 (35, 1999).

34. DDoC III, 32, 44 (34, 82).

35. DV IV, 3, 4 (43, 155).

36. It is sufficient to cite just the following: R II, 18 (32, 637–638); I, 7, 5 (32, 593); DCD XVIII, 48 (41, 611).

37. Augustine takes over these words of Cyprian, DB IV, 1, 1 (43, 155).

38. CLP III, 55, 67 (43, 384).

39. Böhringer, *Augustinus,* I, 178.

40. E 60, 1 (33, 228).

41. JE 41, 10 (35, 1697).

42. Harnack, *History of Dogma,* V, 163.

43. Dorner, *Augustinus,* p. 288.

44. CEP II, 13, 28 (43, 70).

45. DBC 24, 32 (40, 394).
46. S 137, 8, 8 (38, 759).
47. DCD XX, 10 (41, 676).
48. Harnack, *History of Dogma*, V, 150.
49. Alticozzi, *Summa aug.*, II, 207–216.
50. S 46, 13, 31 (38, 288).
51. S 17, 1, 1 (38, 124).
52. E 194, 1, 1 (33, 874).
53. S 356, 8 (39, 1577).
54. DGsE 1 (43, 697).
55. Cf. E 59, 1 (33, 226); E 129, 7 (33, 493).
56. DH 53 (42, 40).
57. E 82, 4, 33 (33, 290).
58. Such was the contention of Langen.
59. This theory was proposed in Herzog, *Realencyclopädie*, 1st ed., I, 624.
60. See pp. 30–32.
61. Specht, *Lehre von der Kirche*, pp. 124–186.
62. DB II, 1, 2 (43, 127).
63. Herzog, *Die kirchliche Sündenvergebung nach der Lehre der hl. Augustin*, Berne, 1902, p. 33.
64. JE 124, 5 (35, 1973).
65. Cf. Alticozzi, *Summa aug.*, III, 155–319; Schwane, *Dogmengeschichte*, II, 86; Specht, *Lehre von der Kirche*, pp. 154–187.
66. CEM 4, 5 (42, 175).
67. E 53, 1, 2 (33, 196).
68. PD (43, 30).
69. E 43, 3, 7 (33, 163).
70. *Ibid.*
71. See pp. 120–121.
72. *Ibid.*
73. DUC 17, 35 (42, 91). Cf. E. 118, 5, 32 (33, 448).
74. EnP 103, 17 (34, 1350).
75. DSy 6, 14 (40, 635).
76. S 294, 18, 17 (38, 1346).
77. EnP 56, 1 (36, 662).
78. DNu I, 20, 22 (44, 427).
79. EnP 9, 12 (36, 122).
80. E 190, 6, 22 (33, 865). Cf. DB VII, 53, 102 (43, 243).
81. DB II, 3, 4 (43, 128–129).
82. S 294, 21, 20 (38, 1348).
83. DB I, 7, 9 (43, 114).

84. DB II, 9, 14 (43, 135).

85. Different opinions are discussed by J. Ernst, "Augustins Plenar-concil über die Ketzertauffrage," *Zeitschrift für kath. Theol.*, Innsbruck, 1900, pp. 292–325.

86. Cf. E 43, 7, 19 (33, 169).

87. DB II, 3, 4 (43, 129).

88. E 176 (33, 762–764).

89. Cf. Mansi, IV, 334–336.

90. E 177 (33, 764–772).

91. E 176, 5 (33, 764).

92. *Ibid.*

93. E 181, 1 (33, 780); E 182, 2 (33, 784).

94. E 186, 2 (33, 817).

95. CJ I, 4, 13 (44, 648).

96. S 131, 10, 10 (38, 734).

97. CJ III, 1, 1 (44, 701).

98. DCD XX, 9, 2 (41, 673).

99. E 43, 5, 16 (33, 167).

100. S 146, 1, 1 (38, 796).

101. DB VII, 51, 99 (43, 241).

102. AD 4, 6 (43, 656).

103. AD 20, 28 (43, 669). Cf. EnP 101, sermon 1, 2 (37, 1295).

104. E 157, 3, 22 (33, 685).

105. QH V, 39 (34, 764).

106. DB I, 17, 26 (43, 123).

107. DVR 6, 11 (34, 128).

108. See pp. 26–27.

CHAPTER XIV. THE SACRAMENTS

1. DCD X, 5 (41, 282).

2. E 54, 1, 1 (33, 200).

3. E 55, 1, 2 (33, 205).

4. S 228, 3 (38, 1102).

5. S 227 (38, 1100).

6. Harnack, *History of Dogma*, V, 157, quoting Hahn, *Die Lehre von den Sakramenten*, 1864, p. 12.

7. CF XIX, 13 (42, 355); 16 (42, 356).

8. See pp. 24, 50–54.

9. DB III, 17, 22 (43, 149); 23 (43, 150).

10. DB I, 10, 14 (43, 117).

11. CEP II, 11, 24 (43, 67).

12. DB IV, 10, 16 (43, 164).

13. DB III, 10, 13 (43, 144). Cf. CEP II, 11, 24 (43, 68).

14. DB I, 12, 18 (43, 119).

15. CC IV, 16, 19 (43, 559).

16. Reuter, *Aug. Studien*, p. 264.

17. Cf. CEP II, 13, 29 (43, 71).

18. E 98, 5 (33, 362).

19. DB V, 23, 33 (43, 193).

20. The documents are collected in *Monumenta Germanica, Libelli de lite imperatorum et pontificum*, Hanover, 1890–1897, vols. I–III; C. Mirbt, *Die Stellung Augustins in der Publicistik*, Leipzig, 1888, gives a list of the texts from Augustine used by either side.

21. CF XIX, 13 (42, 355).

22. E 54, 1 (33, 200).

23. EnP 103, sermon 1, 9 (37, 1343).

24. CLP II, 104, 239 (43, 342).

25. J 3, 5 (35, 2000).

26. CF XIX, (42, 356).

27. Loofs, "Abendmahl," *Realencyclopädie*, I, 61–63.

28. Harnack, *History of Dogma*, V, 159.

29. Cf. *Revue d'histoire et de litt. relig.*, 1901, p. 535.

30. See the recent works of Wilden, Stentrup, *Synopsis de eucharistia,* pp. 42–49; also the bibliography of Schanz.

31. Loofs, *Leitfaden*, p. 137.

32. Ambrose, *De mysteriis* 8–9 (16, 419–426).

33. E 147, 23, 52 (33, 621).

34. S 307, 2, 3 (38, 1407). Cf. S 131, 1, 1 (38, 729); S 132, 1, 1 (38, 734); especially E 140, 19, 48 (33, 558).

35. EnP 98 9 (37, 1265).

36. Ambrose, *De Spiritu Sancto*, III, 11, 79 (16, 828–829).

37. EnP 33, sermon 1, 10 (36, 306).

38. EnP 33, sermon 2, 2 (36, 308).

39. Harnack, *History of Dogma*, V, 159.

40. Dorner, *Augustinus*, p. 272.

41. S 234, 2 (38 1116).

42. CF XX, 13 (42, 379).

43. DT III, 4, 10 (42, 874).

44. *Ibid.*, 10, 21 (42, 881).

45. S 71, 11, 17 (38, 453); DB V, 8, 9 (43, 181). The whole context of the sermon must be read.

46. Harnack, *History of Dogma*, V, 160.

47. C IX, 13, 36 (32, 778).

48. *Ibid.*, 12, 32 (32, 777).
49. CF XX, 18 (42, 382–383).
50. QE II, 33 (35, 1346).
51. S 227 (38, 1100).
52. DCD XVII, 22, 2 (41, 556).
53. *Ibid.*
54. EnP 33, sermon 1, 6 (36, 303).
55. Dorner, *Augustinus*, p. 269.
56. S 9, 10, 14 (38, 85).
57. CF XII, 10 (42, 259).
58. EnP 3, 1 (36, 73).
59. E 98, 9 (33, 364).
60. DCa 26, 50 (40, 344).
61. DDoC III, 16, 24 (34, 74–75).
62. EnP 98, 9 (37, 1265).
63. *Ibid.*
64. JE 27, 11 (35, 1621); DDoC III, 16, 24 (34, 74–75).
65. EnP 98, 9 (37, 1265).
66. JE 26, 12 (35, 1612).
67. JE 27, 3 (35, 1616). Cf. 2–5 (35, 1616–1618).
68. S 131, 1, 1 (38, 729).
69. *Ibid.*
70. *Ibid.*
71. EnP 98, 9 (37, 1264–1265).
72. See page 249.
73. S 272 (38, 1247).
74. *Ibid.* (38, 1248).
75. See note 29.
76. S 57, 7, 7 (38, 389); S 227 (38, 1099–1101); S 229 (38, 1103); JE 26, 13–15 (35, 1612–1614); E 185, 11, 50 (33, 815).
77. JE 26, 13 (35, 1613).
78. JE 27, 4 (35, 1617).
79. DPB I, 24, 34 (44, 129).
80. S 227 (38, 1099).
81. *Ibid.* (38, 1099–1100).
82. Cf. Harnack, *History of Dogma*, V, 37.
83. See pp. 283–285.
84. This idea is developed in S 351 and S 352 (39, 1535–1560); CJ II, 8, 23 (44, 689).
85. DSy (40, 636).
86. DSy 7, 15 (40, 636).

87. *Ibid.*

88. E 153, 5, 15 (33, 659); S 9, 11, 17 (38, 88).

89. En 69, 19 (40, 265).

90. DSy 7, 15 (40, 636).

91. En 65, 17 (40, 262).

92. *Ibid.*

93. *Ibid.* (40, 263).

94. En 66, 17 (40, 263); 83, 22 (40, 272).

95. S 352, 3, 8 (39, 1558).

96. Cf. ER 16 (35, 2100).

97. S 278, 12, 12 (38, 1273). Cf. DSy 7, 15 (40, 636); DAC 31, 33 (40, 308); DCD XX, 9, 2 (41, 674); DDoC I, 18, 17 (34, 25); S 295, 2 (38, 1349), a very important passage; DB III, 18, 23 (43, 150).

98. JE 124, 5 (35, 1973).

99. Charles Lea, *A History of Auricular Confession*, Philadelphia, 1896, I, 116–118. Cf. H. Casey, S.J., *Notes on a History of Auricular Confession*, 2nd ed., Philadelphia, 1899, pp. 68–78.

100. DSy 7, 15 (40, 636).

101. Rottmanner, *Historisches Jahrbuch*, 1898, p. 895.

102. See S 17, 5, 5 (38, 127).

103. S 351, 3, 6 (39, 1541–1542).

104. S 56, 7, 11 (38, 381–382).

105. *Ibid.*

106. See the texts cited in notes 87–90.

107. En 69, 19 (40, 265). Cf. DSy 7, 15 (40, 636) and especially DFO 26, 48 (40, 228).

108. En 71, 19 (40, 265).

109. S 278, 12, 12 (38, 1273).

110. *Ibid.*

111. DSy 7, 15 (40, 636).

112. See Rottmanner, *Historisches Jahrbuch*, 1898, p. 895; Vacandard, "La discipline pénitentielle," *Revue du clergé français*, 1901, XXVII, 611 ff.

113. DFO 26, 48 (40, 228).

114. Cf. Collet, *De poenitentia*, III, *De satisfactione*, chap. 6, n. 110; Harent, "La confession," *Etudes*, 1899, LXXX, 600; Vacandard, "Discipline," *Revue du clergé*, 1901, XXVII, 611–612.

115. S 351, 4, 9 (39, 1545).

116. See page 76.

117. For example, S 82, 6–8, 9–11 (38, 510–511); En 65, 17 (40, 262).

118. DD83 26 (40, 18). Cf. DCG 15, 46 (44, 944).

119. See Batiffol, *Etudes d'histoire de théologie positive*, pp. 162–163, which recall a decision of Pope St. Leo in 458. Cf. Jaffé, *Regesta*, n. 544; Leo, *Epistola* 168, 19 (54, 1209).

120. Batiffol, *Etudes*, pp. 211, 217.

121. Loofs, *Leitfaden*, p. 195.   Cf. S 82, 8, 11 (38, 511). Cf. Vacandard, *La confession*, 1902, p. 21.

122. En 65, 17 (40, 263).

123. S 351, 4, 9 (39, 1545).

124. Jaffé, *Regesta*, n. 674.

125. Cf. DD83 26 (40, 17–18).

126. S 351, 4, 9 (39, 1545).

127. E 228, 8 (33, 1016).

128. S 352, 3, 8 (39, 1558).

129. En 65, 17 (40, 262).

130. E 228, 8 (33, 1016).

131. Mansi, III, 885. Cf. Mansi, III, 735 (canon 43 of the *Collectio africana*); Hefele, II, 1, 100; Lauchert, *Die Canones der . . . altkirchliche Concilien*, 1896, p. 167.

132. E 153, 3, 7 (33, 656).

133. *Ibid.*

134. *Ibid.* (33, 655).

135. Jaffé, *Regesta*, n. 255.

136. Specht, *Lehre von der Kirche*, p. 109.

137. Dorner, *Augustinus*, p. 286.

138. DCD XX, 9, 2 (41, 673).

139. Harnack, *History of Dogma*, V, 161.

140. *Ibid.*, 160. Cf. En 65, 17 (40, 263).

141. DB V, 20, 28 (43, 190).

142. DB III, 16, 21 (43, 149).

143. DB V, 23, 33 (43, 193).

144. Such is the opinion of Duchesne, *Liber pontificalis*, I, 167. See Morin, *Commentarius historicus de disciplina . . . poenitentiae*, Paris, 1651, IV, 643–650.

145. See page 66.

146. Schanz, *Die Lehre von den Sakramenten*, p. 731.

147. JE 9, 2 (35, 1459).

148. DBC 24, 32 (40, 394).

149. DNu I, 10, 11 (44, 420).

150. DBC 24, 30 (40, 394).

151. DCj I, 13, 14 (40, 459).

152. DNu I, 17, 19 (44, 424).

153. See page 67.

154. DSD I, 14, 39 (34, 1249).
155. DFO 19, 35 (40, 221).
156. R II, 38 (32, 646).
157. R II, 57 (32, 653). Cf. R I, 19, 6 (32, 616).
158. DNu I, 11, 12 (44, 420); CJ V, 12, 46 (44, 810); CF XXIII, 8 (42, 471).

CHAPTER XV. ST. AUGUSTINE'S MORAL THEOLOGY

1. En 2, 1 (40, 231). Cf. DCD XIV, 28 (41, 436); DSL 13, 22 (44, 214).
2. See page 66.
3. Cf. DBe (32, 959–976); DME I, 3–11, 4–19 (32, 1312–1320).
4. C, especially II, 6, 12–13 (32, 680); IV, 12, 18–19 (32, 700–701); V, 4, 7 (32, 708–709); X (32, 779–810).
5. DT XII 4–8, 4–13 (42, 1000–1005).
6. DCD XIV (41, 403–436); XIX (41, 621–658).
7. S 150 (38, 807–814); EnP 118, sermon 1 (37, 1501–1504); sermon 12 (37, 1531–1535); sermon 13 (37, 1535–1538); sermon 22 (37, 1562–1566).
8. DLA III, 8, 23 (32, 1282); DCD XI, 27 (41, 340).
9. DT XIII, 4, 7 (42, 1018).
10. S 150 (38, 808–814).
11. C 7, 11, 17 (32, 742).
12. EnP 134, 6 (37, 1742).
13. DME I, 8, 13 (32, 1316).
14. EnP 62, 34 (36, 928).
15. DDoC I, 5, 5 (34, 21).
16. Cf. DMu VI, 14, 46 (32, 1187).
17. Peter Lombard, I *sententiarum*, d. 1, c. 2.
18. Cf. Bonaventure, *In* I *sententiarum*, d. 1, a. 1–2, Quarrachi, I, 30; Thomas, *ibid*., q. 2.
19. See pp. 103–104.
20. DME I, 14, 24 (32, 1322).
21. Nourrisson, *Philosophie d'Augustin*, II, 389.
22. DDoC III, 14, 22 (34, 74).
23. R I, 13, 8 (32, 605).
24. Weber, *Histoire de la philosophie européenne*, p. 175.
25. CML 15, 31 (40, 540).
26. CF XXII, 27 (42, 418). The entire chapter is important.
27. DDu 11, 15 (42, 105). The same expression occurs in DGnI 1, 3 (34, 221).
28. S 278, 8–10, 8–10 (38, 1272–1273).

29. S 9, 10, 15 (38, 87).

30. Cf. S 278, 9, 9 (38, 1273).

31. Bindemann, *Augustinus*, III, 935.

32. Dorner, *Augustinus*, pp. 194-195.

33. See page 93.

34. DSL 32, 56 (44, 237); S 53, 10, 11 (38, 369).

35. DFO 14-27, 21-49 (40, 211-230). See pp. 65-66. Also DUB 10, 17 (43, 604); DB IV, 19, 26 (43, 171); EnP 31, sermon 2, especially n. 6 (36, 261).

36. DD83 76 (40, 87-89).

37. R I, 23, 2 (32, 621).

38. C IX, 13, 34 (32, 778). Cf. DGrL 1, 1 (44, 881); DCD XIV, 26 (41, 435); E 194, 5, 19 (33, 880).

39. Loofs, *Leitfaden*, p. 226.

40. En 121, 32 (40, 288).

41. DME I, 15, 25 (32, 1322).

42. DCD XIV, 28 (41, 436).

43. DDoC III, 10, 15 (34, 71). See also DDoC III, 10, 16 (34, 71); E 231, 6 (33, 1025); S 103, 4 (38, 614); DP 23, 20 (40, 622); especially E 167 (33, 733-741).

44. CD II, 9, 21 (44, 586). Cf. DGrC 18, 19 (44, 370).

45. S 349, 2, 2 (39, 1530).

46. Cf. S 349, 7, 7 (39, 1532); DCD XIV, 9 (41, 413-415); EnP 79, 13 (36, 1026); DT VIII, 10, 14 (42, 960); E 167, 4, 15 (33, 739).

47. EnP 36, sermon 2, 13 (36, 371).

48. CJ IV, 3, 33 (44, 756).

49. DGrL 18, 37 (44, 903).

50. S 150, 8, 9 (38, 812). Cf. DME I, 15, 25 (32, 1322); S 21, 8 (38, 146-147); J 6, 3 (35, 2021); 8, 1 (35, 2035-2036).

51. EnP 55, 17 (35, 658).

52. *Ibid.*, 16 (36, 657).

53. *Ibid.*, 17 (36, 658).

54. EnP 72, 33 (36, 928).

55. EnP 93, 24 (37, 1211). Cf. DCD V, 16 (41, 160); XIV, 9 (41, 413). EnP 93, 24-25 (37, 1211-1213); EnP 136, 15 (37, 1770); E 138, 3, 17 (33, 533); especially DCa 27, 27 (40, 331).

56. J 9, 5 (35, 2049).

57. Cf. S65, 5, 6 (38, 429); S 156, 13-14, 14-15 (38, 857-858); S 161, 8, 8 (39, 882); DS 38, 39 (40, 418); DGrL 18, 39 (44, 904-905); DCa 5, 9 (40, 316); OJ VI, 40 (45, 1599-1604).

58. De San, *Tractatus de poenitentia*, chap. 18, Bruges, 1900, pp. 503-521.

59. SO I, 6, 13 (32, 877).
60. DME I, 25, 46 (32, 1330).
61. S 334, 3 (38, 1469).
62. S 331, 4, 4 (38, 1461).
63. E 140, 18, 45 (33, 557).
64. E 155, 4, 13 (33, 672).
65. DME I, 26, 48 (32, 1331).
66. DDoC III, 10, 16 (34, 72).
67. Leibniz, *Letter to Magliabecci*, June, 1698.
68. CA III, 16, 35–36 (32, 952–954).
69. E 47, 4 (33, 186).
70. *Ibid.* Cf. DLA I, 5, 13 (32, 1228).
71. CML 15 (40, 540).
72. CF XX, 21 (42, 384).
73. Cf. DCM (40, 591–610).
74. C IX, 12–13, 29–36 (32, 776–779).
75. S 172 (38, 936–937); S 239 (38, 1127–1130).
76. DCD XIX, 12 (41, 637–640).
77. E 155, 1, 4 (33, 668).
78. QH I, 153 (34, 590).
79. Cf. DCj II (40, 471–486); DBC (40, 373–396).
80. JE 6, 24–26 (35, 1436–1437).
81. Barbeyrac, *Traduction de Puffendorf*, p. 297, quoted by Nourrisson, *Philosophie d'Augustin*, II, 401.
82. Wyclif, *De civili dominio*, I, n. 5, London, 1885, p. 5.
83. E 153, 6, 26 (33, 665).
84. S 317, 1, 1 (38, 1435). Cf. S 311, 13–15, 13 (38, 1418–1419).
85. E 220, 10 (33, 996).
86. DCD XIX, 15 (41, 643).
87. S 21 (38, 142–148).
88. S 361 (39, 1599–1611).
89. Cunningham, *Saint Augustine*, London, 1886, pp. 193–195.
90. DCD IV, 4 (41, 115).
91. *Ibid.*, 3 (41, 114).
92. DLA I, 15, 31 (32, 1238); DCD XIX, 21 (41, 648); DVR 31, 58 (34, 148).
93. DLA I, 6, 14 (32, 1229).
94. CF XXII, 75 (42, 448).
95. DCD XIX, 17 (41, 646).
96. ExR 72 (35, 2083).
97. Harnack, *History of Dogma*, V, 231.
98. C XII, 19, 24 (32, 855).

99. DS 14, 14 (40, 402).

100. E 157, 4, 36–37 (33, 691).

101. DOM 16, 19 (40, 564).

102. The unknown author of the pseudo-Augustinian *Liber de vera et falsa poenitentia*, 18, 34 (40, 1128). See page 74. Cf. Ambrose, *De paradiso*, 14, 71 (14, 328).

103. SS (34, 994).

104. DSy 7, 15 (40, 636). Cf. En 69–71, 18–19 (40, 265); DFO 26, 48 (40, 228); DCD XIX, 27 (41, 657); XXI, 27, 4 (41, 748–749).

105. DCD XXI, 26–27 (41, 743–752).

106. See page 188. Cf. En 71, 19 (40, 265); DCD XIX, 27 (41, 657).

107. DNG 38, 45 (44, 269).

108. See pp. 295–298.

109. DNG 70, 84 (44, 290).

110. En 111, 29 (40, 284).

111. See page 66.

112. OJ IV, 122 (45, 1418).

113. DOM (40, 549–592).

114. S 148, 2, 2 (38, 799); S 224, 3, 3 (38, 1094); E 127, 6 (33, 486).

115. E 150 (33, 645). This was a letter to Demetria when she solemnly took the veil.

116. E 211 (33, 958–965); DME I, 31, 67 (32, 1338). This presents an attractive picture of the monasteries of Egypt.

117. DOM 25, 32 (40, 572).

118. S 356, 8–10 (39, 1577–1578).

119. Cf. DME I, 35, 78 (32, 1343); DSD II, 17, 57 (34, 1294); S 39, 2, 3–4 (38, 242). See page 282.

120. S 39, 2, 4 (38, 242).

121. C XIII, 9, 10 (32, 849).

122. DQ 33–35, 70–79 (32, 1073–1079).

123. *Ibid.*, 35, 79 (32, 1079).

124. *Ibid.*, 33, 76 (32, 1076).

125. DOR II, 18, 48 (32, 1017).

126. See page 104.

127. Cf. DUC 16, 34 (42, 89); SO I, 6, 12–13 (32, 875–876); DD83 46, 2 (40, 30).

128. SO I, 6, 13 (32, 876).

129. DOR II, 19, 51 (32, 1019).

130. DQ 33, 76 (32, 1076).

131. C IX, 10, 23–26 (32, 773–775). Cf. Nourrisson, *Philosophie d'Augustin*, I, 247–252.

132. Ritschl, "Die Methode der ältesten Dogmengeschichte," *Jahrbuch für deutsche Theologie*, 1871.
133. Harnack, *History of Dogma*, V, 138.
134. *Ibid.*, 135.

CHAPTER XVI. ESCHATOLOGY

1. DCD XXI, 27, 6 (41, 751).
2. *Ibid.*, 17 (41, 731).
3. Jaffé, *Regesta*, n. 276.
4. *Ibid.*, n. 282. Cf. Hergenröther, *Histoire de l'Eglise*, II, 221.
5. DCD XX, 7, 1 (41, 667).
6. S 259, 2 (38, 1197).
7. DCD XX, 9, 1–4 (41, 672–675).
8. Ambrose, *Expositio in Lucam*, X, 92 (15, 1919).
9. Thomas Burnet, *De statu mortuorum et resurgentium*, London, 1726, p. 71.
10. *Opera S. Bernardi*, ed. Mabillon, note in *P. L.*, CLXXXIII, 465.
11. Petavius, *Dogmatica theologia*, VII, *De Deo*, 14, 10, Paris, 1865, p. 622.
12. Gener, *Theologia dogmatica scholastica*, II, 100.
13. Turmel, "Eschatologie à la fin du IVe siècle," *Revue d'histoire*, 1900, pp. 2–3, 59.
14. *Ibid.*, p. 59.
15. Muratori, *De paradiso, non expectata corporum resurrectione*, p. 164. This is a refutation of Burnet's work.
16. Schwane, *Dogmengeschichte*, II, n. 76.
17. DPS 12, 24 (44, 977–978).
18. En 109, 29 (40, 283).
19. JE 49, 10 (35, 1751).
20. DGnL XII, 32, 60 (34, 480).
21. S 109, 4, 4 (38, 638).
22. JE 49, 10 (35, 1751).
23. QE II, 38 (35, 1351).
24. QE II, 38 (35, 1350).
25. S 280, 5, 5 (38, 1283).
26. DGnL XII, 33, 63 (34, 482).
27. E 187, 2, 6 (33, 834). Cf. E 164, 3, 8 (33, 712); S 178, 3, 3 (38, 962).
28. EnP 119, 6 (37, 1602).

29. JE 91 (35, 1860). The translator was not able to find this reference.

30. C IX, 3, 6 (32, 765).

31. *Ibid*.

32. S 319, 3, 3 (38, 1441).

33. E 164, 3, 8 (33, 712).

34. *Ibid*.

35. C 329, 1–2 (38, 1455).

36. S 298, 3, 3 (38, 1366).

37. S 331, 2, 1 (38, 1459).

38. DCD XX, 9, 2 (41, 674).

39. *Ibid*. Cf. JE 49, 10 (35, 1751): Martyrs, apostles, virgins, and the other saints are together in the same place of rest.

40. EnP 36, 10 (34, 361). Cf. En 109, 29 (40, 283).

41. EnP 30, sermon 3, 8 (36, 252).

42. Cf. E 187, 3, 7 (33, 835).

43. R I, 14, 2 (32, 606); JE 49, 10 (35, 1751).

44. S 280, 4–5, 4–5 (38, 1282–1283).

45. S 280, 5, 5 (38, 1283).

46. S 328, 5–6, 5–6 (38, 1454).

47. DGnL XII, 35, 68 (34, 483).

48. Rudolf Hofmann, "Fegfeuer," *Realencyclopädie für prot. Theol. und Kirche*, V, 790.

49. Ambrose, *Expositio in psalmum 118*, sermon 3, 17 (15, 1293).

50. DCD XXI, 13 (41, 728).

51. *Ibid*., 16 (41, 731).

52. *Ibid*., 24, 2 (41, 738).

53. DGnM II, 20, 30 (34, 212).

54. EnP 37, 3 (36, 397).

55. See pp. 67, n. 100, and 280–281.

56. C IX, 13, 35 (32, 778).

57. S 172, 2, 2 (38, 936).

58. En 110, 29 (40, 283). Cf. DH 53 (42, 40).

59. DCD XXI, 26 (41, 743–746); En 68, 18 (40, 264); DFO 16, 27–28 (40, 216).

60. DCD XXI, 26, 1–3 (41, 743–744); DFO 16, 27 (40, 216).

61. DCD XXI, 26, 4 (41, 745).

62. DCD XX, 26, 1 (41, 701).

63. DCD XXI, 26, 4 (41, 745).

64. *Ibid*.

65. En 69, 18 (40, 265).

66. En 110, 29 (40, 283).

67. Bellarmine, *De purgatorio*, II, 10.

68. EnP 37, 3 (36, 397).

69. En 110, 29 (40, 283). Cf. DOD II, 1–4 (40, 157–158).

70. DCD XXI, 16 (41, 730).

71. DCD XXI, 13 (41, 728). Cf. DCD XXI, 16 (41, 730).

72. DCD XX, 25 (41, 699–700).

73. See S 361, 4, 4 (39, 1600).

74. En 84–92, 23 (40, 272–275); DCD XXII, 5 (41, 755–757); 12–29 (41, 775–801).

75. EnP 88, 5 (37, 1134).

76. *Ibid.*

77. DCD XXII, 5 (41, 756).

78. E 102, 1, 5 (33, 372).

79. En 89, 23 (40, 273).

80. En 84, 23 (40, 272).

81. En 85–87, 23 (40, 272–273).

82. DOD III, 3 (40, 159). Cf. DOD III, 4–6 (40, 160–161); E 193, 4, 9–13 (33, 872–874).

83. DSy 4, 12 (40, 634).

84. En 92, 23 (40, 274–275).

85. S 256, 2 (38, 1192).

86. S 264, 6 (38, 1217).

87. S 243, 6–8 (38, 1146–1147).

88. S 242, 7, 10 (38, 1142). Cf. En 91, 23 (40, 274).

89. E 197 (33, 899–901); E 199 (33, 904–925); DCD XX (41, 657–708).

90. DCD XX, 4 (41, 662); 23–29 (41, 694–704); DAC 32, 29 (40, 305). Cf. S 110, 4, 4 (38, 640); E 217, 5, 16 (33, 984); *Ibid.*, 22 (41, 986).

91. DCD XX, 6, 1 (41, 665); 30, 1 (41, 705).

92. CF V, 4 (42, 222). Cf. DT I, 13, 31 (43, 844); E 147, 11, 28 (33, 609).

93. DCD XX, 14 (41, 680).

94. Ittameyer, "Augustins Stellung zur Frage nach der Nähe des Weltendes," *Zeitschrift für kirchliche Wissenschaft*, 1881, pp. 570–581.

95. E 197, 5 (33, 901). Cf. E 197, 1–2 (33, 899–900); E 198, 5 (33, 903).

96. E 199, 12–13, 46–54 (33, 922–925).

97. *Ibid.*, 12, 46–50 (33, 923–924). Cf. E 197, 4 (33, 900).

98. DCD XXI, 17–27 (41, 731–752).

99. DCD XXI, 17 (41, 731–732); 23 (41, 735–736).

100. E 102, 4, 22–26 (33, 379–381).

101. En 113, 29 (40, 284).

102. In 413, DFO 14–27, 21–49 (40, 211–230); En 67–69, 18 (40, 263–265); in 422, DOD I, 1–13 (40, 149–157).

103. Cf. DFO 14, 21 (40, 211).

104. DCD XXI, 27, 6 (41, 750).

105. Turmel, "Eschatologie," *Revue d'histoire*, 1900, pp. 14, 109.

106. See page 188.

107. En 67, 18 (40, 263).

108. En 112, 29 (40, 284).

109. En 67, 18 (40, 263).

110. DOD I, 14 (40, 156).

111. DGnL XII, 33, 63 (34, 481). Cf. DCD XVII, 11 (41, 544).

112. E 164, 1, 1 (33, 709).

113. *Ibid.*, 3, 7 (33, 711).

114. One of the heresies he lists in his work on the subject is that of those who believe that Christ delivers unbelievers from hell, DH 79 (42, 45).

115. E 164, 5, 14 (33, 715).

116. *Ibid.*, 5–6, 16–18 (33, 715–716).

117. En 110, 29 (40, 283).

118. En 112, 29 (40, 285). Cf. Faure, notes on chap. 110 of the *Enchiridion*, pp. 208–210.

119. En 113, 29 (40, 285).

120. DCD XXI, 24, 3 (41, 739).

121. *Ibid.*, 2 (41, 737).

122. Peter Lombard, IV *sententiarum*, d. 45 (192, 948).

123. Thomas, *In IV sententiarum*, d. 45, q. 2.

124. See the wise statement of Petavius, *De angelis*, III, chap. 8.

125. DCD XXI, 9, 2 (41, 724).

126. *Ibid.*, 10, 1 (41, 724).

127. *Ibid.*

128. *Ibid.*, 16 (41, 731).

129. DCD XXII, 29, 1 (41, 797).

130. E 92, 6 (33, 320).

131. E 147, 21–22, 50–53 (33, 619–622).

132. E 148, 1, 1–2 (33, 622–623).

133. E 162, 8 (33, 707).

134. S 277, 14–16 (38, 1265–1266).

135. DCD XXII, 29, 3 (41, 798–799).

136. *Ibid.*, 6 (41, 801).

137. R II, 41 (32, 647).

138. Nourrisson, *Philosophie de Augustin*, II, 319.

CHAPTER XVII. GENIUS OF ST. AUGUSTINE

1. Zahm, *Bible, science et foi*, p. 56.
2. Schaff, *Augustin*, p. 97.
3. Bougard, *Vie de sainte Monique*, 1879, p. 497.
4. C III, 6, 10 (32, 187).
5. DD83 9 (40, 14).
6. DCD VIII, 1 (41, 225).
7. See pp. 90–91.
8. SO I, 2, 7 (32, 872).
9. C VII, 17, 23 (32, 744).
10. *Ibid.* (32, 745).
11. *Ibid.*
12. C X, 6, 8 (32, 782).
13. *Ibid.*, 9 (32, 783).
14. Feuerlein, "Über die Stellung Augustins in der Kirchen- und Kulturgeschichte," *Historische Zeitschrift*, Sybel, 1869, XXII, 270–313.
15. Quoted *ibid.*, p. 281.
16. Eucken, *Lebensanschauungen*, p. 211.
17. C I, 1, 1 (32, 661).
18. See pp. 170–172.
19. Eucken, *Lebensanschauungen*, p. 210.
20. Harnack, *History of Dogma*, V, 64.
21. Harnack, *What Is Christianity?*, pp. 264–265.
22. Böhringer, *Augustin*, p. 428.
23. Eucken, *Lebensanschauungen*, p. 213. Cf. Harnack, *What Is Christianity?*, p. 264.
24. Schaff, *Augustin*, p. 96.
25. See page 178.
26. L. Becker, *Revue d'histoire ecclésiastique*, Louvain, 1902, p. 379.
27. Bonaventure, *In II sententiarum*, d. 33, a. 3, q. 1, ad 1, Quarrachi, 1885, II, 794. Cf. Thomas, *De malo*, q. 5, a. 2, ad 1.
28. Schaff, *Augustin*, p. 102.

CHAPTER XVIII. AUTHORITY OF ST. AUGUSTINE

1. Vincent of Lerins tried to monopolize this phrase to his own advantage, *Commonitorium*, II, 32 (50, 684).
2. Text given in Mansi, IV, 455. Cf. Jaffé, *Regesta*, n. 381; Denzinger, *Enchiridion*, n. 128; *P. L.*, XLV, 1756; L, 530.

3. Text given in Mansi, IV, 462. Cf. Denzinger, *Enchiridion*, 142; *P. L.*, XLV, 1760; L. 537.

4. Viva, *Theses damnatae ab Alexandro VIII*, prop. 30.

5. Prosper of Aquitaine, *Liber contra collatorem*, 31, 58 (45, 1831).

6. In earlier editions of Denzinger, *Enchiridion*, these *Chapters* were divided into eleven headings. They are now correctly divided into ten. Cf. *Ibid.*, nn. 130–142.

7. Hergenröther, *Kirchengeschichte*, II, n. 123.

8. Hormisdas, *Epistola ad Possessorem*, 3 (45, 1778).

9. Peter, *Epistola Petri diaconi*, 7, 7 (45, 1776).

10. *Monitum in subsequentem epistolam*, 10 (50, 527).

11. Gelasius, *Epistola ad Episcopos per Picenum*, 8 (45, 1771); Mansi, VIII, 29. Cf. Thiel, *Epistolae romanorum pontificum*, I, 325; Jaffé, *Regesta*, n. 621.

12. Text given in Mansi, VIII, 497; *P. L.*, XLV, 1776.

13. Text given in Mansi, VIII, 498–500; *P. L.*, LXIII, 490–493; XLV, 1778; Thiel, *Epistolae*, p. 926; Jaffé, *Regesta*, n. 850.

14. This has an uncertain origin. Cf. Bardenhewer, *Patrologie*, III, 142.

15. Listed in *P. L.*, LIX, 164.

16. Text given in *P. L.*, LXIII, 493.

17. Petavius, *De Tridentino concilio et Augustini doctrina*, chap. 5.

18. DPS, 18, 37 (44, 987).

19. Boniface, *Epistola ad Caesarium*, 2 (45, 1790); (65, 31); Mansi, VIII, 736; Jaffé, *Regesta*, n. 881.

20. Mansi, VIII, 804; *P. L.*, LXVI, 21; Jaffé, *Regesta*, n. 885.

21. Cf. Gotti, *Theologia scholastica dogmatica*, I, *De Deo sciente*, q. 4, dub. 5, Venice, 1750, p. 230.

22. No reference given in original.

23. Marcelli, O.S.A., *Institutiones theologicae*, V, *De gratia*, p. 91.

24. See the text in Gotti above, note 21, or Serry, *Historia congregationis de auxiliis*, 1740, p. 95.

25. Jansenius, *Augustinus*, chap. 30.

26. *Ibid*.

27. Jansenius, *De statu naturae purae*, III, chap. 22, II, 403.

28. "Alexandre VIII," DTC, I, 762.

29. A. Koch, *Der h. Faustus von Riez*, 1895, pp. 129–191.

30. Diego Alvarez, *De auxiliis divinae gratiae*, d. 10, n. 3, p. 49.

31. Cf. the documents in Serry, *Historia congregationis de auxiliis*, 2nd ed., Venice, 1760, appendix, p. 249.

32. *Ibid.*, 213.

33. See page 312.

34. Quesnel, *Opera S. Leonis Magni*, d. 3, p. 2, c. 2.

35. CD III, 8, 24 (44, 606).

36. See page 190.

37. Noris, *Vindiciae augustinianae*, 8 (47, 828).

38. See Serry, *Historia congregationis*, 2nd ed., appendix, pp. 91–112.

39. This document is given by Schneemann, *Controversiarum de divina gratia*, Freiburg im Breisgau, 1881, p. 296.

40. Denzinger, *Enchiridion*, n. 1526.

41. Melchior Cano, *De locis theologicis*, VII, 3, 3, Padua, 1734, p. 217.

42. Bañez, *In I$_{am}$*, q. 22, a. 5.

43. Noris, *Vindiciae*, 5, 10 (47, 773–782).

44. Suarez, *De gratia*, Prolegomena VI, 6, 16.

45. Denzinger, *Enchiridion*, n. 128.

46. Koch, *Faustus von Riez*, pp. 135–138.

47. DT III, 2 (42, 869).

48. E 193, 4, 10 (33, 873). Cf. DT II, 1 (42, 845); E 147, 1, 2 (33, 597); 16, 39 (33, 614); 23, 53–54 (33, 621–622).

49. E 82, 1, 3 (33, 277). Cf. E 82, 4, 32 (33, 289).

50. E 148, 4, 15 (33, 629).

51. See pp. 177–178.

52. See pp. 196–204.

53. Bossuet, *Défense de la tradition et des saints Pères*, especially I, chaps. 7–8, Versailles, 1820, V, 22–30.

54. See page 312.

55. Cf. Melchior Cano, *De locis theologicis*, VII, 1–4; Fessler, *Institutiones patrologiae*, I, 41–47.

56. Thomassin, *Consensus scholae de gratia*, I, chap. 10, *Dogmata theologica*, Paris, 1870, VI, 28.

57. See pp. 221–222.

The Works of St. Augustine

DATE	TITLE	CSEL¹	PL²	NUMBER³
	First period: Augustine's writings while a catechumen (386–Easter, 387)			
386	Contra academicos, III	63, 3–81	32, 905–958	4
386	De beata vita	63, 89–116	32, 959–976	5
386	De ordine, II	63, 121–185	32, 977–1020	6
387	Soliloquia, II	...	32, 869–904	7
387	De immortalitate animae	...	32, 1021–1034	8
387	De grammatica (a fragment)	...	32, 1385–1408	11
387–391	De musica, VI	...	32, 1081–1194	12
	Second period: Baptism to priesthood (387–391)			
387–388	De quantitate animae	...	32, 1035–1080	9
388	De moribus ecclesiae Catholicae et de moribus Manichaeorum, II	...	32, 1309–1378	22
388–390	De Genesi contra Manichaeos, II	...	34, 173–220	67
388–395	De libero arbitrio, III	...	32, 1221–1310	27
389	De magistro	...	32, 1193–1220	10
389–391	De vera religione	...	34, 121–172	14
389–396	De diversis quaestionibus, LXXXIII	...	40, 11–100	86

¹ CSEL=Corpus scriptorum ecclesiasticorum Latinorum, Vienna, 1866 ff.
² PL= Patrologiae cursus completus, series Latina, ed. J. P. Migne, Paris, 1844–1864, vols. 32–47.
³ This number corresponds to the marginal number of the work in chapter four of this book.

Third period: Priesthood to episcopal consecration (391–396)

DATE	TITLE	CSEL	PL	NUMBER
391–392	De utilitate credendi	25, 3–48	42, 63–92	15
391–392	De duabus animabus contra Manichaeos	25, 51–80	42, 93–112	23
392	Disputatio contra Fortunatum	25, 83–112	42, 111–130	24
393	De fide et symbolo	41, 3–32	40, 181–196	83
393–394	De Genesi ad litteram liber imperfectus	28, I, 459–503	35, 219–246	68
393–396	De sermone Domini in monte, II	...	34, 1229–1308	76
393–396	Psalmus contra partem Donati	51, 3–15	43, 23–32	34
393–396	Contra Adimantum Manichaei discipulum	25, 115–190	42, 129–172	25
393–396	Expositio quarumdam propositionum ex Epistola ad Romanos	...	35, 2063–2088	79
394	Expositio Epistolae ad Galatas	...	35, 2105–2148	81
394	Epistola ad Romanos inchoata expositio	...	35, 2087–2106	80
394	Epistola 28 ad Hieronymum de nova Veteris Testamenti versione	34, I, 103–113	33, 111–114	...
394–395	De mendacio	41, 413–466	40, 487–518	92
394–395	De continentia	41, 141–183	40, 348–372	94

Fourth period: Episcopacy to the Pelagian controversy (396–412)

DATE	TITLE	CSEL	PL	NUMBER
396–397	De diversis quaestionibus VII ad Simplicianum	...	40, 101–148	87
397	De agone christiano	41, 101–138	40, 289–310	84
397	Contra epistolam Manichaei quam vocant Fundamenti	25, 193–248	42, 173–206	26
397	De doctrina christiana, III (Liber IV, 426)	...	34, 15–122	66
397–400	Quaestiones Evangeliorum ex Matthaeo et Luca, II	...	35, 1321–1364	75

Date	Work			
397–400	Annotationes in Job	28, II, 509–628	34, 825–886	72
400	De catechizandis rudibus	...	40, 309–348	102
397–401	Confessiones, XIII	33, 1–388	32, 659–868	1
400	Contra Faustum Manichaeum, XXXIII	25, 251–797	42, 207–518	28
400	De consensu Evangelistarum, IV	43, 1–418	34, 1041–1230	74
400	Epistolae 54–55 ad Januarium	34, II, 158–213	33, 199–223	...
400	De opere monachorum	41, 531–596	40, 547–582	101
400	De fide rerum quae non videntur	...	40, 171–180	16
400	Contra epistolam Parmeniani, III	51, 19–141	43, 33–108	35
400	De baptismo contra Donatistas, VII	51, 145–375	43, 107–244	36
400	De bono conjugali	41, 187–231	40, 373–396	95
400–401	De sancta virginitate	41, 235–302	40, 397–428	96
400–401	Contra litteras Petiliani Donatistae, III	52, 3–227	43, 245–388	37
400–402	Ad Catholicos epistola de unitate ecclesiae	52, 231–322	43, 391–446	38
402	De Trinitate, XV	...	42, 819–1098	89
400–416	De Genesi ad litteram, XII	28, I, 3–435	34, 245–486	69
401–415	De actis cum Felice Manichaeo, II	25, 801–852	42, 519–552	29
404	De natura boni contra Manichaeos	25, 855–889	42, 551–572	30
405	Contra Secundinum Manichaeum	25, 905–947	42, 577–602	31
405–406	Epistola 82 ad Hieronymum	34, II, 351–387	33, 275–291	...
406	Contra Cresconium grammaticum partis Donati, IV	52, 325–582	45, 445–594	39
406	De divinatione daemonum	41, 597–618	40, 581–592	17
406–411	Epistola 93 ad Vincentium de haereticis vi coercendis	34, II, 445–496	33, 321–347	...
408, 408–409	Epistola 102 ad Deogratium, sex quaestiones contra paganos	34, II, 544–578	33, 370–386	18
409	Epistola 108 ad Macrobium de non iterando baptismo	34, II, 612–634	33, 405–417	41

DATE	TITLE	CSEL	PL	NUMBER
410	Epistola 118 ad Dioscorum de philosophiae erroribus	34, II, 665–698	33, 432–449	19
410	Epistola 120 ad Consentium de Trinitate	34, II, 704–722	33, 452–462	90
410	De unico baptismo contra Petilianum	53, 3–34	43, 595–614	40
411	Breviculus collationis cum Donatistis	53, 39–92	43, 613–650	42
412	Liber contra Donatistas post collationem	53, 97–162	43, 651–690	43

Fifth period: From the Pelagian controversy to his death (412–430)

DATE	TITLE	CSEL	PL	NUMBER
412	Epistola 137 ad Volusianum de Incarnatione	44, 96–125	33, 515–525	...
412	Epistola 138 ad Marcellinum de Incarnatione	44, 126–148	33, 525–535	...
412	Epistola 140 ad Honorium de gratia Novi Testamenti	44, 155–234	33, 538–577	...
412	De peccatorum meritis et remissione et de baptismo parvulorum, III	60, 3–151	44, 109–200	46
412	De spiritu et littera	60, 155–229	44, 201–246	47
413	De fide et operibus	41, 35–97	40, 197–230	91
413	Epistola 147 ad Paulinum de videndo Deo	44, 274–331	33, 596–622	...
413–426	De civitate Dei, XXII	40, I, 3–660; 40, II, 1–670	41, 13–804	13
414	De bono viduitatis ad Julianam	41, 303–343	40, 429–450	97
414	Epistola 157 ad Hilarium de Pelagianismo	44, 449–488	33, 674–693	...
415	De natura et gratia contra Pelagium	60, 233–299	44, 247–290	48
415	De perfectione justitiae hominis	42, 3–48	44, 291–318	49
415	Epistola 166 ad Hieronymum de origine animae hominis	44, 545–584	33, 720–733	...
415	Epistola 167 ad Hieronymum de sententia Jacobi	44, 586–609	33, 733–741	...

DATE	TITLE	CSEL	PL	NUMBER
421	Contra Julianum haeresis Pelagianae defensorem, VI	...	44, 641–674	57
421	Enchiridion ad Laurentium de fide, spe, charitate	...	40, 231–290	85
421	De cura pro mortuis gerenda	41, 621–660	40, 591–610	100
422	De octo Dulcitii quaestionibus	...	40, 147–170	88
423	Epistola 211 ad moniales	57, 356–371	33, 958–965	...
426–427	De gratia et libero arbitrio ad Valentinum	...	44, 881–912	59
426–427	De correptione et gratia ad eundem	...	44, 915–946	60
426–427	Retractationes, II	36, 7–205	32, 583–656	2
427	Epistola 217 ad Vitalem de Pelagianismo	57, 403–425	33, 978–989	61
427	Speculum de Scriptura sacra	12, 3–285	34, 887–1040	82
428	Collatio cum Maximino Arianorum episcopo	...	42, 709–742	65
428	Contra Maximinum Arianorum episcopum	...	42, 743–814	65
428	De haeresibus ad Quodvultdeum	...	42, 21–50	21
428	Tractatus adversus Judaeos	...	42, 51–64	20
428–429	De praedestinatione sanctorum ad Prosperum et Hilarium	...	44, 959–992	62
428–429	De dono perseverantiae ad eosdem	...	45, 993–1034	63
429–430	Opus imperfectum contra Julianum, VI	...	45, 1049–1608	58
391–430	Sermones 1–363	...	{38, 23–1484; 39, 1493–2354	103
386–430	Epistolae 1–270	Vols. 34, 44, 57, 58	33, 61–1162	3
391–430	Enarrationes in Psalmos	...	36, 67–1028; 37, 1033–1968	73

Selected Bibliography

The titles which follow include all the works cited by Portalié, although in some instances complete bibliographical information was not supplied in his reference and could not be filled in from other sources. Besides these works, other significant books written since Portalié's time have been added. These latter are marked with an asterisk.

The symposia which appeared on the anniversaries of Augustine's birth and death in 1954 and 1930 appear at the beginning of this bibliography, since it is felt that they represent the latest thought in Augustinian scholarship.

References in parentheses throughout this volume are to the complete works of Augustine in *Patrologiae cursus completus, series latina*, ed. J. P. Migne, vols. 32–47. Thus (34, 720–724) indicates volume 34, columns 720–724. Many of Augustine's works have been critically reedited in the *Corpus scriptorum ecclesiasticorum latinorum* (CSEL). These will be found in the chronological list of writings given in the appendix.

A more extensive bibliography of older books can be found in the *Dictionnaire de Théologie Catholique* (DTC) at the end of the various sections of the Augustine article. For more recent books, see E. Gilson, *Introduction à l'étude de s. Augustin*, 3rd ed., Paris, 1949, pp. 324–351; E. Nebreda, *Bibliographia augustiniana seu operum collectio quae divi Augustini vitam et doctrinam quadantenus exponunt*, Rome, 1928; F. Van Steenberghen, "La philosophie de s. Augustin d'après les travaux du centenaire (430–1930)," *Revue néoscolastique de philosophie*, XXXIV (1932) 366–387; XXXV (1933) 106–126, 230–281. See also the annual lists in the same journal since that time.

AUGUSTINE SYMPOSIA

Acta Hebdomadae Augustino-Thomisticae. Rome: 1930.
Augustiniana: Dissertationes et Orationes. Averbode: 1930.
Augustinus: Feestnemmer van de Studia Catholica. Nijmegen: 1930.
Aurelius Augustinus: Festschrift der Görres-Gesselschaft. Cologne: 1930.
Etudes sur saint Augustin: Archives de Philosophie. Paris: 1930.
Le XV. centenaire de saint Augustin: Documentation Catholique. Paris: 1930.
Mélanges Augustiniennes: Revue de Philosophie. Paris: 1931.

Miscellanea Agostiniana: Testi e Studi. 2 vols. Rome: 1930–1931.

Miscellanea Augustiniana: Gedenkenboek. Rotterdam: 1930.

Monument to Saint Augustine. London, 1930.

XV centenario de la muerte de S. Agustin. Madrid: 1931.

Saint Augustin: Cahiers de la Nouvelle Journée. Paris: 1930.

Saint Augustin: La Vie Spirituelle. Juvisy: 1930.

S. Agostino: Revista di Filosofia Neoscolastica. Milan: 1931.

St. Augustinus: A.D. 430–1930. Würzburg: 1930.

Sw. Augustyn. Poznan: 1930.

Augustiniana. Louvain: 1954.

Augustinus Magister: Etudes Augustiniennes. 3 vols. Paris: 1954.

Giornale di Metafisica. Turin: 1954.

Pensamiento. Madrid: 1954.

Saint Augustin parmi nous, ed. H. Rondet et al. Paris: 1954.

San Agustin y la espiritualidad cristiana. Madrid: 1955.

Santo Agostinho no XVI Centenario do seu nascimento. Braga: 1955.

OTHER WORKS

*Adam, K., *Die geheime Kirchenbusse nach dem hl. Augustin.* Kempten: 1931.

*———, *Saint Augustine, the Odyssey of His Soul.* New York: 1932.

Alexandre, Noël, "De concilio plenario quod controversiam de baptismo haereticorum diremit juxta sententiam Augustini," *Historia ecclesiastica,* IV, 165–168. Venice: 1778.

*Alfaric, P., *L'Evolution intellectuelle de saint Augustin.* Paris: 1918.

Alticozzi, Laurent, *Summa augustiniana ex collectis, disputatis explicatisque sententiis d. Aur. Augustini.* 6 vols. Rome: 1755.

anon., *De humanae cognitionis ratione anecdota quaedam s. Bonaventurae et nonnullorum ipsius discipulorum.* Quaracchi: 1883.

*Armas, G., *La moral de San Agustin.* Madrid: 1955.

*Arquillière, H. X, *L'Augustinisme politique. Essai sur la formation des théories politiques du moyen âge.* Paris: 1934.

*Bardy, G., *Saint Augustin: l'homme et l'œuvre,* 6th ed. Paris: 1946.

*Barion, J., *Plotin und Augustinus: Untersuchungen zum Gottesproblem.* Berlin: 1935.

*Battenhouse, R., ed., *A Companion to the Study of St. Augustine.* New York: 1955.

*Battifol, P., *Le Catholicisme de s. Augustin.* Paris: 1920.

Baur, *Die christliche Kirche vom Anfang.* 1859.

*Baynes, N., *The Political Ideas of St. Augustine's "De Civitate Dei."* London: 1936.

Becker, L., *Revue d'histoire ecclésiastique.* Louvain: 1902.

Beelen, J., *Dissertatio theologica qua sententiam vulgo receptam esse sacrae Scripturae multiplicem interdum sensum litteralem, nullo fundamento satis firmo niti demonstrare conatur.* Louvain: 1845.

Bestmann, J., *Qua ratione Augustinus notiones philosophiae graecae ad dogmata anthropologica describenda adhibuerit.* Erlangen: 1877.

*Bigg, C., *The Christian Platonist of Alexandria.* London: 1886.

Bindemann, C., *Der heilige Augustin.* Berlin: 1844.

Böhringer, F., "Aurelius Augustin," *Die Kirche Christi und ihre Zeugen,* 2nd ed., I, 97–774. Stuttgart: 1877–1878.

Boissier, G., "La conversion de s. Augustin," *La Fin du paganisme,* I, 339–379. Paris: 1891.

Bonifas, F., *Histoire des dogmes.* Paris: 1886.

Bonwetsch, N., "Donatismus," *Realencyclopädie für protestantische Theologie und Kirche,* 3rd ed., ed. Herzog. IV, 788–789. Leipzig: 1897.

Bossuet, *La Défense de la tradition de saints Pères,* ed. Lebel. Versailles: 1815.

Bougard, *Vie de sainte Monique.* 1879.

*Bourke, V., *Augustine's Quest of Wisdom.* Milwaukee: 1945.

*Bovy, L., *Grâce et liberté chez s. Augustin.* Montreal: 1939.

*Boyer, C., *Christianisme et néo-platonisme dans la formation de s. Augustin.* Paris: 1920.

*————, *L'Idée de vérité dans la philosophie de s. Augustin.* Paris: 1921.

*————, *Saint Augustin.* Paris: 1932.

*Brucculeri, A., *Il pensiero sociale di S. Agostino.* Rome: 1932.

Bruckner, A., "Julian von Eclanum, sein Leben und seine Lehre," *Texte und Untersuchungen,* XV. Leipzig: 1897.

Burkitt, "The Old Latin and Itala," *Texts and Studies,* IV (1896) 55–78. Cambridge.

*Burleigh, J., *The City of God: A Study of St. Augustine's Philosophy.* London: 1944.

*Burnaby, J., *Amor Dei: A Study of the Religion of St. Augustine.* London: 1938.

Burnet, T., *De statu mortuorum et resurgentium.* London: 1726.

*Busch, B., *De initiatione christiana secundum doctrinam S. Augustini.* Rome: 1939.

*Butler, C., *Western Mysticism.* London: 1927.

Cabrol, *Revue des questions historiques,* XLVII (1890) 232–243.

*Capanaga, V., *La teologia agustiniana de la gracia.* Madrid: 1933.

*Carney, J., *The Doctrine of St. Augustine on Sanctity.* Washington: 1945.

Casey, H., *Notes on a History of Auricular Confession,* 2nd ed. Philadelphia: 1899.

Caspari, *Briefe und Abhandlungen und Predigten.* Christiana: 1890.

Cave, *Scriptorum ecclesiasticorum historia litteraria,* I, 290–299. Basle:
  1741–1745.

*Cayré, F., *La contemplation augustinienne: principes de la spiritualité
  de s. Augustin.* Paris: 1927.

*———, *Initiation à la philosophie de s. Augustin.* Paris: 1947.

*———, *Introduction générale aux oeuvres de s. Augustin.* Paris: 1947.

*———, *Les sources de l'amour divin: la divine présence d'après s.
  Augustin.* Paris: 1933.

Ceillier, R., *Histoire générale des auteurs sacrés et ecclésiastiques,* XI.
  Paris: 1744.

*Chapman, E., *St. Augustine's Philosophy of Beauty.* New York: 1939.

Clausen, N., *Aurelius Augustinus Hipponensis, S. Scripturae interpres.*
  Copenhagen: 1827.

*Cochrane, C., *Christianity and Classical Culture: A Study of Thought
  and Action from Augustus to Augustine.* Oxford: 1940.

*Combès, G., *La Charité d'après s. Augustin.* Paris: 1934.

*———, *La Doctrine politique de s. Augustin.* Paris: 1927.

*Costello, *St. Augustine's Doctrine on the Inspiration and Canonicity
  of Scripture.* Washington: 1930.

*Courcelle, P., *Recherches sur les Confessions de s. Augustin.* Paris:
  1950.

Cremer, *Studien und Kritik.*

Cunningham, W., *S. Austin and His Place in the History of Christian
  Thought.* London: 1886.

Cupetioli, A., *Theologia moralis et contemplativa S. Augustini.* 3 vols.
  Venice: 1737.

Denzinger, H., and Bannwart, C., *Enchiridion symbolorum,* 26th ed.,
  ed. J. Umberg. Freiburg i.B.: 1947.

Dorner, A., "Augustine," *A Religious Encyclopedia,* ed. P. Schaff.
  I, 173 ff. Edinburgh: 1883.

———, *Augustinus, sein theologisches System und seine religions-
  philosophische Anschauung.* Berlin: 1873.

Douais, "Saint Augustin et la Bible," *Revue biblique,* 1893, pp. 62–81,
  351–377; 1894, pp. 110–135, 410–432.

*Durkin, E., *The Theological Distinction of Sins in the Writings of
  St. Augustine.* Mundelein: 1952.

Ebert, *Histoire de la littérature du moyen âge,* 2nd ed., I, 229–272.
  Paris: 1883.

*Eger, H., *Die Eschatologie Augustins.* Paderborn: 1933.

Ernst, J., "Die Werke und Tugenden der Ungläubigen nach hl. Augustin," *Zeitschrift für katholische Theologie*, 1895, p. 117.

———, "Der heilige Augustine über die Entscheidung der Ketzertauffrage durch ein Plenarconcil," *Zeitschrift für katholische Theologie*, 1900, pp. 282–325.

Eucken, R., *Die Lebensanschauungen der grossen Denker*. Leipzig: 1902.

Faure, J., *Annotationes super Enchiridion*, 2nd ed., ed. Passaglia. Naples: 1847.

Fénelon, *Lettres sur divers sujets de métaphysique et de religion*, ed. Lebel. 1820.

Fessler, J., *Institutiones patrologiae*, 2nd ed., ed. Jungmann. II, 250–404. Innsbruck: 1896.

Feuerlein, E., "Über die Stellung Augustins in der Kirchen- und Kulturgeschichte," *Historische Zeitschrift*, XXII (1869) 270–313.

*Figgis, J., *Political Aspects of St. Augustine's City of God*. London: 1921.

Frantz, A., *Das Gebet für die Todten . . . nach den Schriften des Augustinus*. Nordhausen: 1857.

Franzelin, J., *De Deo uno*. Rome: 1870.

*Frend, W., *The Donatist Church*. Oxford: 1952.

*Garvey, M., *Saint Augustine: Christian or Neo-Platonist?* Milwaukee: 1939.

*Gendreau, A., *Sancti Augustini Doctrina de Baptismo*. Baltimore: 1939.

*Geyser, J., *Augustin und die phaenomenologische Religionsphilosophie der Gegenwart*. Münster: 1923.

*Gibb, J., and Montgomery, W., *The Confessions of Augustine*. Cambridge: 1908.

*Gilson, E., *Introduction à l'étude de s. Augustin*, 3rd ed. Paris: 1949.

*———, *Philosophie et Incarnation selon s. Augustin*. Montreal: 1947.

Gottschick, J., "Augustins Anschauung von der Erlöserwirkungen Christi," *Zeitschrift für Theologie und Kirche*, 1901, pp. 97–213.

Gourdon, L., *Essai sur la conversion de s. Augustin*. Cahors: 1900.

*Grabmann, M., *Die Grundgedanken des hl. Augustinus über Seele und Gott*. Cologne: 1929.

*Grabowski, S., *The All-Present God: A Study in St. Augustine*. St. Louis: 1954.

*———, *The Church: An Introduction to the Theology of St. Augustine*. St. Louis: 1957.

Grandgeorge, *S. Augustin et le néoplatonisme*. Paris: 1896.

*Greenslade, S., *Schism in the Early Church*. London: 1953.

Gretillat, *Dogmatique.*

*Grou, *Morality Extracted from the Confessions,* introd. by R. Hudleston. London: 1934.

*Guitton, J., *Le Temps et l'éternité chez Plotin et s. Augustin.* Paris: 1933.

*Guzzo, A., *Agostino contro Pelagio.* Turin: 1934.

Haag, *Histoire des dogmes chrétiennes.*

Hahn, *Bibliothek der Symbole,* 3rd ed.

Harnack, A., *Abhandlungen Al. von Ottingen gewidmet.* Munich: 1898.

———, *History of Dogma,* trans. by J. Millar, W. M'Gilchrist, N. Buchanan, and E. Speirs. 7 vols. London: 1894-1899.

———, *Monasticism and the Confessions of St. Augustine,* trans. by E. Kellett and F. Marseille. London: 1901.

———, *What Is Christianity?,* trans. by T. Saunders, 3rd ed. New York: 1904.

*Harvey, J., *Moral Theology of the Confessions of St. Augustine.* Washington: 1951.

Hefele, C., *Histoire des conciles,* trans. by Goschler et Delarc, II. Paris: 1908.

*Hendriks, E. *Augustins Verhältnis zur Mystik.* Würzburg: 1936.

*Henry, P., *La vision d'Ostie.* Paris: 1950.

Hergenröther, J., *Handbuch der allgemeinen Kirchengeschichte.* 4 vols. Freiburg i.B.: 1879.

Hertling, G., *Der Untergang der antiken Kultur, Augustin.* Mainz: 1902.

Herzog, E., *Die kirchliche Sündenvergebung nach der Lehre des hl. Augustin.* Bern: 1902.

*Hessen, J., *Augustins Metaphysik der Erkenntnis.* Berlin: 1931.

*———, *Die unmittelbare Erkenntnis nach dem hl. Augustinus.* Paderborn: 1919.

*Hofmann, F., *Der Kirchenbegriff des hl. Augustinus.* Munich: 1933.

Hofmann, R., "Fegfeuer," *Realencyclopädie für protestantische Theologie und Kirche,* 3rd ed., ed. Herzog. V, 788-792. Leipzig: 1897.

*Hodgson, L., *The Doctrine of the Trinity.* London: 1943.

Holtzmann, *Historische Zeitschrift.* Sybel: 1879.

Huemer, "Der Grammatiker Augustinus," *Zeitschrift für österreichische Gymnasien,* IV, 1886.

*Humphries, E., *Politics and Religion in the Days of Augustine.* New York: 1927.

*Hymnen, J., *Die Sakramentlehre Augustins.* Bonn: 1905.

Ittameyer, "Augustins Stellung zur Frage nach der Nähe des Weltendes," *Zeitschrift für kirchliche Wissenschaft*, 1881.

Jaffé, P., *Regesta Pontificum Romanorum*, ed. Wattenbach. 2 vols. Leipzig: 1885. Reprinted from same plates, Graz: 1956.

*Janssen, J., *Die Entstehung der Gnadenlehre des hl. Augustins*. Rostock: 1936.

Janssens, L., *Praelectiones de Deo uno*. Rome: 1899.

*Jolivet, R., *Le Problème du mal chez s. Augustin*. Paris: 1936.

*———, *Saint Augustin et la néoplatonisme chrétien*. Paris: 1932.

*Kälin, B., *Die Erkenntnislehre des hl. Augustinus*. Sarnen: 1920.

*Kaufmann, N., "Les éléments aristotéliciens dans la cosmologie et la psychologie de s. Augustin," *Revue néoscolastique de philosophie*, II (1904), 140–156.

Koch, A., *Der hl. Faustus von Riez*. 1895.

*Körner, F., *Das Prinzip der Innerlichkeit in Augustins Erkenntnislehre*. Würzburg: 1952.

*Kreuger, A., *Synthesis of Sacrifice according to St. Augustine*. Mundelein: 1950.

Kurtz, *Histoire de l'Eglise*, 9th ed. 1885.

Lea, H., *A History of Auricular Confession*. Philadelphia: 1896.

*Leahy, D., *St. Augustine on Eternal Life*. New York: 1939.

*Le Blond, J., *Les conversions de s. Augustin*. Paris: 1950.

Le Camus, *Saint Augustin, de l'ouvrage des moines*. Rouen: 1633.

*Lehaut, A., *L'Eternité des peines de l'enfer dans s. Augustin*. Paris: 1912.

Lepidi, *Examen philosophico-theologicum de ontologismo*. Louvain: 1874.

Loesche, *De Augustino plotinizante in doctrina de Deo disserenda*. Jena: 1880.

Loofs, F., "Abendmahl," *Real. für prot. Theol. und Kirche*, I, 61–63.

———, "Augustin," *Real. für prot. Theol. und Kirche*, II, 257–285.

———, *Leitfaden zum Studium der Dogmengeschichte*, 3rd ed. Halle: 1893.

*McCabe, J., *St. Augustine and His Age*. London: 1902.

*McKeough, M., *The Meaning of the Rationes Seminales in St. Augustine*. Washington: 1926.

Mansi, J., *Sacrorum conciliorum nova et amplissima collectio*. Florence: 1759–1798.

Margival, H., *Revue d'histoire et de littérature religieuses*. 1889.

*Marrou, H., *Saint Augustin et la fin de la culture antique*. Paris: 1949.

Marrou, *St. Augustine and His Influence through the Ages*, trans. by Patrick Hepburne-Scott. New York: n.d. [1958].

*Marshall, R., *Studies in the Political and Socio-Religious Terminology of the "De Civitate Dei."* Washington: 1952.

Martin, A., *S. Augustini philosophia*, 2nd ed. Paris: 1863.

*Martin, J., *Doctrine spirituelle de S. Augustin.* Paris: 1901.

——, *Saint Augustin.* Paris: 1901.

*Mausbach, J., *Die Ethik des hl. Augustinus.* 2 vols. Paderborn: 1928.

Mercator, M., *Commonitorium super nomine Coelestii.* (48, 63–108).

——, *Liber subnotationem in verba Juliani.* (48, 109–172).

Mirbt, *Die Stellung Augustins in der Publicistik der Gregorianischen Kirchenstreits.* Leipzig: 1888.

Moehler, *Dogmatik.*

Monceaux, *Histoire littéraire de l'Afrique chrétienne.* Paris: 1901.

*Montgomery, W., *St. Augustine.* London: 1914.

*Morgan, W., *The Psychological Teaching of St. Augustine.* London: n.d.

Morin, G., *Revue bénédictine*, 1894, pp. 49–77.

——, *Revue d'histoire et de littérature religieuses*, 1902.

*Mullany, K., *Augustine of Hippo, "The First Modern Man."* New York: 1930.

Muratori, *De paradiso regnique caelestis gloria.* Verona: 1738.

Neander, *Kirchengeschichte.*

Noris, *Vindiciae augustinianae.* (47, 270–378).

Nourrisson, J., *La philosophie de s. Augustin*, 2nd ed. 2 vols. Paris: 1866.

*O'Connor, W., *The Concept of the Soul According to St. Augustine.* Washington: 1921.

Ohlmann, D., *De s. Augustini dialogis in Cassiciaco scriptis.* Strasburg: 1897.

*Oman, J., *Grace and Personality*, 3rd ed. Cambridge: 1925.

*O'Meara, J., *The Young Augustine.* London: 1954.

Orosius, P., *Liber apolgeticus de arbitrii libertate.* (31, 1174–1212).

*O'Toole, C., *The Philosophy of Creation in the Writings of St. Augustine.* Washington: 1944.

Ott, W., *Über die Schrift des hl. Augustinus De magistro.* Hechingen: 1898.

Patrizzi, *De interpretatione Scripturae.* Rome: 1844.

*Pera, L., *La creazione simultanea e virtuale secondo S. Agostino.* Florence: 1928.

*Pereira, B., *La doctrine du mariage selon s. Augustin.* Paris: 1930.

Petavius, *Dogmata Theologica: De Tridentino concilio et Augustini doctrina*, IV, 659–702. Paris: 1866.

*Pincherle, A., *La formazione teologica di S. Agostino*. Rome: 1948.

*Platz, P., *Der Römerbrief in der Gnadenlehre Augustins*. Würzburg: 1937.

Plotinus, *Plotin Ennéades*, ed. Bréhier. 3 vols. Paris: n.d.

*Polman, A., *De Predestinatie van Augustinus, Thomas van Aquino, en Calvijn*. Franeker: 1936.

*Pope, H., *Saint Augustine of Hippo*. Westminster, Md.: 1949.

Possidius, *Indiculus librorum tractatuum et epistolarum S. Augustini*. (46, 5–22).

——, *Vita S. Aurelii Augustini*. (32, 33–66).

*Przywara, E., *An Augustine Synthesis*, introd. by C. C. Martindale. New York: 1936.

Raab, L., *Disquisitio historica de libris Hypognosticon*. Altdorf: 1735.

Regnon, *Etudes de théologie positive*.

*Reuter, A., *S. Augustini doctrina de bonis matrimonii*. Rome: 1942.

Reuter, H., *Augustinische Studien*. Gotha: 1887.

Ritschl, "Die Methode der ältesten Dogmengeschichte," *Jahrbuch für deutsche Theologie*. 1871.

*Roland-Gosselin, B., *La morale de s. Augustin*. Paris: 1925.

*Rondet, H., *Gratia Christi: essai d'histoire de dogme et de théologie dogmatique*. Paris: 1948.

Rönsch, "Die lateinischen Bibelübersetzungen in christlichen Afrika zur Zeit des Augustinus," *Zeitschrift für die historische Theologie*. 1867, pp. 606 ff.; 1870, 91 ff.

Rottmanner, O., *Der Augustinismus*. Munich: 1892.

——, "S. Augustin sur l'auteur de l'Epitre aux Hébreux," *Revue bénédictine*, July, 1901.

——, *Historisches Jahrbuch*. 1898.

*Saint-Martin, J., *La pensée de s. Augustin sur la prédestination*. Paris: 1930.

Schaff, P., *Saint Augustin*. Berlin: 1854.

*Schanz, *Die Einheit der Kirche nach dem hl. Augustinus*. Neuburg: 1885.

——, *Die Lehre von den Sakramenten*.

Schanz and Rottmanner, O., *Theologische Quartalschrift*, LXXVII (1895) 269–276.

Scheeben, M., *La dogmatique*.

Scheel, O., *Die Anschauung Augustins über Christi Person und Werk*. Leipzig: 1901.

Schiesl, J., *Der objective Unterscheid zwischen Tod und lässlicher Sünde*. Augsburg: 1891.

*Schilling, O., *Die Staats- und Soziallehre des hl. Augustinus*. Freiburg i.B.: 1910.

*Schmaus, M., *Die psychologische Trinitätslehre des hl. Augustinus*. Münster: 1927.

Schmid, *Quaestiones selectae ex theologia dogmatica*. Paderborn: 1891.

Schönemann, C., *Bibliotheca histor. litter. Patrum latinorum*. (47, 9–197).

*Schubert, A., *Augustins Lex-aeterna-Lehre nach Inhalt und Quellen*. Münster: 1924.

Schwane, *Dogmengeschichte*, 2nd ed. Freiburg i.B.: 1894.

*Sciacca, M., *S. Agustino. La vita e l'opera. L'itinerario della mente*. Brescia: 1949.

Scipio, K., *Des Aurelius Augustinus Metaphysik in Rahmen seiner Lehre vom Übel*. Leipzig: 1886.

Seeberg, *Lehrbuch der Dogmengeschichte*, I, 252–332. Erlangen: 1895.

Sell, *Aus der Geschichte der Christentum*. 1888.

*Sihler, E., *From Augustus to Augustine*. London: 1924.

*Simon, P., *Aurelius Augustinus: Sein geistiges Profil*. Paderborn: 1953.

Simon, R., *Histoire critique des commentateurs du Nouveau Testament*. Rotterdam: 1693.

Sixtus of Sienna, *Bibliotheca sancta*. Cologne: 1576.

*Sokolowski, P., *Der hl. Augustin und die christliche Zivilisation*. Halle: 1927.

*Spaneddo, G., *Il misterio della Chiesa nel pensiero di Sant' Agostino*. Sassari: 1944.

*Sparrow-Simpson, W., *St. Augustine and African Church Divisions*. London: 1910.

Specht, *Die Einheit der Kirche*. 1884.

Specht, T., *Die Lehre von der Kirche nach dem hl. Augustinus*. Paderborn: 1892.

Stentrup, *De Verbo incarnato, soteriologia*, I, 387–416.

Stilting, J., *Acta sanctorum Augusti*, VI. Antwerp: 1743.

Stöckl, A., *Geschichte der christlichen Philosophie zur Zeit der Kirchenväter*. Mainz: 1891.

——, *Geschichte der Philosophie des Mittelalters*. 3 vols. Mainz: 1864.

*Svoboda, K., *L'Esthétique de s. Augustin et ses sources*. Paris: 1933.

Teuffel, *Geschichte der römische Literatur*, 5th ed.

*Theiler, W., *Porphyrios und Augustin*. Halle: 1933.

Thiel, *Epistolae romanorum pontificum*.

Tillemont, L., *Mémoires sur les six premiers siècles de l'Eglise*, XII and XIII. Paris: 1710.

*Tolley, W., *The Idea of God in the Philosophy of St. Augustine*. 1930.

Turmel, J., "Le dogme du péché originel dans s. Augustin," *Revue d'histoire et de littérature religieuses*, 1901, pp. 385–426; 1902, 128–147, 209–231, 289–322, 510–534.

———, "L'Eschatologie à la fin du IV siècle," *Revue d'histoire et de littérature religieuses*, 1900.

Vacandard, "La discipline pénitentielle," *Revue du clergé français*, XXVII (1901) 611 ff.

*Webb, C., *God and Personality*. London: 1918.

Weber, A., *Histoire de la philosophie européenne*, 4th ed. 1886.

Weihrich, F., *Die Bibelexcerpte de divinis Scripturis und die Itala des hl. Augustinus*. Vienna: 1893.

*Weinand, H., *Die Gottesidee, der Grundzug der Weltanschauung der hl. Augustinus*. Paderborn: 1910.

*Whitely, W., ed., *The Doctrine of Grace*. London: 1932.

Wilden, M., *Die Lehre des hl. Augustinus vom Opfer der Eucharistie*. Schaffhausen: 1864.

*Williams, N. *The Grace of God*. London: 1934.

*Willis, G., *Saint Augustine and the Donatist Controversy*. London: 1950.

Wolfsgruber, C., *Augustinus*. Paderborn: 1898.

*Wolfson, H., *The Philosophy of the Church Fathers*. Cambridge, Mass.: 1956.

*Woods, H., *Augustine and Evolution*. New York: 1924.

Wörter, F., *Die Geistesentwickelung des hl. Aur. Augustinus bis zu seiner Taufe*. Paderborn: 1892.

Zahm, *Bible, science et foi*. Paris: 1894.

———, *L'Evolution et le dogme*. Paris: 1897.

*Zarb, S., *Chronologia Operum s. Augustini*. Rome: 1934.

Zigliara, *Della luce intellectuale e dell' ontologismo secondo la dottrina dei SS Agostino, Bonaventura e Tommaso*. 2 vols. Rome: 1874.

TRANSLATIONS

The more important of Augustine's works have appeared frequently in English translation, although his entire works are yet to be translated. The various series listed here contain most of the major selections.

Defarrari, R., et al., eds., *The Fathers of the Church*. New York.

Quasten, J., and Plumpe, J., eds., *Ancient Christian Writers*. Westminster, Maryland.

Schaff, P., ed., *A Select Library of the Nicene and Post-Nicene Fathers of the Christian Church*, vols. I–VIII. New York: 1886–1887 Republished from the same plates, Grand Rapids, Mich.: 1956.

INDEX

Index

A = St. Augustine